T5-BAM-978

The evolving modern world is characterized by two opposing trends: integration and segregation. On the one hand, we witness strong forces for segregation on the basis of nationality, ethnicity, religion, and culture in the former Soviet Union, the former Czechoslovakia, the former Yugoslavia, as well as in Northern Ireland, Spain, and Canada. These forces are quite strong and, in some cases, violent. On the other hand, the European Union and NAFTA represent the tendency for integration motivated primarily by economic considerations (such as gains from trade and scale economies). In fact, these opposing trends can be explained by the concepts developed in modern club theory, local public finance, and international trade. For example, club theory explains the advantages of the forming of homogeneous consumption groups, while international trade theory emphasizes the gains from trade among heterologous economies. The outcome of such forces may be a system of overlapping "functional clubs," one in which an individual can belong simultaneously to several clubs, each fulfilling a different purpose.

This volume presents recent developments in urban geography, club theory and local public finance, and international trade which contribute to the explanation of these recent opposing trends. Part I is concerned with the role of transportation costs, crowding, and preferences for a large variety of goods in shaping the main features of urban geography. Positive and normative aspects of agglomerative economic forces are examined in the two contributions. Part II contains four contributions on fundamental issues associated with the provision of collective goods (club goods and local public goods) by use of a game-theoretic approach. Part III is devoted to issues associated with the production, pricing, and the consumption of congested public goods. The articles discuss the financing of transportation infrastructure (which is a special case of a congested public facility) in an intertemporal framework, the efficiency of monopolistic provision of congested public goods, the positive and normative aspects of the "musical-suburbs" problem, and the influence of secession forces on federations. Part IV deals with several interesting tax issues that have arisen in a world where economic borders are gradually being removed.

Topics in public economics

Topics in public economics

Theoretical and applied analysis

EDITED BY

DAVID PINES
Tel Aviv University

EFRAIM SADKA
Tel Aviv University

ITZHAK ZILCHA
Tel Aviv University

PUBLISHED BY THE PRESS SYNDICATE OF THE UNIVERSITY OF CAMBRIDGE
The Pitt Building, Trumpington Street, Cambridge CB2 1RP, United Kingdom

CAMBRIDGE UNIVERSITY PRESS
The Edinburgh Building, Cambridge CB2 1RP, United Kingdom
40 West 20th Street, New York, NY 10011-4211, USA
10 Stamford Road, Oakleigh, Melbourne 3166, Australia

First published 1998

Printed in the United States of America

Typeset in Times Roman

Library of Congress Cataloging-in-Publication Data
Topics in public economics / edited by David Pines, Efraim Sadka, Itzhak Zilcha.
p. cm.
Includes bibliographical references.
ISBN 0-521-56136-1
1. Finance, Public. 2. Urban economics. 3. Public goods.
I. Pines, David II. Sadka, Efraim III. Zilcha, Itzhak.
HJ117.T67 1997
336—dc20 96-20417
CIP

A catalog record for this book is available from the British Library

ISBN 0 521 56136 1 hardback

Contents

Dedication ix
HAIM BEN-SHAHAR

In memory of Eitan Berglas xiii
ELHANAN HELPMAN

Acknowledgments xvii

The contributors xix

Introduction 1
DAVID PINES, EFRAIM SADKA, AND ITZHAK ZILCHA

Part I: New perspectives on urban development

1 A "slime mold" model of city formation 15
PAUL KRUGMAN

2 The size of regions 33
ELHANAN HELPMAN

Part II: The economics of clubs

3 First and second welfare theorems for economies with collective goods 57
VICKY BARHAM AND MYRNA H. WOODERS

4 Anonymous pricing in Tiebout economies and economies with clubs 89
JOHN P. CONLEY AND MYRNA H. WOODERS

5 Decentralization in club economies: How multiple private goods matter 121
ROBERT P. GILLES AND SUZANNE SCOTCHMER

6 Agglomeration and incentives: Some modeling problems 139
ROGER GUESNERIE

Part III: The provision of public goods

7 Self-financing of congestible facilities in a growing economy 161
RICHARD ARNOTT AND MARVIN KRAUS

8 The monopolistic provision of congested public goods 185
WILLIAM H. OAKLAND

9 Imperfect solutions to the musical-suburbs problem 197
JOHN DOUGLAS WILSON

10 Nationalism and secession 220
DANIEL H. BERKOWITZ

Part IV: Taxation and distribution

11 Why is there corporate taxation in a small open economy? The role of transfer pricing and income shifting 237
ROGER H. GORDON AND JEFFREY K. MacKIE-MASON

12 Patterns of tax arbitrage and decentralized tax autonomy 262
BERND GENSER

13 Destination- and origin-based taxation under international capital mobility 286
A. LANS BOVENBERG

14 Factor mobility, risk, inequality, and redistribution 314
DAVID E. WILDASIN

Index 341

Eitan Berglas

Dedication

Haim Ben-Shahar

More than two years have elapsed since the passing of our dear friend, Prof. Eitan Berglas.

Many scholars were acquainted with him, either personally or through his scientific work. I had the privilege of knowing Eitan for a long time, and our collaboration as colleagues and personal friends goes back a long way. Eitan was an outstanding human being. Probably the best way to pay tribute to him is simply by briefly telling his life story.

I first met Eitan in 1957 when, at the age of twenty-two, he was a first-year student. He had come to Jerusalem with his wife, Hadassah, to work full-time at the Ministry of Finance and to study nights at the Hebrew University, which he did, intensively. He already had a career behind him – that of treasurer of a kibbutz – a role that required him to carry the heavy financial burden of the kibbutz on his young shoulders.

Eitan's academic talents became apparent immediately, and three years later he was accepted into the Ph.D. program in economics at the University of Chicago. By 1963, Eitan had received his Ph.D. degree and returned to Israel. He was the only young economist I ever knew to turn down Prof. Don Patinkin's proposal to join the Faculty of the Department of Economics at the Hebrew University. Eitan believed that he could serve the country better by accepting another offer, to establish the Economics Department at the Ministry of Defense. He hoped to introduce new modes of rational choice economic analysis to the Ministry and, by so doing, to influence decision making on major defense policy issues.

Eitan spent over three years in the Ministry of Defense and, concurrently, taught part-time at the Hebrew University. He was thoroughly devoted to his major assignment at the Ministry of Defense. Unfortunately, he gradually became frustrated at the lack of impact despite his efforts. In 1967, he decided to resign. His decision was made exactly at the time that Tel Aviv University was establishing its Department of Economics and searching for faculty members. We both joined the new Department, with the understanding that Eitan would be its first Chairman.

With this decision, Eitan began what he considered to be the most important activity of his life – the inauguration, nurture, and upgrading of the Department of Economics at Tel Aviv University, a department that has since earned worldwide recognition and one that was recently elevated to a school, rightfully bearing his name. Eitan embarked on this mission head-on, knowing that some of the best young talents of the time, such as Yoram Ben-Porath, David Levhari, and Eytan Sheshinsky, among others, were committed to the Hebrew University. He initiated a search for younger promising talents and in the process discovered Jacob Frenkel, Elhanan Helpman, Efraim Sadka, and Assaf Razin, who were then at the very early stages of their academic careers.

Eitan knew that he had lost precious years by not conducting scientific research and therefore, three years later, he decided to nominate one of the young faculty members as Chairman in his place and devote more of his time to academic research. However, from that time on, he remained the unofficial chairman, guide, teacher, and mentor of every young faculty member and of the Department of Economics as a whole. No major decision was made without consulting him. He never willfully intervened; on the contrary, he was always approached for guidance, which he readily gave. The affairs of the department continued to receive the highest priority among his many other activities.

In 1974, when he took his sabbatical leave at the University of Rochester, he had already made a breakthrough in the theory of clubs. He found such pleasure and gratification in his research. During every meeting we had, he would talk like an enthusiastic youngster about his new ideas and accomplishments. It was apparent that academic work gave him immense satisfaction.

Upon returning to Israel, Eitan and I found ourselves immersed once more in close collaboration; this time at Tel Aviv University, where I was President and he was Deputy Rector. That period was especially difficult for the university due to the drastic government budget cuts following the 1973 Yom Kippur War. Eitan's wise advice and assistance, given in a friendly manner and with a great deal of care, were tremendously helpful.

In 1978, Eitan was asked to head the Budget Division at the Ministry of Finance, a challenge he had to face, seeing it as an opportunity to exert a major impact on national economic policy. However, this turned out to be one of the most frustrating experiences of his career. Two years later he resigned and returned to the university to pursue his academic interests. By then, the Department of Economics had begun to take off. Eitan derived a great deal of pleasure from watching his "home base" flourish. Unfortunately, however, he could not enjoy it for long because Hadassah became ill. For two years Eitan and Hadassah struggled with the illness, initially with great hope. That hope soon faded, and in 1984 Hadassah passed away. From that time on, Eitan increased the ever-devoted attention he gave to his children.

In 1985, Eitan started his new career as Chairman of Bank Hapoalim, a career that made him a national figure. In this position, he was responsible for the largest bank in Israel at a time when it and the entire banking system were suffering from a deep crisis. Eitan had to confront many difficulties and deal with all of them simultaneously. He soon became the principal adviser of the bank's new CEO, Amiram Sivan. Eitan's wisdom, poise, and effectiveness helped bring Bank Hapoalim out of its crisis and, together with Sivan, he led the bank into a new era of prosperity. Eitan's unique qualities and skills were eminently realized in this position.

Eitan's contributions did not stop there. He was closely involved in advising the government on the stabilization plan of 1985. He handled macroeconomic issues as well as the bank's business responsibly and in a nonpartisan manner. All this made him a highly respected figure among government and political circles as well as in the business sector. Eitan's voice on national matters and banking issues was always respected, and his views were often accepted due to his sound reasoning and persuasiveness.

All the while, and in spite of his heavy involvement with the bank, the Department of Economics retained its place among Eitan's priorities. He always found time to deal with departmental affairs and handled them as devotedly as if they were his most important responsibility. He consistently participated in faculty seminars and committee meetings and found time to sit in his university office in order to meet with young faculty members. And he never gave up teaching, if only on a part-time basis.

When I reflect about Eitan's personality and rare qualities, a stream of adjectives and descriptive phrases come to my mind. Eitan was modest but conscious of his capabilities. He was a natural leader who never forced himself on others. He was loved and admired for his integrity, discretion, and wisdom, a man of his word who would not compromise on principles or values. Highly talented and capable of learning any complex subject quickly and in depth, Eitan expressed views that were thoroughly based on common sense coupled with incisive thinking. Although he did not possess rhetorical capabilities, he always expressed himself clearly and logically. He never attempted to accept a position solely to satisfy other people. Eitan was a man of substance, not of images or of public relations. He projected credibility, solidity, and, most of all, reliability. Despite his varied interests and career, his main love was academia, centered on the Department of Economics.

Eitan's malignant disease was discovered shortly after the death of his wife. He faced his illness with his usual poise and bravely fought it for many years. Eitan often underwent difficult medical treatments while he was the Chairman of Bank Hapoalim; however, this did not affect his performance. He functioned in that demanding position as any healthy person would. His illness remained a discreet and well-guarded private affair. Most of those who came in contact with Eitan as he fulfilled his duties at the bank or participated in university affairs and other public forums, knew nothing of his illness. Even when hospitalized for treatment, he would function over the telephone as if he were operating out of his own office. No one suspected that he was working from a hospital bed. Eitan maintained his usual workload up until his last week, when he was hospitalized with a very high fever. Who would have thought at the time that Eitan would leave us in just a matter of days?

It has been very difficult without Eitan; the passage of time has not made it any easier.

In memory of Eitan Berglas*

Elhanan Helpman

Eitan Berglas affected the lives of many. He had an engaging personality, a striking intelligence, and unprecedented humility in a profession that worships competition, and a rare kindness. Most of my professional life he was beside me, initially as a teacher, later on as a mentor, a colleague, a friend. He taught me economics in the classroom (my first courses in Public Economics and International Trade), during my tenure as his research assistant (working on income distribution and on an econometric model of the Israeli economy), during policy discussions and the heated debates over research topics. But most of all I learned from him *how to be an economist*, by which I mean how to view economic problems, how to mix theory with fact, how to evaluate solutions in a broad context, how to breath life into economic reasoning. This is the type of economist he was, and I have tried to follow in his footsteps.

In Israel, Eitan was widely known for his contributions to the formation of public policy. Initially as economic advisor to the ministry of defence, later on as director of the budget in the Treasury, and finally as the Chairman of the board of directors of Bank Hapoalim. Each of these jobs he performed with skill, honesty, wisdom, and great devotion. In each role, his influence greatly exceeded the confines of his authority. He quickly became a public figure, sought after by cabinet ministers, parliament members, business men, journalists, TV reporters, and numerous others. All this fame notwithstanding, he maintained a modest life style, friendly composure, and constant devotion to his family and friends. Despite his many duties in the public and business sectors, he always remained active at the university, showing up at the economists' lunch table, at faculty meetings, and in the classroom. For no matter what he did at the moment, Eitan always remained a scholar at heart.

Eitan's research spanned many topics. He wrote about monetary issues, exchange rates, the balance of payments, investment and productivity, taxes, the government budget, international trade, and economic integration. Despite the fact that much of the time he was deeply immersed in very practical problems, his research was mostly theoretical, although generally with practical implications. Much of his thinking was rooted in public economics. When he worked

* Translated from remarks, made in Hebrew, at the memorial service held in Tel Aviv, June 6, 1995.

on exchange rates, he emphasized the relationship between the real exchange rate and the government budget; when he wrote about economic integration, he made a point of emphasizing taxation issues. Broad as his interests were, however, one subject was by far his favorite: the theory of clubs. He returned to this subject he returned time and again, until the very end.

One may wonder how a person with such broad interests in economics focused on a subject that appears so narrow. The answer is that Eitan viewed it as very broad indeed. In his perception, the canonical example of a country club with limited membership was only a metaphor. He saw clubs everywhere. Every company or public department that provides an assortment of services by means of a common facility is a club. As a result, clubs include schools, fire departments, health maintenance organizations, power companies, and telephone companies. Even cities can be viewed as clubs. Assortments of goods and services whose joint supply is cost effective, and which are subject to congestion, are natural candidates for economic clubs. Such goods and services can be supplied by private companies or by the public sector. Indeed, the study of the efficient organization of their supply, including the division of labor between the private and public sectors, comprised the core of his research program.

In 1965, James Buchanan published the first important paper on club theory. He described the conditions for an optimal structure of a club, and suggested a role for the public sector in the supply of club goods. Importantly, Buchanan also mentioned the possibility that the private sector may play a constructive role in the supply of club goods, but he did not explore this option. This is the point from which Eitan began his explorations. Eleven years after Buchanan, he published a paper that turned him into the leading exponent of club theory. The central argument of the paper was that the private sector can efficiently supply club goods in a competitive environment. However, in the domain of such goods, competition does not take the form of price taking for each good and service; rather, competition implies taking as given the utility level that a club needs to provide to prospective members because individuals choose their club association by seeking the highest reward in terms of their overall utility level. Eitan also extended the concept of club goods by distinguishing between their public and private dimensions. This ingenious distinction helped greatly in clarifying the role of market institutions in the supply of such goods; it has become part and parcel of the literature. This paper laid the foundations of modern club theory and has been widely cited over the years.

Eitan's main arguments can be summarized as follows. Competitive firms choose to supply their products at minimum cost, and firms that supply club goods are no exception. For the same reason, they have an incentive to price their products efficiently. To be sure, competition in club goods involves non-linear pricing. He particularly emphasized the point that clubs compete in the *structure* of their pricing scheme, not just in the pricing of each service separately. It is then in the interest of each supplier to price her products efficiently. Moreover, clubs compete in a number of other dimensions as well, a particularly important one being the quality of services, which depends on the size of the available facility and on the number of visits made by members. Taking into account this multidimensional view of competition, he argued that the market can provide an efficient mix of clubs.

From this point, Eitan began a long and detailed exploration of the generalizability of his main insight. He sought to identify broad circumstances in which competition leads the private sector to supply club goods efficiently, and the necessary modifications that arc called for in order to secure this outcome. In this vein, he showed that flat membership fees do not constitute an efficient pricing scheme when club members can alter the number of visits, and that in a population with heterogeneous preferences, separate clubs will be formed for each group having similar preferences. The latter result caused him great concern, because despite the tendencies for separation, it appears that in practice, economic clubs have substantially mixed populations. This seems to be particularly so in local communities, such as urban neighborhoods and small townships. Taking local communities as the relevant unit, he decided to investigate possible reasons for mixing populations. For this purpose, he constructed a model in which people differ in tastes on the one hand and in innate abilities on the other. The latter was designed to proxy differences in the ability to contribute to the local community, especially through the labor supply. Building on these features he showed that with sufficient complementarity of different skills, mixed communities are called for in an efficient allocation. These insights attracted much attention, and recent research is still occupied with their implications.

The next question that arose in this context was how to decentralize an efficient allocation with mixed communities when individuals migrate between them to better themselves and when local authorities compete for residents. He showed that as long as local authorities do not seek to redistribute income, they adopt similar tax structures and support an efficient allocation with mixed communities. But if local authorities aim to redistribute income among different types of people, and if they employ local taxation for this purpose, then the resulting tax competition prevents the attainment of an efficient allocation and, moreover, it produces severe instability in the structure of the communities.

These results have far-reaching implications. First, they explain why income distribution policies are best pursued by national governments rather than by local governments. Authorizing local governments to engage in income redistribution produces migration flows in response to tax policies, which generate budgetary difficulties, economic instability, and harmful consequences for the overall efficiency of the economic system. Examples of two-tier governments to which this tension applies include the central government and the municipalities in Israel, the federal and state governments in the United States, as well as the federal and provincial governments in Canada. A similar point arose in the 1992 program of the European Community which, among its many aims, also sought to enhance labor mobility across member countries. Its architects were urged to include tax harmonization as part of the program in order to avoid such instability.

Much of the work that I have described so far was done prior to Eitan's service as Director of the Budget in the Ministry of Finance. Upon his return to the university, he also returned to his beloved research topic: the theory of clubs. This time, he joined forces with David Pines. Together they produced a fascinating synthesis of club theory, the theory of local public goods, urban economics, and transportation economics. Their 1981 joint paper has become a classic; and both of them have become the leading experts on this important subject.

Academic economists tend to be judged by their publications and Eitan achieved renown on this front. In addition, he contributed to the creation of a major department of economics, at Tel Aviv University, he significantly influenced the making of public policy in Israel – including the design of the very successful stabilization program of 1985 – and he was instrumental in leading a major bank from crisis to striking success during his chairmanship of the board of directors. Very few people can claim this much. In fact, his influence reached far beyond these achievements. His wise advice was sought by many; he thereby played a central role in major aspects of Israeli public life. He was a true public servant, with a strong commitment to doing good. He will be greatly missed.

Acknowledgments

David Pines

Efraim Sadka

Itzhak Zilcha

This volume, dedicated to the memory of Prof. Eitan Berglas, is the product of the efforts of three Tel Aviv University institutions: the Pinhas Sapir Center for Development, the Eitan Berglas School of Economics, and the Faculty of Social Sciences. The project began with the decision to dedicate the 10th Annual Sapir Conference in memory of Prof. Berglas and to invite papers closely related to the late Prof. Berglas' interests. We sincerely thank these institutions for their active support and cooperation.

We would also like to thank our English language editor, Nina Reshef, for all her efforts.

The contributors

Richard Arnott, Professor, Department of Economics, Boston College. Prof. Arnott specializes in urban economics, public finance, and the economics of uncertainty and information. His most recent research has concentrated on the economics of urban traffic congestion and urban housing markets.

Vicky Barham, Assistant Professor, Department of Economics, University of Ottawa. Prof. Barham's research interests are focused on nonmarket-mediated economic activity, particularly on the ways in which groups of individuals structure their economic relationships so as to provide themselves with both pure and local public goods. In this context, she has devoted special attention to the influence of population heterogeneity on equilibrium efficiency and to the degree of consistency between decentralized approaches to provision of such goods and the pursuit of equity objectives. Prof. Barham's other interests include the economics of health, education, and the family.

Daniel Berkowitz, Assistant Professor, Department of Economics, University of Pittsburgh. Prof. Berkowitz conducts theoretical and empirical research on the transitions to a market economy taking place among former socialist countries. He is currently studying the impact of fiscal decentralization on market integration and changes in regional cost-sharing arrangements adopted by these economies as well as researching the impact of local government policies on the emerging private sector. Prof. Berkowitz has taught economics and conducted field work in Russia and the Czech Republic.

A. Lans Bovenberg, Deputy Director, the Central Planning Bureau, the Netherlands, and Professor of Public Policy, the Research Center for Economic Policy (OCFEB), Erasmus University. Prof. Bovenberg is also Senior Research Fellow at the Center for Economic Research, Tilburg University. Prof. Bovenberg has worked extensively on tax policy in open economies and, in recent years, has focused on environmental taxation and its impact on employment and growth. His current research interests include the fiscal aspects of the European Monetary Union, the economic and fiscal implications of aging, and taxation in imperfect labor markets.

John P. Conley, Assistant Professor, Department of Economics, University of Illinois, Champaign. Prof. Conley's interests lie in the application of modern tools of general equilibrium and game theory to classic problems in public economics. His goal is to discover exactly when the presence of nonconvexities, externalities, and public goods leads to market failure, and how market efficiency can be recovered. Most recently, he has been occupied with exploring Tiebout's hypothesis on market provision of local public goods and general equilibrium versions of the Coase theorem.

Bernd Genser, Professor of Public Economics, Faculty of Economics and Statistics, University of Konstanz. Prof. Genser teaches public economics, including international taxation, environmental economics, and the economics of the European Union. His research interests include the economics of taxation, particularly international taxation, tax policy in multilevel fiscal systems, and applied fiscal policy analysis. Prof. Genser also heads the research project on public finance and increasing international interdependence with the Internationalization of the Economy Program at the University of Konstanz.

Robert P. Gilles, Assistant Professor, Department of Economics, Virginia Polytechnic Institute and State University. Among Prof. Gilles' varied, current research interests are general equilibrium theory, with a concentration on economies having non-Samuelsonian public goods and club economies, the economics of transaction costs, cooperative game theory, and the theory of the firm.

Roger H. Gordon, Professor, Department of Economics, University of Michigan. Prof. Gordon's research has been centered on normative and positive studies of tax policy, with a sidelong view on the reform process in transition economies. During the last few years, his work has focused on tax policy in open economies, especially on the role of the corporate tax in such a setting. Prof. Gordon has also spent three years as co-editor of the *American Economic Review* and is beginning a term as co-editor of the *Journal of Public Economics*.

Roger Guesnerie, Director of Research, CNRS, Director of Studies, EHESS, and Director of DELTA, Paris. Prof. Guesnerie has been intensely involved in the study of government intervention in the economy, beginning with its role in the allocation of resources. Second-best taxation has received special attention within his analysis of government intervention vis-à-vis income distribution. Prof. Guesnerie's current interests include the study of the foundations of the rational expectations hypothesis and its crucial role in the assessment of stabilization policies.

Elhanan Helpman, Professor, the Eitan Berglas School of Economics, Tel Aviv University. Prof. Helpman is the Archie Sherman Professor of International Economic Relations at Tel Aviv University, Fellow of the Canadian Institute for Advanced Research, Research Associate of the National Bureau of Economic Research, and Research Fellow of the Center for Economic Policy Research.

His research has converged on international trade, economic growth, and political economy.

Marvin Kraus, Professor, Department of Economics, Boston College. Prof. Kraus' current research is concerned with efficient pricing and investment policies for congestible facilities. This study, conducted jointly with Prof. Richard Arnott, is proceeding along two lines: The first is concerned with extending the results of the chapter in this volume to environments with uncertainty; the second investigates the implications of unobservable heterogeneity in peak-load models with schedule delays and congestion costs.

Paul Krugman, Professor, Department of Economics, Massachusetts Institute of Technology. Beginning with the study of international trade, Prof. Krugman's research later turned to the subject of trade in the presence of increasing returns, a phenomenon often displaying multiple equilibria. More recently, he has directed his attention to the subject of economic geography in general, especially the ways in which economies spontaneously generate spatial structure.

Jeffrey K. MacKie-Mason, Associate Professor of Economics and Public Policy, Department of Economics and School of Public Policy, University of Michigan, Ann Arbor. Prof. MacKie-Mason has investigated a number of the effects of domestic and international tax policies on corporate behavior: financial choices, choice of organizational form, transfer pricing, income shifting, and investment. His recent research has concentrated on information network economics, especially the economics of Internet.

William H. Oakland, Professor of Economics, Department of Economics, Tulane University. Prof. Oakland's major research interests lie in the areas of public goods, local public finance, and international tax competition. He is currently engaged in developing optimal business tax structures for subnational governments.

Suzanne Scotchmer, Professor of Economics and Public Policy, Lecturer in Law, University of California, Berkeley. Prof. Scotchmer has devoted her research to the study of public goods and club economies, intellectual property, evolutionary game theory, and cooperative game theory.

David E. Wildasin, Professor, Department of Economics, Vanderbilt University. Prof. Wildasin's research concerns lie in the areas of public economics and urban economics. He has recently been working on the implications of economic integration for public economics.

John Douglas Wilson, Professor and former Chairman, Department of Economics, Indiana University. Prof. Wilson's primary research interests are centered on the open-economy aspects of public economics. He has published extensively in the area of local public economics, including several articles on interjurisdictional tax competition. His research has also covered international policy issues, including optimal income taxation in the presence of migration and the political economy of trade protection. He serves on the editorial boards of *Economics and Politics*, the *Journal of International Economics*, and the *Journal of Urban Economics,* and is a past member of the editorial board of the *American Economic Review*.

Myrna H. Wooders, Professor of Economics, Department of Economics, University of Toronto. The broad range of Prof. Wooders' research interests cover the conditions under which large economies, including economies with public goods, clubs, and hedonic coalitions are "market-like," as well as the modeling of abstract economies as coalitional games and the study of their market-like properties. More recently, Prof. Wooders has investigated cooperation and coalition formation with incomplete information, evolutionary models of human behavior and group formation, partnerships, and the stability of commonwealths when member states have the option of secession. Prof. Wooders also actively participates in professional conference organization.

Introduction

The evolving modern world is characterized by two opposing trends: integration and segregation. On the one hand, we witness strong forces for segregation on the basis of nationality, ethnicity, religion, and culture in the former Soviet Union, the former Czechoslovakia, the former Yugoslavia, as well as in Northern Ireland, Spain, and Canada. These forces are quite strong and, in some cases, violent. On the other hand, the European Union and NAFTA represent the tendency for integration motivated primarily by economic considerations (such as gains from trade and scale economies). In fact, these opposing trends can be explained by the concepts developed in modern club theory, local public finance, and international trade. For example, club theory explains the advantage of forming homogeneous consumption groups, while international trade theory emphasizes the gains from trade among heterogeneous economies. The outcome of such forces might be a system of overlapping "functional clubs," one in which an individual may belong simultaneously to several clubs, each fulfilling a different purpose.

It appears natural, therefore, that the growth of a body of literature dealing with the rationale driving these forces and their consequences should be observed. Indeed, in evaluating trends in the contents of the *Journal of Public Economics* for a period of 21 years, Atkinson (1993) writes that the provision of local public goods, income redistribution as a local public good, and the financing of local government are prominent examples of topics which have remained of continuing importance. He also notes that "elsewhere in the profession, there is more concern with open economies and the implications of international movement of capital." This volume is devoted to these two interrelated subjects: that is, economies of size, club theory, and local public finance; and the theory of taxation in the presence of free international movements of commodities, labor, and capital. Parts I to III are dedicated to the first topic, and Part IV to the second. Specifically, Part I is concerned with the roles of transportation costs, crowding, and preferences for a large variety of goods in shaping the main features of urban geography. Positive and normative aspects of the agglomerative forces are studied in the two contributions in this section. Part II contains four contributions dealing with fundamental issues associated with the provision of collective goods (club goods and local public goods), all of which employ a game-theoretic approach. Part III covers issues associated with the production, pricing, and consumption of congested public goods. It includes a discussion of the financing of transportation infrastructure (which is a special case of a congested public facility) in an intertemporal setup; efficiency aspects of providing congested public good by a monopoly; positive and normative aspects of the "musical-suburbs" problem; and secession forces in federations. Finally, Part IV deals with several interesting tax issues that have arisen in a world in which economic borders are rapidly being removed.

Part I contains two contributions concerned with the role of agglomerative forces in shaping urban geography. Krugman (1991) has motivated thinking about the formation of cities as spurred by increasing returns-to-scale technology in the production of differentiated products. As in his earlier work, the model presented in this volume contains two types of commodities: homogeneous (agricultural) products produced with constant returns-to-scale technology, and differentiated products manufactured with increasing returns-to-scale technology (a composite of large numbers of symmetric differentiated products). There are two types of agents involved: immobile farmers versus workers in the differentiated products sector who can move from one city to the other. Locations are evenly spaced around a circle and transportation takes place on the circle's perimeter only. Again, Krugman assumes zero transport costs for the agricultural goods, but positive transport costs for manufactured goods. Transport costs have Samuelson's "iceberg" form, namely, if one unit of a manufactured good is shipped from one location to another part, the shipment gets lost, depending on the distance. Consumers in this economy have identical Cobb-Douglas preferences between agricultural goods and manufactured aggregate goods.

The framework employed in the current chapter takes firms to be myopic over space and time, that is, the decision to move to neighboring locations is dictated solely by whether or not real wages are higher there than in the current location. In their decision whether to move, firms ignore opportunities available in distant locations as well as strategic considerations regarding the state of the economy in the long run. Moreover, the dynamics of this system are crucially affected by the following assumption: A positive probability exists that the firm will move in the "wrong" direction due to some randomness introduced into the decision-making process. Thus, while the expected direction of motion is toward higher real income, the firm may move to the wrong location. We should point out here that, due to the assumption of zero transport cost for agricultural goods, all farmers have the same real wage.

For any given distribution of firms across locations, a dynamic general equilibrium problem arises and it is shown that, under the proper choice of parameters, the economy reaches an equilibrium where the real income of each type of firm is determined at each location. In this stochastic dynamic spatial model as in the other models used by Krugman (1991), we observe two opposing forces: centripetal forces generated by the incentive for firms to move toward suppliers of manufactured goods, and centrifugal forces generated by the "market potential," namely, the incentive to move toward large markets. Nonetheless, we also observe the tendency to disperse due to the immobility of the farmers: When manufacturers are concentrated, it might be beneficial for them to disperse since competition is weaker in the rural markets. The chapter itself focuses on cases where the initial distribution of manufacturing firms is almost flat. Since a flat distribution is an unstable equilibrium, when conditions which guarantee strong incentives arise, the system evolves into a highly uneven spatial structure.

Helpman's chapter follows Krugman's (1991) previous study and investigates the role of agglomerative and disagglomerative economic forces which, when applied in an appropriate dynamic framework, result in the formation of cities. As in Krugman's model, the agglomerative force in Helpman's model relies on the advantage of accessibility to a wide variety of goods that characterizes large urban areas. However, unlike Krugman, where the disagglomerative force is the geographically dispersed demands of the immobile farmers, Helpman takes this force to be a result of the disadvantage of crowding in cities, an outcome reflected in a decline of housing supply per capita with increasing population size. It is in this sense that Helpman shifts the emphasis from the Löcshian setup, where the shape of human settlement is based on agricultural production, to the premise of modern urban economics.

On the positive side, three types of stable equilibria emerge. With a high elasticity of substitution among varieties and/or high housing preferences, the population (in a stationary equilibrium) tends to disperse. With a small elasticity of substitution and/or low preference for housing, the outcome depends on transportation costs. In these circumstances of very high transportation costs, the population tends to concentrate in one city. Assuming an intermediate level of transportation cost, in a stable equilibrium, there results a tendency for the population to be unequally distributed in two cities, one big and one small, both of which are stable. In the last case, with an unequal population distribution, the allocation is suboptimal; hence, everyone can be better off by relocating from the small to the large city, which means the market tends to generate insufficient agglomeration. Obviously, this reflects the external effect associated with the advantage of a large selection of varieties. More precisely, when the individual moves from the small to the large city, the range of available varieties there increases and, consequently, the welfare of the population in the large city as well as in the small city increases.

Although the models used by Krugman and Helpman are motivated in different ways, the dynamics in both models, which result from two opposing forces, yield stable long-run equilibria. Their studies consequently shed light on the economic aspects of the interesting phenomenon of self-organization.

Part II deals with fundamental issues of club and local public good theories, using a game-theoretical approach. The Barham and Wooders and Conley and

Wooders chapters are complementary and cover much of the club theory literature. Both discuss issues associated with decentralization of optimal allocations. The first concentrates on nondifferentiated (anonymous) crowding while the second focuses mainly on a crowding types model, where agents are only affected by the numbers and observable crowding types of other agents. Gilles and Scotchmer discuss the effects of introducing multiple private goods (rather than only one good) into the club model. In particular, they explore the effect of multiple private goods on the optimal club system and the possibility of its decentralization. While these three chapters are focused on formation of consumption groups under first-best regime and the possibility of decentralizing this allocation, Guesnerie's chapter is mainly concerned with the formation of such groups under a second-best regime, where optimal taxation is not feasible.

Barham and Wooders address three different sorts of price systems – anonymous Tiebout equilibrium admission pricing, and Lindahl pricing with either anonymous prices (not dependent on tastes) or nonanonymous prices (dependent on tastes) under two different conditions of production: constant returns to scale within jurisdictions and concave production within jurisdictions. Their results illustrate that the more restrictive the price system, the more restrictive the conditions required on the environment to obtain core-equilibrium equivalence. It is perhaps especially interesting that the nonanonymous Lindahl equilibrium outcomes are equivalent to the admission equilibrium outcomes even when the anonymous Lindahl outcomes are only a strict subset (possibly empty) of the core.

One of Barham and Wooders' contributions is the extension of the Second Welfare Theorem for club economies by applying it not only to cases where individuals attain their type-optimal utility, but also to every equal-treatment Pareto-optimal state of the economy achieved by redistribution of endowments.

Conley and Wooders extend the scope of the analysis to include situations where consumers differentiate between other consumer types on the basis of their crowding effects. The authors show that in the crowding types model, anonymous admission prices decentralize the core. They argue that this result proves the Tiebout hypothesis that large economies with public goods and effective small groups are "market-like" – that is, the core can be supported by a price-taking equilibrium where prices depend on publicly observed information.

Conley and Wooders elaborate on three distinct equilibrium concepts: admission equilibrium, Lindahl equilibrium, and uniform Tiebout equilibrium. The authors report that the equivalence of the nonanonymous Lindhal pricing and nonanonymous admission pricing, shown in several papers in the literature on differentiated crowding, extends to the crowding types model. The anonymous Lindahl and anonymous admission price equilibria are not equivalent in the crowding types model. Thus, with anonymous pricing, there is a significant difference between Lindahl and admission equilibrium in terms of their ability to decentralize the state of the economy in the core.

There is an aspect of the Barham and Wooders and Conley and Wooders chapters that might fruitfully be further investigated. Whether anonymous or nonanonymous pricing is used, Lindahl equilibrium is more information-efficient than admission equilibrium since Lindahl equilibrium only requires a finite number of prices. Therefore, it would be interesting to have an existence result for the Lindahl equilibrium which is less restrictive than in Barham and Wooders for the nondifferentiated crowding model. Another open issue is whether it is possible to define groups with different crowding types but with the same demands for public goods. Such a definition may be possible under restrictive conditions only, since the demand depends on the crowding profile, not only on the preferences (e.g., the crowding profile determines the income when individuals are complementary in production, and the demand depends not only on the preferences but also on income).

Gilles and Scotchmer show that extending the club model to include more than one private good matters, whenever the MRS between some pair of the private goods is affected by the characteristics of the club. In particular, optimal equal-utility allocation implies that more than one type of club should prevail. A similar observation has already been demonstrated by Wilson (1987) for a local public good model with land, where, in the case of multiple private goods, homogeneous jurisdictions structure cannot be optimal. However, the discussion of Gilles and Scotchmer provides different reasoning which is relevant to club models without production as well.

In fact, the superiority of the heterogeneous structure stems from the interplay of similar forces in both Wilson's local public good and Gilles and Scotchmer's club models: the tradeoff between the *gains from trade* on the one hand, and the *loss from inefficient group size* (a jurisdiction's or club's size), on the other. The difference between Gilles and Scotchmer's club and Wilson's local public good specifications, however, is that in the latter, the gains from trade always exceed the losses from inefficient group size, while in the former they may not.

Gilles and Scotchmer show that achieving gains from trade requires a club composition that allows markets to clear. This condition implies that the emphasis when proving decentralization of the optimal allocation should be shifted from the concept of optimal club size to that of an "optimal economy," within which the optimal gains from trade can be achieved with market clearing. This condition, however, aggravates the integer problem (emptiness of the core): Not only should the optimal club membership size be an integer number, but the population of the economy as a whole should be an integer replication of the "optimal economy." This observation is relevant, of course, to Wilson's case as well.

Guesnerie's framework is similar to that of Jehiel and Scotchmer (1994) in that the fragmentation of the population into groups (jurisdictions) is motivated by an inefficient tax system ("disagglomeration forces"). The collective good is pure; therefore, the efficient group size is the total population ("the grand coalition"). Since the relevant information (regarding the individual type) is not available, a Lindahl equilibrium cannot be established and, instead, a distortive tax system is applied (an identical head tax in the case of Jehiel and Scotchmer and a commodity tax in the case of Guesnerie). Guesnerie shows that even in nonpathological cases, the efficient "grand coalition," comprised of the whole population, may not be achievable because an inefficient fragmentation of the population into smaller groups may be stable. Stability, however, is not guaranteed unless some restrictive conditions are imposed on the individual's preferences.

On the basis of his simple model, Guesnerie touches upon fundamental informational issues associated with the formation of blocking coalitions. The second-best tax structure is explained by lack of information (otherwise a Lindahl tax system could have been imposed with a Pareto improving Lindahl tax system). Guesnerie then raises the following question: If information is not available so as to create the grand coalition (to establish a Lindahl equilibrium), how can blocking coalitions having some internal distributional patterns be formed? Referring to his work with Demange, Guesnerie defines two concepts of a core, one based on full information and the other on only partial information. He then discusses the implication of each concept of the core on the stability of the allocations. As in many other models with private information, the following issue is raised: Can we apply the information revealed by the creation of such stable groups for a taxation pattern that will result in the formation of the grand coalition?

Part III is devoted to issues related to the production, pricing, and consumption of congested public goods. Arnott and Kraus elaborate on the financing of transportation infrastructure – which is a special case of a congested public facility – in an intertemporal framework; Oakland discusses the efficiency of monopoly provision of a congested public good; Wilson deals with the nonexistence of equilibrium and efficiency issues associated with interjurisdictional migration and induced by the failure to implement marginal-cost pricing (the "musical-suburbs" problem); and Berkowitz analyzes secession trends in federations.

Arnott and Kraus extend the self-financing of transportation infrastructure result (when the long-run average cost function reflects constant returns to scale) in static models to a variety of intertemporal environments, using the present value criterion. The self-financing result is obtained when the user-cost function exhibits zero homogeneity in volume of traffic and the capacity-cost function exhibits linear homogeneity. (In fact, by inversion, these assumptions are equivalent to assuming that the volume of traffic is a linear homogeneous function of the infrastructure (fixed input) and the total user-cost (variable input), which is a standard result in microeconomics). With appropriate interpretation, Arnott and Kraus show that this result applies equally to a dynamic setup. However, in any time interval, the self-financing result does not hold on a cash basis: The toll revenue need not equal the cash outlay for maintaining and investing in infrastructure. Rather, the present value of the toll revenue equals the present value of the stream of outlays for maintenance and investment. During any time interval, current toll revenue plus capital gains equals the interest cost on capital plus depreciation and maintenance.

The self-financing result (with several extensions) remains robust if the production technologies exhibit constant returns to scale. For example, introducing an adjustment cost exhibiting homogeneity of degree one in the infrastructure and its rate of change modifies the self-financing result only slightly by including profits from investment, evaluated at shadow prices, on the revenue side. The only exception is the case of fixed increment to capacity, such as runways. Although the chapter directly refers to transportation capacity, the analysis applies equally to any congestible public facility characterized by constant returns to scale.

Oakland studies the provision of a local public good by a monopoly. Starting from Knight's (1952) claim that the monopoly provision is likely to be as efficient as in the free entry case, Oakland demonstrates that, under quite general assumptions, it is actually inefficient. Moreover, it is not impossible to fully characterize the nonoptimality of the price or the capacity of a public facility in this case. However, using a weakly separable utility function (between the private good and the characteristics of the public good), he shows that when "demand compensation" (i.e., the price reduction required to compensate for an increase in congestion) is uncorrelated across types of consumers, the nondiscriminating monopolist's price will be "too low," which may look counterintuitive, and the capacity will fall below the socially efficient level. On the other hand, if the public facility monopolist chooses the efficient capacity, it sets the price above the efficient level, as in the standard case of monopoly-supplying of a private or pure public good. As Oakland shows in his work, the monopolist can exploit any imperfect substitutability between a congested good and other goods. The absence of a contending firm capable of offering consumers some combination of price and congestion that would increase their utilities, without incurring a loss, is the major reason for the inefficiency.

Turning to Wilson's contribution, it is well known in the literature on local public goods that matching residents' tax payments with their marginal congestion costs is, in many cases, infeasible and, in the event of free migration, may result in the nonexistence of a competitive equilibrium. Those with high congestion/tax ratios tend to join communities with low congestion/tax ratios.

The latter, then, tend to secede and form another community just to realize that they are being joined again. For example, if the tax base equals property values, those with low demand for housing tend to join communities exhibiting high demand for housing. Wilson begins the analysis of this "musical-suburb" problem and its solution by assuming that there are two types of individuals, differing from each other by the congestion costs they generate. These costs, however, are unobservable for taxation purposes. He shows that with perfect foresight, an inefficient equilibrium exists where communities with low cost/tax ratios deviate from the Samuelson criterion for supplying public goods in order to exclude the individuals with high cost/tax ratios. Thus, in contrast to the earlier literature, Wilson shows that an equilibrium exists with homogeneous communities, each accommodating unique types of cost/tax ratios. However, in excluding the potential free riders, the allocation is distorted. Wilson then demonstrates that, with some qualifications, appropriate head transfers from individuals in the low cost/tax to the high cost/tax communities can induce a Pareto improvement. The reason this works is that such transfers make the communities with high cost/tax ratios more attractive and, hence, a smaller deviation from the Samuelson criterion is required to keep individuals with high cost/tax ratios from entering. This diminished distortion may more than offset the loss from the transfer. Wilson extends the analysis by introducing a case where monitoring congestion is possible but costly, as well as a case where the "musical-suburb" problem is created by a property tax.

The chapter by Daniel Berkowitz presents a study of the viability of a fiscal federation. He distinguishes between the economic (non-nationalistic) and noneconomic (nationalistic) considerations of policy makers. Suppose that a fiscal federation of certain regions is a Pareto improving institution, that is, all the regions belonging to the federation gain from membership. Obviously, if all regional governments are motivated solely by economic (non-nationalistic) considerations, the federation prevails. However, when there is some risk that the nationalistic forces will gain power in some regions of this economically viable federation, then non-nationalistic governments in other regions, those motivated only by economic gains and losses, may nevertheless choose to secede. This results from their concern regarding the loss of part of the resources they contributed, either voluntarily or through taxes, to the dissolving federation. Hence, *non-nationalistic* regional government may secede from an *economically viable* federation.

Part IV deals with several practical issues of taxation in open economies. The chapter by Roger Gordon and Jeffrey MacKie-Mason reexamines the question of why countries levy corporate taxes in small open economies. Existing theories suggest, following the Diamond-Mirrlees aggregate production efficiency theorem, that it is optimal for a small open economy to equate its domestic marginal product of capital to the world's real rate of interest. Therefore, it should levy the same tax rate on the capital income of its residents whether they invest at home or abroad. When enforcement of a tax on foreign-source income is problematic, one would expect small open economies to exempt corporate and other capital income from taxation or, at least, levy a relatively low tax rate. This conclusion is reinforced by the ability of multinationals to shift their accounting profits from high-tax countries to low-tax countries via appropriate transfer pricing schemes.

Yet, Gordon and MacKie-Mason point out, not only are corporate tax rates nonzero, but in recent years they tend to be roughly comparable with the top personal tax rate in each country. Must the inevitable conclusion be that countries are following suboptimal policies?

Gordon and MacKie-Mason offer some other explanations. A possible rationale for the corporate tax is to protect the personal income tax base. The absence of a corporate tax creates a strong incentive for individuals to conduct their trade or even provide their labor services through closely held corporations; retain earnings rather than pay them out as wages; and sell some of their shares or distribute dividends, making their earnings subject to effectively low capital gains or dividend tax rates rather than labor income tax rates. Other issues, such as credits versus deductions for taxes paid abroad, postponement of taxes on foreign-source profits until they are repatriated, etc., are also examined.

The chapters by A. Lans Bovenberg and by Bernd Genser deal with several issues associated with the relationship between destination-based and origin- (or source-) based indirect taxation. The main instrument of this type of taxation nowadays is the value-added tax (VAT), so attention is focused upon it. Two principles, or some mixture of them, govern the application of the VAT in the international arena: the destination principle and the origin (or source) principle. According to the first principle, a country levies the tax on all goods and services destined for final consumption in that country, regardless of the source (origin) of production. Specifically, imports are taxed and exports are exempted (or, more accurately, zero-rated). According to the second principle, a country levies the tax on all goods and services produced in that country, irrespective of their final destination.

When two countries adopt the destination principle for their VAT, the *producer* (pretax) prices of the consumer goods are equal in the two countries. If they adopt the origin principle, then the *consumer* (post-tax) prices of the consumer goods are equal in the two countries. Suppose there is a factor of production which is mobile between the two countries, so that its price is the same in the two countries. Now, if the VAT rates differ in the two countries, then equal producer prices in the two countries imply unequal consumer prices; and equal consumer prices in the two countries imply unequal producer prices. Therefore the two taxation principles are not equivalent. The destination principle yields equal producer prices and production efficiency, but unequal consumer prices and consumption inefficiency; whereas the origin principle yields equal consumer prices and consumption efficiency, but unequal producer prices and production inefficiency. However, when factors of production are *internationally immobile*, their domestic prices will adjust to absorb the aforementioned difference in consumer prices (with the destination principle) or the aforementioned difference in producer prices (with the origin principle). Therefore, in this case, the destination principle and the origin principle become equivalent to each other.

The chapter by Bernd Genser follows this line of thought to establish some equivalences between certain mixtures of the two aforementioned (pure) principles. These equivalences have practical relevance in light of the ongoing debate on international tax coordination. Specifically, Genser shows that a mixed VAT system, which follows the origin principle within the European Union, and the destination principle between the European Union and the rest of the world, is equivalent to a pure destination regime. The chapter by Bovenberg extends the analysis of the two taxation principles to a dynamic framework. The non-equivalence between these two principles in the presence of international factor mobility now holds not only with respect to the *international* distribution of resources, but also with respect to the *intergenerational* distribution of resources.

David Wildasin's contribution may be viewed as an open economy version of the branch of the literature, originating in the work of Domar and Musgrave, concerned with the role as well as the scope of income taxation as a means of social insurance. Redistributive taxation in a closed economy with technological risk can be very useful in sharing that risk among the various factors of production (or their owners). But such taxation cannot reduce the economy-wide level of risk: When total output is uncertain, total consumption is equally uncertain; taxation can only help in pooling the risk among the many agents in the economy. However, in an open economy, the existence of mobile factors can reduce the level of risk for the economy as a whole by out-migration in the case of a low realization of output, and in-migration in the case of a high realization of output. By doing so, the mean return to the immobile factor may also rise. Redistributive taxation may interfere with the insurance role of migration in such a case, thereby becoming inefficient. Finally, the fiscal implications of factor market integration for developed and developing countries are discussed.

The contributions in this volume not only present developments in important areas in urban, public, and international economics, they also provide new directions to be pursued in future research. For example, the subject of economic geography is still in its childhood. Much more work is needed to fully understand the forces that shape human settlement over space. The study of the size distribution of cities presented here would benefit by accompanying research on the spatial distribution of cities. Furthermore, an integration of this analysis with a discussion of local public finance is essential for evaluating the conceptions of fiscal federalism underlying the present reforms of local government structure taking place in both Western and Eastern Europe. Similarly, as Guesnerie has pointed out, further research on the role of information and its diffusion will enhance our understanding of the creation and dissolution of coalitions. We hope that this volume will serve to motivate such research.

References

Atkinson, A.B. (1993) "*The Journal of Public Economics* at 21 Ycars and 50 Volumes: A Personal View." *The Journal of Public Economics,* Master Index: Vols. 1–50, 1–7.

Jehiel, P. and S. Scotchmer (1994) "*On the Right of Exclusion in Jurisdiction Formation.*" *(Unpublished).*

Knight, F. (1952) "Some Fallacies in the Interpretation of Social Cost." Reprinted in G Stigler and K. Boulding, eds., *Readings in Price Theory*, Vol. VI. Homewood: Irwin, 160–79.

Krugman, P. (1991) "Increasing Returns and Economic Geography." *Journal of Political Economy*, 99, 483-99.

Wilson, J. O. (1987) "Trade in a Tiebout Economy." *American Economic Review,* 77(3), 431–41.

PART I

NEW PERSPECTIVES ON URBAN DEVELOPMENT

CHAPTER 1

A "slime mold" model of city formation

Paul Krugman

1. Introduction

It has often been observed that a city is like a living thing. In particular, like an organism that continually replaces its cells yet somehow retains its identity, a city contains an ever-changing population yet remains a well-defined unit. But what sort of organism does a city most resemble? This paper will suggest that a good answer may be that cities are not too unlike slime molds.

Why slime molds, aside from their delightful name? (When I suggested the analogy to one Washington-based acquaintance, he said that whatever its general applicability, the analogy certainly applied pretty well to our nation's capital). Because the slime mold has been widely used as a motivating biological example in the growing interdisciplinary literature on self-organizing systems.

By a self-organizing system, these researchers mean a system in which the interactions of small individual units lead to the emergence of collective behavior that shows large-scale order. A slime mold, for example, exists in two forms. When food is abundant, it consists of many independent amoebas, single-cell units that move about randomly. When food is scarce, however, these amoebas begin emitting chemical signals that lead them to coalesce, eventually forming large units that move across the landscape in "search" of more favorable conditions. What researchers such as Goodwin (1994) have pointed out is that the process of coalescence in slime molds is qualitatively very similar to that of self-organizing chemical systems – such as the famous Beloussov-Zhabotinski reaction – and that essentially the same mathematical model can be used to simulate both. Thus the slime mold becomes a sort of advertisement for the proposition that there are common principles of self-organization that apply to complex dynamic systems in many different fields of activity.

It would be too much to hope for that the process of city formation could be represented as an exact analogy with either chemical reactions or slime mold aggregation. In particular, it seems unreasonable to try to impose on a model of economic behavior the kind of restriction to purely local interaction that comes naturally in both chemical and biological models. Yet there are nonetheless some clear similarities. Despite the presence of some large developers, urban concentrations arise in large part as the result of the independent movements of large numbers of individual households and firms; the dynamics that lead to city formation arise from the interactions among these individuals. Spatial economic models normally involve a tension between "centripetal" and "centrifugal" forces, not too different from the tension between positive and negative feedback that is central to many models of biological, chemical, and physical self-organization. And the distribution of firms and households across the landscape surely can be viewed as an "excitable medium" of the type that Goodwin claims is the generic representation of self-organizing spatial systems.

At any rate, in this paper I will develop a model of agglomeration that shares a number of the features typical of models of self-organization in chemical and biological systems. In particular, while we begin with simulation results, it turns out to be possible to understand those results using an analytical approach originally suggested in a classic analysis by none other than Alan Turing (1952). The model is closely related to that in a companion analysis (Krugman, 1996), which is, in turn, part of an ongoing sequence of work I have done on economic geography (Krugman 1991, 1993). In this case, however, the basic model allows for discrete firms (as opposed to the continuum of firms assumed in the companion paper) and introduces some randomness in the dynamics. As we will see, the model exhibits a "symmetry breaking" when this randomness falls below a critical level, with cities emerging from a near-uniform spatial distribution of activity much like crystals precipitating out of a solution.

The remainder of this paper is organized as follows: Section 2 sets out a dynamic model of a spatial economy and shows how that model can be solved. Section 3 describes some simulation experiments with that model; it then offers a preliminary explanation of the behavior found in those simulations. Section 4 shows how the heuristic analysis of the second part can be given a more formal statement. Finally, Section 5 contains concluding remarks.

2. A dynamic spatial model

The first step in describing a spatial economy must be to specify its "geometry." For the purposes of this paper, it will be helpful if we consider a geometry with two characteristics. First, all locations are symmetric, so that the emergence of cities is a case of pure self-organization, rather than reflecting inherent advantages (such as centrality) of particular sites. Second, space is one-dimensional – because one dimension is much simpler to work with than two. The geometry that satisfies both of these criteria is, of course, a "racetrack" economy in which locations are evenly spaced around a circle, and transportation must take place along that circle's rim.

We consider such an economy in which there are J locations, indexed by $j = 1, \dots, J$. We let D_{jk} be the (shortest!) distance between any pair of locations j and k.

In this economy, there are two kinds of producer: immobile "farmers" and mobile "firms." Farmers are rooted in their locations; in order to leave any emergent spatial structure as completely endogenous, they will be assumed to be equally divided among the locations. It will turn out to be convenient to choose units so that there are $1 - \mu$ farmers.

Everyone in this economy shares the same tastes, which may be represented by a two-level structure. At the upper level, there are Cobb-Douglas preferences between agricultural goods and a manufacturing aggregate:

$$U = C_M^{\mu} C_A^{1-\mu} \tag{1-1}$$

At the lower level, manufacturing is a CES composite of a large number of symmetric differentiated products:

$$C_M = \left[\sum_v C_v^{(\sigma-1)/\sigma} \right]^{\frac{\sigma}{\sigma-1}} \tag{1-2}$$

where σ is the elasticity of substitution.

Farmers produce the homogeneous agricultural good with constant returns to scale. Firms produce differentiated manufactured goods; in particular, each firm produces one unit of a single differentiated product in a single location, and each firm produces a different product. Clearly, this assumption implicitly relies on some kind of economies of scale. In fact, the model is closely based on a series of related papers in which mobile "workers" are employed by monopolistically competitive firms. For current purposes, however, it will be useful to bury the details of market structure inside the assumption that there are simply discrete units called firms, selling differentiated products, that can change their location over time.

We also introduce transport costs. For the sake of tractability, there are assumed to be zero transport costs for agricultural goods. Transport costs on manufactured goods are of Samuelson's "iceberg" form. If one unit of a manufactured good is shipped from location j to location k, only $\exp(-\tau D_{jk})$ units arrive, with τ the transportation cost per unit distance.

If we take the spatial distribution of firms as given, what we have just described is simply a general equilibrium model. The equilibrium of that model includes an equilibrium level of the real income of a typical firm at each location; differences in these real incomes are what drive the economy's dynamics.

The assumed dynamics in this model are ad hoc, but similar to those used in many simulations of self-organizing systems (see, for instance, the examples described in Resnick [1994]). Firms are assumed to be myopic over both time and space. They tend to move to neighboring locations that currently offer real incomes that are higher than those at their current location, ignoring both more distant locations and possible future changes in the economy. (The assumption of only local movement differs from the assumed dynamics in Krugman 1993, 1996). Also, some randomness is introduced into firms' behavior: While their expected direction of movement is toward higher real income, there is some possibility that they will move in the "wrong" direction.

This behavior is specifically modeled as follows. Let ω_j be the real income earned by a firm at location j; and let ω_{j+1} be the real income at the location to the right (clockwise) of j, ω_{j-1} the income to the left. Then we assume that the probability that the firm moves one location right in the next period is

$$pr\,(j, j+1) = \frac{\exp(\gamma\omega_{j+1})}{\exp\,(\gamma\omega_{j+1}) + S\exp\,(\gamma\omega_j) + \exp\,(\omega_{j-1})} \tag{1-3}$$

and, similarly, that the probability that the firm moves one location left is

$$pr\,(j, j-1) = \frac{\exp(\gamma\omega_{j-1})}{\exp\,(\gamma\omega_{j+1}) + S\exp\,(\gamma\omega_j) + \exp\,(\omega_j - 1)} \tag{1-4}$$

That is, the firm's choice among the three locations j, $j+1$, and $j-1$ can be represented with the kind of logit formulation often used in empirical studies of discrete choice.

Two points should be noted about the formulation of dynamics in Eqs. (1-3) and (1-4). First, the parameter S is in effect a "slowing" parameter: It introduces a bias toward staying put. In simulation experiments of the kind reported in Part 3, it is essentially an inverse rate of adjustment. When we consider the limiting case of continuous time, we will find that S drops out of the analysis.

The parameter γ, by contrast, plays an essential role. It determines how much "noise" there is in firms' choices. If γ is small, firms are almost as likely to move in the wrong as in the right direction; if it is large, they will almost always move in the direction of higher real incomes. As we will see, there is a critical value of γ (depending on the other parameters of the model), at which the qualitative behavior of the economy changes from randomness to emergent order.

The dynamic behavior of this model, then, can be thought of as a sequence of general-equilibrium problems. For any given distribution of firms across locations, the economy reaches an equilibrium that determines the real income of a typical firm at each location. This vector of real incomes then determines, via Eqs. (1-3) and (1-4), the distribution of firms in the next period, and so on.

To solve the instantaneous general-equilibrium problem, we begin by defining p_j as the f.o.b. price charged by a typical firm at location j, measured in terms of the agricultural good.

We now proceed in stages. First, we note that since transport costs for agricultural goods are zero, all farmers will earn the same wage; let us use this common wage as the numeraire. Then the total income earned at any given location is

$$Y_j = \frac{1-\mu}{J} + \mu\, n_j p_j \tag{1-5}$$

Next, we develop an equation for the price at any given location. Let c_{vj} be consumption of variety v at location j, and let d_{vj} be the delivered (c.i.f.) price of that variety at that location. Then, since a share μ of income is spent on manufactures, it must be true that

$$\mu Y_j = \sum_v c_{vj}\, d_{vj} \tag{1-6}$$

Pick any variety, say variety 1; then the consumption of every other variety relative to that variety depends on the ratio of their prices,

$$\frac{c_{vj}}{c_{1j}} = \left(\frac{d_{vj}}{d_{1j}}\right)^{-\sigma} \tag{1-7}$$

Substituting Eq. (1-7) into Eq. (1-6) and rearranging, we can derive an expression for the total expenditure of location j residents on good 1:

$$c_{1j}\, d_{1j} = \mu\, Y_j \frac{d_{1j}^{\,1-\sigma}}{\sum_v d_{vj}^{\,1-\sigma}} \tag{1-8}$$

Equation (1-8) may be simplified by defining the true or ideal price index of manufactures at location j:

$$T_j = \left[\sum_v d_{vj}^{\,1-\sigma}\right]^{\frac{1}{1-\sigma}} \tag{1-9}$$

Then Eq.(1-8) may be rewritten (and applied to any variety v) as

$$c_{vj}\, d_{vj} = \mu Y_j \left[\frac{d_{vj}}{T_j}\right]^{1-\sigma} \tag{1-10}$$

But now bear in mind that n_j varieties are produced in each location j; that the f.o.b. price of any good produced in location j is p_j; and that the c.i.f. price of that good in any other location, say k, is $p_j \exp(\tau D_{jk})$. It then follows that the true price index of manufactures at location j is

$$T_j = \left[\sum_k n_k \,(p_k\, e^{\tau D_{jk}})^{\,1-\sigma}\right]^{\frac{1}{1-\sigma}} \tag{1-11}$$

It may be worth noting that if all locations have similar f.o.b. prices, a shift of manfacturing toward locations that are close to region j – that is, locations for which D_{jk} is small – will tend to lower the price index of manufactures there. This is the source of one of the "centripetal" forces in this model, a "forward linkage" in which firms want to be close to other firms that supply them with consumption goods.

Turn next to the equilibrium prices. We note that the total expenditure on a manufactured good produced at j (including the fraction of the good which melts in transit), which must equal the f.o.b. value of that good, is

$$p_j = \mu \sum_k Y_k \,(p_j\, e^{\tau D_{jk}}/T_k)^{\,1-\sigma} \tag{1-12}$$

Rearranging, we get the price equations

$$p_j = [\mu \sum_k Y_k\, T_k^{\sigma-1}\, e^{-\tau(\sigma-1)D_{jk}}]^{1/\sigma} \tag{1-13}$$

Equation (1-13) may be regarded as a rigorously derived version of the ad hoc "market potential" functions that are widely used to predict location decisions in empirical work in economic geography (see, for example, Dicken and Lloyd [1990:181-185]). Market potential functions generally assign a location a potential that depends positively on income at all other locations, but with a weight on each location that declines in distance. A typical market potential function might be of the form

$$M_j = \sum_k Y_k / D_{jk} \tag{1-14}$$

Here, the functional form is different, and an additional set of variables, true price indices – which in effect capture competition from other regions – enter. Nonetheless, there is a distinct family resemblance.

In this case, however, the market potential functions arise in the context of a full general equilibrium model. That model's instantaneous equilibrium may be derived by simultaneously solving Eqs. (1-5), (1-11), and (1-13). (Bear in mind that each of these equations applies to all J locations; thus $3J$ equations must be solved simultaneously).

Once we have derived the instantaneous equilibrium, we can apply the dynamic rules, Eqs. (1-3) and (1-4) to see how the system evolves. This rule, however, requires that we compute real incomes of firms; Eq. (1-13) computes prices in terms of the agricultural numeraire. But this is straightforward: Since manufactures are a share m of consumption, the real income at location j is

$$\omega_j = p_j T_j^{-\mu} \tag{1-15}$$

We have now set out a dynamic, stochastic model of a spatial economy. As pointed out in Krugman (1991), this model economy, like the real economy, is characterized by a tension between centripetal and centrifugal forces. The centripetal forces are the incentive for firms to move toward suppliers of manufactured goods – the "forward linkage" that can be observed in Eq. (1-11); and the incentive to move toward large markets – the "backward linkage" captured by the "market potential" equation, Eq. (1-13). Against these forces works the general incentive to disperse that arises from the immobility of the farmers: If manufacturing is geographically concentrated, it may be to the advantage of firms to move away from that concentration, so that they can sell to a rural market for which they face little competition.

Unfortunately, while these forces are fairly clear, the model defies analytic solution when there are more than two regions. We will see later in the paper that it is possible nonetheless to learn quite a lot from a novel analytical approach; but as a first step we turn to some simulations.

3. Self-Organization: Simulations and heuristic analysis

If one is willing to turn to numerical methods, it is straightforward to simulate this model. One must first specify the number of locations J and the distances between them; one must also specify the parameters τ, σ, μ, S, and γ; and one must specify the initial distribution of firms among locations. (I always begin with firms randomly allocated among locations.) One then solves Eqs. (1-5),

(1-11), and (1-13) – something most easily done simply by making initial guesses at Y, p, and T and cycling until convergence. This then allows one to calculate real wages, and by applying the random adjustment rules, Eqs. (1-3) and (1-4), to produce a new distribution of firms; and so on.

It quickly becomes apparent that the results of such a simulation crucially depend on the parameter γ.

Figure 1-1 shows the results of a typical simulation of the model when γ is below what we will soon see is a critical value. The economy in this case consists of 12 locations, like the numbers on a clock face. (The number 12 was chosen because it is a fairly small number with a large number of divisors.) Thus location 12 is next to location 1. The locations were spaced one unit apart. The parameters for this run were $\sigma = 4$, $\mu = .2$, $\tau = .2$, $S = 2$, and $\gamma = 40$. There were 200 firms.

The figure shows a simulation lasting 70 periods, beginning with a random allocation of firms to locations. The x axis represents location; the y axis the number of firms at that location; and the z axis time.

The figure shows quite a lot of movement, but no clear pattern. There is certainly no obvious tendency toward self-organization.

But now let us run the same experiment with a somewhat larger value of γ, $\gamma = 60$. The result is shown in Fig. 1-2. The economy now organizes itself into a very clear spatial pattern, in which the great majority of firms are either in or near two peaks, at locations 4 and 10.

It may not seem surprising that the economy forms agglomerations in this fashion. What is somewhat surprising, however, is the regularity of the result. Notice that the two locations 4 and 10 are 6 apart; that is, they are precisely opposite one another on the circle. I did not choose this picture because it has

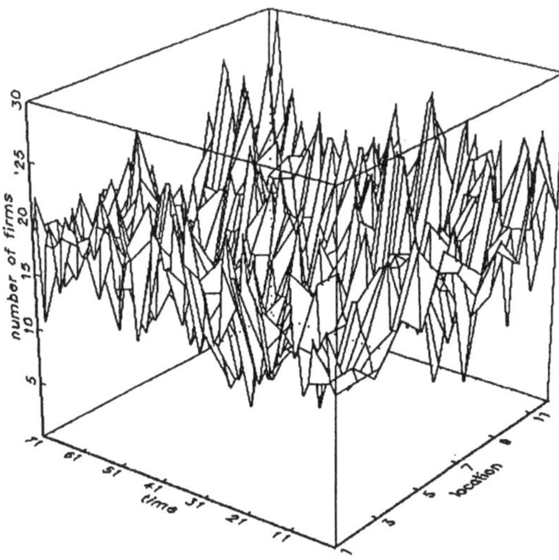

Figure 1-1

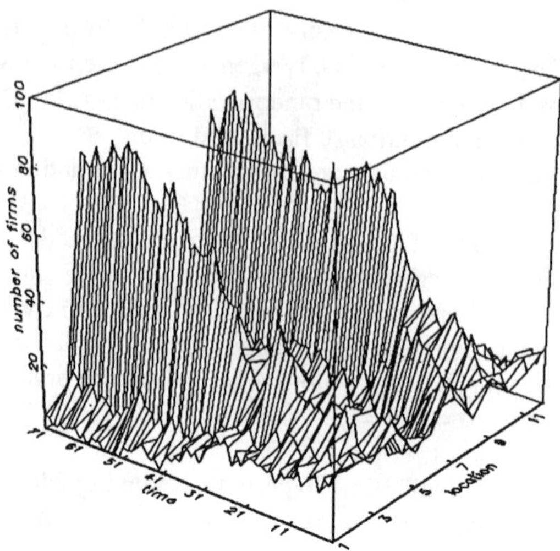

Figure 1-2

this outcome: When the model is run with these parameters, it consistently yields two manufacturing concentrations, exactly opposite one another (although which pair get the manufacturing is random).

The major question we will try to answer in this section and the next is where this regularity comes from. In the process, we will also arrive at a better understanding of the reasons why the initially almost flat distribution undergoes a process of self-organization.

The basic approach we will take is to focus on the behavior of the model *near a completely flat distribution of manufacturing*. A flat distribution of firms is always an equilibrium; but as we will argue, when firms respond sufficiently strongly to economic incentives, it is an unstable equilibrium. The nature of that instability turns out to be the key to the emergence of spatial order.

To analyze the model, it is helpful to "smooth" it in several ways. As stated and as simulated, this is a model in which a finite number of discrete firms move among discrete locations in discrete time. To understand what happens, however, we will successively approximate all of these discrete variables by continuous ones, so that a continuous distribution of firms across a continuous space evolves over continuous time. As we will see, this reformulation actually makes things simpler!

To begin with, it would be helpful if we normalize distances so that the circumference of the circle is $2\pi R$, with locations a distance δ apart. In our first continuum assumption, we let $\lambda(x)$ be the concentration of manufacturing, measured as a continuous variable, at location x. Then, it is clear from the logic of the model that the rate of change of $\lambda(x)$ depends only on the concentration of manufacturing at other locations. That is, we can write a reduced form of the model, in which

$$\frac{d\lambda(x)}{dt} = F[\lambda(x - N\delta), \ldots \lambda(x), \ldots \lambda(x + N\delta)] \tag{1-16}$$

for any x.

Now consider a linear approximation to this reduced form in the vicinity of a uniform distribution of manufacturing. The linearized dynamics now become

$$\frac{d\lambda(x)}{dt} = \sum_{-N}^{N} F_z [\lambda(x + \delta z) - \bar{\lambda}] \tag{1-17}$$

where, owing to the symmetry of the model, $F_Z = F_{-Z}$.

Equation (1-17) defines a system of linear differential equations. To analyze such a system, we look for eigenvectors and their associated eigenvalues.

Let us simply posit a solution of the form

$$\lambda(x) - \bar{\lambda} = e^{i\varphi x} \tag{1-18}$$

(Ignore for the moment the impossibility of complex numbers of firms at each location.) Such a solution is only possible, of course, if it implies an integer number of cycles around the circle. That is, we consider only values of φ such that φR is an integer.

Substitute Eq. (1-18) into Eq. (1-17), and we find

$$\begin{aligned} \frac{d}{dt}[\lambda(x) - \bar{\lambda}] &= \sum_{-N}^{N} F_z e^{i\varphi(x + \delta z)} \\ &= e^{i\varphi x} \sum_{-N}^{N} F_z e^{i\varphi \delta z} \end{aligned} \tag{1-19}$$

Now invoke the equality between F_Z and F_{-Z}, and we find

$$\frac{d}{dt}[\lambda(x) - \bar{\lambda}] = [\lambda(x) - \bar{\lambda}]\left[1 + 2\sum_{1}^{N} F_z \cos(\varphi \delta z)\right] \tag{1-20}$$

But the term in brackets is independent of x. Thus we have just learned that any sinusoidal fluctuation in the density of manufacturing (with a period that is an integer multiple of the circumference) is an eigenvector of the linearized system near the flat equilibrium, with an eigenvalue (the term in brackets) that depends on the frequency of that fluctuation.

In general, the actual deviation of the distribution of manufacturing from perfect flatness will not be a perfect sinusoidal fluctuation. However, as long as it is sufficiently smooth, that deviation can be represented as a Fourier series of the form

$$\lambda(x) - \bar{\lambda} = \sum_{m=1}^{\infty} \left(A_m e^{i(m/R)x} + B_m e^{-i(m/R)x}\right) \tag{1-21}$$

That is, it can be represented as a sum of sinusoidal fluctuations. And since these fluctuations are eigenvectors, we can in effect represent the evolution of the economy as the parallel, independent evolution of a set of economies whose initial distribution of manufacturing *is* perfectly sinusoidal.

What, then, is the condition for spatial self-organization – that is, for an almost flat distribution of manufacturing to spontaneously evolve into a highly uneven spatial structure? The condition required is that at least one of the fluctuations into which the initial distribution can be decomposed be unstable; that is, that at least one of the eigenvalues determined by Eq. (1-21) be positive.

But we can say more than this. Suppose we start with a set of parameters such that all eigenvalues are negative, so that the economy does not tend to form any structures. Now change a parameter in such a way that one of the eigenvalues becomes positive. Then the distribution of firms will become increasingly non-uniform as the density fluctuation, whose frequency corresponds to that eigenvalue, grows. The peaks of that fluctuation will, of course, be regularly spaced, and the number of peaks will equal the frequency of that fluctuation.

This explains both the regularity and the predictability of the result shown in Fig. 1-2. The reason one always gets two peaks, exactly opposite each other, is that the unstable eigenvector that is produced when γ is increased from 40 to 60 has a frequency of 2.

But what determines which wavelength fluctuation is the first to become unstable when γ is increased? And why does an increase in γ create instability?

The first question is fairly complex to approach analytically. We will carry out a formal analysis of the relationship between the frequency of fluctuations and their stability in the next section. Let us begin, however, with a heuristic exposition.

As we have seen, this model is characterized by both centripetal and centrifugal forces. Let us restate our loose definition of these forces in terms of the way that the density of manufacturing at one location affects the real income of a firm at some other location. Suppose that there is an above-average density of manufacturing at some location at a distance D from my location. This has both positive and negative effects on my real income. On the one hand, that concentration provides a larger market for my product (backward linkage) and a larger supply of products I consume (forward linkage). On the other, that concentration competes with me for the agricultural market. (Note that the effects of a reduction in the density of manufacturing at some other location are precisely the reverse: weaker linkages but less competition).

Both the positive and negative spillovers from manufacturing decline with distance. However, we can loosely argue that the *effective range* of the negative effects is larger than that of the positive effects. Suppose that goods can on average economically be shipped 200 miles. (In the model, of course, there is no fixed range of shipment, just rising transport costs; but think of this as some average distance of shipment). Then a concentration of manufacturing can provide forward and backward linkages only if it is less than 200 miles away; but it can still compete with me in some markets even if it is 400 miles away.

Now consider a fluctuation of a very high frequency. Is the peak of such a fluctuation a desirable place for firms to be? Well, with such a short wavelength, every positive effect from an above-average concentration in the range of positive spillovers will be more or less canceled by the negative effect of a neighboring region of below-average concentration; and the same will be true within the range of negative spillovers. Thus both peaks and troughs of very high-frequency fluctuations will offer only roughly the average real income to firms; that is, there is no reason for high-frequency fluctuations to grow.

On the other hand, consider a very low-frequency fluctuation. In this case, there will be above-average density of manufacturing at all locations relevant to each peak of the fluctuation; there will be positive effects from the range of positive spillovers, and negative effects from the range of negative spillovers. As long as the negative spillovers are sufficiently strong relative to the positive – which as we will see reduces to a simple condition in terms of the model's parameters – a peak of a very low-frequency fluctuation will be a place of *below*-average real income. Such very low-frequency fluctuations will therefore tend to shrink.

But, finally, consider an intermediate-wavelength fluctuation. If the wavelength has been chosen correctly, such a fluctuation will be one in which density is above-average in the range of positive spillovers, which tends to make the real wage high at the peak, and below-average in the range of negative spillovers, which *also* tends to make the real wage high at the peak. So such an intermediate-wavelength fluctuation will have high real wages at its peaks, low real wages at its troughs. It therefore has the best prospect for growth.

But will it actually grow? Not necessarily because, due to the random element in the dynamics, there is another force operating in this model: *diffusion.*

Consider again the dynamics implied by Eqs. (1-3) and (1-4), but now imagine that the number of firms is large enough so that we can treat the number at any one location as a continuous variable, and the expected rate of change as a deterministic variable. Now ask: What determines the expected rate of change of n_j? Recall that $pr\ (j, j+1)$ is the probability that a given firm moves from location j to $j+1$; then

$$\Delta n_j = n_{j-1}\, pr\,(j-1, j) - n_j\,[pr\,(j, j-1) - n_j\, pr\,(j, j+1)\,] \qquad (1\text{-}22)$$
$$+ n_{j+1}\, pr\,(j+1, j)$$

But Eqs. (1-3) and (1-4) define expressions for these probabilities, which can be substituted into Eq. (1-22). The resulting equation can be made somewhat simpler if we take a linear approximation in the vicinity of the average concentration of firms and the average real income of firms; it now becomes

$$\Delta n_j = \frac{1}{2+S}(n_{j-1} - 2n_j + n_{j+1}) + \frac{\gamma}{(2+S)^2}[-\omega_{j-2} \qquad (1\text{-}23)$$
$$-(2+2S)\,\omega_{j-1} + (4+4S)\,\omega_j - (2+2S)\,\omega_{j+1} - \omega_{j+2}]$$

We can simplify further by moving to continuous time. Bear in mind that S is a sort of inverse speed of adjustment. If we make the period dt very short, we should think of S as growing very large; indeed, since the probability of moving out of a location when the wage is uniform is $1/(2+S)$, when dt is small S must be of the order $1/dt$. It will therefore do no harm to assume $S = 1/dt$. Let dt be very small; then Eq. (1-23) becomes

$$\frac{dn_j}{dt} = (n_{j-1} - 2\,n_j + n_{j+1}) + \gamma(-2\,\omega_{j-1} + 4\,\omega_j - 2\,\omega_{j+1}) \tag{1-24}$$

or, rewriting,

$$\frac{dn_j}{dt} = [\,(n_{j+1} - n_j) - (n_j - n_{j+1})\,] - 2\,\gamma\,[\,(\omega_{\gamma+1} - \omega_j) - (\omega_j - \omega_{j-1})\,] \tag{1-25}$$

Finally, imagine that locations are very close, so that we can approximate the density and real incomes of firms by continuous functions of location. Then Eq. (1-25) becomes

$$\frac{dn\,(x)}{dt} = \lambda''\,(x) - 2\,\gamma\,\omega''\,(x) \tag{1-26}$$

For a sinusoidal fluctuation with frequency φ, we know immediately that

$$n''(x) = \varphi^2\,[n\,(x) - \bar{n}] \tag{1-27}$$

We can also conclude from the fact that such a deviation is an eigenfunction that (in the linear approximation near a flat distribution of firms) the deviation of the real wage from its actual value is proportional to the deviation of density from the average:

$$\omega\,(x) - \bar{\omega} = a_\omega\,(\varphi)\,[n\,(x) - \bar{n}] \tag{1-28}$$

with the coefficient depending on the other parameters of the model. So a fluctuation of frequency φ is unstable if and only if

$$1 - 2\,a_\omega\,(\varphi)\lambda < 0 \tag{1-29}$$

Our earlier discussion suggests, however, that the relationship between the frequency of a fluctuation and the coefficient a_ω should have an inverted U shape. Very low-frequency fluctuations should have $a_\omega < 0$; very high-frequency fluctuations should have a_ω near 0; and intermediate-frequency fluctuations should have $a_\omega > 0$. And there should be a particular "preferred" frequency that will be the first to become unstable if γ is sufficiently large; the distance between emergent manufacturing concentrations will equal the wavelength corresponding to that frequency.

We now have an intuitive story about the process of self-organization in this model, based on the idea of shifting our focus from a direct analysis of the growth of particular locations to that of the growth of fluctuations of different wavelengths. This shift in focus has three very attractive features. First, it offers a satisfying way to think about what might otherwise seem to be the impossibly complex dynamics of a model with an arbitrary number of locations. Second, it explains the surprisingly orderly structures that emerge from simulations with random initial conditions. Finally, it allows us to relate the issue of the sizes and distances between emergent manufacturing concentrations to the underlying economics.

At this point, however, the analysis is still only heuristic. In the next section we turn to the fairly laborious but in the end rewarding task of using the fluctuations approach to analyze the formal model of Section 2.

4. How fluctuations grow

To carry out a formal analysis in terms of fluctuations, it turns out to be easier to work from the beginning with a model in which firms and farmers are spread continuously around the circle rather than being distributed in a number of discrete locations. It also helps to change the normalizations slightly.

Let us, then, consider a circular economy of circumference $2\pi R$ in which farmers are evenly spread. It will now be convenient to choose units so that there are $1 - \mu$ farmers per unit of circumference, so that if firms were spread evenly there would be μ firms per unit of distance. We now define λ as the ratio of the actual density to that uniform density, and w as the ratio of the price charged by each firm to the price they would receive if evenly spread. It follows that the income at any location x is

$$Y(x) = 1 - \mu + \mu\lambda(x)\, w(x) \tag{1-30}$$

The rest of the basic equations of the model follow by analogy. The true price index of manufactures at location x is

$$T(x) = \left[\int_z \lambda(z)\, w(z)^{1-\sigma} e^{\tau(1-\sigma) D_{xz}}\, dz \right]^{1/1-\sigma} \tag{1-31}$$

The price equation now becomes

$$p(x) = \left[\int_z Y(z)\, T(z)^{\sigma - 1} e^{-\tau(\sigma-1) D_{xz}}\, dz \right]^{1/\sigma} \tag{1-32}$$

And real income is simply

$$\omega(x) = w(x)\, T(x)^{-\mu} \tag{1-33}$$

There is an equilibrium, albeit possibly an unstable one, with $\lambda(x) = 1$ everywhere. It is straightforward to show that, in this equilibrium

$$\overline{Y} = 1 \tag{1-34}$$

$$\overline{w} = 1 \tag{1-35}$$

$$\overline{T} = \left[\frac{2}{\tau(\sigma - 1)} (1 - e^{-\tau(\sigma-1)\pi R}) \right]^{1/1-\sigma} \tag{1-36}$$

and

$$\overline{\omega} = \overline{T}^{-\mu} \tag{1-37}$$

We next take a linear approximation of this system in the vicinity of these equilibrium values. The linearized system is

$$Y(x) - \overline{Y} = \mu\,[\lambda(x) - 1] + \mu\,[w(x) - \overline{w}] \tag{1-38}$$

$$\begin{aligned} T(x) - \overline{T} = & \frac{1}{1-\sigma}\overline{T}^{\sigma}\int_z e^{-\tau(\sigma-1)D_{xz}}\,[\lambda(z) - 1]\,dz \\ & + \overline{T}^{\sigma}\int_z e^{-\tau(\sigma-1)D_{xz}}\,[w(z) - \overline{w}]\,dz \end{aligned} \tag{1-39}$$

$$\begin{aligned} w(x) - \overline{w} = & \frac{1}{\sigma}\overline{T}^{\sigma-1}\int_z e^{-\tau(\sigma-1)D_{xz}}\,[Y(z) - \overline{Y}]\,dz \\ & + \frac{\sigma-1}{\sigma}\overline{T}^{\sigma-2}\int_z e^{-\tau(\sigma-1)D_{xz}}\,[T(z) - \overline{T}]\,dz \end{aligned} \tag{1-40}$$

and

$$\omega(x) - \overline{\omega} = [w(x) - \overline{w}]\,\overline{T}^{-\mu} - \mu\,\overline{T}^{-\mu-1}\,[T(x) - \overline{T}) \tag{1-41}$$

This system of equations does not, at first sight, appear especially promising! But now hypothesize a solution given that

$$\lambda(x) - \overline{\lambda} = e^{i\varphi x} \tag{1-42}$$

Our discussion in the previous section suggests that there should be a solution of the form

$$Y(x) - \overline{Y} = a_Y\,[\lambda(x) - \overline{\lambda}] \tag{1-43}$$

$$T(x) - \overline{T} = a_T\,[\lambda(x) - \overline{\lambda}] \tag{1-44}$$

$$w(x) - \overline{w} = a_w\,[\lambda(x) - \overline{\lambda}] \tag{1-45}$$

and

$$\omega(x) - \overline{\omega} = a_\omega\,[\lambda(x) - \overline{\lambda}] \tag{1-46}$$

In other words, we should be able to use only four simultaneous linear equations to solve for the ratio of each of the model's variables to the deviation of density from uniformity,

$$\frac{d\lambda(x)}{dt} = \gamma\,[\omega(x) - \overline{\omega}] = \gamma a_\omega\,[\lambda(x) - \overline{\lambda}] \tag{1-47}$$

To solve for these parameters, we substitute Eqs. (1-42)–(1-46) back into Eqs. (1-38)–(1-41). Two equations fall out immediately. First, we have

$$A_Y e^{i\varphi x} = \mu e^{i\varphi x} + \mu a_w\, e^{i\varphi x} \tag{1-48}$$

or

$$a_y = \mu + \mu a_w \tag{1-49}$$

Similarly, we find that

$$a_\omega = \overline{T}^{-\mu} a_w - \mu \overline{T}^{-\mu-1} a_T \tag{1-50}$$

The other two equations are a bit more difficult. It is useful to define a variable G, where

$$G = \int_z e^{-\tau(\sigma-1)D_{xz}} e^{i\varphi(z-x)}\, dz = \frac{2\tau(\sigma-1)}{\tau^2(\sigma-1)^2+\varphi^2}\left\{1 - e^{-\tau(\sigma-1)\pi R}\left[\cos(\varphi\pi R)+\sin(\varphi\pi R)\right]\right\} \tag{1-51}$$

This definition may be somewhat simplified if we recall that φ cannot take on arbitrary values, but is restricted to values for which φR is an integer. Sin($n\pi$), with n an integer, is always zero; cos($n\pi$) is 1 or –1, depending on whether n is odd or even. So we have

$$G = \frac{2\tau(\sigma-1)}{\tau^2(\sigma-1)^2+\varphi^2}\left[1 - e^{-\tau(\sigma-1)\pi R}(-1)^{\varphi R}\right] \tag{1-52}$$

We can now state the remaining equations:

$$a_T = \frac{1}{1-\sigma}\overline{T}^{\sigma} G + \overline{T}^{\sigma} G a_w \tag{1-53}$$

$$a_w = \frac{1}{\sigma}\overline{T}^{\sigma-1} G a_Y + \frac{\sigma-1}{\sigma}\overline{T}^{\sigma-2} G a_T \tag{1-54}$$

Given G, Eqs. (1-46), (1-47), (1-50), and (1-51) can be solved for the coefficients. The results are still too messy, in general, for easy analysis, particularly because of the integer constraint on the frequency: When φR is small, G bounces up and down as it alternates between odd and even.

We can, however, get much more insight by making one more assumption – that the economy is very large, that is, by taking the limit as R goes to infinity. This has the immediate effect of allowing us to ignore the integer constraint on φ. It also leads to a considerable simplification of the equations. As R becomes arbitrarily large, we have

$$\overline{T} = \left[\frac{2}{\tau(\sigma-1)}\right]^{1/1-\sigma} \tag{1-55}$$

and

$$G = \frac{2\tau(\sigma-1)}{\tau^2(\sigma-1)^2+\varphi^2} \tag{1-56}$$

Define a new variable,

$$H = \overline{T}^{\sigma-1} G = \frac{\tau^2(\sigma-1)^2}{\tau^2(\sigma-1)^2+\varphi^2} \tag{1-57}$$

H clearly varies between 1 and 0 as φ varies between 0 and infinity. Now we can write the simplified equations

$$a_T = \frac{1}{1-\sigma}\overline{T}H + \overline{T}H a_w \tag{1-58}$$

$$a_w = \frac{1}{\sigma} Ha_Y + \frac{\sigma - 1}{\sigma} \overline{T}^{-1} Ha_T \tag{1-59}$$

and we can solve directly to find that

$$a_w = \frac{H(\mu - H)}{\sigma - \mu H - (\sigma - 1) H^2} \tag{1-60}$$

and

$$a_w = \overline{T}^{-\mu} H \left[\frac{(1 - \mu)(\mu - H)}{\sigma - \mu H - (\sigma - 1) H^2} + \frac{\mu}{\sigma - 1} \right] \tag{1-61}$$

Since H is a monotonic function of φ, we are finally home: Eq. (1-58) is a tractable equation relating the frequency of density fluctuations to a_ω.

Does this relationship have the inverse-U shape we hypothesized? Consider first very high-frequency fluctuations. In that case, $H \geq 0$, and it is immediately apparent that the a_ω is also 0. That is, very high-frequency fluctuations have a near zero. Suppose, on the other hand, that we consider very long wavelength fluctuations, $\varphi \geq 0$, so that $H \geq 1$. Then

$$a_\omega = \overline{T}^{-\mu} \left[\frac{\mu}{\sigma - 1} - (1 - \mu) \right] \tag{1-62}$$

This will be negative – that is, very long wavelength fluctuations will die out no matter how little noise there is in the system – provided that

$$\mu \frac{\sigma}{\sigma - 1} < 1 \tag{1-63}$$

This is a familiar condition found, for example, in Krugman (1991). It amounts to saying that aggregate economies of scale – economies of scale in the manufacturing sector multiplied by the share of that sector in income – are not so strong that an increase in the number of firms in some location actually raises their real wages even in the absence of trade with other locations.

Given this condition, then, we know that a_ω is negative when H is 1, zero when $H = 0$. Is there an intermediate positive range? Evaluate the derivative of $a_\omega$with respect to H in the vicinity of $H = 0$:

$$\frac{da_\omega}{dH} = \frac{\mu(1 - \mu)}{\sigma} + \frac{\mu}{\sigma - 1} > 0 \tag{1-64}$$

So there must be an upward-sloping region near the origin, and the relationship between H and a_ω is an upside-down U.

Clearly, there is some value of H, corresponding to some frequency of fluctuation, for which a_ω is maximized. How does this preferred frequency depend on the model's parameters? Note that we can rewrite H as

$$H = \frac{(\sigma - 1)^2}{(\sigma - 1)^2 + \varphi^2/\tau^2} \tag{1-65}$$

Table 1-1. Preferred values of ϕ/τ

	μ	.2	.3	.4
σ				
4		5.83	4.48	3.60
5		7.76	6.11	5.00
6		10.00	7.64	6.25

This allows us to conclude directly that the preferred frequency is proportional to transport costs, and hence that the preferred wavelength is inversely proportional – which should be obvious because, in this model, doubling transport costs is fully equivalent to doubling the unit of distance.

It is more difficult to derive analytical results for the other two parameters, σ and μ. However, we might expect that an increase in σ, because it reduces the monopoly power of firms and the implied importance of scale economies, should tend to increase φ, that is, to lead to more closely spaced urban concentrations; an increase in μ, by reducing the importance of the agricultural market, should tend to reduce φ, leading to more widely spaced cities. It is easy to numerically confirm that this is the case, as shown in Table 1.1.

5. Conclusions

In a way, it is surprising that there have not (to my knowledge) been any previous efforts to apply some variant of the reaction-diffusion models that have become so influential in the study of chemical and biological phenomena to the formation of cities. After all, an economy with cities is definitely a self-organizing spatial system, indeed arguably one of the premier examples of such a system; if the parallels with chemical reactions or slime molds are not exact, they are surely strong enough to warrant exploring.

In any case, this paper (and its companion piece, Krugman [1996]) offer what is intended as a provocative attempt to apply something like a Turing model to a spatial economy. The details of the model are different from those appropriate to chemistry or biology: While the dynamics are ad hoc, the statics are based on a fully specified if very special general equilibrium model. Nonetheless, the general behavior of the model – symmetry-breaking when noise is reduced below a critical level, followed by spontaneous evolution of a spatial pattern, with a characteristic wavelength determined by the underlying parameters – is very much in the spirit of the related literature in other fields.

To make this a truly convincing model, of course, considerable work is needed. Perhaps the most obvious task is to extend the analysis to two dimensions, something that is not at all easy, even if one is interested only in simulation results (a two-dimensional model with comparable "resolution" turns out to require several hundred times as much computation for each run). We would also like to introduce different types of firms, perhaps generating an urban hierarchy. Beyond this is the problem of making the underlying model less unrealistic, by introducing transportation costs for agricultural goods, for example. And there are deeper issues, such as whether it is possible to derive dynamics from some kind of explicit rational choice model without making the analysis completely intractable.

Nonetheless, the model as it stands is already highly suggestive. It shows that the dynamic behavior of a model seemingly offers a huge range of possible equilibria that can exhibit surprising regularities; and that it is possible to obtain analytical insights into the model by approaching it from a different perspective. Above all, it offers hope that there may in fact be useful spillovers between economics and the study of self-organizing systems in other fields.

References

Dicken, P. and P. Lloyd (1990) *Location in Space: Theoretical Perspectives in Economic Geography*. New York: Harper Collins.

Fujita, M., P. Krugman, and T. Mori (1994) "On the Evolution of Hierarchical Urban Systems." Mimeo. Philadelphia: University of Pennsylvania, Department of Regional Science.

Goodwin, B. (1994) *How the Leopard Changed Its Spots*. New York: Basic Books.

Krugman, P. (1991) "Increasing Returns and Economic Geography." *Journal of Political Economy*, 99, 483-99.

Krugman, P. (1993) "On the Number and Location of Cities." *European Economic Review* 37, 293-98.

Krugman, P. (1996) *The Self-Organizing Economy*. Cambridge, MA: Blackwell.

Resnick, M. (1994) *Turtles, Termites, and Traffic Jams: Explorations in Massively Parallel Microworlds*. Cambridge, MA: MIT Press.

Turing, A. M. (1952) "The Chemical Basis of Morphogenesis." *Philosophical Transactions of the Royal Society of London*, 236, 5-72.

CHAPTER 2

The size of regions

*Elhanan Helpman**

1. Introduction

Regional scientists and urban economists have studied many forces that shape urban and regional structures. They have emphasized the availability of usable land, of local amenities such as beaches or climate; the provision of local public goods such as roads and schools; commuting costs, congestion, pollution; localized economies of scale in production; and more. These factors help us to understand differences in layouts of cities and in city size as well as regional differences in population density or the concentration of manufacturing facilities. They can also be used to explain differences in the economic geography of countries.

Some of these elements, such as the availability of land or congestion, push for the dispersion of economic activity. Others, such as the provision of local public goods or localized economies of scale in production, push for agglomeration. The observed outcomes reflect the balance of these forces. Tolley and Crihfield (1987) suggest that market forces tend to generate too much agglomeration, and their view is quite common among urban economists.

My purpose in this chapter is to take a fresh look at the problem of agglomeration by examining a model of two regions in which the availability of housing (land) is the main driving force behind dispersion of economic activity, typical to regional and urban economics. In addition, I will introduce an industrial sector into the model that supplies differentiated products that are traded between the regions at a cost. These goods are produced with brand-specific economies of scale. As a result, the industrial sector provides the main driving force for agglomeration. An industrial sector of this sort has been extensively utilized by Paul Krugman in his work on economic geography (e.g., Krugman 1991).

Although each of these centrifugal and centripetal forces has been studied before, their combination provides some new insights. In particular, as simple as this model may be, it produces interesting equilibrium outcomes: Each region may be occupied in proportion to (or as a function of) its relative amount of

* Tel Aviv University and the Canadian Institute for Advanced Research. I am grateful to David Pines for generously providing advice on the content of this paper. I am also grateful to Yossi Hadar for research assistance.

housing; or regions may be unequally populated even when they have equal amounts of housing. Importantly, in the latter type of equilibrium, there is too little agglomeration; in the former, the degree of agglomeration is efficient. The simplicity of the model enables us to explain these results by means of the intensity of preferences for differentiated products, the degree of substitution across brands, and the level of transport costs.

The formal model is developed in Section 2. Section 3 is then devoted to an analysis of equilibrium outcomes. It is shown that whenever transport costs are low, a unique stable equilibrium exists in which both regions are occupied. Population density is determined by the relative availability of housing. If the amount of housing is the same in both regions, half of the population resides in each of them. When the demand for housing is high or the elasticity of substitution across brands is high, the same type of unique, stable equilibrium prevails for all levels of transport costs. When the demand for housing is low, however, or the elasticity of substitution across brands is low, there exist two asymmetric equilibria with regions of unequal size in each one of them, even when the supply of housing is the same in both locations. The higher the transport costs, the more unequal the regions, while the inequality in the size of regions rises very rapidly with transport costs. These results are different from Krugman's (1991) regarding the link between agglomeration and transport costs. Explanations for the differences are provided in Section 6, in which the two models are compared in some detail.

Before the reader reaches this section, however, two additional issues are studied. First, I examine the welfare properties of the resulting equilibria in Section 4. An important conclusion reached is that there is either too little agglomeration or the amount of agglomeration is just right. The former occurs at the asymmetric equilibria. It follows that whenever regions differ in size as a result of endogenous economic pressures rather than inherent differences, it is desirable to make their inequality even more pronounced.

As mentioned at the beginning of this introduction, there are many potential forces of agglomeration and dispersion. My model focuses on just two of them. In order to see whether it produces results that are peculiar to economies in which differentiated products that are costly to transport provide the incentive to agglomerate, I examine an alternative model with no transport costs and with regional external economies of scale in the production of a homogeneous product in Section 5. The model produces equilibria that are similar to the equilibria of the model described in Section 2. This indicates that there is nothing unusual in my results.

Much of what is discussed in this chapter applies to cities, regions, and countries. For concreteness, however, I will refer to each location as a *region*, where a region is characterized by a fixed supply of housing (although we could replace housing by any other good or service that is not traded across regions).[1] The differentiated products can be produced anywhere, but they are traded across regions at a cost. And finally, people move across regions in search of higher welfare. Clearly, this type of model also applies to cities, although in the study of cities one may want to specify their layouts in more detail. It also applies to countries that allow free migration. These interpretations should be kept in mind in reading what follows.

2. The basic model

In this section I develop a simple model of regions that focuses on the tradeoff between the supply of housing – which is not traded across regions and serves as a centrifugal force – and the manufacturing of differentiated industrial products with increasing returns to scale. As these products are footloose but costly to transport, their manufacture serves as a centripetal force. Suppliers of manufactured products engage in monopolistic competition while suppliers of housing are competitive.

Each region has a fixed stock of housing and people can choose in which region to reside. Poeple who live in a region purchase housing services and all manufactured products therein, both locally produced and imported brands. A person works in the region of residence. As a result, labor supply in a region is determined by its population. Labor supply determines, in turn, the local output of differentiated products, including the number of brands. A more populated region is supplied with a larger variety of locally manufactured goods while imported brands are costly to transport. This raises the local standard of living. On the other hand, housing costs are higher in a more populated region, which reduces the local standard of living. These two forces produce a tension between the tendency to agglomerate and the tendency to disperse. Individuals migrate from regions with a low standard of living to regions with a higher standard of living. Therefore, in equilibrium, the standard of living is the same in all populated regions.

My analysis is confined to the case of two regions and it focuses on the following questions:

- What determines the distribution of the population across regions?
- Do lower transport costs lead to more or less agglomeration?
- Is the resulting degree of agglomeration efficient relative to the market structure?

[1] I treat the supply of housing in a region as a given constant. Urban economic models that treat the supply of housing endogenously emphasize intra-city commuting costs as a main determinant of its availability.

In order to address these questions, I now develop a formal model.

There are N identical individuals, each having a Cobb-Douglas utility function

$$u = h^{\beta} d^{1-\beta} \tag{2-1}$$

where h represents consumption of housing services and d represents a consumption index of differentiated products. This index is given by

$$d = \left[\int_0^n x(j)^{\alpha} \, dj \right]^{1/\alpha}, \quad 0 < \alpha < 1 \tag{2-2}$$

where n is the available number (measure) of brands and $x(j)$ represents consumption of brand j. As is well known, these preferences imply a constant price elasticity of demand $\varepsilon = 1/(1-\alpha) > 1$ for each brand, where ε also represents the elasticity of substitution between them. As a result, the price of a brand equals $1/\alpha$ times marginal costs.

Assume that it takes $a + x$ units of labor to manufacture x units of a single brand, where a represents fixed costs in terms of labor. Then in Region i, with a wage rate w_i, the mill price of each locally produced brand equals

$$p_i = \frac{1}{\alpha} w_i \tag{2-3}$$

In addition, free entry of manufacturers ensures zero profits on each brand, or

$$p_i = \left(\frac{a}{x} + 1 \right) w_i$$

which states that the price equals average costs. Taken together with Eq. (2-3), this free entry condition implies a constant output level for each brand, the same in both regions,

$$x = \frac{\alpha a}{1 - \alpha} \tag{2-4}$$

The production function $a + x$ also implies that labor demand in Region i equals $(a + x)n_i$, where n_i represents the number of brands that are manufactured in Region i. Since labor demand equals labor supply in each region, considering Eq. (2-4), a region that is populated with N_i individuals, each one endowed with one unit of labor, manufactures the following number of brands:

$$n_i = \frac{1 - \alpha}{a} N_i \tag{2-5}$$

2.1 *Relative prices*

Now assume that a resident of Region i pays the mill price p_i for every locally manufactured brand and the price tp_j, $t > 1$ for a brand imported from Region $j \neq i$. I will use the "melting iceberg" interpretation of transport costs. Namely, in order to consume one unit of an imported brand an individual has to buy t

units of the good from the supplier. Next, let E_i represent aggregate income of the residents in Region i. It follows from the preferences, the structure of transport costs, and Eq. (2-4), that the condition in which aggregate demand for a brand produced in Region i equals its supply can be represented by

$$\frac{\alpha a}{1-\alpha} = \frac{p_1^{-\varepsilon}}{n_1 p_1^{-\varepsilon} + n_2 (t p_2)^{1-\varepsilon}} (1-\beta) E_1 + \frac{t\,(t\,p_1)^{-\varepsilon}}{n_1 (t\,p_1)^{1-\varepsilon} + n_2 p_2^{1-\varepsilon}} (1-\beta) E_2 \tag{2-6}$$

where the left side represents supply and the right side represents demand. A similar condition holds in the other region.

Each individual spends a fraction β of personal income on housing (due to the Cobb-Douglas preferences). Therefore, the aggregate value of housing services equals βE, where $E = \Sigma_i E_i$. On the other hand, aggregate spending equals aggregate income, which is composed of labor income $\Sigma_i w_i N_i$ plus income from housing βE. It follows that aggregate income from housing equals $\beta(\Sigma_i w_i N_i)/(1-\beta)$. I assume that the housing stocks are equally owned by all individuals. Hence, income from housing by residents of Region i equals the fraction N_i/N of the total income from housing. As a result, spending by residents of Region i equals

$$E_i = w_i N_i + \frac{\beta N_i}{(1-\beta) N} \sum_k w_k N_k \tag{2-7}$$

Substituting this equation together with Eq. (2-3) and Eq. (2-5) into Eq. (2-6), we obtain the reduced-form equilibrium condition

$$1 = \frac{f q^{1-\varepsilon}}{f q^{1-\varepsilon} + (1-f)\, t^{1-\varepsilon}} \left[1 - \beta + \beta\left(f + \frac{1-f}{q}\right)\right] + \frac{(1-f)\,(t\,q)^{1-\varepsilon}}{f\,(t\,q)^{1-\varepsilon} + 1 - f}\left[\frac{1-\beta}{q} + \beta\left(f + \frac{1-f}{q}\right)\right] \tag{2-8}$$

where $f = N_1/N$ represents the fraction of individuals that reside in Region i and $q = p_1/p_2 = w_1/w_2$ represents the relative mill price of a brand in Region i as well as the relative wage in Region i.

The right side of Eq. (2-8) declines in q. Therefore, this equation provides a unique solution to relative prices for each allocation of the population across regions; i.e., q is a *function* of f. Inspection of Eq. (2-8) reveals the following properties:

1. The relative price depends on the fraction of the total population living in each region and, importantly, does not depend on the population's size or the supply of housing.

2. When half of the population lives in each region, the relative price equals 1, independently of transport costs.

The first property is self-evident. The second property can be examined by substituting $f=1/2$ and $q=1$ on the right side of Eq. (2-8). The latter stems from the fact that equally populated regions supply the same number of brands and the same quantity of each. In addition, income per capita is the same in both regions if and only if the relative price equals 1.[2] When income per capita is equalized, the composition of demand for differentiated products in terms of local versus imported goods is the same in each region. Therefore, we have both symmetric demand and symmetric supply, ensuring market clearing. As for housing, the residents of a region spend a fraction β of their income on housing. In this event the aggregate housing budget is the same in both regions. If the supply of housing is also the same in both, then housing prices are equalized. Otherwise, the price of housing is higher in the region with a lower stock of housing, but the value of the housing stock is the same in both.

2.2 Relative utilities

Region i's housing stock provides a fixed flow of services, H_i. As a result, consumption of housing per resident equals H_i/N_i. In addition, spending per resident on manufactured products equals $(1-\beta)\,E_i/N_i$. Therefore, the utility level of an individual that resides in Region i [see Eqs. (2-1) and (2-2)] equals

$$u_i = \left(\frac{H_i}{N_i}\right)^{\beta} \left[\frac{(1-\beta)\,E_i}{N_i\,P_{di}}\right]^{1-\beta} \qquad (2\text{-}9)$$

where P_{di} is the price index of differentiated products in Region i, given by

$$P_{di} = [n_i\,p_i^{1-\varepsilon} + n_j\,(t\,p_j)^{1-\varepsilon}]^{1/(1-\varepsilon)}, \qquad j \neq i$$

Using the pricing condition Eq. (2-3), the equilibrium number of brands Eq. (2-5), and the levels of spending Eq. (2-7), we compute from Eq. (2-9) the relative utility level $v = u_1/u_2$

$$v = \left(\frac{H_1}{H_2}\,\frac{1-f}{f}\right)^{\beta} \left[\frac{(1-\beta)\,q + \beta\,(f\,q + 1 - f)}{1-\beta+\beta\,(f\,q+1-f)}\right]^{1-\beta} \times \left[\frac{f\,q^{1-\varepsilon} + (1-f)\,t^{1-\varepsilon}}{f(tq)^{1-\varepsilon} + 1 - f}\right]^{\frac{1-\beta}{\varepsilon-1}} \qquad (2\text{-}10)$$

[2] Recall that income per capita from the ownership of housing is always equal while labor income per capita depends on the wage rate and that relative wages are also represented by q.

Solving from Eq. (2-8) the relative price for each allocation of people f, and substituting the result into Eq. (2-10) enables us to trace out relative utility levels for each f. This relationship is useful for the study of equilibria.[3]

3. Region size

In order to identify equilibrium configurations, we now study the relationship between relative utility levels and the fraction of the population living in Region i. The equilibrium size of regions consists of those values of f that ensure equal utility levels in each region, or a higher utility level in a single region that contains the entire population.

To begin with, consider the limiting case with no transport costs: That is, $t \Rightarrow 1$. In this case, the relative price q equals 1 for all values of f [see Eq. (2-8)]. As a result, relative utilities [see Eq. (2-10)] are given by

$$v = \left(\frac{H_1}{H_2} \frac{1-f}{f} \right)^{\beta}$$

It follows that the relative utility in a region declines with the relative size of its population. This relationship is exhibited in Fig. 2-1 for the case of equal housing stocks in both regions. Here a unique equilibrium configuration exists, described by point A, at which half of the population lives in each region. In this allocation, the utility level is the same everywhere. With any other distribution of population across regions, the utility level is higher in the smaller region. I assume that individuals living in a region with a lower utility level gradually migrate to the

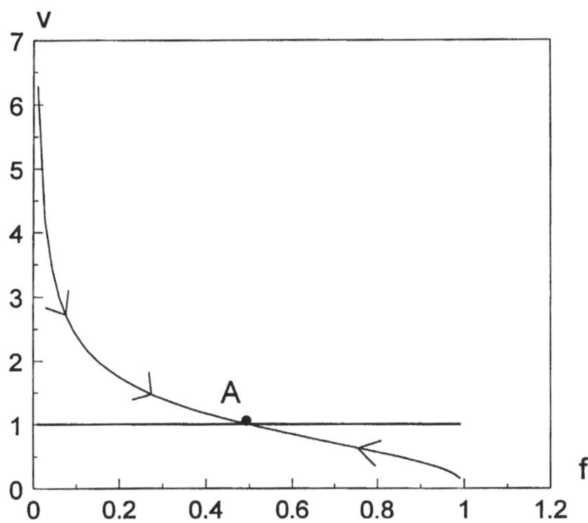

Figure 2-1. Relative utility with low transport costs (t close to 1 or $\beta\varepsilon > 1$)

[3] Krugman (1991) uses a similar approach.

region with the higher utility level. This adjustment process will be used below to study the stability of equilibria. It follows that whenever regions differ in population size, individuals migrate from the larger to the smaller region, as indicated by the arrows. We conclude that point *A* describes a unique globally stable equilibrium. Finally, if regions have different stocks of housing, the unique stable equilibrium consists of an allocation of population that is proportional to each region's housing stock.

To understand this result, observe that in the absence of transport costs, an individual has access to all brands of the differentiated product at prices that do not depend on the region in which the individual chooses to live. Personal income is also the same in either region. Therefore, people migrate to the region with the lower housing costs. But the region with disproportionately fewer residents has the lower price of housing. The result is that people migrate from the region with a disproportionately larger population to the region with a disproportionately smaller population, until each region's population becomes proportional to its housing stock.

The next thing to observe from Eq. (2-8) is that as the fraction of people living in the first region approaches zero, the relative price of brands q approaches $t^{-(\varepsilon-1)/\varepsilon}$, which is finite for finite transport costs. In view of this fact, Eq. (2-10) implies that the relative utility of residents of Region 1 approaches infinity as the fraction of people residing in Region 1 approaches zero. This means that for all finite levels of transport costs, the v curve is asymptotic to the vertical axis, as shown in Fig. 2.1. My simulations show that the curve is also downward sloping for all levels of transport costs whenever the elasticity of substitution between brands, ε, is large or the expenditure share on housing, β, is large, so that $\beta\varepsilon > 1$. In this event, there exists a unique stable equilibrium in which a region's population is a function of its relative housing stock.[4] On the other hand, whenever the elasticity of substitution or the expenditure share on housing are small, so that $\beta\varepsilon < 1$, a region's relative welfare rises with its relative population when the distribution of the population across regions is almost equal. Figure 2.2 depicts an extreme outcome, when transport costs are infinite (and the housing stock is the same in each region). In this case, three equilibria exist, one in which half of the population lives in each region, and two in which all people live in one region, either in Region 1 or Region 2. As can be seen from the figure,

[4] Equality of utility levels implies the equilibrium relationship

$$\frac{N_1}{N_2} = \left(\frac{H_1}{H_2}\right)^{\frac{\beta(\varepsilon-1)}{\beta\varepsilon-1}}$$

Since the exponent on the right side is larger than 1, it follows that whenever the housing stocks differ across regions, the equilibrium distribution of people is more skewed than the distribution of housing.

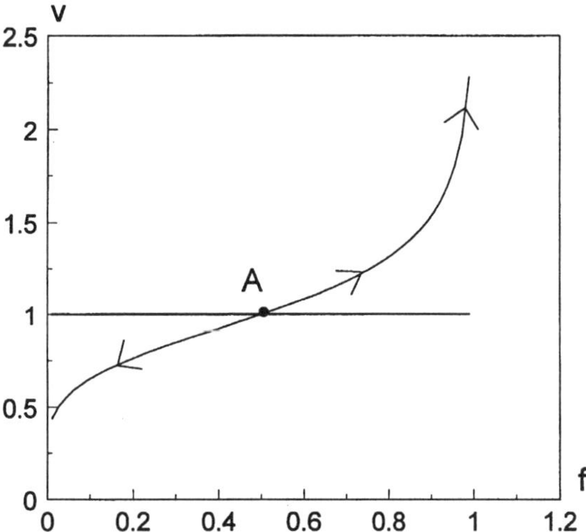

Figure 2-2. Relative utility with infinite transport costs (t unbounded and $\beta\varepsilon < 1$)

however, when the population is not the same in both regions, welfare is higher in the larger region. As a result, people migrate from the smaller to the larger region, as indicated by the arrows in Fig. 2.2. The end result is that everyone lives in the same region. It follows that the two equilibria in which a single region is occupied are locally stable while the equilibrium in which both regions are occupied is unstable. Moreover, whichever region has more people to begin with grows in size until it absorbs the entire population.

Our discussion of the case of unbounded transport costs has revealed the important roles of the elasticity of substitution and the intensity of preferences for housing. We have seen that whenever they are large, both regions are occupied in equilibrium, while only one region is occupied when they are small. To understand this result, observe that with unbounded transport costs an individual who resides in Region i consumes only brands that are manufactured in that region. If the elasticity of substitution between brands is high, the individual cares little about the available variety choice and therefore is not particularly attracted to a densely populated region with many brands of the differentiated product. But the individual is attracted to a region with low housing costs, which happens to be thinly populated. And the latter attraction is more important the more housing is preferred over differentiated products (the larger β). These pressures lead to an equilibrium in which the entire housing stock is used, which requires both regions to be occupied. On the other hand, individuals with a low elasticity of substitution between brands are willing to pay a premium for a large variety of choice. They are attracted to a densely populated region with many brands of the differentiated product. This attraction is even more powerful when they care little about housing, because in densely populated regions housing costs are high. Individuals of this type tend to bunch together, producing large agglomerations. And in equilibrium all of them end up living in the same region.

We have seen that whenever brands of the differentiated product are highly substitutable for each other and the demand for housing is high (i.e., $\beta\varepsilon > 1$), the relative utility in a region declines with its population when transport costs are either nil or infinite. In both cases, there exists a unique globally stable equilibrium in which the population of a region is distributed according to its housing stock, as depicted in Fig. 2-1. Moreover, my simulations show that the relative utility in a region declines with its relative population for all intermediate values of transport costs. As a result there exists in this case a unique globally stable equilibrium for every level of transport costs, and both regions are occupied in these equilibria. When the housing stock is the same in both regions, half of the population lives in each one of them.[5]

Next observe that whenever brands of the differentiated product are poorly substitutable for each other and the demand for housing is low (i.e., $\beta\varepsilon < 1$), the relative utility in a region declines with its population when transport costs are negligible and rises with its population when transport costs are prohibitive. In the former case, there exists a unique stable equilibrium in which both regions are occupied while in the latter case, in a stable equilibrium, the entire population lives in one region. These extreme cases show that whenever $\beta\varepsilon < 1$, the degree of agglomeration depends on transport costs; it is low for negligible transport costs and high for prohibitive transport costs. However, for the intermediate range of transport costs, the relative utility of a region declines with its population when the region is very small, rises with its population when the region expands, and eventually declines again when a large fraction of the population lives in the region, as exhibited in Fig. 2-3 (in this figure as well the housing stocks are taken to be equal in both regions). Evidently, three equilibria now exist, indicated by points A, B, and C, except that the middle equilibrium at point B is unstable (see the arrows of the adjustment process). An interesting property of the stable equilibria is that, despite the fact that the same stock of housing is available in both regions, the regions differ in size. Moreover, simulations show that the relative size of the larger region increases with transport costs. This is, therefore, a case in which the tradeoff between the centrifugal forces of housing and the centripetal forces of differentiated products is most significant. In this equilibrium, the utility level in the larger region is the same as in the smaller region because residents of the larger region consume a better choice of brands which is just sufficient to compensate them for the lower consumption of housing services.

[5] Observe that whenever $f = 1/2$ and $q = 1$, the equilibrium condition for the relative price Eq. (2-8) is satisfied for all transport costs and that Eq. (2-10) implies that the utility level is the same in both regions independently of transport costs.

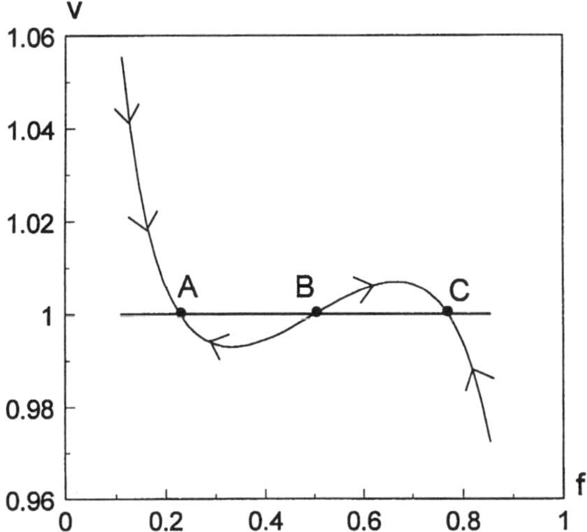

Figure 2-3. Relative utility with intermediate transport costs ($\varepsilon = 2$, $\beta = 0.4$, $\beta\varepsilon < 1$, $t = 6$)

Importantly, Fig. 2-3 describes the generic structure for $\beta\varepsilon < 1$. As transport costs rise, point A shifts to the left and point C shifts to the right. At the limit, as transport costs rise to infinity, point A approaches the vertical axis and C approaches the vertical line through $f = 1$. Namely, higher transport costs lead to more unequal regions and at the limit, everyone lives in the same region. My simulations show that the inequality in the size of regions rises rapidly with transport costs. As a result, for even moderate levels of transport costs, the smaller region is very small relative to the larger one.

Figure 2-4 describes the fraction of people that live in Region 1 in stable equilibria, when both regions have the same stock of housing. When transport costs are low, half of the population lives in each region. For the range $t \geq \underline{t}$, one region is more populated than the other, and the relative size of the larger region is greater the higher the transport costs. At the limit, as transport costs approach infinity, the entire population lives in one region.

We have seen that as simple as this model of regional formations might be, it produces a rich set of equilibrium outcomes and helps to shed light on the roles of a small number of critical parameters in shaping geographical structures. In the next section I examine the extent to which these structures are efficient and, in particular, whether it is possible to improve the resulting degree of agglomeration.

4 Welfare

One of two types of equilibria emerges in our two-region economy, as depicted by Figs. 2-1 and 2-3 (Fig. 2-2 is a limiting case of 2-3). Are these equilibria efficient relative to the existing market structure? Namely, taking as given the fact that housing services are competitively supplied while the market for differentiated products is characterized by monopolistic competition, is it possible to reallocate people across regions and have the winners compensate the losers in a way that raises the welfare level of all individuals? We will shortly see that some of these equilibria are efficient in this sense, while others are not. For the purpose of this analysis, however, we first need to compute the utility level of a representative individual in each region for a given allocation of the population across them.

Substituting the pricing Eq. (2-3), the number of brands Eq. (2-5), and the expenditure levels Eq. (2-7) into the utility specification Eq. (2-9), we obtain the utility level in each region as a function of the fraction of the population living in Region 1, f, and the relative price q:

$$u_1 = A\left(\frac{H_1}{f}\right)^{\beta}\left(\frac{(1-\beta)\,q+\beta\,(fq+1-f)}{[fq^{1-\varepsilon}+(1-f)\,t^{1-\varepsilon}]^{1/(1-\varepsilon)}}\right)^{1-\beta} N^{(1-\beta\varepsilon)/(\varepsilon-1)} \tag{2-11}$$

$$u_2 = A\left(\frac{H_2}{1-f}\right)^{\beta}\left(\frac{1-\beta+\beta\,(fq+1-f)}{[f\,(tq)^{1-\varepsilon}+1-f]^{1/(1-\varepsilon)}}\right)^{1-\beta} N^{(1-\beta\varepsilon)/(\varepsilon-1)} \tag{2-12}$$

where $A = \alpha^{1-\beta}\,[(1-\alpha)/a]^{(1-\beta)/(\varepsilon-1)}$ and $N = N_1 + N_2$ represents the size of the entire population. By solving from Eq. (2-8) the relative price q for each allocation f and substituting the result into these equations, we can trace out the utility levels in each region as functions of the fraction of the population living

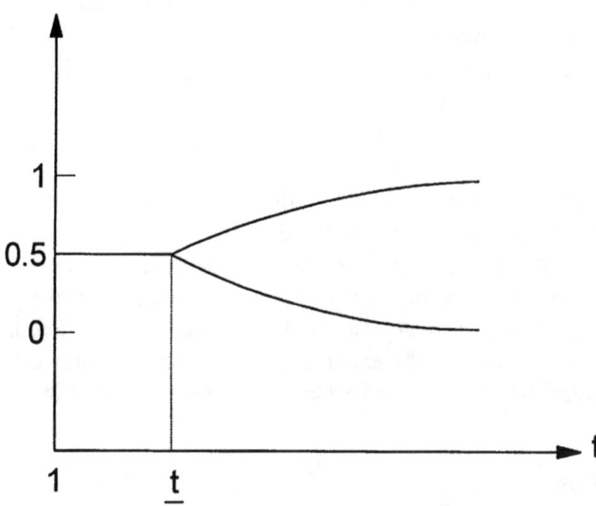

Figure 2-4. Stable equilibrium allocations for different levels of transport costs ($\beta\varepsilon < 1$)

in Region 1. These curves shed light on the efficiency issue, as I will shortly describe.

Before we proceed to a discussion of this issue, observe that the welfare level in each region is proportional to $N^{(1-\beta\varepsilon)/(\varepsilon-1)}$, while the solution to the relative price does not depend on the size of the population. It follows that in this economy, welfare rises with population size if and only if $\beta\varepsilon < 1$.[6] Namely, when the demand for housing is low and brands of the differentiated product poorly substitute for each other, the economy is better off with a larger population. A low elasticity of substitution represents a situation in which individuals highly value variety. Under these circumstances they prefer a larger population because a larger population raises variety of choice. True, a larger population raises housing prices as well, but given that these individuals place little weight on housing costs and much on variety of choice, the eventual decline in the consumption of housing services as a result of the population's expansion is more than compensated for by the larger variety of choice. When $\beta\varepsilon > 1$, however, housing is important enough relative to variety to cause general distress when the population expands.

First consider the case in which transport costs are low or people have a strong preference for housing and a weak preference for variety (i.e., $\beta\varepsilon > 1$). Also suppose that the regions have equal housing stocks. There then exists a unique stable equilibrium in which half of the population lives in each region, as described in Fig. 2-1. Moreover, under these circumstances, the utility in each

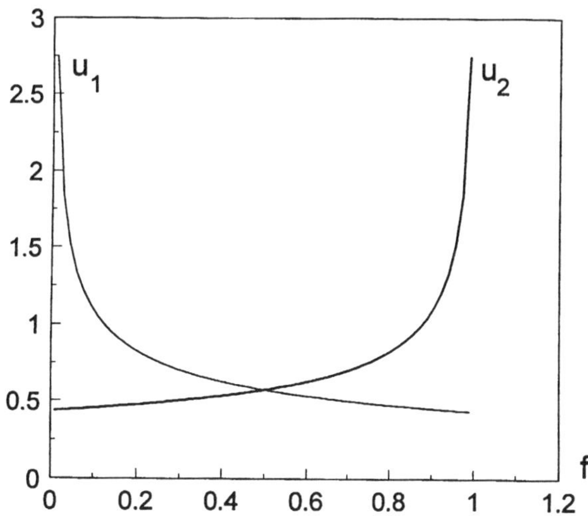

Figure 2-5. Relationship of utility to size of regions: Low transport costs (t close to 1 or $\beta\varepsilon > 1$)

6 Recall that this same condition determines whether prohibitive transport costs lead to an equilibrium with a single occupied city.

region declines with its relative size, as depicted in Fig. 2-5. Therefore, a reallocation of people away from the equilibrium point raises the utility level of those that end up living in the smaller region and reduces the utility level of those that end up living in the larger region. Evidently, such reallocations are not Pareto improving. Next, suppose that we tax individuals in the smaller region and subsidize individuals in the larger region, using lump-sum taxes and subsidies to equalize their well-being. At what value of f will the common utility level be highest? Simulations show that it is highest at the equilibrium point, and that it declines the more the regions are unequal in size. This is so because in the absence of a tax-transfer scheme, the few individuals that live in the smaller region are better off; they need to be highly taxed in order to compensate the many individuals that live in the larger region in order to equalize utility levels. This tax turns out to be too high to make all of them better off. We conclude that in this case, the equilibrium allocation is efficient.

Next consider the case of intermediate transport costs and $\beta\varepsilon < 1$, which yields the relative utility curve depicted in Fig. 2-3. The resulting utility levels as functions of the fraction of the population living in Region 1 are depicted in Fig. 2-6 (the housing stocks are again taken to be the same in both regions). Points A, B, and C in this figure correspond to the equilibrium points A, B, and C in Fig. 2-3. As argued before, only A and C are stable. Evidently, if the economy is at a stable equilibrium and people are reallocated from the larger to the smaller region, then the well-being of everyone rises. This shows that the stable equilibria are not efficient. Since a more skewed distribution of region size raises everyone's welfare, we conclude that *market forces do not generate enough agglomeration.*

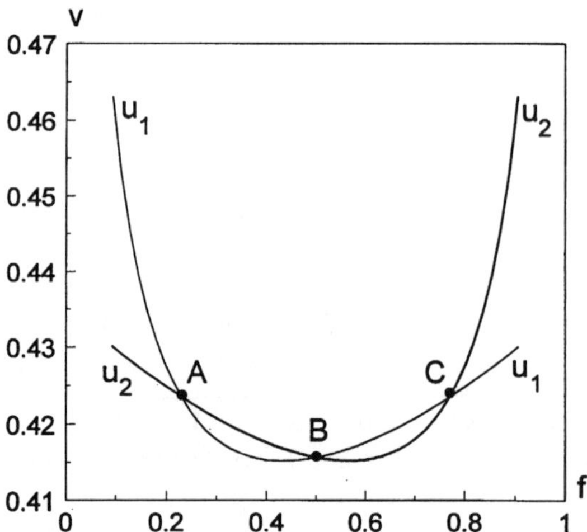

Figure 2-6. Relationship of utility to size of regions: Intermediate transport costs ($\varepsilon = 2$, $\beta = 0.4$, $\beta\varepsilon < 1$, $t = 6$)

Now refer to Fig. 2-4, which describes stable equilibrium allocations for different levels of transport costs. Our welfare analysis has shown that whenever transport costs are relatively low, that is, $t \leq \underline{t}$, then regions are of equal size and contain an efficient degree of agglomeration. But whenever transport costs are finite and higher than $\underline{t}$, it is efficient to increase the population in the larger region and reduce it in the smaller one. Therefore, in this range, the market provides too little agglomeration.

5. External economies

Regional structures are shaped by many forces. Urban economists have emphasized a variety of centrifugal forces that generate congestion, such as intra-regional commuting costs [see for example Muth (1961) and Alonso (1964)], as well as a variety of centripetal forces that generate regional economies of scale, such as the supply of local public goods [see for example Stiglitz (1977)]. My model has focused on the tradeoff between two such forces: the centrifugal force of available housing and the centripetal force of available variety. Do our results depend in a critical way on the particular variables that were chosen to represent these forces? The answer is no. Each one of them can be replaced with other forces that perform similar functions in the shaping of regions. In order to demonstrate these possibilities, in this section I develop an alternative model in which a homogeneous product that is produced with external economies of scale replaces the differentiated products. The equilibria of this model are similar to the equilibria of the original model, as demonstrated below. Both models share an important feature – they have economies of scale that are not internalized. In this section, the lack of internalization will become self-evident. In the previous sections it resulted from the fact that available variety had properties similar to a public good, and individuals did not consider the effect of their migration decisions on the supply of variety.

Preferences are again given by Eq. (2-1) where, as before, h represents consumption of housing services. The supply of housing is fixed in every region. This time, however, d stands for the consumption of a homogeneous product that is manufactured with labor and supplied competitively. A business firm that manufactures the homogeneous product in Region i has a production function $d = A_i l$, where l is the firm's employment of labor. Therefore, the marginal product of labor equals A_i in Region i and the regional wage rate w_i equals $p A_i$, where p represents the price of the product. This price is the same in both locations because there are no transport costs.

Now let there be regional external economies of scale, as a result of which $D_i^{\delta/(1+\delta)}$, $\delta > 0$, where D_i represents aggregate output of the homogeneous product in Region i. Then

$$D_i = N_i^{1+\delta}$$

and

$$w_i = p\,N_i^{\delta} \tag{2-13}$$

I maintain the original assumption about the ownership of housing (i.e., the housing stock in each region is equally owned by all individuals). As a result, regional expenditure levels are given by Eq. (2-7). Substituting Eq. (2-13) into Eq. (2-7), we can now compute the relative utility level $v = u_1/u_2$:

$$v = \left(\frac{H_1}{H_2}\,\frac{1-f}{f}\right)^{\beta}\left(\frac{(1-\beta)\,f^{\delta} + \beta\,[f^{1+\delta} + (1-f)^{1+\delta}]}{(1-\beta)\,(1-f)^{\delta} + \beta\,[f^{1+\delta} + (1-f)^{1+\delta}]}\right)^{1-\beta} \tag{2-14}$$

This equation describes a direct relationship between the fraction of the population residing in Region 1, f, and the relative utility of the residents in that region.

Two important properties emerge directly from Eq. (2-14):

1. When the external economies are small (that is, δ is close to zero) or people spend a large share of their budget on housing (that is, β is close to one), the relative utility of a region declines with its relative population size. This case is similar to the case depicted in Fig. 2-1. As a result, there exists a unique stable equilibrium in which both regions are occupied. The population is equally divided between the regions whenever the housing stocks are of equal size.
2. When the external economies are large (i.e., δ is large) or people spend a small share of their budget on housing (i.e., β is close to zero), the relative utility of a region rises with its relative population size. This case is similar to the case depicted in Fig. 2-2. In this event, there exist two stable equilibria, with the entire population living in one region in each one of them.

Similar equilibria were identified in the original model. In fact, these equilibria are driven by similar forces. A strong preference for housing leads to an equilibrium in which housing is utilized up to its capacity and people allocate themselves across regions according to the availability of housing. This is true in both models. On the other hand, large localized external economies lead to a concentration of people in one location. This ensures the highest real wage rate. In the model with external economies this feature is self-evident, with δ representing the local degree of economies of scale. In the original model, however, the elasticity of substitution across brands drives the local economies of scale; a lower elasticity of substitution generates stronger economies of scale in the supply of *variety*. Herein lies the analogy between these alternative specifications.

What happens for intermediate values of preferences for housing and external economies? There do exist values (such as $\delta = 0.5$ and $\beta = 0.25$) for which the plot of Eq.(2-14) looks similar to Fig. 2-3. In this event, regions in a stable equilibrium differ in size even when they have the same supply of housing. Moreover, there is too little agglomeration in such cases because the regional utility levels, as functions of f, are similar to Fig. 2-6. Namely, it is most efficient to concentrate the entire population in one region. Unfortunately, in this allocation, people have an incentive to migrate to the empty region. Therefore, complete agglomeration is not an equilibrium outcome.

This completes our discussion of the analogy between the models.

6. Comparison with Krugman

Krugman (1991) was the first to construct a model with differentiated products and transport costs that can address the tradeoff between a centrifugal and a centripetal force in the shaping of regional structures. My assumptions about the differentiated product have been borrowed from his work. He also assumed that the other commodity is homogeneous but, unlike my model (see Section 2), he assumed instead that the homogeneous product is freely traded across regions. He also assumed that the ownership of the homogeneous product (in his case, agriculture) is concentrated in the hands of people who do not supply labor and that because these people do not move across regions, their consumption takes place in the region in which they own the homogeneous product. Clearly, these assumptions are not suitable to describe housing. There appear therefore to be two main differences between Krugman's model and mine:

1. He assumed that the homogeneous product is freely traded across regions while I have assumed that it is not.
2. He assumed that the income derived from the homogeneous product that is located in Region i is spent entirely in Region i while I have assumed that this income generates demand in each region in proportion to the number of people who reside within it.

These differences in assumptions produce differences in results. Krugman has shown that whenever transport costs of differentiated products are small enough, the relative utility of residents in Region 1 rises with the fraction of the population living in this region, as depicted in Fig. 2-2. In this case, there exist two stable equilibria, with all the population living in one region in each of them. It can be shown that whenever $\beta\varepsilon < 1$, the relative utility level also rises for large transport costs. On the other hand, whenever $\beta\varepsilon > 1$ and transport costs are large enough, the relative utility curve declines, as depicted in Fig. 2-1. As a result, there exists a unique stable equilibrium in which both regions are occupied.

When the homogeneous product is in equal supply in both regions, half of the population lives in each one of them.[7] These relationships between the structure of equilibria and the level of transport costs are just the opposite of the results obtained in Section 3. Namely, while in Krugman's model low transport costs lead to agglomeration and high transport costs lead to dispersion, in my model, low transport costs lead to dispersion and high transport costs lead to agglomeration. Given that there exist two differences between the models, one wonders which one of them drives the differences in results.

It can be shown that the differences in assumptions about the regional distribution of purchasing power derived from the ownership of the homogeneous product do not cause the differences in results described above. By this I mean to say that if we were to assume in our model, that instead of equal ownership of the housing stocks by mobile workers, there exist three groups of people, that is, (i) workers who are mobile across regions; (ii) owners of housing in Region 1 who live and consume in Region 1; and (iii) owners of housing in Region 2 who live and consume in Region 2, then the same type of equilibria that exist in the model in Section 2 would emerge in the modified model.[8]

[7] Using our notation, the equilibrium conditions in Krugman's model can be represented by the following three equations:

$$\frac{1}{1-\beta}=\frac{q^{1-\varepsilon}}{fq^{1-\varepsilon}+(1-f)\,t^{1-\varepsilon}}\left(f+\frac{q_{H2}H_1}{\alpha\, q\, N}\right)+\frac{(tq)^{1-\varepsilon}}{f(t\,q)^{1-\varepsilon}+1-f}\left(\frac{1-f}{q}+\frac{q_{H2}\,H_2}{\alpha\, q\, N}\right)$$

$$\frac{1}{1-\beta}=\frac{t^{1-\varepsilon}}{fq^{1-\varepsilon}+(1-f)\,t^{1-\varepsilon}}\left(qf+\frac{q_{H2}H_1}{\alpha N}\right)+\frac{1}{f(t\,q)^{1-\varepsilon}+1-f}\left(1-f+\frac{q_{H2}\,H_2}{\alpha N}\right)$$

$$v=q\left[\frac{fq^{1-\varepsilon}+(1-f)\,t^{1-\varepsilon}}{f(tq)^{1-\varepsilon}+1-f}\right]^{(1-\beta)/(\varepsilon-1)}$$

where $\alpha=(\varepsilon-1)/\varepsilon$ and $q_{H2}=p_H/p_2$. The price of H equals p_H in both locations due to the free tradeability of this good. The first two equations describe market clearing in each region while the third describes the relative utility of the mobile workers. Recall that the owners of H live and consume in the region in which they own the good. The first two equations provide solutions for q and q_{H2} as functions of the fraction of mobile workers that live in Region 1, f. Substituting the resulting solution for the relative price q into the third equation we obtain the relative utility v as a function of f.

[8] It can be shown that with the proposed modification of the structure of demand the equilibrium condition Eq. (2-8) for the relative price q would be replaced with

$$1=\frac{fq^{1-\varepsilon}}{fq^{1-\varepsilon}+(1-f)\,t^{1-\varepsilon}}+\frac{(1-f)\,t^{1-\varepsilon}\,q^{-\varepsilon}}{f(t\,q)^{1-\varepsilon}+1-f}$$

and the equation for the relative utility level Eq. (2-10) would be replaced with (*cont.*

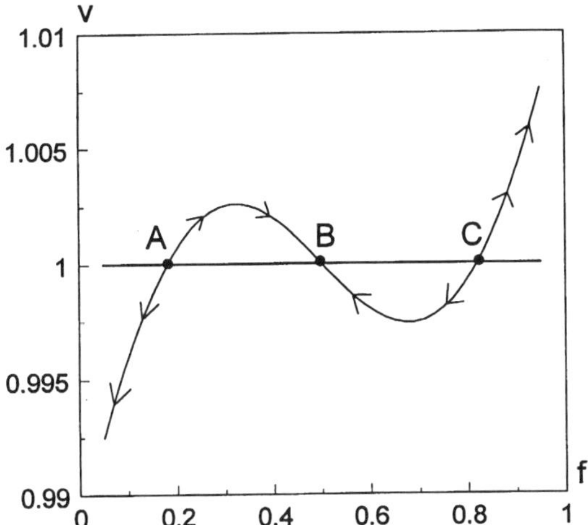

Figure 2-7. Relative utility for intermediate values of transport costs (Re: Krugman; $\varepsilon = 4$, $\beta = 0.7$, $\beta\varepsilon > 1$, $t = 1.666$)

I conclude that the fact that Krugman assumed that the homogeneous product is freely traded across regions while I assume that it is not is responsible for the differences in results. Moreover, under the assumption of a freely traded homogeneous product, his additional assumption that some demand is tied to each location is essential for the presence of a centrifugal force. Namely, while in my model dispersion is driven by region-specific supplies (of nontraded housing services), in his model, dispersion is driven by region-specific demands (of owners of the homogeneous product). Can Krugman's model produce an intermediate case in which regions with an equal supply of the homogeneous product differ in size?[9] Figure 2-7 presents a plot of the relative utility in his model for intermediate values of transport costs given $\beta\varepsilon > 1$. In this example the amount of H is the same in both regions. As we see, there are three stable equilibria; either both regions are of equal size or all the population lives in one

(*cont.*)

$$v = \left(\frac{H_1}{H_2}\frac{1-f}{f}\right)^{\beta}\left[\frac{f q^{1-\varepsilon} + (1-f)\, t^{1-\varepsilon}}{f\,(t\,q)^{1-\varepsilon} + 1 - f}\right]^{\frac{1-\beta}{\varepsilon-1}} q^{1-\beta}$$

It follows that v declines with f for small levels of transport costs. It also declines with f for large transport costs whenever $\beta\varepsilon > 1$. Finally, simulations show that for intermediate values of transport costs and $\beta\varepsilon < 1$ the relative utility curve takes on the shape that is depicted in Fig. 2-3.

[9] Krugman (1991) raises this possibility in Footnote 3 but does not pursue it.

region. There do exist two additional equilibria at points A and C, in which regions differ in size, but those equilibria are unstable.

For the case of equal regional endowments of the homogeneous product, my simulations show that in Krugman's model there exist two equilibria for all values of transport costs, with the entire population living in one region in each, whenever $\beta\varepsilon < 1$. On the other hand, for $\beta\varepsilon > 1$, the relationship between equilibrium regional structures and transport costs is as depicted in Fig. 2-8. Namely, for low transport costs $t < \underline{t}_K$, there exist two stable equilibria with extreme agglomerations. For high transport costs $t > \bar{t}_K$, there exists a single stable equilibrium with regions of equal size. Finally, for intermediate values of transport costs there exist three stable equilibria: two with extreme agglomerations and the third with regions of equal size.

To close this section, let us examine the intuition behind Krugman's results in order to understand why they differ from mine. For this purpose, it suffices to focus on the extreme cases. When transport costs are nil, every allocation of mobile workers across regions constitutes an equilibrium in his model because, under these circumstances, every product can be bought for the same price at each location and wages are the same everywhere. As a result, workers are indifferent as to where they live no matter how many of them reside in each region (that is, the v curve is flat at 1). Now suppose that the same amount of the homogeneous product is supplied in each location and half of the workers

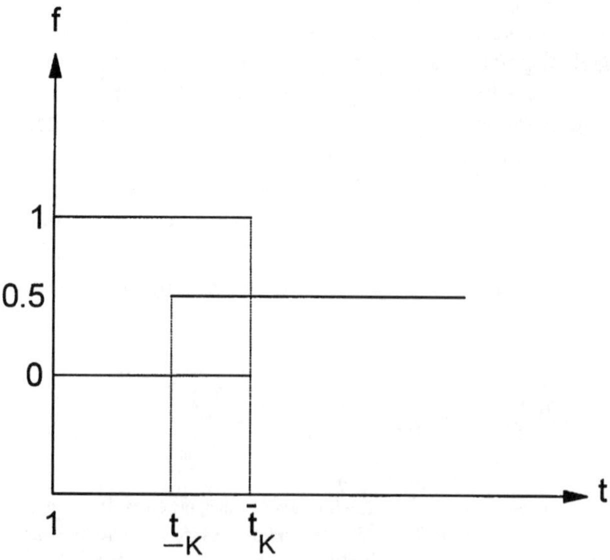

Figure 2-8. Stable equilibrium allocations for different levels of transport costs (Re: Krugman; $\beta\varepsilon > 1$)

live in each region, while transport costs are small but positive. In this case as well, workers have no incentive to switch locations. But suppose that some of them nevertheless move from Region 1 to Region 2. Then variety of choice is larger in Region 2 and more workers will be attracted to that region. Manufacturers of the differentiated product will shift production to Region 2 in order to serve a larger market. With sufficiently low transport costs, the demand for differentiated products by the owners of the homogeneous product in Region 1 is not sufficient to raise wages of workers in Region 1 so as to compensate them for the larger variety of choice available in Region 2. As a result, the cumulative process of migration will continue until all workers reside in Region 2.

We have thus seen why low transport costs cause the relative utility of mobile workers in a region to rise with the fraction of workers that live in it. What happens when transport costs are large and, for the sake of concreteness, suppose that they are prohibitive? Let us start again from an allocation with equally populated regions and equal levels of well-being of workers in both locations. Now suppose that some workers move from Region 1 to Region 2. Then again there is more variety in Region 2 which makes it attractive to live there. Except that this time, manufacturers of differentiated products in Region 2 cannot serve the owners of the homogeneous product in Region 1. As a result, they have an incentive to locate some production in Region 1. Is the demand by owners of the homogeneous product in Region 1 sufficiently high to induce production of differentiated products in that region at wages sufficiently high to keep production workers in Region 1? To retain workers in Region 1, the wage rate has to be high enough to compensate them for the lower variety of choice in that region. It follows that the answer depends on two things: First, how high the income level of the owners of the homogeneous product is; and second, how important variety of choice is. If people spend a small fraction of their income on the homogeneous product, the income level of its owners in Region 1 will be small and they will not generate enough demand to compensate workers for a lower variety of choice. If, in addition, the elasticity of substitution across products is small, workers require high compensation in the form of wages in order to forgo a better variety of choice in Region 2. Therefore, whenever $\beta\varepsilon < 1$, the utility of workers is higher in the region that has more of them (the v curve slopes upwards), which leads to a cumulative process of migration from the smaller to the larger region. On the other hand, whenever the demand for the homogeneous product is high, the demand level by its owners in Region 1 is large. Furthermore, if the elasticity of substitution across brands is large, workers request little compensation for loss of variety of choice. In this event – which happens when $\beta\varepsilon > 1$ – workers are better off in the smaller region (the v curve slopes downward). As a result, workers migrate to the smaller region until a symmetric equilibrium is attained.

7. Concluding comments

By providing a new framework for the analysis of regional structures, Krugman's work on economic geography has generated renewed interest in regional economics. His approach emphasizes the centripetal force of a manufacturing sector that supplies costly transported differentiated products, and builds on a centrifugal force consisting of regional demand levels driven by immobile individuals. The latter is particularly suitable for societies in which agriculture plays a major role, and in which farmers are tied to their land.

I have examined an alternative framework in this chapter, in which agriculture is replaced with housing. A prominent feature of housing services is that they are traded within a region but not across regions. As a result, locally supplied housing services produce the major centripetal force. This framework seems to be closer to standard urban economic models.

Importantly, while low transport costs in Krugman's framework lead to extreme agglomerations and higher transport costs may reduce the degree of agglomeration, in my framework low transport costs lead to little agglomeration while higher transport costs may lead to larger agglomerations. Since each one of these alternative frameworks is suitable in different circumstances, it is important to understand the economic forces that drive their results. I have tried to clarify them. Finally, I have shown that in economies of this type, if anything, free markets provide too little agglomeration.

These findings result from a focus limited to a small number of features, which limits their role in explaining urban and regional structures. It is therefore necessary to broaden the scope of such investigations in order to obtain a better understanding of these problems. Standard elements of regional and urban economics, such as spatial layouts, commuting costs, and congestion, are natural candidates for incorporation in the analysis.

References

Alonso, W. (1964) *Location and Land Use*. Cambridge, MA: Harvard University Press.

Krugman, P. (1991) "Increasing Returns and Economic Geography." *Journal of Political Economy*, 99(3), 483-99.

Muth, R. F. (1961) "The Spacial Structure of the Housing Market." *Papers and Proceedings of the Regional Science Association*, 7, 207-20.

Stiglitz, J. (1977) "The Theory of Local Public Goods." In M. S. Feldstein and R. P. Inman (eds.), *The Economics of Public Services*. London: Macmillan Press.

Tolley, G. and J. Crihfield (1987) "City Size and Place as Policy Issues." In E. S. Mills (ed.), *Handbook of Regional and Urban Economics*, Vol. II. Amsterdam: Elsevier.

PART III

THE ECONOMICS OF CLUBS

CHAPTER 3

First and second welfare theorems for economies with collective goods*

Vicky Barham and Myrna H. Wooders

1. Introduction

In a seminal contribution, Tiebout (1956) argued that local public goods could be efficiently provided by a competitive system of communities. Tiebout conjectured that in a large economy, the problem of reconciling the different demands of different types of participants disappears. Since different types of participants can choose to reside in distinct jurisdictions, each jurisdiction can cater to the preferences of its particular type of resident. Tiebout's insight has proved extraordinarily fecund and has been widely applied to economic models with collectively produced and consumed commodities, such as models of economies with local governments or clubs. Indeed, much research focusing on the problem of decentralization in economies with congestible public goods derives from what we suggest may be referred to as Phase I of the "Tiebout Program." Specifically, Phase 1 has sought to formally characterize the conditions under which the First Fundamental Theorem of Welfare Economics holds in large economies with local public goods or congestible public facilities.

Although different approaches to examining this question have been pursued (for more recent references, see the survey by Sandler and Tschirhart [1980] or Barham [1992]), a particularly fruitful avenue of investigation has been the study of the equivalence between the core and equilibrium outcomes. Wooders (1978a) introduces a model of an economy with nondifferentiated crowding – that is, participants are crowded only by the numbers of other participants with whom they share the public goods[1] – and defines a notion of competitive equilibrium in which both firms and participants act as price takers with respect to an anonymous price system. It is proven that if participants can be "optimally"

* Both authors wish to thank the Social Sciences and Humanities Research Council of Canada for financial support. The first author also acknowledges support received from the University Research Scholarship program of the University of Ottawa. Preliminary versions of this paper were presented at the 1993 meeting of the Regional Science Association and at the 1994 meetings of the Public Choice Society and North American Econometric Society, as well as at the Second International Meeting of the Social Choice and Welfare Society in Rochester, New York. We thank participants in those sessions, including Julien Manning and Marcus Berliant, for their comments. We especially thank an anonymous referee for helpful comments, John Conley for helpful discussions and for permitting us to refer to research results that are as yet unpublished, and David Pines for stimulating discussions.

[1] Our term "differentiated crowding" is motivated by the literature on differentiated commodities, cf. Mas-Colell (1975), since consumer types are differentiated in the same way as differentiated commodities.

partitioned, the core is non-empty. Moreover, if small groups are strictly effective – that is, all gains to collective activities can be realized with groups bounded in size – and the production technology available to each jurisdiction satisfies constant returns to scale, then the core and the set of competitive equilibrium allocations are equivalent. The existence of the equilibrium and the equivalence of the core and equilibrium outcomes justifies the equilibrium concept.

The nature of different price systems in economies with public goods has generated significant interest. The price system in Wooders (1978a) has one per-unit price for the public good within each jurisdiction. It might be described as an anonymous Lindahl equilibrium – anonymous because prices for public goods do not depend on private information, and Lindahl because the prices are per unit and it can be shown that prices equal marginal rates of substitution in equilibrium. Any profits in production are shared among the members of a jurisdiction. In contrast, Berglas and Pines (1980) and Scotchmer and Wooders (1987) use an admission price system, which lists a price for each level of public good provision in each jurisdiction, and imposes a zero profit condition. One manifestation of the differences between these price systems is that Wooders (1978a) requires only a finite number of prices whereas Berglas and Pines (1980) and Scotchmer and Wooders (1987) require an infinite number of prices for each jurisdiction. In this chapter, we introduce a nonanonymous Lindahl equilibrium, where prices depend on tastes.

To gain insight into the properties of price systems in economies with crowded public goods, we systematically investigate the difference between the core-equilibrium equivalence theorems that hold under the three different price systems in different economic contexts, all with nondifferentiated crowding. A form of strict small-group effectiveness is required throughout the chapter. The economic contexts discussed differ primarily in whether or not constant returns to scale in production are required. We show that when production within each jurisdiction is subject to constant returns to scale, then Wooders' (1978a) equilibrium outcomes, the admissions equilibrium outcomes of Berglas and Pines (1980) and Scotchmer and Wooders (1987), the nonanonymous Lindahl equilibrium outcomes, and the core all coincide.

But if we relax the assumption of constant returns to scale within jurisdictions, an example due to Conley and Wooders (1994b) shows that the core may be strictly larger than the set of Wooders' equilibrium outcomes; in particular, Wooders' (1978a) equilibrium may not exist even though the core is nonempty. Thus, with only concavity of the production function available to a jurisdiction, the set of *nonanonymous* Lindahl equilibrium outcomes is equivalent to the core and to the set of admission equilibrium outcomes but not to Wooders' equilibrium outcomes. This is a particularly interesting result. In the context of the standard differentiated crowding model, several papers have discussed the equivalence of nonanonymous admission pricing and nonanonymous Lindahl pricing [Scotchmer and Wooders (1986), Wooders (1991, 1993), and Scotchmer (1994)].[2] Previous research thus failed to identify any compelling reason for preferring one sort of price system over the other, except that Lindahl pricing requires only a finite number of prices whereas admission pricing requires an infinite number. In contrast, the results presented here and the example of Conley and Wooders (1994b) show that, in general, this equivalence *requires* the *nonanonymity* of Lindahl prices.

To summarize, with constant returns to scale within jurisdictions, all three different pricing systems lead to the same outcomes. When the assumption of constant returns to scale is relaxed but the requirement of anonymity of the price system is maintained, the more robust notion of admission equilibrium is required for equivalence of the core and the set of equilibrium outcomes. If the assumption of constant returns to scale and the requirement of anonymity of the price system are relaxed, then the core and the equilibrium outcomes with nonanonymous per-unit Lindahl prices and wages coincide.[3] Besides illuminating the different properties of different price systems, these results show, as suggested by other results in the literature, that the appropriate choice of equilibrium concept depends on the environment being studied and the questions being asked.[4]

To prepare for our discussion of competitive equilibrium, we review several theorems from Wooders (1978a) and strengthen two of its results. Recall that Wooders (1978a) shows that when a core state of the economy has participants of each type in at least two jurisdictions, then core jurisdictions consist only of individuals with the same "type-optimal demands" for public goods and crowding. We strengthen this result to provide a necessary and sufficient result. Specifically, we show that when a state of the economy has participants of each type in at least two different jurisdictions, then that state is in the core *if and only if* all individuals are receiving their type-optimal utilities. We also show that the core is nonempty *if and only if* all participants of each type receive their type-optimal utilities.[5] Note that this implies that all states of the economy in the core have the equal-treatment property; that is, all participants of the same type have the same utility levels.

[2] The admission prices and Lindahl prices of these papers are nonanonymous since they depend on the taste types of participants, which are private information.

[3] The importance of the anonymity of the price system is emphasized by Bewley (1981) and Conley and Wooders (1994a; 1994b; 1996). It is reasonable to suppose that tastes are private information and thus a nonanonymous Lindahl equilibrium may not be implementable. Nevertheless, the nonanonymous Lindahl equilibrium and its equivalence to an anonymous Lindahl equilibrium is of theoretical interest.

[4] For example, Ellickson (1973) shows that standard Lindahl equilibrium outcomes are not necessarily Pareto-optimal in the presence of crowded public goods.

[5] These "if and only if" results depend, of course, on the assumption that there is only one private good (or that the prices of private goods are fixed).

The second part of this chapter is concerned with Phase II of the "Tiebout Program" – the conditions under which the Second Welfare Theorem holds in economies with congestible public goods. Remarkably, relatively little research has addressed this issue. Scotchmer and Wooders (1987) consider situations with only two types of consumers, and prove only a restricted version of the Second Welfare Theorem. Specifically, Scotchmer and Wooders show that every equal-treatment Pareto-optimal state of the economy in which all participants receive their type-optimal utility levels is an equilibrium state. In this chapter we prove a Second Welfare Theorem for an economy with nondifferentiated crowding and with an admission equilibrium price system. Specifically, we show that every equal-treatment Pareto-optimal outcome is an admission equilibrium outcome. With additional conditions on production, our Second Welfare Theorem holds for nonanonymous Lindahl equilibrium and Wooders' (1978a) equilibrium. Underlying our Second Welfare Theorem are the results that, when small groups are effective, (a) all equal-treatment Pareto optima are in the core for some (re)distribution of endowments, and (b) a state of the economy is in the core if and only if all participants receive their type-optimal utility levels.

The equal-treatment property plays an important part in the study of economies with crowded public goods since equal treatment is a feature of the behavior of competitive markets. Our result that a state of the economy is a Pareto-optimal equal-treatment state if and only if it is in the equal-treatment core (for an appropriate distribution of endowments) hinges crucially on our assumption that small groups are strictly effective. Thus, we discuss a number of different assumptions of strict small group effectiveness, all of which ensure the equal-treatment property.

The outline of this chapter is as follows. In the remainder of this section we describe the model. In Section 2, we discuss the core. Section 3 treats equilibrium and the core. Section 4 presents our Second Welfare Theorem, and Section 5 contains our conclusions.

1.1 Goods, agents, jurisdictions, endowments

In our model a consumption bundle has three components: a private good x, a partially nonrivalrous collective good y, and a number of participants m with whom the collective good is jointly consumed. It is both possible and costless to exclude participants from sharing in the consumption of the collective good.

Each participant of type t has a positive endowment e^t of the private good. There are no endowments of the collective good.

Participants are distinguished by their *type* t, $t = 1 \ldots T$. The number of participants of type t in the economy is denoted by N_t and the total number of participants in the economy is denoted by

$$\|N\| := \sum_{t=1}^{T} N_t.$$

Let Z^T_+ denote the T-fold Cartesian product of the set of non-negative integers Z. A group of participants is described by its *profile*, a vector $s = (s_1, ..., s_T) \in Z^T_+$, where s_t denotes the number of participants of type t in the group. Note that the profile of the total population is thus given by $N = (N_1, ..., N_T)$.

A *jurisdiction* is a group of participants who collectively consume the public good. Like other groups, a jurisdiction is described by its profile $s = (s_1, ..., s_T)$. A jurisdiction structure describes a partition of the population into jurisdictions; thus a *jurisdiction structure* of a group s is a collection of jurisdictions $(s^j)^J_{j=1}$ such that $\sum_j s^j = s$. A jurisdiction structure of the total population N is denoted by $n = (n^1 ..., n^G)$. Letting n^g_t denote the number of type t participants belonging to jurisdiction n^g, it holds that $\sum_g n^g_t = N_t$. Also, $\sum_g n^g = N$.

Let u^t denote the utility function of a participant of type t. The utility level achieved by a participant depends on his allocations of x (the private good) and y (the collective good) and on m (the total number of participants with whom the public good is jointly consumed). Thus, a *consumption plan* (x, y, m) is a vector where $x, y \in \mathbf{R}+$ and m is a non-negative integer. We assume that utility functions are quasi-concave and monotonically increasing in x. The assumption that u^t depends only on the total number m of participants jointly consuming the collective good reflects the feature that *crowding is nondifferentiated* – participants do not care about the names and/or preferences of those participants with whom they share consumption of the collective good.[6]

As stated above, it is assumed that consumption of the collective good is partially non-rivalrous.

1.2 Production

We assume that for each positive integer m there is a well-behaved production technology described by a cost function $z = c(m, y)$, where z denotes the amount of the private good required to produce y units of the public good for the collective consumption of m participants, and where $c(m, 0) = 0$.

We might think of the cost function as showing the cost of providing a given level of public good y to m consumers, or we might think of the cost function as showing the cost of providing y when the jurisdiction (firm, or club) has m workers, all of whom reside in the jurisdiction. Thus, there is an aspect of the model that permits us to regard members of a jurisdiction as inputs to the production process.

For most of our results we do not require any assumptions linking the cost functions for the public goods produced in different jurisdictions. However, to

[6] We choose the term "nondifferentiated" rather than "anonymous" since, even when agents of different types crowd differently, crowding can still be anonymous in the sense that identities of particular participants are irrelevant. Our usage here is consistent with the differentiated commodities literature and is also suggested by other works on economies with clubs, cf., Berglas and Pines (1980). Note also that our model is a special case of the crowding types model of Conley and Wooders (1994b).

ensure that the public good does not become free, for each positive output y the limit of the average cost $c(m,y)/m$ as m becomes large is bounded away from zero. For some results we will require that the production technology underlying the cost function is concave (implying decreasing average costs) and, for others, that the production technology exhibits constant returns to scale (implying constant average costs).

1.3 States of the economy

Let s be a jurisdiction. An *allocation for s* is a list $[(x_{tq}, y, \|s\|); q = 1, \dots s_t, t = 1, \dots, T]$ where, for any type t with $s_t > 0$, x_{tq} denotes consumption of the private good by the qth participant of that type ($q = 1, \dots, s_t$), y denotes public good consumption, and $\|s\|$ denotes the number of participants in the jurisdiction.[7] Notice that our description allows different participants of the same type to receive different allocations of private goods. Observe also that if $s_t = 0$, then the allocation for s does not include consumption plans for agents of type t (since there are none).

Let n be a jurisdiction structure. An *allocation relative to n*, which we denote by $[(x^g_{tq}, y^g, \|n^g\|); q = 1, \dots N_t, t = 1,\dots,T, g = 1,\dots,G]$ or simply $(x^g_{tq}, y^g, \|n^g\|)_{tq,g}$, consists of an allocation for each jurisdiction n^g in the jurisdiction structure n.

A *state of the economy* ε consists of a jurisdiction structure n of N and an allocation relative to n; thus

$$\varepsilon = [n, (y^g, z^g), (x^g_{tq}, y^g, \|n^g\|)_{tq,g}] \tag{3-1}$$

where, for each g, $z^g = c(n^g, y^g)$. The state of the economy ε is *feasible* if the resources required to satisfy the prescribed production and consumption plans do not exceed the total supply; that is,

$$\text{for each } n^g \in n,\ z^g = c\,(\|n^g\|, y^g) \tag{3-2a}$$

(production plans are in accordance with the production function), and

$$\sum_{g=1}^{G} \left[\left(\sum_{t=1}^{T} \sum_{q=1}^{n^g_t} x^g_{tq} \right) + z^g \right] \le \sum_{t=1}^{T} N_t e^t \tag{3-2b}$$

(feasibility).

Observe that since n is a jurisdiction structure for N it holds that all participants are assigned to jurisdictions; that is, for each type t,

$$\sum_{g=1}^{G} n^g_t = N_t.$$

[7] Indexing private goods consumptions enables us to avoid indexing the participants individually.

1.4 Type-optimal jurisdictions

In investigating both the core and equilibrium outcomes, it is useful to characterize the consumption plans (x,y,m) that maximizes the utility of a representative participant of type t, given his endowment and given equal sharing of costs. This is useful since, under the conditions of our results, all states of the economy in the core and also all equilibrium states will have the equal-treatment property. A *type-optimal configuration for participants of type t*, relative to endowment e^t, is a triple (x^{*t},y^{*t},m^{*t}) satisfying

$$(x^{*t},y^{*t},m^{*t}) \text{ maximizes } u^t(x,y,m) \tag{3-3a}$$

subject to

$$z^t = c(m^t,y^t) \tag{3-3b}$$

and

$$m^t x^t \leq m^t e^t - z^t \tag{3-3c}$$

We denote the *type-optimal utility level for type-t participants with endowment* e^t as $u^{*t}(e^t)$. These optimal values may not be uniquely determined; hence, we denote the set of triples of optimal private good consumptions, collective good consumptions and group sizes for participants of type t by $[x^{*t}(e^t),y^{*t}(e^t),m^{*t}(e^t)]$. Note that each $m^{*t}(e^t)$ will be a positive integer since we are maximizing over consumption plans admitting only positive-integer-sized jurisdictions. Also observe that a type-optimal configuration is defined relative to a particular distribution of endowments; if endowments change, due to the imposition of lump-sum redistributive taxes, for instance, then the type-optimal jurisdiction size (and level of collective good production) may also change. This will play an important role in establishing subsequent results.

In developing our analysis we need to ensure that the number of participants of each type is sufficiently large. This is an important assumption; it ensures that continuum limit or "large economy" results obtain in finite economies, regardless of the population distribution. Specifically, we assume that the number of participants of each type is sufficiently large so that, for each type, there are type-optimal jurisdictions whose size is smaller than the total number of participants of that type. Formally, for each type t,

$$N_t > \sup_{e^t} \min_{m} \left\{ m : m \in m^{*t}(e^t) \right\} \tag{A1}$$

where the supremum is taken over all positive real numbers e. Throughout the remainder of the chapter we maintain this assumption, which ensures that all gains to type t group formation can be exhausted by strict subsets of the total population of type t – that is, small groups are strictly effective.

2. The core

A state of the economy is in the core if no subset of participants, using only the resources with which they are endowed, can improve upon the outcome for its members. Since there is only one private good and thus, in a core state of the economy, no trade between jurisdictions, if a coalition can improve upon a state of the economy then a jurisdiction can also improve upon that state. Therefore, to define the core we need consider only improvement by jurisdictions. Let $\varepsilon = [n,(y^q,z^g), (x^g_{tq},y^g,n^g)_{tq,g}]$ be a feasible state of the economy.[8a] A jurisdiction s can improve upon the state of the economy ε if, for each t with $s_t \neq 0$, there is a one-to-one mapping θ^t from a subset $S(t)$ of the set $\{(t,q,g) : q = 1, ..., n^g_t, g = 1, ...,G\}$ to the set $\{(t,q) : q = 1, ..., s_t\}$, such that

$$u^t(x'_{\theta^t(t,q,g)},y',\|s\|) \geq u^t(x^g_{tq},y^g,\|n^g\|) \tag{3-4}$$

for each $(t,q,g) \in S(t)$, with strict inequality for at least one member of $S(t)$, where

$$z' = c\,(\|s\|,y') \tag{3-5a}$$

and

$$\sum_t s_t e^t = \sum_{(t,q,g) \in S} x'_{\theta^t(t,q,g)} + z'. \tag{3-5b}$$

The first condition Eq. (3-4) means that each participant $\theta^t(t,q,g)$ judges the allocation $(x'_{\theta^t(t,q,g)},y',\|s\|)$ to be at least as attractive as the allocation $(x^g_{tq},y^g,\|n^g\|)$ that he receives in the state of the economy ε, while at least one participant finds his improving allocation $(x'_{\theta^t(t,q,g)},y',\|s\|)$ more attractive than the allocation $(x^g_{tq},y^g,\|n^g\|)$. The conditions Eq. (3-5a) and Eq. (3-5b) require that the improving allocation is feasible for the coalition S; coalition S is an *improving coalition* of participants.

A state of the economy ε is in the *core of the economy* if no jurisdiction s can improve upon ε.

A state of the economy ε satisfies the criterion of *equal treatment* if all individuals of the same type receive the same payoff; that is, for each t there is a constant $\bar{u}^t$ such that for all q=1, ..., n_t^g,

$$u^t\,(x^g_{tq},y^g,\|n^g\|) = \bar{u}^t. \tag{3-6}$$

The *equal-treatment core* consists of those states of the economy in the core with the equal-treatment property.

[8a] Our definition of an improving coalition is standard and is equivalent to that of Conley and Wooders in this volume. Unlike Conley and Wooders, however, we "keep track" of the initial juridisctions of residence of the agents in the improving coalition. This allows us to consider allocations that are not equal-treatment.

The following result, that states of the economy in the core assign proof of this sort of result, has become standard. A general form of the result is provided in Wooders (1983, Theorem 3). The proof is by contradiction. First suppose that two agents of the same type in two different jurisdictions are treated differently. The jurisdiction containing the best-off of the two agents could form a new jurisdiction by replacing the best-off agent with the worst-off agent. This would permit the new jurisdiction to make all its members better off, giving us the required contradiction for this case.[8b]

Proposition 1. [Wooders 1978a: Theorem 3(i)]. The equal-treatment property of the core. *Let* $\varepsilon = [n, (y^g, z^g), (x^g_{tq}, y^g, n^g)_{tq,g}]$ *be a state of the economy in the core. Assume that for each type t there are at least two jurisdictions* n^g *and* $n^{g'}$ *such that* $n^g_t \neq 0$ *and* $n^{g'}_t \neq 0$*. Then, for each t and all* $q, q' = 1, ..., n^g_t$ *and* $g, g' = 1, ..., G$, *it holds that*

$$u^t(x^g_{tq}, y^g, \|n^g\|) = u^t(x^{g'}_{tq'}, y^{g'}, \| n^{g'} \|). \tag{3-7}$$

That is, ε *has the equal-treatment property.*

Proof. Let $\varepsilon = [n, (y^g, z^g), (x^g_{tq}, y^g, n^g)_{tq,g}]$ be a state of the economy in the core. Suppose that for some t', q', q'', and g', g'', it holds that

$$u^{t'}(x^{g'}_{t'q'}, y^{g'}, \|n^{g'}\|) > u^{t'}(x^{g''}_{t'q''}, y^{g''}, \|n^{g''}\|). \tag{3-8}$$

First, let us assume that $g' \neq g''$. Consider a jurisdiction s with the same profile as $n^{g'}$. We replace participant $t'q'$ in $n^{g'}$ with participant $t'q''$ in $n^{g''}$ to form an improving coalition. To do this, define the set of participants S consisting of the members of $n^{g'}$ minus $t'q'$ and plus $t'q''$:

$$S = \{ (t,q,g') : q = 1, ..., n^{g'}_t, t = 1, ..., T, (t,q,g') \neq (t',q',g') \} \cup \{ (t',q'',g'') \}. \tag{3-9}$$

Next, define the map θ with domain S by

$$\theta(t',q'',g'') = (t',q') \tag{3-10a}$$

and

$$\theta(t,q,g') = (t,q) \text{ for } (t,q,g') \in S, (t,q,g') \neq (t',q',g'). \tag{3-10b}$$

It is now clear that Eq. (3-4) is satisfied by taking $y' = y^{g'}$ and $x'_{\theta^t(t,q,g')} = x^{g'}_{tq}$ for each (t,q) with $n^{g'}_t \neq 0$ and $q = 1, ..., n^{g'}_t$. This contradicts the assumption that ε is in the core.

Now let us suppose that $g' = g''$. By assumption, there is another jurisdiction n^{g*} with $n^{g*}_t \neq 0$. Then for some $q*$ it holds that either

$$u^{t'}(x^{g'}_{t'q'}, y^{g'}, \|n^{g'}\|) > u^{t'}(x^{g*}_{t'q*}, y^{g*}, \|n^{g*}\|)$$

[8b] We note that with some forms of strict small group effectiveness, such as the "minimum efficient scale for coalitions" used for Wooders' (1983) equal-treatment Theorem, it is not necessary to suppose that there are participants in at least two jurisdictions to obtain the result. Even if the two agents are in one jurisdiction, there is a third agent in another jurisdiction who must be treated better or worse than one of the two agents who are treated unequally. This permits the contradiction described above.

or

$$u^{t'}(x^{g*}_{t'q*}, y^{g*}, \|n^{g*}\|) \geq u^{t'}(x^{g'}_{t'q'}, y^{g'}, \|n^{g'}\|) > u^{t'}(x^{g''}_{t'q''}, y^{g''}, \|n^{g''}\|).$$

In either case, by proceeding as above, we can again obtain a contradiction. ■

The condition that for each type *t* there are at least two jurisdictions containing members of that type is not required if we assume that coalitions containing all members of any one type can be improved upon by individual participants. In this case, it is a result that a state of the economy in the core has at least two jurisdictions containing participants of each type (Wooders [1978a: Theorem 5]). Alternatively, we can assume that the only feasible jurisdictions are those uniformly bounded in size. Then, a corollary of Proposition 1 and condition (A1) is that all states of the economy in the core have the equal-treatment property, since every feasible state has participants of each type in at least two jurisdictions. Other definitions of (strict) small-group effectiveness lead to equal treatment even though there are not necessarily members of each type in two or more jurisdictions, cf., Conley and Wooders (1994a). The essential feature is that for each type *t*, every state of the economy capable of improvement can be improved upon by a coalition not containing all the participants of that type.[9]

The notion of the core employed in this chapter requires that in an improving coalition *at least one participant* be better off. Another notion of the core requires that *all participants* in an improving coalition be better off. Equivalence of these two notions of improvement holds under the assumptions that there is an infinitely divisible good that is essential (necessary for survival) and with which all participants are positively endowed (see, for example, Wooders [1980, 1993]).

As the preceding remarks indicate, a number of different assumptions ensure that all states of the economy in the core have the equal-treatment property. Since the equal-treatment property drives a number of our results, we will consider only economies satisfying the property that all states of the economy in the core are equal-treatment. This is what is meant, in this chapter, by (strict) small-group effectiveness.

We also make use of the following result, stating that all core jurisdictions are "demand-homogeneous." This result, of fundamental importance, underlies the fact that competitive equilibrium requires only one price for each jurisdiction (or for each jurisdiction and level of provision of the public good) and this price is not type-dependent. The sufficiency part of Proposition 2 was proved in Wooders (1978a: Theorem 3[iv]).[10] The necessity part of the result, stating that

[9] This assumption was introduced in Wooders (1978b) for games with side payments – games derived from economies with quasilinear utilities. Variations appear in a number of papers.

[10] Berglas and Pines (1981) independently showed that a Pareto-optimal state of the economy with jurisdictions consisting only of consumers with the same preferences cannot be improved upon by a jurisdiction containing more than one taste type. The Berglas-Pines result is implied by Wooders' result. Both results were presented at a conference in 1978 at Queen's University. Demand homogeneity has subsequently been discussed by a number of authors.

if participants all receive their type optimal utilities then the state of the economy is in the core, is new to this chapter.

Proposition 2. Equivalence of the set of type-optimal allocations and the core. *Let* $\varepsilon = [n,(y^g,z^g),(x^g_{tq},y^g,n^g)_{tq,g}]$ *be a feasible state of the economy. Assume that for each type t there are at least two jurisdictions,* n^g *and* $n^{g'}$*, such that* $n^g_t \neq 0$ *and* $n^{g'}_t \neq 0$*. Then* ε *is in the core if and only if for each g, all* $t = 1, ..., T$*, and* $q = 1, ..., n^g_t$ *it holds that*

$$(x^g_{tq},y^g,\|n^g\|) \in \{ [x^{*t}(e^t),y^{*t}(e^t),m^{*t}(e^t)] \} \tag{3-11a}$$

and

$$u^t(x^g_{tq},y^g,\|n^g\|) = u^{*t}(e^t); \tag{3-11b}$$

that is, all participants of each jurisdiction receive their type-optimal payoffs.

Proposition 2 establishes that all participants in each jurisdiction have the same "demands" for the public good and for crowding.

Proof. We provide only a sketch of the proof since the sufficiency part of the proof already appears in Wooders (1978a) and the ideas of the arguments are by now familiar.

Let $\varepsilon = [n, (y^g,z^g), (x^g_{tq},y^g,n^g)_{tq,g}]$ be a state of the economy in the core. Since ε is in the core, it follows immediately from (A1) that $u^t(x^g_{tq},y^g,\|n^g\|) \geq u^{*t}(e^t)$ for each t; otherwise, a jurisdiction s with $s_t = m^{*t}(e^t)$ and $s_{t'} = 0$ for all $t' \neq t$ could improve upon the state. Now suppose for some jurisdiction n^g there are types t and t' such that $n^g_t \neq 0$ and $n^g_{t'} \neq 0$ and either

$$(x^g_{tq},y^g,\|n^g\|) \notin \{x^{*t}(e^t),y^{*t}(e^t),m^{*t}(e^t)\}$$

or

$$(x^g_{t'q},y^g,\|n^g\|) \notin \{x^{*t'}(e^{t'}),y^{*t'}(e^{t'}),m^{*t'}(e^{t'})\}$$

or both. In such a case at least one type must contribute more than its per capita share toward the cost of provision of the public good because otherwise the other type would realize less than its type-optimal utility and could improve upon the state. But if participants of one type contribute more than their per capita share, then those participants will realize less than their type-optimal per capita utilities. This is a contradiction.

Now suppose that ε is a state of the economy satisfying the conditions of Proposition 2 and all participants of each type receive their type-optimal utilities. Suppose in addition that ε is not in the core. Then there exists an improving jurisdiction s. But s cannot consist of agents of only one type, from the fact that participants in ε receive type-optimal allocations. Therefore ε must contain at least two types. But then at least one type must contribute more than average to the production of the public good and realize *less* than its type-optimal utilities, a contradiction. ■

It is easy to show that if (A1) holds (an assumption maintained throughout this chapter) and a state of the economy in the core has the equal-treatment property, then the conclusion of the above result holds. We leave the proof of the following closely related proposition to the reader; the proof of sufficiency can be found in Wooders (1978a: Theorem 3[iii]).

Proposition 2'. *Let* $\varepsilon = [n,(y^g,z^g), (x^g_{tq},y^g,n^g)_{tq,g}]$ *be an equal-treatment state of the economy. Then* ε *is in the core if and only if for each g, all* t=1, ..., T *and* q=1, ..., n^g_t it holds that

$$(x^g_{tq},y^g,\|n^g\|) \in \{(x^{*t}(e^t),y^{*t}(e^t),m^{*t}(e^t)\} \tag{3-12a}$$

and

$$u^t(x^g_{tq},y^g,\|n^g\|) = u^{*t}(e^t), \tag{3-12b}$$

that is, all participants of each jurisdiction receive their type-optimal payoffs.

It is important to have a result showing that under some reasonable set of conditions the core is nonempty. The nonemptiness of the core depends on whether or not consumers can be partitioned into type-optimal jurisdictions. Part (a) of the following result extends Wooders (1978a: Theorem 3 [iv]) to show that the partitioning condition is necessary as well as sufficient for nonemptiness while part (b) uses an additional idea from that paper. For part (a) it is important to keep in mind that we have assumed that there are "many" consumers of each type [assumption (A1)].

Proposition 3. Nonemptiness of the core. *(a) The equal-treatment core is nonempty if and only if the set of agents can be partitioned into type-optimal jurisdictions. (b) Assume that for each type there are at least two relatively prime type-optimal jurisdiction sizes, such as consecutive integers. Then for all economies containing a sufficient number of agents of each type, the core is nonempty.*

To demonstrate a sufficiently large lower bound on the required number of agents of each type in the economy, let n' and n'' denote two relatively prime type-optimal group sizes for type t, for example, two consecutive integers. Then, if the total number of type t agents in the economy is greater than or equal to $(n'-1)(n''-1)$, the set of agents of type t can be partitioned into type-optimal groups. Thus, under reasonable economic assumptions – that there is a range of optimal group sizes and that for every one agent there are many other agents with similar demands – the core is nonempty.

The proof of Proposition 3 (a) follows techniques that are now standard, so we leave it to the reader. The second part of the proposition follows from a well-known result in number theory.

3. Competitive equilibrium

We first discuss Wooders' (1978a) notion of an anonymous two-part price-taking equilibrium concept with per-unit prices. Recall that, as noted in the introduction, this might also be viewed as an anonymous Lindahl equilibrium since prices for public goods do not depend on tastes and, like Lindahl prices, the prices are "per unit." (When small groups are strictly effective it is a consequence – not an assumption – that these prices are equal to marginal rates of substitution.) Next, we introduce our notion of a nonanonymous Lindahl equilibrium with participation prices and show that the equilibrium outcomes are equivalent to the core. Finally, we consider equilibrium with admission prices (or taxes) and relate the three equilibrium outcomes to the core.

3.1 A wage and price-taking equilibrium for economies with collective goods

In our model, output of the public good depends both on the input of the private good and on the number of participants in the jurisdiction for whom the public good is produced. In our presentation we first discuss the equilibrium which is obtained when profits arising from production are distributed as wages or, equivalently, profit shares, to members of the jurisdiction. We call this a "two-part equilibrium."

Because different jurisdictions of the same size may provide different levels of the public good, and because the production technology is a concave function of the input, different prices and wages may be required for jurisdictions of the same size in equilibrium. Consequently, both wages and prices must be defined relative to a jurisdiction structure. (We return to this aspect of the equilibrium below.) In addition, the equilibrium notion requires that prices for the collective good as well as wages be posted for all jurisdiction sizes, including jurisdiction sizes that do not arise in the equilibrium jurisdiction structure.

Let n be a jurisdiction structure. Let $w(n^g) \in \Re$ denote a wage in jurisdiction n^g. Thus the list $[w(n^g) : g=1, ..., G]$ states a wage for each jurisdiction in the jurisdiction structure n. It is also necessary to specify wages for all potential jurisdictions sizes. A *wage structure* relative to n is denoted by w and is given by

$$\mathbf{w} = \{w(s) : w(s) = w(n^g) \text{ for } g = 1, ..., G, \tag{3-13a}$$

and, for all jurisdictions s and s'

$$\text{with } \|s\| = \|s'\| \neq \|n^g\| \text{ for any } g, w(s) = w(s')\}. \tag{3-13b}$$

Note that a wage is specified for each jurisdiction n^g in the equilibrium jurisdiction structure and for each potential jurisdiction s with $\|s\| \neq \|n^g\|$. Given a jurisdiction size $m \neq \|n^g\|$, it is required that $w(s) = w(s')$ for all jurisdictions s and s' with $\|s\| = \|s'\|$; thus, for jurisdictions with sizes different than those in the equilibrium jurisdiction structure, wages depend only on jurisdiction sizes.

A price system for the public good is similarly defined. Let n be a jurisdiction structure. Let $p(n^g) \in \Re$ denote a wage in jurisdiction n^g. Thus the list $\{p(n^g) : g=1, ..., G\}$ states a price for each jurisdiction in the jurisdiction structure n. A *price system* is a vector p where

$$\mathbf{p} = (p(s): \quad s = n^g \text{ for } g = 1, ..., G \text{ and,} \tag{3-14}$$

for all jurisdictions s and s' with $\|s\| = \|s'\| \neq \|n^g\|$ for any g,

$$p(s) = (p(s)).$$

In interpretation, $p(s)$ is a price per unit of the public good in jurisdiction s. Thus, the price system stipulates a price for the public good for each jurisdiction in the equilibrium jurisdiction structure and for each jurisdiction size which does not appear among the equilibrium jurisdiction sizes.

A *two-part equilibrium* $e^W=(\varepsilon,\mathbf{p},\mathbf{w})$, consists of a feasible state of the economy $\varepsilon = [n,(y^g,z^g),(x^g_{tq},y^g,n^g)_{tq,g}]$, a price system $\mathbf{p}$ and a wage structure $\mathbf{w}$, both relative to n, which satisfy the following properties:

(i) For each jurisdiction n^g and for all pairs (y,z) such that $z = c(m,y)$ it holds that

$$\|n^g\|p(n^g)\, y^g - w(n^g)\|n^g\| - z^g = 0 \geq \|n^g\|p(n^g)y - w(n^g)\|n^g\| - z \tag{3-15}$$

(profit maximization in public goods production).

(ii) For each profile s with $\|s\| \neq \|n^g\|$ for any g,

(a) for all pairs (y,z) such that $z = c\,(\|s\|,y)$,

$$0 \geq \|s\|p(s)y - w(s)\|s\| - z \tag{3-16a}$$

(no profitable entry), and

(b) for some pair (y',z') with $z' = c\,(\|s\|,y')$

$$\|s\|p(s)y' - w(s)\|s\| - z' = 0 \tag{3-16b}$$

(the possibility of zero profit).

(iii) For each jurisdiction n^g, each type t and each $q = 1, ..., N_t$,

$$p\,(n^g)y^g + x^g_{tq} = e^t + w\,(n^g) \tag{3-17a}$$

and for all (x,y,s) such that

$$u^t(x,y,s) > u^t(x^g_{tq},y^g,n^g), \tag{3-17b}$$

it holds that

$$p(s)y + x > e^t + w(s) \tag{3-17c}$$

(participants maximize utilities and do not wish to move).

Clearly, an important aspect of the equilibrium is the prices posted for potential jurisdictions, that is, those jurisdictions not in the equilibrium jurisdiction structure. The fact that, at the given prices, no participant benefits by moving to a potential jurisdiction and no firm can make a positive profit in a potential jurisdiction ensures that the equilibrium jurisdiction structure is optimal.[11]

It can be verified by inspection that our equilibrium concept is the same as that of Wooders (1978a: Definition 10). In that definition, the wage distribution is called a profit distribution and profits are tied to jurisdiction membership just as wages are tied to jurisdiction participation in the present paper. The difference is simply one of interpretation of the participation prices for players. Our interpretation here is that the jurisdictions are formed by profit-maximizing firms. In Wooders (1978a), the interpretation given is more in the spirit of club theory, where the members of a club are more typically regarded as owners of the club rather than as workers in a firm. Note especially that the equilibrium requires neither "utility taking" nor cooperation. As we discuss below, the equilibrium can be viewed as describing an outcome of a market economy, a labor-managed coalition production economy where workers share the surplus generated by the firm, or a club economy where the members of the club take profits as given and share them among themselves. For large economies with small effective groups, nondifferentiated (anonymous) crowding and free entry, club distribution rules of equal profit-sharing and competitive market rules of wage distribution give the same set of outcomes.[12]

Note also that if production $z = c(m,y)$ exhibits constant returns to scale within jurisdictions, then all wages are zero and, as in Wooders (1978a), all profit shares are zero; the subtleties caused by the potential for positive wages/profits disappear.[13]

In proving subsequent results, we make use of the following theorem.

Proposition 4. [Wooders (1978a: Theorem 1)]. Two-part equilibrium outcomes are in the core. *Let* $e^W=(\varepsilon,\mathbf{p},\mathbf{w})$ *be a two-part equilibrium. Then* ε *is in the core.*

We will not provide a proof since the argument of the proof is very similar to that of Proposition 6 to follow.

Observe next that since a state of the economy that can be improved upon by any coalition can be improved upon by a jurisdiction, it follows from Proposition 3 that a competitive equilibrium state of the economy is Pareto-optimal, i.e., the First Theorem of Welfare Economics holds.

Remark. It is possible that two different types of participants t and t' have the same type-optimal demands for jurisdiction size but different demands for

[11] Wooders (1978a) provides an example showing that if there is not a sufficiently large menu of choices (and prices for these choices) available, then an equilibrium may not satisfy the First Theorem of Welfare Economics. See also the discussion of complete price systems in Conley and Wooders (1997, this volume).

[12] The interpretation of the lump sum participation prices as profits or wages is similar to the classic interpretation of the profits of a firm as wages for entrepreneurial ability.

[13] That is, if for any positive real number $\lambda > 0$,

$$c\,(m,\lambda y) = \lambda c\,(m,y).$$

crowding, that is, $m^{*t}(e^t) = m^{*t'}(e^{t'})$ but $x^{*t}(e^t) \neq x^{*t'}(e^{t'})$. To enable an equilibrium to support such situations, the equilibrium must permit two same-sized jurisdictions to post different prices for public goods as well as different wages. The admission equilibrium to be introduced later has a similar aspect – the admission price to a jurisdiction of size m depends on the amount of public goods provided. Also note that, because of the feature that two different jurisdictions of the same size in the equilibrium jurisdiction structure may charge different prices, the equilibrium is not "fully anonymous" in the sense of Conley and Wooders (1994b, 1996). The price system is anonymous, however, since the same prices are available to all participants.

Let ε be a state of the economy. The state ε is a *two-part equilibrium state* if there is a price system p and a wage system w such that (ε,p,w) is a competitive equilibrium.

Proposition 5. Equivalence of the core and the equilibrium outcomes [Wooders (1978a: Theorem 4)]. *Assume that all states of the economy in the core have the equal-treatment property and that production is subject to constant returns to scale. Then the core coincides with the set of two-part equilibrium states.*

Proof. Let ε be a state of the economy with the equal-treatment property. Suppose ε is in the core. From Proposition 2, all participants receive type-optimal utilities for their types. Thus, for each jurisdiction n^g and each t with $n^g_t \neq 0$, it holds that $u(x^g_{tq}, y^g, \|n^g\|) = u(x^*(e^t), y^*(e^t), m^*(e^t))$.

Define $w(n^g) = 0$ and $w(s) = 0$ for each jurisdiction s with $\|s\| \neq \|n^g\|$ for any $g = 1, ..., G$. For each $g = 1, ..., G$, define

$$p(n^g) = \frac{1}{\|n^g\|y} c(n^g, y)$$

for any $y > 0$ and, for each jurisdiction s with $\|s\| \neq \|n^g\|$ for any $g = 1, ..., G$, define

$$p(s) = \frac{1}{\|n^g\|y} c(s, y)$$

(From constant returns to scale, it holds that the prices $p(n^g)$ and $p(s)$ are well-defined.) From the fact that all participants are realizing their type-optimal utilities and that ε is in the core, it follows that for each n^g and for all types t with $n^g_t \neq 0$, $p(n^g) = e^t - x^g_{tq}$. It is straightforward to verify ε is an equilibrium with all wages equal to zero and prices equal to average costs, as constructed.■

As was previously noted, the above result does not necessarily hold when the assumption of constant returns to scale is relaxed. See Conley and Wooders (1994b) for an example demonstrating this point.

3.2 Lindahl equilibrium

For situations where all gains to collective activities can be exhausted by strict subgroups of the population, equilibrium outcomes of (nonanonymous) Lindahl pricing are equivalent to the core. One might suppose that the two-part equilibrium only separates participants with different demands into different jurisdictions because there is only one price for each jurisdiction. The Lindahl equilibrium has the interesting aspect that *even when jurisdictions offer different prices for different types of participants, the Lindahl prices for jurisdictions in the equilibrium jurisdiction structure are the same for all types of participants contained in a jurisdiction.* This result contrasts with apparently accepted thinking on Lindahl pricing.

A *(nonanonymous) Lindahl price system,* denoted by γ, consists of two parts, prices for each jurisdiction in the equilibrium jurisdiction structure and prices for each potential jurisdiction whose profile is not included within the equilibrium jurisdiction structure. Given a jurisdiction structure $n = (n^g)$, define γ by

$$\begin{aligned}\gamma = \{(\gamma_{tq}(s) : q = 1, ..., s_t, t = 1, ..., T, s = n^g \text{ for } g = 1, ..., G,\\ \text{or } \|s\| = m \text{ for some integer } m \leq \|N\|, m \neq \|n^g\| \text{ for any } g\}.\end{aligned} \tag{3-19}$$

We typically denote a Lindahl price system by $\gamma = (\gamma_{tq}(s))$. Note that the Lindahl prices are personalized. We have allowed personalized prices, rather than only type-dependent prices, as this makes our results more striking. We show, rather than assume, that all participants in the same jurisdiction face the same Lindahl price in equilibrium.

A *Lindahl equilibrium* $e^L = (\varepsilon, \gamma, \mathbf{w})$ consists of a feasible state of the economy $\varepsilon = [n, (y^g, z^g), (x^g_{tq}, y^g, n^g)_{tq,g}]$, a Lindahl price system $\gamma = (\gamma_{tq}(s))$, and a wage system w such that:

(i) For each jurisdiction n^g and for all pairs (y,z) with $z = c(m,y)$ it holds that

$$\begin{aligned}&\sum_{t=1}^{T} \sum_{q=1}^{n^g_t} \gamma_{tq}(n^g)y^g - w(n^g)\|n^g\| - z^g = 0\\ &\geq \sum_{t=1}^{T} \sum_{q=1}^{n^g_t} \gamma_{tq}(n^g)y - w(n^g)\, \|n^g\| - z\end{aligned} \tag{3-20}$$

(profit maximization).

(ii) For each profile s with $\|s\| \neq \|n^g\|$ for any g, and for all pairs (y,z) such that $z = c\,(\|s\|,y)$

$$0 \geq \sum_{t=1}^{T} \sum_{q=1}^{s_t} \gamma_{tq}(s)y - w\,(s)\|s\| - z \tag{3-21}$$

(no profitable entry).

(iii) For each jurisdiction n^g, each type t and each $q = 1, ..., N_t$,

$$\gamma_{tq}(n^g)y^g + x^g_{tq} = e^t + w(n^g) \tag{3-22a}$$

and for all (x,y,s) such that

$$u^t(x,y,s) > u^t(x^g_{tq}, y^g, n^g), \tag{3-22b}$$

it holds that

$$\gamma_{tq}(s)y + x > e^t + w(s) \tag{3-22c}$$

(participants maximize utilities subject to their budget constraints and do not wish to move).

A state of the economy ε is a *Lindahl equilibrium state* if there is a Lindahl price system γ and a wage system w such that $(\varepsilon,\gamma,\mathbf{w})$ is a Lindahl equilibrium. Foley (1970) showed that with constant returns to scale, the Lindahl equilibrium (with no crowding and all consumers residing in one jurisdiction) is in the core. This also holds for a Lindahl equilibrium with multiple jurisdictions and participation prices; constant returns to scale, however, are not required.

Proposition 6. Lindahl equilibrium outcomes are in the core. *Let* $(\varepsilon,\gamma,\mathbf{w})$ *be a Lindahl equilibrium state of the economy. Then* ε *is in the core of the economy.*

Proof. Suppose the proposition is false. Then there exists a Lindahl equilibrium $(\varepsilon,\gamma,\boldsymbol{w})$ with the property that ε is not in the core of the economy. This means that there is a jurisdiction s and, for each t with $s_t \neq 0$, there is a one-to-one mapping θ^t from a subset $S(t)$ of $\{(t,q,g) : q = 1, \dots n_t^g, g = 1, \dots, G\}$ to $\{(t,q) : q = 1, \dots, s_t\}$ such that for each $(t,q,g) \in S := \cup_t S(t)$

$$u^t(x'_{\theta^t(t,q,g)}, y', \|s\|) \geq u^t(x^g_{tq}, y^g, \|n^g\|) \tag{3-23}$$

with strict inequality for at least one $(t,q,g) \in S$, and where y' *satisfies*

$$z' = c(\|s\|, y') \tag{3-24a}$$

and

$$\sum_{t=1}^{T} s_t e^t = \sum_{(t,q,g)\in S} x_{\theta^t(t,q,g)} + z'. \tag{3-24b}$$

From profit maximization in public goods production it holds that

$$\sum_{t} \sum_{q=1}^{s_t} \gamma_{tq}(s)y' - z' - w(s)\|s\| \leq 0 \tag{3-25}$$

From feasibility, $z' = \sum_t \sum_{q=1}^{s_t} e^t s_t - \sum_t \sum_{q=1}^{s_t} x'_{\theta^t(t,q,g)}$.

The above, and Eq. (3-25), imply that

$$\sum_{t=1}^{T} \sum_{q=1}^{s_t} \gamma_{tq}(s)y' + \sum_{t=1}^{T} \sum_{q=1}^{s_t} x'_{\theta^t(t,q,g)} \leq \sum_t e^t s_t + w(s)\|s\|. \tag{3-26}$$

From (iii) of the definition of the Lindahl equilibrium, however, it holds that

$$\sum_{t=1}^{T} \sum_{q=1}^{s_t} \gamma_{tq}(s)y' + \sum_{t=1}^{T} \sum_{q=1}^{s_t} x'_{\theta^t(t,q,g)} > \sum_t e^t s_t + \|n^g\| w(n^g). \tag{3-27}$$

This is a contradiction.■

The following corollary is an immediate consequence of Proposition 6 and depends, of course, on the feature that there is only one private good in the economy.[14]

Corollary 1. *Assume that all states of the economy in the core have the equal-treatment property. Then all Lindahl states of the economy have the equal-treatment property and all individuals of the same type in the same jurisdiction in the equilibrium jurisdiction structure have the same Lindahl prices.*

Our next proposition states that when small groups are effective, the core is equivalent to the set of Lindahl equilibrium outcomes. Note that Proposition 7 does not require constant returns to scale in the production of the public good.

Proposition 7. Equivalence of the core and the Lindahl outcomes. *Assume that all states of the economy in the core have the equal-treatment property and that the production technology underlying the cost function is concave. Then the core coincides with the set of Lindahl equilibrium outcomes.*

Proof. The result is a special case of Conley and Wooders (1996), Theorem 2.[15] ■

We can now state the first major result of this chapter. Recall that we are assuming equal-treatment rather than any one of a number of other assumptions that would lead to this result.

Theorem 1: Equivalence of equilibrium concepts. *Assume that all states of the economy in the core have the equal-treatment property. Let* $(\varepsilon,\gamma,\mathbf{w})$ *be a Lindahl equilibrium. Then:*

(i) *for each g, and for all t, t′ with* $n_t^g \neq 0$ and $n_{t'}^g \neq 0$, *it holds that*

$$\gamma_{tq}(n^g) = \gamma_{t'q}(n^g) \tag{3-28}$$

(all participants in the same jurisdiction in the equilibrium jurisdiction structure pay the same Lindahl price); and

(ii) there is a two-part equilibrium $e^W = (\varepsilon, p, \mathbf{w})$, *consisting of the same feasible state of the economy* $\varepsilon = [n, (y^g,z^g), (x_{tq}^g, y^g, n^g)_{tq,g}]$, *a price system* **p** *and a wage structure* w *such that*

$$p(n^g) = (\gamma_{tq}(n^g)) \text{ for any } t \text{ with } n_t^g \neq 0. \tag{3-29}$$

Proof. The result is immediate from the facts that the core coincides with both the competitive equilibrium states of the economy and the Lindahl equilibrium states of the economy. ■

14 Wooders (1994b) elaborates this point and provides additional results on nonanonymous Lindahl pricing and the equal-treatment property.

15 Related results appear in Scotchmer and Wooders (1986) and Scotchmer (1994), in which the price systems are nonanonymous with type-dependent rather than name-specific Lindahl prices. Our result is stronger since, although we allow name-specific prices, we show that, with small effective groups, all individuals in the same jurisdiction pay the same price.

3.3 Tiebout equilibria and contestability

Implicit in the discussion by Tiebout (1956) is the notion of lump-sum taxes for admission to jurisdictions and access to the collective goods provided within the jurisdictions. One interpretation of this notion, in Wooders (1980, 1989) is based on the idea of contestability (Baumol, Panzer, & Willig [1982]); that is, a state of the economy is a Tiebout equilibrium state if no firm/jurisdiction can profitably provide the collective goods or, alternatively, where prices for private goods are given, no group of consumers can benefit from "opting out" of the system and providing its own collective goods. Such equilibria are investigated in Wooders (1980), where it is shown that Tiebout equilibrium states converge to the nonanonymous Lindahl equilibrium states as defined above.[16] The motivation underlying an admission tax equilibrium and its designation as a Tiebout equilibrium comes from the fact that a variety of procedures may be used by governments (or firms or clubs) to determine the distribution of costs and benefits resulting from membership. As emphasized by Tiebout, competition between jurisdictions forces local governments to raise tax revenues optimally.

3.4 Admission equilibrium

A different notion of a Tiebout equilibrium specifies an admission price for each level of the public good in each jurisdiction, and thus involves an infinite number of prices.

An *admission price system* is a collection of prices

$$\Lambda = \left\{ \lambda\,(s,y) \in \Re : s \leq N \text{ and } y \in \Re_{+} \right\} \tag{3-30}$$

where $\lambda\,(s,y) = \lambda\,(s,y')$ if $\|s\| = \|s'\|$; that is, an admission price system specifies a price for each level of the public good for each possible jurisdiction. Note that, like a two-part equilibrium, two jurisdictions of the same size in the equilibrium jurisdiction structure can charge different prices – provided they offer different levels of the public goods. It is immediately clear, however, that if two different jurisdictions in the equilibrium jurisdiction structure of a two-part equilibrium charge different prices they *must* provide different levels of the public goods.

A *Tiebout admission equilibrium* is, therefore, an ordered pair $e = (\varepsilon, \Lambda)$, consisting of a feasible state of the economy

$$\varepsilon = [n, (y^g,z^g), (x^g_{tq},y^g,n^g)_{tq,g}]$$

and an admission price system Λ such that:

(i) for each jurisdiction n^g

$$\|n^g\|\lambda\,(n^g,y^g) - z^g = 0, \tag{3-31a}$$

(zero profits in the jurisdictions in n);

[16] Similar results are obtained in Wooders (1981, 1989) for a significantly more general model.

(ii) for each profile $s \leq n$ and for all (y,z) such that $z = c(s,y)$,

$$0 \geq \|n^g\| \lambda\,(s,y)y - z \tag{3-31b}$$

(profit maximization);

(iii) for each jurisdiction n^g and for each participant tq in n^g it holds that

$$\lambda\,(n^g,y^g) + x^g_{tq} = e^{tq}$$

and for all $(x,y,\|s\|)$ such that

$$u^t\,(x,y,\|s\|) > u^t\,(x_t,y^g,\|n^g\|), \tag{3-31c}$$

it holds that

$$\lambda\,(s,y) + x > e^{tq}. \tag{3-31d}$$

Let ε be a state of the economy. Then ε is a *Tiebout admission equilibrium state of the economy* if there is a set of admission prices Λ such that (ε,Λ) is a Tiebout admission equilibrium.

The set of admission equilibrium outcomes includes the set of two-part equilibrium outcomes.

Proposition 8. Two-part equilibrium outcomes are admission equilibrium outcomes. *Let ε be a two-part equilibrium state of the economy. Then ε is an admission equilibrium state of the economy.*

Proof. Suppose that ε is a two-part equilibrium state of the economy. Then there is a price system $\mathbf{p}$ and a wage system $\mathbf{w}$ such that $(\varepsilon,\mathbf{p},\mathbf{w})$ is a two-part equilibrium. To construct an admission equilibrium price system for each jurisdiction s define $\lambda\,(s,y) = p\,(s)\,y - w\,(s)$ and define Λ by $\Lambda = \{\,\lambda\,(s,y) : s$ is a jurisdiction and $y \in \Re_+\}$. It is easy to verify that (ε,Λ) is an admission equilibrium. ■

Recall that a two-part equilibrium is defined relative to a jurisdiction structure. This is required since two jurisdictions of the same size may provide different levels of the public good and charge different prices. In an admission equilibrium, this possibility is built into the price function (for this reason, prices can be a function of jurisdiction size and the level of public good provided).

The following result will enable us to establish Theorem 2. The result is a special case of a result established by Conley and Wooders (1994a) since the nondifferentiated crowding model employed here is a special case of their model.[17]

[17] Since it concerns an admission equilibrium and our model has nondifferentiated crowding, this result is similar in some respects to the core-equilibrium equivalence result in Scotchmer and Wooders (1987). That paper allows variable intensity of consumption of the public good within jurisdictions and thus the Conley and Wooders result is more directly applied.

Proposition 9. (Conley and Wooders 1994a). Equivalence of the core and the Tiebout admission equilibrium outcomes. *Let* ε *be a state of the economy with the equal-treatment property. Then* ε *is a Tiebout admission equilibrium state if and only if* ε *is in the core.*

We are now able to state the following theorem.

Theorem 2: *Let* ε *be a state of the economy with the equal-treatment property. Then the following two statements are equivalent:*

1. ε *is a Tiebout admission equilibrium state of the economy.*
2. ε *is in the core.*

If the production technology is concave, then the above statements are equivalent to the statement that

3. ε *is a Lindahl state of the economy.*

Moreover, if production satisfies the constant returns to scale condition within jurisdictions, then the above three statements are equivalent to the following statement.

4. ε *is a two-part equilibrium state of the economy.*

Proof. The proof is immediately clear from our preceding propositions. ■

An interesting aspect of this result is that it indicates that, informally, more prices "substitute" for more conditions on the economy.

4. The Second Welfare Theorem: Pareto optima are competitive equilibria

A feasible state of the economy ε with jurisdiction structure n is a *Pareto optimum* if it is impossible to find some other state of the economy such that no participant is worse off and at least some (possibly one) participant is better off. That is, ε is a Pareto optimum if there does not exist some other feasible state ε' with jurisdiction structure n' (not necessarily distinct) and, for each t, a one-to-one mapping θ^t from $\{(q,g) : q = 1, \ldots, n_t^g, g = 1, \ldots, G\}$ to $\{(q',g') : q' = 1, \ldots, n_t', g' = 1, \ldots, G'\}$ such that, for each $n^g \in n$ and each $q = 1, \ldots, n_t^g$,

$$u^t(x_{tq'}^{g'}, y^g, \|n^g\|) \geq u^t(x_{tq}^{g}, y^g, \|n^g\|) \tag{3-32}$$

where $\theta^t(q,g) = (q',g')$ with strict inequality for at least one tq.

The results established in this section often require us to redistribute resources across participants. It is therefore useful to introduce terminology which describes the construction of these new allocations. An *equal-treatment redistribution* is a vector $\tau \in \mathbf{R}^T$ satisfying

$$\sum_t N_t \tau^t = 0. \tag{3-33}$$

In interpretation, τ^t is the amount of the tax imposed on each individual of type t. Obviously, if τ^t is greater than zero, then type t players pay a tax; if τ^t is less than zero, they receive a subsidy.

Our next theorem is concerned with the relationship between the distribution of endowments and the distribution of utilities at Pareto optima. It should be recalled that the fact that ε is a Pareto optimum provides no information about the way in which the costs of providing the collective good in each jurisdiction are shared among the participants in the economy. In particular, it may be true that, given their endowments e^t, the utility level achieved by some participants will be less than they could earn in a type-optimal club, whereas others may earn more. What the following theorem establishes, however, is that for any Pareto optimum, an *equal-treatment redistribution* can be constructed so that, relative to post-tax endowments, each player type earns exactly its type-optimal utility.

As the proof of Theorem 3 is fairly long, it is useful to provide a "road map." It is first shown that if a state of the economy ε is a Pareto optimum, then it cannot be true that, relative to their endowments, all participants obtain either less or more utility than in type-optimal clubs. The difficulty arises if some participants earn less utility, while others earn more, than in type-optimal clubs. The next step is then to show that by applying appropriately determined lump-sum taxes to those participants earning less, and by appropriately redistributing (as lump-sum payments) this tax revenue to those earning more, then all types earn exactly their type-optimal utilities relative to their post-tax endowments; in effect, the redistribution reconciles participants' payoffs and their capacity to pay. It is interesting to note that the proof of the theorem relies only on feasibility arguments and does not require interiority assumptions. It is also useful to point out that the jurisdiction structure remains fixed throughout the redistribution process. Although participants' payoffs in ε are compared to what they could obtain in a type-optimal club given their (post-tax) endowments, the comparisons are drawn between what participants obtain in actually existing jurisdictions and what they could obtain in fictional homogeneous jurisdictions.

Theorem 3: *Let ε be a Pareto optimum with the equal-treatment property. Then there exists an equal-treatment redistribution τ such that for each type t, each participant receives his type-optimal utility relative to the endowment $e^t + \tau^t$, that is,*

$$u^t(x^g_{tq}, y^g, \|n^g\|) = u^{*t}(e^t + \tau^t). \tag{3-34}$$

Proof. Suppose this condition does not hold. Let ε be a Pareto optimum with jurisdiction structure $\aleph$. Assume that at ε, players of type t have endowments e^t. There are three possible cases: given their endowments, all participants of each type obtain less utility than in their type-optimal clubs; all obtain more utility than in type-optimal clubs, or some types obtain more while others obtains less utility than in type-optimal clubs. We consider each case in turn.

Clearly, if in state ε every type obtains less than its type-optimal utility relative to endowments e^t, then an alternative allocation is to assign all agents to (homogeneous) type-optimal clubs; in this case, all will be better off than at ε, and so ε cannot be a Pareto optimum, which is a contradiction.

Next, observe that if for any $n^g \in n$, $u^t(x^g_{tq}, y^g, \|n^g\|) > u^{*t}(e^t)$ – if type t participants, given their endowments, are better off at ε than in their type-optimal jurisdictions – then it must be true that

$$x^g_{tq} > e^t + w(n^g) - \frac{z^g}{\|n^g\|}. \tag{3-35}$$

This follows from the fact that if the consumption plan followed by agents of type t at ε is preferred by them to the plan available in a type-optimal club, it must then be true that this consumption plan is not attainable given their own resources. But if the above expression is true for each t, then ε is not feasible, a contradiction.

We now consider the case in which at ε, some types obtain more utility than $u^{*t}(e^t)$, while others obtain less. By appropriate relabeling of participant types, we can suppose that for all $t < t_o$, $u^t(x^g_{tq}, y^g, \|n^g\|) < u^*(e^t)$ and for all $t \geq t_o$, $u^t(x^g_{tq}, y^g, \|n^g\|) \geq u^*(e^t)$.

Our next step is to calculate the maximum amount of tax revenue that can be extracted from those participants who at ε earn less than their type-optimal utility levels relative to their endowments; to this end, we calculate the difference between their actual endowment and the resources they would require to attain their payoff at ε in a homogeneous club. For all $t < t_o$, solve the following program:

$$\text{for } t < t_o, \max_{\tau^t} \quad R^t = e^t - \tau^t$$

subject to

$$u^{*t}(e^t - \tau^t) \geq u^t(x^g_{tq}, y^g, \|n^g\|).$$

Let $R_o = \sum_{t<t_o} N_t R^t$; R_o is the total tax revenue. We now redistribute this tax revenue to those participants who, given endowments e^t, obtain more utility at ε than they could in a type-optimal jurisdiction. For $t \geq t_o$, define an equal-treatment redistribution according to the following rule:

$$s^t_o = \min\left\{\frac{R_o}{\sum_{t \geq t_o} N_t}, \tau^t_o\right\}, \tag{3-36}$$

where τ^t_o solves $u^t(x^g_{tq}, y^g, \|n^g\|) = u^{*t}(e^t + \tau^t_o)$. If $R_o / \sum_{t \geq t_o} N_t = \tau^t_o$, set $s^t_o = \tau^t_o$.

Therefore, s^t_o assigns to participants of type $t \geq t_o$ the lesser of their per capita share of the tax revenue R_o or the amount necessary to equalize the utility obtained at ε with the utility obtained in a type-optimal jurisdiction, given their endowments and their share of the tax revenue.

Next, implement the following algorithm. This algorithm simply repeats the redistributive procedure used above to redistribute any surplus tax revenue among those players whose payoffs at ε continue to exceed that which they could obtain in a type-optimal club, given their endowments and total after-tax revenue.

Let r count the number of iterations. Start the algorithm at r=1.

Step 1. Relabel participants so that for $t \geq t_r$, $s^t_{r-1} \neq \tau^t_{r-1}$. *Go to step 2.*

Step 2. Define $R_r = R_{r-1} - \sum_{t \geq t_{r-1}} N_t s^t_{r-1}$.

- For $t \geq t_r$, define an equal-treatment redistribution according to the following rule:

$$s^t_r = \min \left\{ \frac{R_r}{\sum_{t \geq t_r} N_t}, \tau^t_r \right\} \tag{3-37}$$

where τ^t_r solves $u^t(x^g_{tq}, y^g, \|n^g\|) = u^{*t}(e^t + \sum_{r=0}^{r-1} s^t_r + \tau^t_r)$. If $R_r / \sum_{t \geq t_r} N_t = \tau^t_r$, set $s^t_r = \tau^t_r$. *Go to step 3.*

Step 3. If $s^t_r = R_{r-1} / \sum_{t > t_r} N_t$ for all t_r, *stop.*

- If $s^t_r = \tau^t_r$ for all t_r, *stop.*
- Otherwise, *go to step 1.*

Observe that since the number of types is finite, the algorithm must eventually terminate. When the algorithm terminates, two possible cases arise; we investigate each in turn. The first is that all of the tax revenue will have been redistributed, but there will be some participant types that still obtain more utility at ε than they could in a type-optimal jurisdiction, given their endowments and total after-tax revenue; we show that this is inconsistent with feasibility. The second is that a redistribution will be constructed such that, relative to their after-tax endowments, all participants earn at ε exactly their type-optimal utilities; we show that when this second case obtains, all the tax revenue must be redistributed.

Case One: After $\hat{r}$ iterations, for all $t \geq t_{\hat{r}}$,

$$s^t_{\hat{r}} = R_{\hat{r}-1} / \sum_{t > t_{\hat{r}}} N_t \quad \text{and} \quad u^t(x^g_{tq}, y^g, \|n^g\|) > u^{*t}(e^t + \sum_{r=0}^{\hat{r}} s^t_r).$$

This means that given their post-tax endowments, in a homogeneous club with $\|n^g\|$ participants, these agents could not afford the consumption plan which they obtain at ε; that is, for $t \geq t_{\hat{r}}$,

$$x^g_{tq} > e^t + w(n^g) + \sum_{r=0}^{\hat{r}} s^t_r - \frac{z^g}{\|n^g\|}. \qquad (3\text{-}38)$$

In contrast, for each $t < t_{\hat{r}}$, there exists some $r'(t) < \hat{r}$ such that

$$u^t(x^g_{tq}, y^g, \|n^g\|) = u^{*t}(e^t + \sum_{r=0}^{r'(t)} s^t_r).$$

Since the consumption plan adopted by the type-optimal club to obtain this utility level is resource-minimizing, it follows that

$$x^g_{tq} \geq e^t + w(n^g) + \sum_{r=0}^{r'(t)} s^t_r - \frac{z^g}{\|n^g\|}. \qquad (3\text{-}39)$$

Summing the above two relations for all participants, and recalling that $\sum_{r=0}^{\hat{r}} s^t_r = R_o$, it is evident that feasibility is violated. Since ε is feasible by assumption, we have shown that if the algorithm terminates after $\hat{r}$ iterations, there does not exist a $t_{\hat{r}}$ such that $u^t(x^g_{tq}, y^g, \|n^g\|) > u^{*t}(e^t + \sum_{r=0}^{r'} s^t_r)$.

Case Two: After $\tilde{r}$ iterations, $R_{\tilde{r}+1} \geq 0$ and for all t,there exists $r''(t) \leq \tilde{r}$ such that $u^t\,(x^g_{tq}, y^g, \|n^g\|) = u^{*t}(e^t + \sum_{r=0}^{r''(t)} s^t_r)$. If $R_{\tilde{r}+1} > 0$ then, by forming homogeneous jurisdictions, it would be possible to achieve the same distribution of utility as at ε using fewer resources, which contradicts our assumption that ε is a Pareto optimum. If $R_{\tilde{r}+1} = 0$, then the algorithm has constructed the required equal-treatment redistribution and our claim is proved. ■

Observe that the proof of Theorem 3 relies only on feasibility conditions and does not require any interiority conditions. Consequently, Theorem 3 is valid even when there are Pareto-optimal allocations in which participants consume only the collective good. However, since all participants in a jurisdiction receive their type-optimal utilities relative to their post-tax endowments, it remains true that even if the membership of a jurisdiction is mixed, all the participants in the jurisdiction have the same "demand" for the collective good.

As a preliminary step to proving our Second Welfare Theorem, it is useful to investigate the relationship between the set of Pareto optima and the set of equal-treatment core allocations. Recall that the core allocations are defined relative to a particular distribution of endowments. If endowments are redistributed via some redistribution τ, then the set of core allocations changes. Our next result establishes an equivalence between the set of Pareto-optimal equal-treatment outcomes and core allocations relative to some equal-treatment redistribution of endowments.[18]

Theorem 4. Equivalence of Pareto-optimal equal treatment outcomes and core allocations relative to redistributions. *Let ε be an equal-treatment state of the economy. Then there exists an equal-treatment redistribution τ and a vector of core utilities* $u(e - \tau) = (u^1(e^1 - \tau^1), \ldots, u^T(e^T - \tau^T))$ *relative to en-*

[18] Of course, it should be clear that our results depend heavily on the assumptions of only one private good and of equal treatment.

dowments $\{(e^t - \tau^t) : t = 1, ..., T\}$ *such that* $u^t(x^g_{tq}, y^g, \|n^g\|) = u^{*t}(e^t - \tau^t)$ *if and only if* ε *is Pareto-optimal.*

Proof. Necessity follows directly from the definition of the core. We will therefore prove sufficiency. Let ε be a Pareto optimum. Then, by Theorem 3, there exists an equal-treatment redistribution τ such that, for each t,

$$u^t(x^g_{tq}, y^g, \|n^g\|) = u^{*t}(e^t - \tau^t).$$

We claim that $[u^t(x^g_{tq}, y^g, \|n^g\|)\,]_{t=1}^T$ is a vector of core utilities $u(e - \tau)$ relative to endowments $e^t - \tau^t$. If the claim is false, then there exists a group of participants who could do better by forming a new jurisdiction, that is, there exists $s = (s^1, ..., s^T)$, $s^t \le n^t$ such that for each t,

$$(x^s_{tq'}, y^s, \|s\|) > (x^g_{tq}, y^g, \|n^g\|)$$

and

$$\sum_{t=1}^{T} \sum_{q'=1}^{s^t} x^s_{tq'} + z^s = \sum_{t=1}^{T} (e^t - \tau^t). \tag{3-40}$$

Observe that since $u^t(x^g_{tq}, y^g, \|n^g\|) = u^{*t}(e^t - \tau^t)$, groups of participants cannot improve upon their payoff at ε by forming homogeneous clubs. Consequently, the composition of any group of participants which can improve its payoff by forming a new jurisdiction must be mixed and, furthermore, for each type t such that $s^t > 0$, $u^t(x^s_{tq'}, y^s, \|s\|) > u^{*t}(e^t - \tau^t)$. But then, for each participant of type t such that $s^t > 0$,

$$x^s_{tq'} > e^t - \tau^t - \frac{z^s}{\|s\|}; \tag{3-41}$$

feasibility is violated. ■

Having established that every Pareto optimum is a core allocation relative to an appropriate redistribution of endowments, we now have all the elements in hand to establish our Second Welfare Theorem. The result in fact follows directly from Theorem 4 and core-equilibrium equivalence.

Theorem 5: A Second Welfare Theorem. *Suppose* ε *is an equal-treatment Pareto optimum. (a) Then there exists some equal-treatment redistribution* t *such that* ε *is an admission equilibrium relative to the after-tax endowments. (b) Suppose in addition that the production technology is concave. Then there exists some equal-treatment redistribution* τ *such that* ε *is a Lindahl equilibrium outcome. (c) Suppose that there are constant returns to scale in production. Then there exists some equal-treatment redistribution* τ *such that* ε *is a two-part equilibrium outcome.*

Proof. By Theorem 4, if ε is a Pareto optimum with the equal-treatment property, then there exists an equal-treatment redistribution τ such that $(u^t(x^g_{tq}, y^g, \|n^g\|))_{t=1}^T$ is an equal-treatment core allocation relative to post-redistribution endowments $e^t - \tau^t$. By Proposition 8, since $(u^t(x^g_{tq}, y^g, \|n^g\|))_{t=1}^T$ is an equal-treatment core allocation, there exists an admission price system Λ such that (ε,Λ) is a competitive equilibrium.

The remainder of the proof is similar to the preceeding propositions. ■

Our Second Welfare Theorem must be compared to those established by Scotchmer and Wooders (1987) and Manning (1992). Scotchmer and Wooders (1987) consider an economy with only two participant types but variable usage of the club, whereas our theorem is for a finite set of types but nonvariable usage. An analogue of our result can be established for the Scotchmer and Wooders (1987) model; the modifications required are easily made. More significantly, the Scotchmer and Wooders result is established for those Pareto-optimal outcomes where individuals all receive their type-optimal utilities. (In fact, their result is more in the spirit of our Proposition 2' and core-equilibrium equivalence than of our Second Welfare Theorem.) In contrast, we prove that any efficient equal-treatment state of the economy is an equilibrium state in which all agents receive their type-optimal utilities (relative to their after-tax endowments). Also, we show that if ε is an efficient state but participants do not achieve core utilities relative to initial endowments, then it is in fact *feasible* to redistribute endowments across participants in a lump-sum fashion so that core utilities are achieved relative to the after-tax endowments. Manning (1992) considers an economy with multiple private and public goods. However, he considers differentiated, nonanonymous crowding – that is, both types and names matter – and so his competitive equilibrium notion uses nonanonymous pricing. In contrast, the price system used here to support Pareto optima is anonymous.

There are still some limitations to our Second Welfare Theorem. The first is that not all Pareto-optimal outcomes are equal-treatment ones and the core may be empty relative to any arbitrary redistribution of endowments. Thus, we may want to consider economies with nonempty cores, such as those of Greenberg and Weber (1986), for example. Alternatively, we might formulate approximate versions of the Second Welfare Theorem. This appears to be a promising direction since approximate cores of large economies are nonempty under mild conditions. The second limitation is that our results are obtained under the assumption of only one private good; this appears to be primarily a technical problem with significant difficulties caused by the complexities of the relationship between the equal-treatment core and demands for private and public goods as endowments change.

5. Conclusions

Our results on equilibrium concepts indicate that, as can be expected, the appropriateness of various concepts of economic equilibrium depends on the economic environment being considered. We emphasize that with constant returns to scale, all the equilibrium concepts considered are equivalent and are equivalent to the core. That, in general, equivalence of admission equilibrium outcomes, Lindahl equilibrium outcomes, and the core requires nonanonymity of Lindahl prices is especially intriguing. It appears that the large of the menu of choices available in an admission equilibrium allows a resolution to the moral hazard problem that the finite number of prices characterizing the Lindahl equilibrium does not permit. This is suggestive of the resolution to a problem of screening with moral hazard advocated by Page (1992), which introduces a large menu of choices. Application of Page's approach may be quite fruitful in the context of economies with public goods.

Our Second Welfare Theorem is a contribution to what might be called Phase II of the "Tiebout Program" – the investigation of conditions under which the Second Welfare Theorem holds in economies with congestible public goods. We show that by constructing an appropriate equal-treatment redistribution, all equal-treatment Pareto optima can be supported as competitive equilibria. An important feature of our proof is that it relies exclusively on feasibility arguments; no interiority conditions are imposed with respect to the private good. It appears that our Second Welfare Theorem may be significantly generalized, providing conditions ensuring nonemptiness of the core for all initial endowments are satisfied.

Our model requires some features that appear very special. We view the restriction to one private good and one public good as technical matters. The requirement that groups bounded in absolute size can realize all or almost all gains to collective activities appears to be a feature shared by any economic structure in which cores converge to cooperative outcomes.[19] Thus, we do not view our assumption that all gains to collective activities can be realized by groups bounded in absolute size as restrictive. The main restriction may appear to be that the crowding effects only depend on the numbers of consumers with whom consumption is joint. Ongoing research indicates that this feature of our model and of our results is not excessively restrictive in the sense that a number of results for the nondifferentiated crowding model extend to the crowding types model of Conley and Wooders (1994a; 1994b; 1996).

The obvious Phase III of the Tiebout Program is the investigation of the game-theoretic foundations of the Tiebout Hypothesis. The game-theoretic analysis initiated in Wooders (1978a) and continued in this chapter is part of this phase. Noncooperative approaches, such as that initiated by Novshek and Sonnenschein (1978) for private goods economies with production, were suggested by Shubik and Wooders (1983), c.f., Scotchmer (1985). Other contributions using noncooperative approaches include Silva and Kahn (1991), Barham, Boadway, Marchand, and Pestieau (1992), Bloch and Ryder (1994), and Lagunoff (1994). By combining general equilibrium theory and theories of collective goods, coalition formation, and problems of social choice and collective decision making by relatively small units in large societies, the Tiebout Program

[19] This has been shown for large games and economies modeled by the pregame framework since within this framework cores converge if and only if small groups are effective; see Wooders (1994a: Section 4).

provides a rich framework within which problems of coordination and collective action can be addressed.

We conclude with a few comments indicating some possible extensions of our results. Our model is quite specialized; there is only one private good and one public good. The results in Wooders (1993) for differentiated crowding, for a model with multiple public goods and, for some results, multiple private goods, indicate that our results will continue to hold as long as small groups are effective and crowding is nondifferentiated. If there are many private goods, however, and/or small groups are not *strictly* effective, then the results will hold only asymptotically, as the economy grows large. The natural extension of the nondifferentiated crowding in our model is not the standard differentiated crowding model, as in Wooders (1993), for example, but the crowding types model of Conley and Wooders (1994a, b, 1996) since in that model, as in this, agents are only crowded by observable characteristics of other agents.[20]

References

Barham, V. (1992) *Issues in Club Theory and Social Equity.* Louvain-la-Neuve: CIACO.

Barham, V., R. Boadway, M. Marchand, and P. Pestieau (1992) "Voluntary Contributions and Club Formation: Nash Equilibrium and Optimality." *Journal of Public Economics* (forthcoming).

Baumol, W. J., J. C. Panzer, and R. D. Willig (1982) *Contestable Markets and the Theory of Industry Structure.* New York: Harcourt Brace Jovanovich.

Berglas, E. and D. Pines (1980) "Clubs as a Case of Competitive Industry with Goods of Variable Quality." *Economics Letters,* 5, 363-366.

Berglas, E. and D. Pines (1981) "Clubs, Local Public Goods, and Transportation Models: A Synthesis." *Journal of Public Economics,* 15, 141-162.

Bewley, T. (1981) "A Critique of Tiebout's Theory of Local Public Expenditure." *Econometrica,* 49, 713-740.

Bloch, F. and H. Ryder (1994) "Two-sided Search, Marriages and Matchmakers." CORE Discussion Paper 9428.

Conley, J. and M. H. Wooders (1994a) "Equivalence of Tiebout Equilibrium and the Core in a Model with Crowding Types." University of Illinois Working Paper (Revised). *Journal of Urban Economics* (forthcoming).

Conley, J. and M. H. Wooders (1994b) "Anonymous Lindahl Pricing in a Tiebout Economy with Crowding Types." University of Illinois Working Paper (Revised 1995).

Conley, J. and M. H. Wooders (1995) "Hedonic Independence and Taste Homogeneity of Optimal Jurisdictions in a Tiebout Economy with Crowding Types," manuscript.

Conley, J. and M. H. Wooders (1997) "Anonymous Pricing in Tiebout Economies and Economies with Clubs." In *Topics in Public Economics,* D. Pines, E. Sadka, and I. Zilcha, eds. New York: Cambridge University Press.

[20] In certain respects the model of this chapter might be thought of as a partial equilibrium version of a crowding types model where there is only one crowding type. Remarkably, however, the homogeneity of demands for crowding and public goods that we observed in this chapter does not necessarily carry over into the crowding types model; see Conley and Wooders (1995).

Ellison, B. (1973) "A Generalization of the Pure Theory of Public Goods." *American Economic Review,* 63, 417-432.

Foley, D. (1970) "Lindahl's Solution and the Core of an Economy with Public Goods." *Econometrica,* 38, 66-72.

Greenberg, J. and S. Weber (1986) "Strong Tiebout Equilibrium with Restricted Preference Domain." *Journal of Economic Theory,* 38, 101-117.

Lagunoff, R. (1994) "On the Dynamic Selection of Mechanisms for Provision of Public Projects." Mimeo, University of Pennsylvania.

Manning, J. (1992) "Local Public Goods: First Best Allocations and Supporting Prices." (Typescript).

Mas-Colell, A. (1975) "A Model of Equilibrium with Differentiated Commodities." *Journal of Mathematical Economics,* 2, 263-295.

Novshek, W. and H. Sonnenschein (1978) "Cournot and Walras Equilibrium." *Journal of Economic Theory,* 19, 223-266.

Page, F. H. Jr. (1992) "Mechanism Design for General Screening Problems with Moral Hazard." *Economic Theory,* 2, 265-282.

Sandler, T. and J. T. Tschirhart (1980) "The Economic Theory of Clubs: An Evaluative Survey." *Journal of Economic Literature,* 18, 1481-1521.

Scotchmer, S. (1985) "Two-tiered Pricing of Shared Facilities in a Free-entry Equilibrium." *Rand Journal,* 16, 456-472.

Scotchmer, S. (1994) "Public Goods and the Invisible Hand." In *Modern Public Finance,* J. Quigley and E. Smolensky, eds. Cambridge: Harvard University Press.

Scotchmer, S. and M. H. Wooders (1986) "Optimal and Equilibrium Groups." Harvard Discussion Paper No. 1251 (and subsequent, incomplete revisions under the title of "Competitive Equilibrium and the Core in Club Economies with Nonanonymous Crowding").

Scotchmer, S. and M. H. Wooders (1987) "Competitive Equilibrium and the Core in Club Economies with Anonymous Crowding." *Journal of Public Economics,* 34, 159-174.

Shubik, M. and M. H. Wooders (1983) "Approximate Cores of Replica Games and Economies; Part I. Replica Games, Externalities, and Approximate Cores." *Mathematical Social Sciences,* 6, 27-48.

Silva, E. C. D. and C. M. Kahn (1991) "Exclusion and Moral Hazard; the Case of Identical Demand." *Journal of Public Economics* (forthcoming).

Tiebout, C. (1956) "A Pure Theory of Public Expenditures." *Journal of Political Economy,* 64, 416-424.

Wooders, M. H. (1978a) "Equilibria, the Core, and Jurisdiction Structures in Economies with a Local Public Good." *Journal of Economic Theory,* 18, 328-348.

Wooders, M. H. (1978b) "A Characterization of Approximate Equilibria and Cores in a Class of Coalition Economies." Stony Brook Department of Economics, Working Paper No. 184.

Wooders, M. H. (1980) "The Tiebout Hypothesis: Near Optimality in Local Public Good Economies." *Econometrica,* 48, 1467-1486.

Wooders, M. H. (1981) "A Limit Theorem on the ε-Core of an Economy with Public Goods." National Tax Institute of Japan, Paper No. 20.

Wooders, M. H. (1983) "The Epsilon Core of a Large Replica Game." *Journal of Mathematical Economics,* 11, 277-300.

Wooders, M. H., (1988), "Stability of Jurisdiction Structure in Economies with Local Public Goods." *Mathematical Social Sciences,* 29-49.

Wooders, M. H. (1989) "A Tiebout Theorem." *Mathematical Social Sciences,* 18, 33-55.

Wooders, M. H. (1991) "Large Games and Competitive Markets; Applications." Sonderforschingsbereich 303 University of Bonn Discussion Paper No. B-196.

Wooders, M. H. (1993) "Equivalence of Lindahl Equilibrium with Participation Prices and the Core." *Economic Theory* (forthcoming).

Wooders, M. H. (1994a) "Large Games and Economies with Effective Small Groups." In J.-F. Mertens and S. Sorin, eds. *Game Theoretic Approaches to General Equilibrium Theory. Dordrecht, Boston, London: Kluwer Academic Publishers, 145-206.*

CHAPTER 4

Anonymous pricing in Tiebout economies and economies with clubs*

John P. Conley and Myrna H. Wooders

1. Introduction

One of the persistent problems in public economics is how to achieve efficient outcomes through market mechanisms in the presence of public goods. The Lindahl equilibrium as formalized by Samuelson (1954) is not in itself a satisfactory solution. Decentralizing efficient allocations through the Lindahl equilibrium notion requires that the prices faced by agents depend upon their preference mappings. As a consequence, self-interested agents may prefer not to reveal their true preferences, relying instead on others to provide the public goods. Solving this "free rider" problem in pure public goods economies typically requires appealing to nonmarket mechanisms.[1]

In his seminal paper, Tiebout (1956) proposed an alternative model. He observed that many types of public goods are "local" rather than "pure." Tiebout suggested that when public goods are provided to agents by a large number of jurisdictions, competition among these jurisdictions for members will lead to market-type efficiency. In effect, agents reveal their preferences by their choice of jurisdiction. Consequently, the free-rider problem disappears and the equilibrium outcome is efficient.

One of the first researchers to address Tiebout's basic insight in detail was Eitan Berglas. In an influential paper, Berglas (1976) introduced a model of an economy with public goods subject to crowding and exclusion and raised important questions on how production techniques, distribution of tastes and skills, and inter-community trade might affect the nature of economic equilibrium. Berglas was especially concerned with the type-homogeneity of optimal jurisdictions. Subsequent researchers in the field owe him a debt of gratitude for drawing attention to this rich and interesting area of research. We will refer to the work of Berglas again below.

The purpose of this chapter is to discuss the different approaches to formalizing Tiebout's hypothesis. There are many possible interpretations. One could reasonably view the Tiebout hypothesis as equivalent to a First Welfare Theorem, a Second Welfare Theorem, an existence theorem, a core/equilibrium

* The authors are indebted to Vicky Barham, Birgit Grodal, Sergiu Hart, David Pines and Karl Vind for helpful discussions and comments, and the Social Sciences and Humanities Research Council of Canada for support.

[1] See Jackson and Moulin (1992) for a recent survey of such mechanisms (as well as an interesting new mechanism).

convergence theorem, or a core/equilibrium equivalence theorem. Before considering any of these possibilities, we must understand what is meant by equilibrium. Specifically, this chapter focuses on the nature of decentralizing price systems. Our main point is that unless prices are anonymous in the sense that they cannot discriminate between agents on the basis of unobservable characteristics (tastes, for example), they do not decentralize in the same sense as competitive prices in private goods markets.

We consider both nondifferentiated crowding and differentiated crowding models.[2] Nondifferentiated crowding implies that agents are directly affected only by the size of the group with whom the public goods are shared. When crowding is differentiated agents are affected by both the size and the composition of the group sharing the public goods. Two sorts of differentiated crowding models are discussed, the standard model and the crowding types model introduced in Conley and Wooders (1994a). In the standard model, agents are affected by the types of other agents, including their taste-types. In the crowding types model, agents are affected only by those aspects of others that are publicly observable — their crowding types. We explore the decentralization theorems available for each of these three models: the nondifferentiated crowding model, the standard differentiated crowding model, and the crowding types model.

The motivation for the crowding types model is to recover anonymous decentralization of core states even when crowding is differentiated. This model distinguishes two sets of characteristics for each agent. The first set consists of tastes and endowments. These are unobservable and do not enter into the objectives or constraints of other agents. The second set consists of crowding characteristics that enter into utility or production functions and therefore affect the welfare of others. We assume that crowding characteristics are observable, and allow their effects to be either positive or negative. For example, gender is a crowding characteristic – we are able to distinguish males from females – and we may have preferences about the proportion of males to females at a dance. On the other hand, preferences for types of music are taste characteristics – we may not be able to determine which band an agent most prefers – but an agent's taste in music does not directly affect the welfare of other agents.[3]

The main result from the crowding types model described above is that when small groups are effective, anonymous decentralizing prices will exist for every state of the economy in the core. (Intuitively, small group effectiveness means

[2] Nondifferentiated and differentiated crowding have also been called anonymous and nonanonymous crowding, respectively. This is somewhat misleading because in the standard differentiated crowding model, where different types may have different crowding effects, crowding is also anonymous. That is, it is not the names of agents that matter to other agents, but rather their crowding types. Within a given type, agents are perfect substitutes and crowd nondifferentially. Our usage is also motivated by the differentiated commodities literature, for example, Mas-Colell (1975).

[3] Although there may be indirect effects when an agent expresses tastes through consumption choices.

that all or almost all gains to collective activities can be achieved by groups whose membership is bounded in absolute or relative size. With sufficient numbers, small group effectiveness is equivalent to per capita boundedness – finiteness of the supremum of average payoff.) Similar results have been obtained for the nondifferentiated crowding model. For the standard differentiated crowding model, however, prices depend upon tastes and are, therefore, not anonymous.

The plan of the chapter is as follows. In Section 2, we formally define and motivate the major modeling approaches. In Section 3, we define the core and consider problems of existence. In Section 4, we discuss different notions of market equilibrium, paying special attention to associated price systems. In Section 5, we discuss different notions of small group effectiveness, which appears to be a fundamental economic condition. In Section 6, we connect local public goods economies to the literature on market games. Section 7 contains concluding remarks.

2. Models of local public goods economies

Tiebout's original contribution has led to two major strands in the literature: local public goods economics and the theory of clubs. The distinction between the two is more traditional than formal, and is based mainly on the type of problem that motivates a particular author, not on the tools or modeling techniques involved.

Authors who write on club economies usually have in mind a private membership club, such as a country club. They are concerned about the extent to which private clubs can effectively provide public goods traditionally supplied by governments. Most papers consider the problem from the standpoint of one profit-maximizing and price-taking club. The general equilibrium question of how to allocate all agents in the economy to clubs does not necessarily arise in this context.[4]

Perhaps the most important feature distinguishing the club from the local public goods approach is that club membership is not particularly associated with the physical location of agents. As a consequence, agents are typically allowed to join more than one club or no club at all. Questions of variable usage of club facilities and how this affects crowding and pricing naturally arise.

Studies of local public goods economies are typically motivated by locational models. We imagine optimizing jurisdictions that competitively offer bundles of public goods and associated tax prices. Agents express their demands indirectly by "voting with their feet" – moving to the locality with their most preferred mix of taxes and public goods. The fact that agents can live in only one location motivates the restriction that agents join exactly one of these local

[4] We emphasize that there is no technical reason why general equilibrium questions could not be addressed in the context of clubs with multiple and overlapping membership. See Shubik and Wooders (1986) and Hochman, Pines, and Thisse (1995) for recent examples.

public goods "clubs." Local public goods models usually focus on the general equilibrium question of how the entire population allocates itself to various jurisdictions in response to market signals. Interesting questions associated with local public goods models include the effects of property rights assignments and how variable land consumption choice and capitalization of the present value of public goods consumption affect the nature and efficiency of the equilibrium.

Our focus is on local public goods economies. Our motivation is simply to choose an approach to examining the Tiebout hypothesis and this should not be construed as a rejection of part of the literature.

In each of the models discussed below, we assume that agents can be members of only one jurisdiction at a time. Using the sort of assumptions introduced by Shubik and Wooders (1986), our results can be extended to club economies. For simplicity, we discuss economies with one private good and L public goods.[5a]

2.1 *Nondifferentiated and differentiated crowding models*

Since nondifferentiated crowding is a special case of differentiated crowding we present a formal model which includes both nondifferentiated and differentiated crowding. Consider an economy with I agents, $i \in \{1, ..., I\} \equiv \mathcal{I}$, each with a preference mapping indexed by $t \in \{1, ..., T\} \equiv \mathcal{T}$, and an associated endowment of private good $\omega_t \in \mathfrak{R}_+$. The total population of agents is denoted by $N = (N_1, ..., N_t, ..., N_T)$, where N_t is the number of agents of type t in the entire economy. A jurisdiction is a group of agents which collectively produces and consumes a common level of public goods. A jurisdiction is identified with a vector $m = (m_1, ..., m_t, ..., m_T)$, where m_t is defined as the number of agents of type t in the jurisdiction. The set of all feasible jurisdictions is denoted by $\mathcal{N}$.

A partition $n = \{n^1, ..., n^K\}$ of the population is a collection of jurisdictions satisfying $\Sigma_k n^k = N$.[5b] We will write $n^k \in n$ when a jurisdiction n^k is in the partition n. Let $\theta : I \to \mathcal{T}$ be a function that indicates the type of a given individual. Thus, if agent i is of type t, then $\theta(i) = t$. With a slight abuse of notation, if individual i is a member of jurisdiction m, we shall write $i \in m$.

For simplicity, we will assume that for each type t, the preferences of an agent of type t can be represented by a continuous utility function.

$$u_t : \mathfrak{R} \times \mathfrak{R}^L \times \mathcal{N}_t \to \mathfrak{R}. \tag{4-1}$$

The value where $\mathcal{N}_t \subset \mathcal{N}$ is the set of jurisdictions m with $m_t \neq 0$. $u_t(x,y,m)$ is interpreted as the utility an agent of type t receives from consuming an amount x of private good and a bundle y of public goods while residing in a jurisdiction with composition m. We note that continuity of utility functions is not necessarily needed for market decentralization of efficient allocations in Tiebout economies.

[5a] Models with differentiated crowding and one or more private goods are treated in Wooders (1981, 1988b, 1989, 1993a, 1993b). Similar techniques can be applied to crowding types model.

[5b] The total number of jurisdictions K is determined endogenously.

On the production side, the cost in terms of private good of producing a bundle y of public goods for a jurisdiction with composition m is given by the function

$$f: \Re_{+}^{L} \times \mathcal{N} \rightarrow \Re_{+}. \tag{4-2}$$

Thus, $f(y,m)$ is the amount of private good necessary to produce the bundle y of public goods in a jurisdiction with composition m. We could also represent this information by a production set, but a cost function is easier to work with when there is only one private good.

Crowding effects are allowed in both production and consumption. There is no requirement in general that these crowding effects be positive, negative, convex, or even monotonic. To make such restrictions would exclude many important economic applications. For example, people at a party may crowd each other positively over some range, and then negatively as it becomes too crowded to dance. In production, we might find that two Spanish-speaking carpenters can build a house just as fast as two English speakers, but one Spanish and one English speaker working together would take much longer. Thus, none of the ordinary assumptions on preferences or production are appropriate in the context of crowding.

Recall that nondifferentiated crowding means agents are affected only by the size – the total number of people – of the jurisdiction they join. The identities or tastes of their neighbors make no difference to them. For instance, on a highway, agents are affected by the total number of drivers on the road, but the favorite colors and musical tastes of the other agents are irrelevant. There are other economic situations in which the assumption of nondifferentiated crowding is not as appropriate. For example, agents are crowded differently by men and women at a dance. One gender may generate positive externalities while the other may crowd negatively. It follows that production costs and utility functions generally depend on the entire profile of agent types instead of simply on the total number of agents in a jurisdiction.

Formally, nondifferentiated crowding is a special case of the crowding types model of differentiated crowding treated below – a nondifferentiated crowding model is a crowding types model with only one crowding type. An economy with nondifferentiated crowding is required to satisfy two conditions called *Nondifferentiated Crowding in Consumption* (NCC) and *Nondifferentiated Crowding in Production* (NCP).

(NCC) For all $m, \hat{m}, \in \mathcal{N}$, if $\sum_t m_t = \sum_t \hat{m}_t$, then for all $x \in \Re_{+}$, $y \in \Re_{+}^{L}$ and all $t \in \mathcal{T}$ it holds that $u_t(x,y,\hat{m})$.

(NCP) For all $m, \hat{m}, \in \mathcal{N}$, if $\sum_t m_t = \sum_t \hat{m}_t$, then for all $y \in \Re_{+}^{L}$ it holds that $f(y, m) = f(y, \hat{m})$.

Typically, the utility and production functions for the nondifferentiated crowding case are written in the reduced forms $u_t(x,y,\sum_t m_t)$ and $f(y,\sum_t m_t)$.

2.2 *The crowding types model*

There is an important sense in which the standard differentiated crowding model is an unsatisfactory generalization of the nondifferentiated crowding model. While it may seem reasonable that different types of agents often crowd each other differently, it is far from clear that the tastes of one agent should directly affect the welfare of another. Consider, for example, the labor complementarity model. The skills that an agent brings to a jurisdiction should affect the cost of producing public goods, but why should the agent's preferences over consumption bundles make any difference? A plumber who likes big cars contributes just as much to production as one who likes compact cars. In the standard differentiated crowding model, an agent's tastes and crowding effects are perfectly correlated. There is no evident reason for this.

An alternative generalization is to explicitly endow agents with crowding characteristics that are formally distinct from their preferences. This is called a "crowding types" model. Agents still possess one of the T different sorts of tastes or preference maps, but agents are also identified as having one of C different sorts of crowding characteristics. The crowding type of an agent is denoted by $c \in \{1, ..., C\} \equiv \mathcal{C}$.[6] No correlation between c and t is assumed. Imagine, for example, a dance in which men and women crowd each other differently, but where some individuals of each gender like country music and others like jazz. The tastes of individuals are private information, but gender is a publicly observable crowding characteristic.

The rest of the crowding types model is a natural extension of the differentiated crowding model stated above. The population of agents is denoted by $N = (N_{11}, ..., N_{ct}, ..., N_{CT})$, where N_{ct} is the total number of agents with crowding type c and taste type t in the economy. A jurisdiction is identified with a vector $m = (m_{11}, ..., m_{ct}, ..., m_{CT})$, where m_{ct} is interpreted as the number of agents with crowding type c and taste type t in jurisdiction m. We will denote by $\mathcal{N}_c$ the set of feasible jurisdictions that contain at least one agent of crowding type $c \in \mathcal{C}$. Formally:

$$\mathcal{N}_c \equiv \{m \in \mathcal{N} : \text{there exists}\, t \in T \,\text{such that}\, m_{ct} > 0\}. \tag{4-3}$$

Two jurisdictions, m and $\hat{m}$, *have the same crowding profile* if, for all $c \in \mathcal{C}$, it holds that $\sum_t m_{ct} = \sum_t \hat{m}_{ct}$. That is, two jurisdictions have the same crowding profile if the number of agents of each crowding type is the same in both jurisdictions. Let $\theta : \mathcal{I} \to \mathcal{C} \times \mathcal{T}$ be a function that indicates the type of a given individual. Thus, if agent i is of crowding type c and taste type t, then $\theta(i) = (c,t)$.

[6] Note that each crowding type may denote a point in a finite (or infinite) dimensional vector

The notion of a crowding type is meant to capture all the characteristics of an agent that enter into the constraints or objectives of any other agents. Tastes may be irrelevant in this respect. We state this formally in the two assumptions, *Taste Anonymity in Consumption* (TAC), and *Taste Anonymity in Production* (TAP).

(TAC) For all $m, \hat{m} \in \mathcal{N}$, if for all $c \in \mathcal{C}$ it holds that

$$\sum_t m_{ct} = \sum_t \hat{m}_{ct},$$

then for all $t \in \mathcal{T}$, $x \in \Re$, and $y \in \Re_+^L$ it holds that

$u_t(x,y,m) = u_t(x,y,\hat{m})$.

(TAP) For all $m, \hat{m} \in \mathcal{N}$, if for all $c \in \mathcal{C}$ it holds that

$$\sum_t m_{ct} = \sum_t \hat{m}_{ct},$$

then for all $y \in \Re_+^L$ it holds that $f(y,m) = f(y,\hat{m})$.

Observe that if we set $C = 1$, this is exactly the nondifferentiated crowding model. Also, if we set $C = T$ and $N_{ct} = 0$ for all $c \neq t$, then we have the standard differentiated crowding model. In words, the crowding types model is equivalent in appearance to the standard differentiated crowding model when crowding types and taste types are perfectly correlated in the population.[7] In that case, each taste type crowds in its own independent way. In interpretation and application, however, the standard differentiated crowding model and the crowding types model are far from equivalent; for example, in the standard model, prices are defined to depend on tastes. Because it can accommodate the prior models of differentiated and nondifferentiated crowding, we will use the crowding types framework to explicate the results in the literature.

A *feasible state of the economy* (X, Y, n) is a partition n of the population, an allocation $X = (x_1, \ldots, x_I)$ of private goods, and public good production plans $Y = (y^1, \ldots, y^K)$ such that

$$\sum_k \sum_{c,t} n_{ct}^k \omega_t - \sum_i x_i - \sum_k f(y^k, n^k) \geq 0. \tag{4-4}$$

We denote the set of feasible states by F. The pair (x,y) is a *feasible allocation for a jurisdiction m* if

$$\sum_{c,t} m_{ct} \omega_t - \sum_{i \in m} x_i - f(y,m) \geq 0. \tag{4-5}$$

[7] Of course, there is no requirement that the same types t have either the same crowding type or the same endowment. Thus, observability of endowments does not imply observability of tastes. Making explicit, however, the separation of crowding type and taste type enables us to obtain new and interesting results.

3. The core

In the one private good case, the definition of the core is especially straightforward. A jurisdiction $m \in \mathcal{N}$ producing a feasible allocation (x,y) improves upon a feasible state $(X, Y, n) \in F$ if:

(i) for all $i \in m$,

$$u_t(x_j, y, m) > u_t(x^k_j, y^k, n^k) \tag{4-6}$$

where $\theta(i) = (c,t)$ and $i \in n^k \in n$ (and n is the partition in the feasible state); and

(ii) for some $j \in m$,

$$u_{\hat{t}}(x_j, y, m) > u_{\hat{t}}(x^k_j, y^k, n^k) \tag{4-7}$$

where $\theta(j) = (\hat{c},\hat{t})$ and $j \in n^{\hat{k}} \in n$.

A feasible state $(X, Y, n) \in F$ is in the core of the economy if it cannot be improved upon by any jurisdiction.

Note that when a jurisdiction improves upon a state, it does so without trading private goods outside the jurisdiction. This restriction is unimportant in the one private good case since no gains from trade are possible. We might interpret such a model as an abstraction of a situation in which prices for all private goods are taken as given and the one private good explicitly in the model is "money." If we allow many private goods in the model, gains from trade become possible. In this case, even if the sizes of jurisdictions are uniformly bounded, equivalence of the core and the equilibrium outcomes will not generally hold in finite economies.[8a] To realize gains from trade in private goods, a defecting coalition typically will form an improving state of the economy with multiple jurisdictions. Even then, the coalition loses the opportunity to trade private goods with the non-defecting agents. This makes direct generalization of some results impossible (unless we have a continuum of traders or some special assumptions on the model).

What appears to be a more serious problem is that regardless of the number of private goods, it is often the case that the core is empty. This is true even in large economies satisfying all the properties that ordinarily guarantee existence (convexity, monotonicity, etc.)[8b] and has been known at least since Pauly (1970). The possible emptiness of the core and other problems[9] led Bewley (1981) to conclude that decentralization is essentially impossible unless public goods are essentially just publicly provided private goods (public services).

The reason for the emptiness of the core is that there will usually exist jurisdictions, smaller than the entire economy, which are optimal in the sense that they maximize the per capita payoff of their memberships. When agents of the various types are not present in numbers that exactly fill out these optimal

[8a] See, however, Wooders (1981, 1989, 1993a, 1993b) for aymptotic equivalence of approximate cores and equilibrium outcomes.

[8b] For an example see Shubik and Wooders (1983, Appendix).

[9] Including the apparent need for prices to depend on preferences.

jurisdictions without any leftovers, we get a cycling problem. Suppose we have the following payoff functions for jurisdictions:[10]

$$\Gamma(m) = \begin{Bmatrix} 0 \text{ if } |m| = 1 \\ 1 \text{ if } |m| = 2 \\ 0 \text{ if } |m| \geq 3 \end{Bmatrix}. \tag{4-8}$$

Observe that two-agent coalitions maximize per capita payoffs. This implies that when there are three agents in the total population, every feasible state can be improved upon. No matter how the two-agent coalition divides its surplus, the agent who is left out can always make at least one of the other agents better off. This same problem appears for every population with an odd number of agents. Although the fraction of leftover agents decreases to zero as the economy gets large, there will still be one leftover. This is enough to generate the same type of cycling, and thus nonexistence of the core, no matter how large the economy.

These problems motivate the study of approximate cores and equilibria of economies with local public goods and of large games, initiated in Wooders (1979, 1980b, 1981, 1983).[11] Fortunately, approximate cores have a very natural interpretation in the context of local public goods economies. Informally, we modify the notion of what it means to improve upon a state to require that it be possible to make defecting agents better off *while paying a small cost of jurisdictional formation.* In other words, agents who defect must each pay a transaction cost of $\varepsilon \geq 0$, which may represent moving or setup costs; in spite of these additional costs, defecting agents must still be better off in the new jurisdiction.

Formally, a jurisdiction $m \in \mathcal{N}$ producing an allocation (x,y) ε-improves *upon* a feasible state $(X,Y,n) \in F$ if:

(i) $$\sum_{c,t} m_{ct}\omega_t - \sum_{i \in m} x_i - f(y,m) \geq \varepsilon \sum_{c,t} m_{ct}; \tag{4-9}$$

(ii) for all $i \in m$,

$$u_t(x_i, y, m) \geq u_t(x_i^k, y^k, n^k) \tag{4-10}$$

where $\theta(i) = (c,t)$ and $i \in n^k \in n$; and

(iii) for some $j \in m$,

$$u_t(x_j, y, m) > u_{\hat{t}}(x_j^k, y^k, n^k) \tag{4-11}$$

where $\theta(i) = (\hat{c},\hat{t})$ and $j \in n^{\hat{k}} \in n$.

A feasible state $(X,Y,n) \in F$ is in the ε-core of the economy if it cannot be ε-improved upon by any jurisdiction.

[10] This matching game is a special case of the more general class of local public goods economies.

[11] The study of approximate cores (especially of nonemptiness) for the important case of private goods exchange economies was initiated in Shapley and Shubik (1966).

To see why ε-cores solve the existence problem, return to the three-agent example above. Consider the ε-core for ε = 1/6. We claim that equal division over all three agents of the surplus produced by the two-person coalition is in the ε-core. Now consider the agents in a two-person coalition. If they defect from the state in which they pay a third of their surplus to the leftover agent, they must pay a cost of 1/3 (two times ε) to set up a new (identical) jurisdiction. Clearly, they are just as well off paying this surplus to the leftover agent as they would be if they were to defect from this state and pay the same amount as a setup cost. The excluded agent, on the other hand, cannot propose an ε-improvement. If this agent forms a jurisdiction with one of the other agents, the new jurisdiction has a surplus of 2/3 to distribute after paying the setup costs, which is just enough to leave these agents exactly as well off as in the original state.

The above intuition applies even when it is only required that the per capita payoff function be bounded. In this case, groups bounded in size can realize nearly all gains to collective activities (Wooders 1980a, 1994b).

The main advantage of the ε-core is that, for an arbitrarily small ε, the ε-core is nonempty for all sufficiently large economies. The intuition is that the number of leftovers becomes an arbitrarily small proportion of the population as the economy gets large. Thus, it is possible to take away a very small amount of private good from each of a large number of agents in optimal or near-optimal jurisdictions and use it to compensate the small fraction of agents who are left out of those jurisdictions. The other advantage of the ε-core is that it makes it possible to treat the many private goods case. Even though defecting coalitions lose the opportunity to trade private goods with the remaining agents, if a defecting coalition is large enough, it can form multiple jurisdictions and internally realize almost all of the gains from trade. Thus, results that are true for the ε-core and ε-equilibrium (defined below) for the one private good case are generally true for the many private goods case as well. This intuition underlies the nonemptiness of the ε-cores of large games. (See Wooders (1994a) for a survey and further references.)

There are several alternative definitions of the ε-core. For example, we could simply ignore a fraction ε of agents, or we could assign agents a probability ε of not being able to find a jurisdiction to join.[12] In all cases, the essential question is how to deal with this small fraction of leftover agents. It is interesting to note, however, that proofs on the nonemptiness of various notions of ε-core and of the existence of approximate equilibrium typically begin by showing nonemptiness of the type of ε-core where a small percentage of players is ignored and then proceed to show how this implies the nonemptiness of the particular notion in question. The appropriateness of any given notion of an approximate core depends on the economic situation being modeled. In some models that elucidate the noncooperative foundations of cooperation, such as Selten (1981) and

[12] See, for example, Kaneko and Wooders (1982), Shubik and Wooders (1983), and Wooders (1988b, 1993b).

Bennett (1991), the natural notion of an approximate core may be one in which a small percentage of players is ignored. On the other hand, for a model of an economy consisting of a federation of separate jurisdictions, it may be that the central government, in order to achieve stability, taxes some jurisdictions by a small amount and uses the revenue to make transfers to less-advantaged jurisdictions. In the remainder of this chapter, we will only treat the notion of the ε-core defined formally above.

It is important to emphasize that the possible emptiness of the core is not related to the indivisibility of agents. Allowing for "fractional" agents, such as part-time members of clubs, does not lead to existence of the core. With nondifferentiated crowding, the core may be empty because the population of agents of some type is not a multiple of a type-optimal group size. We note, however, that under "strict small group effectiveness," – *all* gains to collective activities can be realized by groups bounded in size – there is some multiple of any given population profile for which the core is nonempty: see Wooders (1979, 1983, Theorem 3) and Kaneko and Wooders (1982).

4. Equilibrium and prices

Two major factors that differentiate the many equilibrium notions in local public goods economies are the objectives of the city planners and the method used to decide on public goods levels. City planners have been variously modeled as profit-maximizing entrepreneurs, population-maximizing politicians, and agents of property owners who seek to maximize land values. The decision of how much of a public good to provide may be made either by dictate of a benevolent planner, or by majority rule or similar voting mechanisms. We will treat only the profit maximizing entrepreneur model in the current paper because it is closest to the market mechanism, and therefore seems to address most directly the question of when the market can successfully provide public goods. This should not be interpreted as a rejection of the other models. Indeed, they may even be more appealing than the entrepreneurial model since they may reflect more closely the way public goods levels are chosen in practice.

The structure of the price system also merits careful consideration. There are several properties that the system must have in order to decentralize efficient allocations in a way that is comparable to the price system in markets for private goods.

Full optimization requires that each agent be able to calculate the exact cost of joining every conceivable type of jurisdiction with every feasible level of public goods. In other words, the price system must be *complete.* Such a price system might have an infinite or a finite number of prices. At first, completeness of the price system may seem unreasonably strong. At the very least it means that there must be a price for every possible jurisdiction type, with every possible combination of crowding types. Prices are needed even for jurisdictions that are not formed in equilibrium. This is obviously a large number of prices. On the other hand, it seems to be sufficient to have one price for each good in a private goods economy. The evident simplicity of the price system in the private goods case is, however, very misleading.

Requiring a complete price system in a local public goods economy might appear to be a very strong condition because of the vast array of non-produced commodities that immediately present themselves to our attention. It should come as no surprise that planners who are allowed to consider products that are not traded or priced in equilibrium may be able to find allocations that are Pareto superior to the equilibrium allocations. Of course, it is not hard to imagine nontraded private goods, houses made from recycled tires or a continuum of possible sizes of Mercedes sedans, for example. The literature solves this problem in private goods models by exogenously restricting the commodity space to the set of goods that is traded. To require a similar restriction in a local public goods model would make it impossible to address the central question of whether or not the equilibrium jurisdiction structure will be efficient compared to every other imaginable structure.[13] In short, what is essential for efficiency of the equilibrium in both the local public and private goods cases is that every allocation defined as feasible and considered as a possible Pareto improvement be available to agents through the market.

The second major requirement of a decentralizing price system is that it be anonymous. An *anonymous price system* is one that does not discriminate between agents on the basis of private information. This is, of course, the fundamental difficulty with Lindahl equilibrium in a pure public goods economy. The essence of Tiebout's hypothesis is that when public goods are locally provided, agents will find it is optimal to reveal their preferences by moving to their most preferred jurisdictions. This parallels private goods markets, where prices are anonymous and equally available to all, and agents reveal their preferences by choosing their most preferred consumption bundle. It is the position of the authors that *showing the existence of an anonymous set of prices that decentralize efficient allocations is tantamount to proving the Tiebout hypothesis.* By the same token, equilibrium concepts in which agents with different tastes face different prices depend on agents revealing private information. Decentralizing with such price systems does not solve the free-rider problem in any meaningful way and so should not be taken as confirming Tiebout's hypothesis.

There are two major approaches to pricing, admission prices and Lindahl prices. Informally, admission prices give a single price for each type of agent for every jurisdiction profile, for every possible level of public good. These may be thought of as functions that map each jurisdiction profile and public goods level into a price of admission for agents. A Lindahl price system, on the other hand, lists two prices for each type of agent in each type of jurisdiction

[13] This is very similar to the differentiated product markets literature where the choice of products is endogenous and the central question is which products will be produced in equilibrium.

containing members of his type. The first price is a participation price, which is like an entrance fee. If positive, it may be motivated as a wage, a profit share, or a compensation for positive externalities generated by the agent. If negative, it can be interpreted as the price paid to enjoy the externalities provided by others, or as a Pigouvian tax to compensate others for the negative externalities generated by the agent. The second is a per-unit price for each public good.

Admission prices have a certain amount of appeal since they seem most closely related to the lump-sum taxes suggested by Tiebout. A disadvantage of an admission pricing system is that it requires an infinite number of prices. A Lindahl price system, on the other hand, has the advantage that, in large economies, it conveys the same information as an admission price system but in a more economical way. In particular, only a finite number of prices is required. The Lindahl equilibrium also allows much more flexibility – an agent may pay a property tax, but may also pay a per-hour cost for renting the municipal tennis courts or, instead, only choose to use the community swimming pool. This reflects the commonly observed pricing system of a property tax plus various user charges. The extant literature shows that the equivalence of anonymous admission and anonymous Lindahl equilibrium obtains when crowding is nondifferentiated and production takes place under constant returns to scale. Otherwise, the two concepts are typically not equivalent and it may not be possible to decentralize the core through Lindahl pricing systems. (See Conley and Wooders (1994b) for an example.)

We will treat the admission price system first. For each crowding type $c \in \mathcal{C}$, there is a price function α_c that assigns an admission price to every possible public goods level and jurisdiction pair. Agents may contemplate joining any jurisdiction that contains at least one member of their crowding type. To illustrate, no matter how much Wynton Marsalis may wish it, it is impossible for him to belong to an all-female band. Once he joins, it is no longer an all-female band. Thus, we should provide admission prices for bands that include at least one male, but it makes no sense to provide an admission price to Wynton Marsalis for female-only bands. Formally:

$$\alpha_c : \Re^L \times \mathcal{N}_c \to \Re. \tag{4-12}$$

An *admission price system* is simply a collection of price systems, one for each crowding type.

Notice that we allow different prices for different crowding types but not for different taste types. This is because we are only interested in anonymous prices.

[14] Note that different prices for jurisdictions with identical crowding profiles do not violate anonymity since these prices are still commonly available to all regardless of tastes; see, for example, the discussion of Wooders' two-part equilibrium concept in Barham and Wooders (1997). It turns out that this is not an issue for admission price systems since we demonstrate that the core may be decentralizing with prices satisfying FAP. It is clear that this is not possible for all types of price systems.

Unfortunately, this may not be quite enough for full anonymity. Observe that α gives admission prices for every jurisdiction m. Included in the information is a complete description of the tastes as well as the crowding types of the agents. Thus, without further restrictions, α depends on tastes as well as crowding types. We say that a price system has *Fully Anonymous Prices* (FAP) only if jurisdictions with the same crowding profile and public goods production are priced identically. Formally, we require:[14]

(FAP) For all $m, \hat{m} \in \mathcal{N}$, if for all $c \in \mathcal{C}$ it holds that

$\sum_t m_{ct} = \sum_t \hat{m}_{ct}$, then for all $y \in \Re^L_+$ it holds that $\alpha(y,m) = \alpha(y,\hat{m})$.

Note that in the nondifferentiated crowding model there is only one crowding type and, hence, only one price function. In the standard differentiated crowding model, anonymity is lost since prices are defined to depend on taste type. We are now able to define our first equilibrium notion. An *admission price equilibrium* is a feasible state $(X,Y,n) \in F$ and a price system α such that:

(i) for all $n^k \in n$, all individuals $i \in n^k$ where $\theta(i) = (c,t)$, all alternative jurisdictions $m \in \mathcal{N}_c$, and all levels of public good production $y \in \Re^L_+$,

$$u_t(\omega_t - \alpha_c(y^k, n^k), y^k, n^k) \geq u_t(\omega_t - \alpha_c(y, m), y, m); \tag{4-13}$$

(ii) for all potential jurisdictions $m \in \mathcal{N}$ and all $y \in \Re^L_+$,

$$\sum_{c,t} m_{ct}\alpha_c(y, m) - f(y, m) \leq 0; \tag{4-14}$$

and

(iii) for all $n^k \in n$,

$$\sum_{c,t} n^k_{ct}\alpha_c(y^k, n^k) - f(y^k, n^k)5 = 0. \tag{4-15}$$

Condition (i) states that all agents maximize utility given the price system. Condition (ii) requires that, given the price system, no firm can make positive profits by entering the market and offering to provide any sort of jurisdiction. Condition (iii) dictates that all equilibrium jurisdictions make zero profit, and so cover their costs.[15]

The most widely discussed alternative to admission price equilibrium is the Lindahl price equilibrium. In this type of price system, there is a price function λ_c for each crowding type $c \in \mathcal{C}$ which states a participation price for every jurisdiction an agent of this type can join, and a per-unit price for each public good type. Formally:

$$\lambda_c : \mathcal{N}_c \rightarrow \Re \times \Re^L. \tag{4-16}$$

An *(anonymous) Lindahl price system* is simply the collection of these price systems, one for each crowding type. To satisfy anonymity, Lindahl prices must

[15] Sergiu Hart has pointed out to us that Condition (iii) is implied by Condition (ii) and the definition of feasibility. We continue to state Condition (iii) because we wish to emphasize the competitive nature of club formation.

satisfy a condition similar to FAP or some condition ensuring that the same prices are commonly available to all agents of the same crowding type. We leave the statement of a condition of full anonymity for a Lindahl price system as an exercise for the reader. It is convenient to formally decompose Lindahl prices into two component prices. Thus, $\lambda_c(m) \equiv (p_c(m), q_c(m))$, where $p_c : \mathcal{N}_c \rightarrow \Re$ is the participation price function, and $p_c : \mathcal{N}_c \rightarrow \Re^L$ is the per-unit price function for public goods.

An (anonymous) Lindahl price equilibrium is a feasible state $(X, Y, n) \in F$ and a price system λ such that:

(i) for all $n^k \in n$, all individuals $i \in n^k$ where $\theta(i) = (c,t)$, all alternative jurisdictions $m \in \mathcal{N}_c$, and all levels of public good production $y \in \Re^L_+$,

$$u_t(\omega - p_c(n^k) - q_c(n^k)y^k, y^k, n^k) \geq u_t(\omega_t - p_c(m) - q_c(m)y, y, m); \qquad (4\text{-}17)$$

(ii) for all potential jurisdications $m \in \mathcal{N}$ and all $y \in \Re^L_+$,

$$\sum_{c,t} m_{ct} p_c(m) + \sum_{c,t} m_{ct} q_c(m) y - f(y,m) = 0; \qquad (4\text{-}18)$$

and

(iii) for all $n^k \in n$,

$$\sum_{c,t} n^k_{ct} p_c(n^k) + \sum_{c,t} n^k_{ct} q_c(n^k)\, y^k - f(y^k, n^k) = 0. \qquad (4\text{-}19)$$

Notice that the admission price system bears a strong resemblance to the valuation equilibrium for pure public goods economies.[16] For a given jurisdiction the admission price system is just a general nonlinear function that assigns part of the cost of public goods to each agent. The valuation equilibrium does the same thing except that there is never more than one jurisdiction in the core of a pure public goods economy. The Lindahl price system described above is a natural extension to local public goods economies. For a given jurisdiction, the cost of public goods to an agent is linear in the quantity demanded. A missing piece in this literature is the generalization of the cost share equilibrium to local public goods economies.[17] Here, the cost of public goods to agents is linear in the cost of providing the public good. The cost share equilibrium was introduced by Mas-Colell and Silvestre (1989), and is a generalization of Kaneko's (1977) ratio equilibrium.

An advantage of admission price equilibrium is that, given the nonlinear structure of the price functions, there is no need to assume convexity, continuity or monotonicity of either the utility or cost functions. Lindahl decentralizations appear to require these assumptions for existence to follow from the nonemptiness of the core.

[16] For example, see Manning (1993) for a treatment of the valuation equilibrium in an economy that includes both pure and local public goods as special cases.

[17] We thank Robert Gilles for this observation.

It is possible to define other variants of these equilibrium concepts. One variant makes the prices for players independent of the jurisdiction. The disadvantage of such a pricing system is that it makes existence of an equilibrium less likely. (As a general rule, the more restrictions we place on an equilibrium concept, the more stringent are the conditions required on the economy to obtain existence.)

A uniform price system μ for agents of crowding type $c \in \mathcal{C}$ gives an admission price for each crowding type of agent and each level of public good:

$$\mu_c : \mathfrak{R}^L_+ \to \mathfrak{R}. \tag{4-20}$$

A *uniform Tiebout price system* is simply the collection of such price systems, one for each crowding type.

A *uniform Tiebout equilibrium* is a feasible state $(X,Y,n) \in F$ and a uniform price system μ such that:

(i) for all $n^k \in n$, all individuals $i \in n^k$ with $\theta(i) = (c,t)$, all alternative jurisdictions $m \in N_c$, and all levels of public good production $y \in \mathfrak{R}^L_+$,

$$u_t(\omega_t - \mu_c(y^k), y^k, n^k) \geq u_t(\omega_t - \mu_c(y), y, m); \tag{4-21}$$

(ii) for all potential jurisdictions $m^k \in \mathcal{N}$ and all $y \in \mathfrak{R}^L_+$,

$$\sum_{c,t} n_{ct}\, \mu_c(y) - f(y,m) \leq 0; \tag{4-22}$$

and

(iii) for all $n^k \in n$,

$$\sum_{c,t} n^k_{ct}\, q_c(y^k) - f(y^k,n^k) = 0. \tag{4-23}$$

The conditions of the definition of the uniform Tiebout equilibrium all have the same interpretations as those in the definition of the Tiebout equilibrium, except that the prices, based on crowding types, do not depend on the jurisdiction.

It is clear that a uniform Tiebout equilibrium state of the economy is in the core since a uniform Tiebout equilibrium is a Tiebout equilibrium. A similar modification can be made in the definition of the Lindahl equilibrium to define a uniform Lindahl equilibrium. We leave this to the reader.

Equilibrium allocations are generally in the core. This implies that if the core is empty, equilibrium does not exist. As discussed in Section 3, such observations motivate the study of ε-cores. A corresponding notion of ε-equilibrium (which will generally exist for large economies, since the ε-core generally exists) is needded. The intuition behind the existence of an ε-equlibrium is very similar to that of the ε-core. We modify the definitions of equilibrium to require that agents pay a jurisdiction formation cost of ε when they consider jurisdictions other than the one they occupy in equilibrium. Formally, an **e-admission price equilibrium** is a feasible state $(X,Y,n) \in F$ and an admission price system α such that:

(i) for all $n^k \in n$, all individuals $i \in n^k$ with $\theta(i) = (c,t)$, all alternative jurisdictions $m \in \mathcal{N}_c$, and all levels of public good production $y \in \Re^L_+$,

$$u_t(\omega_t - \alpha_c(y^k,n^k),y^k,n^k) \geq u_t(\omega_t - \alpha_c(y,m) - \varepsilon,y,m); \qquad (4\text{-}24)$$

(ii) for all jurisdictions $m \in \mathcal{N}$ and all $y \in \Re^L_+$,

$$\sum_{c,t} m_{ct}\alpha_c(y,m) - f(y,m) \leq 0; \qquad (4\text{-}25)$$

(iii) for all $n^k \in n$,

$$\sum_{c,t} n^k_{ct}\alpha_c(y^k,n^k) - f(y^k,n^k) = 0. \qquad (4\text{-}26)$$

In the same spirit, an ε-Lindahl price equilibrium is a feasible state $(X,Y,n) \in F$ and a Lindahl price system λ such that:

(i) for all $n^k \in n$, all individuals $i \in n^k$ where $\theta(i) = (c,t)$, all alternative jurisdictions $m \in \mathcal{N}_c$, and all levels of public good production $y \in \Re^L_+$,

$$\begin{aligned} &u_t(\omega_t - p_c(n^k) - q\,(n^k)\,y^k,y^k,n^k) \\ &\qquad \geq u_t(\omega_t - p_c(m) - q_c(m)y - \varepsilon,y,m), \end{aligned} \qquad (4\text{-}27)$$

(ii) for all potential jurisdictions $m \in \mathcal{N}$ and all $y \in \Re^L_+$,

$$\sum_{c,t} m_{ct}\,p_c(m) + \sum_{c,t} m_{ct}\,q_c(m)y - f(y,m) \leq 0; \qquad (4\text{-}28)$$

and

(iii) for all $n^k \in n$,

$$\sum_{c,t} n^k_{ct}\,p_c(n^k) + \sum_{c,t} n^k_{ct}\,q_c(n^k)y^k - f(y^k,n^k) = 0. \qquad (4\text{-}29)$$

Of course, it is possible to define other notions of ε-equilibrium in the same spirit as the alternative notions of the ε-core. We compare these equilibrium notions in more detail in Section 6.

5. Tiebout's assumption six

In Tiebout's original paper, the author laid out seven informal assumptions he believed were sufficient for market decentralization of efficient allocations in a local public goods economy. The sixth assumption required that, "For every pattern of community services ... there is an optimal community size." In other words, economies associated with sharing the costs of producing public goods are eventually overwhelmed by the costs of crowding. This is more a definition of a local public goods economy rather than an assumption on such economies. Roughly, if there is no optimal jurisdiction size, then there is no need for jurisdictions smaller than the grand coalition to form, and thus no possibility of competition between jurisdictions leading to market-type outcomes.[18] In both

[18] We could, however, have situations where "medium-sized" groups are "optimal" from the viewpoint of improvement but where the jurisdiction of the whole, for example, is Pareto-optimal. Thus, this statement is heuristic rather than precise.

the pure public and pure private goods case, the optimal jurisdiction size is equal to the entire population.

For many years the prevailing intuition in the literature was that if public goods are local rather than pure and there are many optimal jurisdictions, then a market-type equilibrium exists and is near-optimal [see, for example, Tiebout (1956) and Berglas (1976)]. It was later recognized that the existence of an optimal group size smaller than the entire population leads to the problem of leftover agents, as discussed earlier, and the possible emptiness of the core and nonexistence of equilibrium. As a result, the view that markets could not be expected to decentralize efficient allocations in such economies became the prevailing wisdom [see, for example, Pauly (1970), Atkinson and Stigliz (1980), and Bewley (1981)]. It has now been shown that the original intuition of Tiebout and Berglas is essentially correct. In large local public goods economies with small optimal jurisdictions, approximate equilibria exist and approximate cores are nonempty.[19] The existence of a minimum efficient scale of jurisdictions ensures competitive outcomes in large local public goods economies just as minimum efficient scale for firms does in large private goods production economies. In fact, in a variety of economic contexts, the assumption of small optimal or near-optimal group sizes is virtually sufficient by itself to obtain nonemptiness of approximate cores, existence of approximate equilibrium, asymptotic equal treatment, and core convergence in large economies.[20]

We now introduce several definitions of small group effectiveness, from the most restrictive of bounded coalitions sizes to the least restrictive of per capita boundedness. Besides explaining the relationships between the definitions, we make the point that the definitions all lead asymptotically to the same results. The choice of definitions is primarily a matter of convenience.[21]

One of the strongest versions of small group effectiveness is strict small group effectiveness. It requires that *all* gains to collective activities, either for the attainment of feasible outcomes or for improvement upon outcomes not in the core, can be realized by groups bounded in size. One form of strict small group effectiveness places a bound on admissible group sizes.[22] Another form

[19] See, for example, Ellickson (1973, 1979), Wooders (1978, 1980b, 1988,1993), and references therein.

[20] These results were first obtained for large economies with quasi-linear utilities modeled as TU games in Wooders (1979a, 1980a) under the assumptions of strict small group effectiveness and then under per capita boundedness. Related literature includes: Shapley and Shubik (1966) on exchange economies, Wooders (1979, 1980a), Kaneko and Wooders (1982), Wooders and Zame (1984, 1987a), and Wooders (1992, 1994a, 1994b), for economies modeled as TU games; Mas-Colell (1979) and Hammond, Kaneko and Wooders (1989) for private goods exchange economies; and Wooders (1983), Kaneko and Wooders (1982, 1986) and Wooders and Zame (1987b) for economies modeled as games without side payments.

[21] If one is interested in necessary and sufficient conditions, then the exact definition is very important. For example, with "thickness," per capita boundedness is necessary and sufficient for core convergence (Wooders 1991).

[22] cf., Kaneko and Wooders (1982, 1994a).

of this assumption places a bound on the size of improving coalitions.[23] In Conley and Wooders (1994a), we state formally that an economy satisfies strict small group effectiveness if there exists a positive integer η^0 such that:

(i) for all positive integers r and economies with population $rN \equiv N'$, if a feasible state (X,Y,n) can be improved upon, then there also exists a jurisdiction $m \in \mathcal{N}'$ with $\sum_{c,t} m_{ct} \leq \eta^0$ that can improve upon (X,Y,n); and

(ii) for all $c \in \mathcal{C}$ and $t \in \mathcal{T}$, either $N_{ct} > \eta^0$ op $N_{ct} = 0$.

The first condition stipulates that for replications of the economy, any state that can be improved upon at all can be improved upon with a jurisdiction containing at most η^0 agents. In other words, small groups are effective in that no new blocking opportunities would arise if the economy were to get larger in this particular way. Thus, the minimum efficient scale, or "optimal community size," can be achieved by a coalition of agents smaller than the entire economy. The second condition states that if there are any agents at all of a given type in the economy, then there are at least η^0 of them. In other words, no type that exists is scarce. This is commonly called a "thickness" assumption. Such thickness is also in the Tiebout tradition since it requires that there be enough agents of each type to form any sort of optimal jurisdiction.

There are many ways to state conditions in the same spirit as the one above. These differ mainly in the extent to which gains from scale are exhausted by relatively small coalitions or coalitions bounded in absolute size. This is especially easy to see in the case of economies with one private good where agents have quasilinear utility functions of the form $u_t(x,y,m) = h(y,m) + x$. For this class of economies we define the *value function*, $V : \mathcal{N} \rightarrow \mathfrak{R}$, as follows:

$$V(m) \equiv \left\{ \max_{y} \sum_{c} \sum_{t} m_{ct}(\omega_t + h_t(y,m)) - f(y,m) \right\}. \tag{4-30}$$

We may now restate part (i) of *strict small group effectiveness* as follows. There is a bound η^0 on coalition sizes such that for all populations N, for some partition $\hat{n}$ of N with $\sum_t \sum_c \hat{n}^k_{ct} < \eta^0$ for all members $\hat{n}^k$of the partition, it holds that

$$\max_{n} \sum_{n^k} V(n^k) - \sum_{\hat{n}^k} V(\hat{n}^k) = 0 \tag{4-31}$$

In other words, all feasible payoffs can be realized with jurisdictions each containing no more than η^0 members.

Strict small group effectiveness could be weakened to *small group effectiveness* which requires only that all or *almost all* gains to collective activities can be realized by groups bounded in absolute size. These sorts of assumptions can also be made in terms of bounds on sizes of coalitions required to realize almost all (within ε per capita) gains to collective activities, either for improvement or

[23] Cf., Wooders (1978, 1979), Kaneko and Wooders (1982), Scotchmer and Wooders (1988), and other papers.

for the attainment of feasible outcomes (see note 19). Our model satisfies *small group effectiveness* (*for the attainment of feasible outcomes*) if given $\varepsilon > 0$, there is a bound $\eta(\varepsilon)$ on coalition sizes such that, for all populations N, for some partition $\hat{n}$ of N with

$$\sum_t \sum_c \hat{n}^k_{ct} < \eta(\varepsilon)$$

for all members $\hat{n}^k$ of the partition, it holds that

$$\max_n \frac{\sum_{n^k} V(n^k)}{\|N\|} - \frac{\sum_{\hat{n}^k} V(\hat{n}^k)}{\|N\|} \leq \varepsilon.^{24} \qquad (4\text{-}32)$$

In other words, almost all feasible per capita utility can be obtained in some state of the economy where each jurisdiction contains no more than $\eta(\varepsilon)$ agents (Wooders 1992, 1994a, 1994b). Almost all gains to group size can be exhausted by groups that become relatively small in growing populations. The model satisfies small group effectiveness (for improvement) if given $\varepsilon > 0$, there is a bound $\eta(\varepsilon)$ on coalition sizes such that for all populations N, for any feasible utility payoff $u = (u_1, ..., u_I)$ not in the ε-core, there is a jurisdiction m with

$$\sum_t \sum_c m^k_{ct} < \eta(\varepsilon)$$

such that

$$V(m) \geq \sum_{i \in m} u_i + \frac{\varepsilon}{2} \|m\| \qquad (4\text{-}33)$$

This formulation of small group effectiveness (Wooders and Zame 1987a) requires *near exhaustion of gains to improvement* in the sense that any outcome that can be significantly improved upon (by ε per capita) can be improved upon by a group bounded in size by $\eta(\varepsilon)$. Engl and Scotchmer (1993) present a closely related definition. The two definitions of small group effectiveness above (and also the condition of Engl and Scotchmer 1993) are asymptotically equivalent; see Wooders (1994a, Proposition 3.8).

An apparently mild form of small group effectiveness is *per capita boundedness* – per capita gains to collective activities are bounded above (Wooders 1980a, 1983, 1994a, 1994b). For our model, per capita boundedness dictates that there be a constant D such that for all total populations N,

$$\max_n \frac{\sum_{n^k} V(n^k)}{\|N\|} < D. \qquad (4\text{-}34)$$

[24] If ε is "small," gains to scale must be nearly exhausted by coaltions smaller than $\eta(\varepsilon)$. Thus, for small ε (unless gains to scale are exhausted by coalitions bounded in size) $\eta(\varepsilon)$ must be "large."

A closely related assumption is that of *asymptotic constant returns to scale* which requires that there is a constant D such that for any given population N and for all positive integers r

$$\max_{n_r} \frac{\sum_{n_r} V(n_r^k)}{\|rN\|} < D \tag{4-35}$$

where n_r denotes a partition of rN (where rN denotes a population containing r times as many agents of each type as N). An assumption of this sort is used in Wooders (1981, 1993).

It is obvious that per capita boundedness implies asymptotic constant returns to scale; in fact, the two conditions are equivalent. When the percentage of agents of each type is bounded away from zero, small group effectiveness and per capita boundedness are equivalent; this is shown for economies with quasi-linear utilities in Wooders (1994a, 1994b). Without market "thickness" assumptions, the conditions of small group effectiveness and per capita boundedness are not generally equivalent.

Clearly, per capita boundedness is a mild yet powerful assumption. If it is not satisfied, then per capita payoffs become infinite in large economies, small groups are not effective and, without additional conditions, we cannot expect nonemptiness of approximate cores and convergence of approximate cores to competitive equilibrium outcomes [see Wooders (1992) for an example of nonequivalence]. But small group effectiveness means that there is "not much" loss of surplus if groups are bounded in absolute size, with a sufficiently large bound. Thus, we have a generalization of the Tiebout hypothesis for large economies with small effective jurisdictions. Any large economy with small effective groups is "market-like." A major conclusion we draw from this discussion is that the particular flavor of small group effectiveness used is largely a matter of convenience, especially for asymptotic results.

6. Results

In this section we briefly survey the literature in the context of the considerations given above. We also describe the main results that have been shown for the three basic formulations of local public goods economies with special focus on the anonymity of the decentralizing prices.

6.1 The nondifferentiated crowding model

A number of non-game-theoretic papers in the literature consider equilibrium and Pareto optimum of economies with nondifferentiated crowding, for example, McGuire (1974), Boadway (1980), and Berglas and Pines (1980, 1981). These papers mainly address the characterization of optimal and equilibrium outcomes.

The formulation of the Tiebout hypothesis for the nondifferentiated crowding case as the convergence of cores to anonymous price-taking equilibrium outcomes is initiated in Wooders (1978, 1980b). In these works, the core can be decentralized with an anonymous Lindahl price system. This result requires that for each given jurisdiction m, the cost function exhibits constant average cost. It follows that, under constant average cost within each jurisdiction, the admission equilibrium states of Berglas and Pines (1980, 1981) and Scotchmer and Wooders (1987) are equivalent to the Lindahl equilibrium states. Conley and Wooders (1994b) provide an example and Barham and Wooders (1996) further discuss of this aspect of the equilibrium concept. In general, if the set of agents can be partitioned into "type optimal" groups, and there are sufficiently many participants of each type, then the core is non-empty and coincides with the admission equilibrium outcomes. Moreover, with strict small group effectiveness, all states of the economy in the core have the equal-treatment property. Since the core may well be empty, it is important to observe that an assumption of small group effectiveness (or per capita boundedness with thickness) ensures that approximate cores are nonempty and converge to equilibrium outcomes (Wooders 1980b and subsequent papers).

As we have noted, another approach to a Tiebout Theorem may be to demonstrate that in economies with local public goods, First and Second Welfare Theorems hold. Since the equilibrium states are in the core, the First Welfare Theorem holds for the model formulated by Wooders (1978). For a closely related model that allows variable intensity of consumption, Scotchmer and Wooders (1987) provide a Second Welfare Theorem showing that every efficient state of the economy in which all agents realize their type-optimal utilities is an equilibrium.[25] Barham and Wooders (1994) show that every equal-treatment Pareto-optimal outcome is an equilibrium outcome in which all agents realize their type-optimal utility levels. Manning (1993) provides a Second Welfare Theorem for the case of (truly) non-anonymous participants in which the actual names of participants matter.

At the heart of the results on cores and equilibria of large economies with effective small groups and nondifferentiated crowding is the feature that agents might "mix" in the same jurisdiction. This can occur in a core state of the economy only if all agents in the jurisdiction have the same "demands" for public goods and crowding.[26] Barham and Wooders (1994) show that even when

[25] Results such as those of Berglas and Pines (1980, 1981), characterizing optimal outcomes by supporting prices, are related in spirit. For a one-private, one-public goods economy, Scotchmer and Wooders (1987) note that if the core relative to a redistribution is nonempty, then a Second Welfare Theorem holds. Coming from the perspective of applied economies rather than game theory, Berglas and Pines did not have available to them the handy tool of the core. One might interpret their work as implicitly assuming existence of equilibrium and the nonemptiness of the set of equal-treatment Pareto-optimal states of the economy.

[26] See Wooders (1978, Theorem 3). Scotchmer and Wooders (1987) provide an analogous result for economies with variable intensity of consumption of the public good. Berglas and Pines (1980, 1981) argue that mixed communities do not dominate optimally-sized homogeneous communities.

we allow different prices for different preference types in the same jurisdiction, the only jurisdictions which succeed in attracting residents are those which charge the same price for all types. The fact that the "demands" of all agents in a jurisdiction are the same for any state of the economy in the core implies that all states of the economy in the core can be supported by price systems where all participants in the same jurisdiction pay the same price.

6.2 The standard differentiated crowding model

The formal modeling and study of differentiated crowding economies was pioneered by Berglas (1976) who focused on the problem of allocating individuals to jurisdictions from the viewpoint of a social planner.[27] Wooders (1981) and several subsequent papers consider convergence of the core and approximate cores to equilibrium outcomes in the presence of several public goods and several private goods. The standard differentiated crowding framework permits only nonanonymous prices and so the price systems referred to in this section are all nonanonymous.

In a model with local public goods satisfying per capita boundedness and conditions on preferences analogous to those in Debreu and Scarf (1963), if markets are "contestable" and all participants take prices for private goods as given, the equilibrium outcomes are contained in the core, and the core converges to the set of equilibrium outcomes (Wooders 1981, 1989). Contestability in this context means that firms can enter and provide public goods, or, if they choose, consumers can "opt out" and provide the public goods for themselves. This convergence result is extended in Wooders (1993a, 1993b) to show that per capita boundedness implies the asymptotic equivalence of Lindahl equilibrium outcomes, the admission equilibrium outcomes, and the core. With strictly effective small groups and one private good, the equivalence holds in finite economies.

Scotchmer and Wooders (1986) discuss and illustrate equilibrium concepts and the equivalence of various equilibrium outcomes. They use a one-public, one-private-good model and assume a form of strict small group effectiveness. This highlights the special properties of economies with local public goods. With linear technology or zero profits within jurisdictions, it is shown that the core, Lindahl equilibrium outcomes, and admission equilibrium outcomes coincide. Very closely related results appear in Scotchmer (1994). The results of Wooders (1993a, 1993b) extend those of Scotchmer and Wooders (1986) to situations with many private and public goods.

[27] An interesting paper by Ellickson (1973) illustrates that when public goods are subject to crowding effects, the nonanonymous Lindahl equilibrium may not exist and the Lindahl equilibrium outcomes may not be in the core. The Lindahl equilibrium concept used by Ellickson, however, does not include participation prices (which are scarcity prices for the agents themselves). Ellickson (1979) treats local public goods as indivisible commodities – no crowding is allowed.

It is an immediate consequence of the results for large NTU games, that in the environments of the above papers, if small groups are strictly effective then the core has the equal-treatment property. In addition, if utilities are quasi-linear, equal treatment and asymptotic equal treatment results for large games with side payments immediately apply.[28]

Some recent related works include McGuire (1991) and Brueckner (1994), who show that if the complementarities between types are not strong, then the incentive to mix across type may be outweighed by the gains to homogeneity of taste within jurisdictions. Cole and Prescott (1994) introduce randomized contracts and show that in club environments where there is a deterministic commodity space and agents maximize expected utility, gains from trade may exist. The introduction of randomized contracts also improves the likelihood that core will exist.[29] Greenberg and Weber (1986) study a related model but do not discuss the optimality of equilibrium. Kahn and Silva (1993) and Wilson (1994) study differentiated crowding models where it is not admissible to charge different prices to different crowding and taste types.

6.3 *The crowding types model*

The crowding types model is introduced in Conley and Wooders (1994a), which studies admission price equilibrium for a transferable utility economy.[30] We show that the First Welfare Theorem is true but that the Second Welfare Theorem is not, mainly because the core may not exist. If the economy satisfies strict small group effectiveness, then the core has the equal treatment property and is equivalent to the set of admission equilibrium states of the economy. To introduce the main ideas, the model of Conley and Wooders (1994a) is restricted to one private good and quasi-linear preferences. A model allowing ordinal preferences and multiple private goods is studied in Conley and Wooders (1996).

In Conley and Wooders (1994b), we find that the equivalence of the anonymous Lindahl equilibria and the core obtains when crowding is nondifferentiated and technology is linear. This result does not obtain in either the standard differentiated or crowding types model – it is not possible in every case to anonymously decompose admission prices into per-unit prices for public goods. If Lindahl prices exist, then it is immediately apparent that they imply a set of admission prices that also decentralize the core. Furthermore, when they exist, the Lindahl equilibrium allocations are contained in the core. The nonanonymous Lindahl equilibria, however, are equivalent to the core in all three models when the technology is linear.

28 See Wooders (1979a, 1983, Theorem 3) for equal treatment of the core in TU and NTU games and Wooders (1979b, 1992, 1994a) for asymptotic equal treatment. Engl and Scotchmer (1993) obtain related results for TU games.

29 Cole and Prescott's model is similar to our crowding types model in that preferences do not directly depend on the tastes of others.

30 The spirit of these results holds much more broadly, but the transferable utility frameworks make exposition especially easy.

The homogeneity properties of the core in the crowding type model are somwhat surprising. In general, mixing of types within jurisdictions is optimal in the differentiated crowding case because some agents may be complementary. Optimal symphony orchestras contain more than just violinists, for example. There is a basic tension between segregating according to type in order to eliminate conflict over what public goods bundle should be produced, and mixing in order to take advantage of the beneficial types of crowding. In the crowding types model, there is no such tension. It is possible to have taste-homogeneous jurisdictions that take advantage of the full array of different skills.

In the example above, intuition might lead us to expect that an orchestra whose members agreed on the best number of concerts to give each year would be able to provide them with more per capita utility than one whose members had different opinions.

Surprisingly, this turns out to be false. Conley and Wooders (1995) give an example which demonstrates that coalitions with several taste types may be strictly better off on a per capita basis than a taste-homogeneous coalition with the same crowding profile. A weaker homogeneity result, however, does hold. Specifically, there is no per capita advantage from having several different taste types within a given crowding type. It may be optimal to mix men who like country music together with women who like jazz, but there is no advantage to mixing men who like jazz with men who like country. Notice that this implies that when there is only one crowding type (as in the nondifferentiated crowding case) no improvement in per capita payoff is possible from mixing together several taste types within a given jurisdiction, the well-known homogeneity results of Wooders (1978) and Berglas and Pines (1980, 1981).[31]

Epple and Romano (1994) consider an applied model of optimal school formation which can be interpreted as a crowding types model. They find that equilibrium schools will typically contain a mix of taste and crowding types, which parallels the results in Conley and Wooders (1995).

7. Market games with crowding types

Some familiarity with the models and results discussed in preceding sections may suggest that there are certain features common to all the models that drive the results. These features are shared by models with coalition production, such as those in Böhm (1974) and Bennett and Wooders (1979) as well as by private goods exchange economies, such as Shapley and Shubik (1969). Roughly, the common features of the economies are superadditivity and small group effectiveness (all or almost all gains to collective activities can be realized by groups of participants bounded in size of membership). Equivalently, when there are "many" commodities of each type and many players similar to each player, then

[31] Berglas and Pines (1981) show that no improvement in per capita payoff is possible from mixing different types. Wooders (1978) shows that in a core state of the economy, agents of different types may mix in the same jurisdiction only if they have the same demands, implying the result of Berglas and Pines. Although Berglas and Pines (1981) was published after Wooders (1978), these papers were formulated concurrently.

the common features can be described as superadditivity and boundedness of per capita payoffs. It has been shown in increasing generality that with the assumptions of superadditivity and small group effectiveness, large economies including ones with coalition production, clubs, local public goods, and collectively consumed and/or produced goods – share familiar properties of exchange economies with concave utility functions.

The approach initiated in Wooders (1979a) shows that when small groups are effective, then large economies behave like competitive markets – there is some set of commodities such that, relative to those commodities, there is a (complete) price system that satisfies virtually all the properties of a competitive equilibrium in a private goods exchange economy. In this section, we review some of the main points of the theory of large games and economies with effective small groups and indicate their application to models of economies.

Let us first consider an example of a game derived from an economy. We will use the economic model with crowding types of this paper but with the assumption of quasi-linear utilities.

Example: We consider exactly the general model introduced above but with the additional assumption that the utility function of each agent is quasi-linear. Recall that a value function $V:\mathcal{N} \rightarrow \Re$ may be defined for such economies. Clearly, a feasible state $(X, Y, n) \in F$ is Pareto efficient if and only if it maximizes $\sum_k V(n^k)$, where $(n^1, ..., n^k) = n$ is a partition. The pair (N, V) is the game induced by the economy.[32]

Recall that a feasible state $(X,Y,n) \in F$ is in the core of the economy if it cannot be improved upon by any jurisdiction. In the context of games with side payments the core is described as a set of utility vectors. A utility vector u is in the *core of the game* (N, V) if there does not exist a coalition $s \subset \mathcal{N}$ such that

$$V(s) > u(s) \equiv \sum_{i \in s} u_i. \tag{4-36}$$

It is easy to see that a state is in the core of the economy if and only if the utility vector associated with that state is in the core of the game.

We now consider general games with side payments (also called "transferable utility" or "TU" games). Recall that a *profile* is a vector of integers in $\Re^T_+$ listing a number of players of each of a finite number T of types; thus the total population vector N is a profile. A *subprofile* s of N is a profile satisfying $s \leq N$.

For a game (N, V), we can define an equilibrium where the equilibrium prices are utility prices or, with quasi-linear utilities, monetary prices. A price vector μ is an *equilibrium price system* if

[32] For a discussion of economies with quasi-linear utilities we refer the reader to Shapley and Shubik (1966, 1975) or Kaneko and Wooders (1996) for a more recent treatment.

$\mu \cdot s \geq V(s)$ for all subprofiles s of N and (4-37)

$\mu \cdot n = V(N)$.

These prices as utility admission prices to groups. The price μ_t for a player of type t states the admission price/wage/profit share required to entice a player of type t to join a group. Note also that prices are linear functions of number of players of each type.

We can view a (utility) price system as a complete price system in a market where all participants have the utility function $V(\cdot)$.

Define

$$V^b(n) = \min_q q \cdot N, \tag{4-38}$$

where the minimum is over all vectors q satisfying $q \cdot s \geq V(s)$ for all profiles $s < n$. The following propositions are taken from Wooders (1979a). Since only outgrowths of these propositions have appeared in the literature, we provide formal statements.[33]

The following proposition is immediate from the Fundamental Duality Theorem of linera programming.

Proposition. *(Wooders 1979a, Theorem 3) A game (N,V) has an equilibrium if and only if one of the following two conditions is satisfied:*

(i) $V^b(N) = V(N)$; and

(ii) *the game (N,V) has a nonempty core.*

A necessary and sufficient condition for the existence of an equilibrium can also be demonstrated in terms of properties of partitions of the total player set into coalitions. This is a generalization of the famous "integer problem" of economies with clubs and/or local public goods.

Proposition. *(Wooders 1979a, Theorem 3). A price vector μ is an equilibrium price vector if and only if there is a partition n of the total player set N into coalitions n^k such that*

(i) $\mu \cdot s \geq V(s)$ *for all subprofiles s of N; and*

(ii) $\mu \cdot n^k = V(n^k)$ for all groups n^k *in the partition.*

In general, equilibrium prices coincide with the equal-treatment core of the game. Note that it is not required that small groups are strictly effective.

Proposition. *(Wooders 1979a, Theorem 6). Let (N,V) be a game. Then μ is an equilibrium price vector for the game if and only if μ is in the equal-treatment core of the game.*

[33] cf. Bennett and Wooders (1979), Wooders (1992, 1994a, 1994b), Scotchmer and Wooders (1988), and other papers. Prior related results appear in Shapley and Shubik (1969).

In Wooders (1979a) it was also shown that if strict small group effectiveness holds, then large games have nonempty approximate cores and payoffs in the approximate core are approximately equal treatment – most players of the same type receive nearly the same payoff. It follows that approximate cores are close to competitive equilibrium price vectors. These results are suggestive of the competitive properties of large economies with small effective groups. In fact, the following "market-like" properties of large games were demonstrated in Wooders (1979a, 1980):

1. Approximate cores are nonempty and the approximation can be made arbitrarily close as the economy becomes large.
2. Approximate price-taking equilibria exist and equilibrium outcomes are in approximate cores.
3. Approximate cores converge to equilibrium outcomes.
4. Approximate cores are asymptotically equal-treatment.
5. When small groups are strictly effective then the core has the equal-treatment property. Core payoffs are monotonic – that is, if the abundance of one type of player increases, then the core payoff to that type does not decrease and may well increase.[34]
6. Additionally, in Scotchmer and Wooders (1988), it is shown that core payoffs are monotonic – that is, if the abundance of one type of player increases, then the core payoff to that type does not decrease and may well increase.[35]

The above results, surveyed in Wooders (1994a), all hold for economies with quasi-linear utility functions. These results can also be shown to hold when player types (or attributes) are continuously divisible (cf. Wooders (1981b), Engl and Scotchmer 1993).[36] With certain assumptions, all of the results above hold for economies modeled as games with nontransferable utilities. A number of the results also hold for economies modeled as games with nontransferable utilities (see Kovolenkov, Wooders, and Zhang 1994 for further references).[35]

[34] Monoticity can be viewed as a consequence of concavity of the utility function representing a game with a nonempty core and of strict small group effectriveness. See Wooders (1988a, 1994a, b) for results showing that the utility function representing a large game is concave.

[35] The results of Engl and Scotchmer (1993), however, do not directly treat cores, approximate cores, and competitive payoffs. Instead, they treat payoffs over groups and then average over groups size. Thus their results are more closely related to the market -game equivalence results of Wooders (1988a, 1994b) than those of Wooders (1979, 1980a, 1994a) on asymptotic equal-treatment and convergence of approximate cores to competitive outcomes.

[36] Other research and work in progress (Wooders and Zame (1987b)) indicates that all the above results extend with remarkable generality. Indeed, in general, there is no need to impose the requirement that there is a finite set of types of players and commodities (or even that there is a topology on the set of player types; cf., Wooders (1994c) and Kovalenkov, Wooders and Zhang (1994) for core convergence).

A number of results in the literature apply the market-games approach to economies with differentiated crowding. The application of the markets-games to crowding type models has not been fully investigated and is the subject of current research.

Conclusions

The results discussed in this paper have been derived primarily for economies with quasi-linear utilities and for games with side payments. A number of papers and research in progress demonstrate that results can be obtained in comparable generality to analogous results for private goods exchange economies. The concept of small group effectiveness also can be broadly extended and applied.

When small groups are effective and payoffs are per capita bounded, then large games/economies have nonempty approximate cores, approximate cores are approximately equal-treatment, approximate equilibria exist (for some definition of the commodity space), and approximate cores converge to equilibrium outcomes. For the case of local public goods economies, these results hold in the context of equilibrium with type-dependent prices. Our results in this paper and in Conley and Wooders (1994a, 1994b) show that when small groups are effective and crowding is differentiated, then prices can be anonymous. If preferences actually depend on the tastes of others, then the same problems of adverse selection arise in economies with differentiated crowding as in economies with private goods only.

References

Atkinson, A. and J. Stiglitz (1980) *Lectures on Public Economics*. New York: McGraw-Hill.

Barham, V. and M. H. Wooders (1997) "First and Second Welfare Theorems for Economies with Collective Goods." This volume.

Barro, R. and Romer, P. (1987) "Ski-Lift Pricing, with Applications to Labor and Other Markets," *American Economic Review* 77, 875–90.

Bennett, E. (1991) "Noncooperative Bargaining." In R. Selten, ed. *Game Equilibrium Models: Strategic Bargaining*. Berlin: Springer-Verlag.

Bennett, E. and Wooders, M. H. (1979) "Income Distribution and Firm Formation." *Journal of Comparative Economics*, 3, 304-17.

Berglas, E. (1976) "Distribution of Tastes and Skills and the Provision of Local Public Goods." *Journal of Public Economics*, 6, 409-23

Berglas, E. and Pines, D. (1980) "Clubs as a Case of Competitive Industry with Goods of Variable Quality." *Economics Letters*, 5, 363-66.

Berglas, E. and Pines, D. (1981) "Clubs, Local Public Goods, and Transportation Models: A Synthesis." *Journal of Public Economics*, 15, 141-62.

Bewley, T. (1981) "A Critique of Tiebout's Theory of Local Public Expenditure." *Econometrica*, 49, 713-40.

Boadway, R. (1980) "A Note on the Market Provision of Club Goods." *Journal of Public Economics*, 13, 131-7.

Böhm, V. (1974) "The Limit of the Core of an Economy with Production." *International Economic Review,* 1, 143-148.

Brueckner, J. (1994) "Tastes, Skills and Local Public Goods." *Journal of Urban Economics,* 35, 201-20.

Cole, H. and E. Prescott (1994) "Valuation Equilibria with Clubs." Federal Reserve Bank of Minneapolis, Staff Report 174.

Conley, J. and M. H. Wooders (1994a) "Equivalence of Tiebout Equilibrium and the Core in a Model with Crowding Types," *Journal of Urban Economics* (to appear).

Conley, J. and M. H. Wooders (1994b) "Anonymous Lindahl Pricing in a Tiebout Economy with Crowding Types." Manuscript.

Conley, J. and M. H. Wooders (1995) "Hedonic Independence and Taste Homogeneity of Optimal Jurisdictions in the Core of a Tiebout Economy with Crowding Types." Manuscript.

Conley, J. and M. H. Wooders (1996) "Tiebout economies with a continuum of agents" (typescript).

Debreu G. and H. Scarf (1963) "A Limit Theorem on the Core of an Economy." *International Economic Review,* 4, 235-46.

Ellickson, B. (1973) "A Generalization of the Pure Theory of Local Public Goods," *American Economic Review,* 63, 417-32.

Ellickson, B. (1979) "Competitive Equilibrium with Local Public Goods," *Journal of Economic Theory* 21, 46–61.

Engl, G. and S. Scotchmer (1993) "The Core and Hedonic Core: Equivalence and Comparative Statics." University of Irvine, Discussion Paper (with other versions dated 1991 and 1992).

Epple, D., R. Filimon, and T. Romer (1984) "Equilibrium among Local Jurisdictions," *Journal of Public Economics* 24, 281–308.

Epple, D. and R. Romano (1994) "Competition Between Private and Public Schools, Vouchers and Peer Group Effects." Manuscript.

Greenberg, J. and S. Weber (1986) "Strong Tiebout Equilibrium under Restricted Preferences Domain." *Journal of Economic Theory,* 38, 101-17.

Hammond, P., M. Kaneko and M. H. Wooders (1989) "Continuum Economies with Finite Coalitions: Core, Equilibria, and Widespread Externalities." *Journal of Economic Theory,* 49, 113-34.

Henderson, V. (1985) "The Tiebout Model: Bring Back the Entrepreneuers," *Journal of Political Economy* 27, 253–79.

Henderson, V. (1991) "Separating Tiebout Equilibria," *Journal of Urban Ecnomics* 29, 128–51.

Hochman, O., D. Pines and J. F. Thisse (1995) "On the Optimal Structure of Local Governments." *American Economic Review,* 85(5) 1224-40.

Jackson, M. and H. Moulin (1992) "Implementing a Public Project and Distributing Its Costs." *Journal of Economic Theory,* 57, 125-40.

Kahn, C. and E. Silva (1993) "Exclusion and Moral Hazard; the Case of Identical Demand." *Journal of Public Economics,* 52, 217-35.

Kaneko, M. (1977) "The Ratio Equilibrium and a Voting Game in a Public Goods Economy." *Journal of Economic Theory,* 16, 123-36.

Kaneko, M. and M. H. Wooders (1982) "Cores of Partitioning Games." *Mathematical Social Sciences,* 3, 313-27.

Kaneko, M. and M. H. Wooders (1986) "The Core of a Game with a Continuum of Players and Finite Coalitions: The Model and Some Results." *Mathematical Social Sciences,* 12, 105-37.

Kaneko, M. and M. H. Wooders (1996a) "Nonemptiness of the Core of a Game with a Continuum of Players." *International Journal of Game Theory,* 25: 245-58.

Kaneko, M. and M. H. Wooders (1996b) "Utility Theories in Cooperative Games." University of Tsukuba, Institute of Socio-economic Planning, Discussion Paper No. 597. In P. Hammond and C. Seidl, eds. *Handbook of Utility Theory.* Dordrecht, Boston and London: Kooner.

Kovolenkov, A., M. H. Wooders and J. K. Zhong (1994) "Approximating cores of games." Manuscript presented at the 1994 University of Illinois International Conference on Game Theory.

Manning, J. (1993) "Local Public Goods: First Best Allocations and Supporting Prices." University of Rochester, Department of Economics. Discussion Paper.

Mas-Colell, A. (1975) "A Model of Equilibrium with Differentiated Commodities." *Journal of Mathematical Economics,* 2, 263-295.

Mas-Colell, A. (1979) "A Refinement of the Core Equivalence Theorem." *Economic Letters,* 3, 307-310.

Mas-Colell, A. and J. Silvestre (1989) "Cost Share Equilibrium: A Lindahlian Approach." *Journal of Economic Theory.* 47, 239-256.

McGuire, M. C. (1974) "Group Segregation and Optimal Jurisdictions." *Journal of Political Economy,* 82, 112-132.

McGuire, M.C. (1991) "Group Composition, Collective Consumption, and Collaborative Production." *American Economic Review,* 81, 1391-1407.

Pauly, M. (1970) "Cores and Clubs." *Public Choice,* 9, 53-65.

Samuelson, P. (1954) "The Pure Theory of Public Expenditures." *Review of Economics and Statistics,* 36, 387-389.

Schweitzer, U. (1983) "Efficient Exchange with a Variable Number of Consumers," *Econometrica* 51, 575–84.

Scotchmer, S. (1994) "Public Goods and the Invisible Hand." J. M. Quigley and E. Smolensky, eds., *Modern Public Finance,* Cambridge: Harvard University Press.

Scotchmer, S. and M. H. Wooders. (1986) "Optimal and Equilibrium Groups." Harvard University Discussion Paper 1251 and incomplete revisions under the title of "Competitive Equilibrium and the Core in Club Economies with Nonanonymous Crowding."

Scotchmer, S. and M. H. Wooders (1987) "Competitive Equilibrium and the Core in Economies with Anonymous Crowding." *Journal of Public Economics,* 34, 159-74

Scotchmer, S. and M. H. Wooders (1988) "Monotonicity in Games that Exhaust Gains to Scale." Stanford University, IMSSS Technical Report No. 525.

Selten, R. (1981) "A Noncooperative Model of Characteristic Function Bargaining." In V. Boehm and H. Nachtkamp, eds., *Essays in Game Theory and Economics in Honor of O. Morgenstern.* Wein-Zurich: Bibliographisches Institut Mannheim.

Shapley, L. S. and M. Shubik (1966) "Quasi-Cores in a Monetary Economy with Nonconvex Preferences." *Econometrica,* 34, 805-27.

Shapley, L. S. and M. Shubik (1969) "On Market Games." *Journal of Economic Theory,* 1, 9-25.

Shapley, L. S. and M. Shubik (1975) "Competitive Outcomes in the Cores of Market Games." *International Journal of Game Theory,* 4, 229-37.

Shubik, M. and M. H. Wooders (1983) "Approximate Cores of Replica Games and Economies: Part I. Replica Games, Externalities, and Approximate Cores." *Mathematical Social Sciences,* 6, 27-48.

Shubik, M. and M. H. Wooders (1986) "Near-Markets and Market Games." *Economics Studies Quarterly,* 37, 129-99.

Tiebout, C. (1956) "A Pure Theory of Local Expenditures." *Journal of Political Economy,* 64, 416-24.

Wilson, J. (1994) "Mobile Households." Presented at the 1994 Tel Aviv conference in honor of Eitan Berglas, Tel Aviv University.

Wooders, M. H. (1978) "Equilibria, the Core, and Jurisdiction Structures in Economies with a Local Public Good." *Journal of Economic Theory,* 18, 328-48.

Wooders, M. H. (1979) "A Characterization of Approximate Equilibria and Cores in a Class of Coalition Economies." (Stony Brook Department of Economics, Working Paper No. 184, revised).

Wooders, M. H. (1980a) "Asymptotic Cores and Asymptotic Balancedness of Large Replica Games." Stony Brook Department of Economics, Working Paper No. 215, revised July 1980.

Wooders, M. H. (1980b) "The Tiebout Hypothesis: Near Optimality in Local Public Good Economies." *Econometrica,* 48, 1467-86.

Wooders, M. H. (1981) "A Limit Theorem onthe ε-core of an Economy with Public Goods," Japan National Tax Institute paper no. 20.

Wooders, M. H. (1983) "The Epsilon Core of a Large Replica Game." *Journal of Mathematical Economics,* 11, 277-300.

Wooders, M. H. (1988a) "Large Games Are Market Games: Large Finite Games," CORE Discussion Paper No. 8842, March 1988.

Wooders, M. H. (1988b) "Stability of Jurisdiction Structures in Economies with Local Public Goods." *Mathematical Social Sciences,* 15, 29-49.

Wooders, M. H. (1989) "A Tiebout Theorem." *Mathematical Social Sciences,* 18, 33-55.

Wooders, M. H. (1991) "On Large Games and Competitive Markets 1." University of Bonn, Sonderforschungsbereich 303, Discussion Paper No. B-195 (revised August 1992).

Wooders, M. H. (1992) "The Attribute Core, Core Convergence, and Small Group Effectiveness; The Effects of Property Rights Assignments on Attribute Games." (Forthcoming in (P. Dubey and J. Geanakoplos, eds. *Essays in Honor of Martin Shubik.*

Wooders, M. H. (1993a) "Convergence of the Core to Competitive Outcomes in Economies with Public Goods." University of Toronto, Department of Economics, Discussion Paper No. 9301.

Wooders, M. H. (1993b) "Equivalence of Lindahl Equilibrium with Participation Prices and the Core." *Economic Theory* 9(1), (forthcoming).

Wooders, M. H. (1994a) "Large Games and Economies with Effective Small Groups." In J. F. Mertens and S. Sorin, eds., *Game-Theoretic Methods in General Equilibrium Analysis,* Dordrecht: Kluwer Academic Publishers.

Wooders, M. H. (1994b) "Equivalence of Games and Markets." *Econometrica,* 62, 1141-1160.

Wooders, M. H. (1994c) "Approximating Games and Economies by Markets." University of Toronto, Department of Economics, Discussion Paper No. 9305, revised 9415.

Wooders, M. H and W. R. Zame (1984) "Approximate Cores of Large Games." *Econometrica,* 52, 1327-1350.

Wooders, M. H and W. R. Zame (1987a) "Large Games; Fair and Stable Outcomes." *Journal of Economic Theory,* 42, 59-93.

Wooders, M. H. and W. R. Zame (1987b) "NTU Values of Large Games." IMSSS, Working Paper No. 503.

CHAPTER 5

Decentralization in club economies: How multiple private goods matter*

Robert P. Gilles and Suzanne Scotchmer

1. Introduction

Club theory (Buchanan 1965) is based on the observation that optimal sharing groups for public goods are often small relative to the economy, and that these small groups should consequently be competitive. The idea that smallness leads to competitiveness has been developed at length, and much of the club theory literature is devoted to the conjecture, now well-established for club economies with one private good, that efficient and core allocations (if they exist) can be decentralized as competitive equilibria.[1] Eitan Berglas was one of the earliest scholars to realize both the scope of club theory, in particular its extension to coalition production, schools, and local public economies, and the fact that optimal allocations could be interpreted as competitive (Berglas 1976, 1981; Berglas and Pines 1980, 1981). His 1976 paper is seminal in recognizing the importance of what is now called "nonanonymous crowding," and his 1981 paper is seminal in establishing the club model with variable intensity of use. In this chapter, we delve into one of the few extensions of club theory that Berglas left relatively untouched, namely, the special problems that arise when the demands for club goods and private goods are interdependent.

The decentralization literature that assumes only one private good overlooks a complication that can only be addressed in a model with several private goods; namely, that there may be strong complementarities between private and club goods in the sense that the consumer's ranking of clubs depends on the consumption of private goods or, alternatively, in the sense that the marginal rates of substitution between private goods depend on the public goods or club goods. Suppose, for example, that the public goods are schools, and that a community must choose between schools that emphasize sports, music, or

* We thank Bob Anderson, Dimitrios Diamantaras, Bryan Ellickson, Shmuel Nitzan, David Pines, Martine Quinzii, Nina Reshef, Joaquim Silvestre and participants at the 10th Pinhas Sapir Conference on Public Economics in Honor of Eitan Berglas at the Berglas School of Economics, Tel Aviv, Israel (January 1995), the Math Econ Seminar at Berkeley (January 1995), and the Economic Theory Seminar at U.C. Davis (February 1995) for useful discussion.

[1] Early decentralization results did not distinguish very clearly between the core and a Pareto optimum, partly because the authors restricted the analysis to equal-treatment allocations where there are no "integer problems," see, e.g., Berglas (1976), Berglas and Pines (1980, 1981), and Boadway (1982). For more explicit treatments with one private good see Brueckner (1994), Scotchmer and Wooders (1987a, 1987b), and Scotchmer (1993, 1994).

mathematics, it not being viable to provide all three. One would expect that the private demand for tennis rackets, musical instruction, and computers would depend heavily on which type of school is provided. In this chapter we summarize work of three papers, Diamantaras, Gilles, and Scotchmer (1996) and Gilles and Scotchmer (1995, 1997), that addresses the interdependencies between club goods and private goods, and discusses the price systems necessary for decentralization. By "decentralization" we mean that an optimal or core allocation is supported by prices such that all agents prefer the optimal allocation to any other allocation, given that their choices are constrained by the decentralizing prices.

Complementarities between private goods and club goods change the problem of decentralization in at least two ways, illustrated below.

- In a pure public goods economy, decentralization may require that consumers conjecture different prices for private goods which depend on the public goods. The same problem carries over to unreplicated club economies. However, conjectural prices can be avoided in an economy that has been replicated sufficiently to "exhaust blocking opportunities."
- One should think in terms of an optimal scale for the economy as a whole, rather than in terms of the optimal club size, or even the optimal club size conditional on agents' characteristics. Because of complementarities between private goods and club goods (public goods or crowding externalities), optimality might require that agents with the same preferences and endowments occupy clubs of different size and trade with each other.[2]

In an unreplicated club economy, not only does decentralization require conjectural prices, but, in addition, admission prices to clubs are individual, because agents provide different externalities. With replication permitting the economy to exhaust blocking opportunities as defined below, the prices required for decentralization look much more like a competitive price system in at least two ways. First, the need for conjectural prices for private goods vanishes, and second, the profit-maximization condition and utility-maximization conditions apply in a global sense, corresponding to how competitive equilibrium is defined in private goods economies.

[2] Previous authors have assumed that there is a unique optimal scale for a club, as is natural in the case of one private good. For example, see Buchanan (1965), Berglas (1976), Berglas and Pines (1980, 1981), and other authors previously referenced. The same idea has been carried over to the context of multiple private goods on the assumption that it will not be optimal for identical agents with identical endowments to trade; for example, see Wooders (1978, 1981), who calls the optimal scale a "distinguished number." Our example in Section 2 shows that such an assumption is unwarranted. It might be optimal to partition a homogeneous population into clubs of different size with identical members trading private goods.

When crowding is nonanonymous, so that members of a club care about the types or characteristics of other members as well as about their number, admission prices required for decentralization will not be anonymous in the sense of Ellickson (1979), Bewley (1981), or Scotchmer and Wooders (1987a). Ellickson required that all members of a club pay an admission price that depends only on the public good provided. Bewley required that admission prices be linked only to an individual's endowment, while Scotchmer and Wooders required the admission prices to depend only on the public goods and number of members, but not on the type or characteristics of the member who joins. With nonanonymous crowding such prices are insufficient. Agents who impose positive externalities will typically have lower admission prices than other members (or they may even be subsidized), while agents who impose negative externalities must pay higher prices for admission. (See Engl and Scotchmer [1996] and Scotchmer [1996], for discussions of how club admission prices can be decomposed as prices for externalities.)

In Section 2 we show how complementarities between private goods and public goods can necessitate conjectural private goods prices in decentralizing an optimum. In Section 3 we present a motivating example to show how replication vitiates the need for conjectural prices, and illustrate that the appropriate notion of "optimal scale" must apply to the economy as a whole. In Section 4 we discuss the nature of competitive prices and the definition of competitive equilibrium. We stress that a definition of competitive equilibrium that is consistent with competitive theory as it applies to private goods economies, has the property that no *conceivable* club, as opposed to no *feasible* club, could make positive profit or increase any agent's utility at the equilibrium prices.

In Section 5 we address existence issues. An obstacle to existence is that while competitive equilibrium inevitably gives the same utility to all agents of the same type (since with anonymous prices they have the same trading opportunities), there might not be a core allocation with this property. We give an example to illustrate the problem, and show that it is avoided if endowments are sufficiently large. A second, and more commonly understood problem for existence is the problem of optimal scale. The problem is fundamental and cannot be avoided except, perhaps, by applying a notion of approximate equilibrium rather than equilibrium; see, for example, Scotchmer (1993).

The work summarized here avoids the assumption of "essentiality" that many authors have employed in decentralization results for clubs.[3] It means that, given an allocation (including both the club structure and the distribution of private

[3] The assumption was introduced by Mas-Colell (1980). See also Diamantaras and Gilles (1994), Hahn and Gilles (1994), Manning (1993a, Assumption 3), Manning (1993b, Assumption 5), Wooders (1989) where the assumption is called "overriding desirability," and Wooders (1993), Assumption [e], called "substitution." It is avoided by Scotchmer (1994).

goods), consumers can be made indifferent between that allocation and any club structure by letting them consume an appropriate amount of private goods. It follows that at zero consumption of private goods, consumers must be indifferent between all club structures. While convenient for writing proofs, the essentiality assumption is very restrictive. For example, unless utility approaches minus infinity as private goods consumption becomes small, it excludes utility functions that are separable between private and public goods. The papers summarized here show that such a strong assumption is not required. Cole and Prescott (1994) also avoid the essentiality assumption in a model where agents randomize on consumption of private and club goods. Here we retain the standard structure of club economies, which is that agents must choose one and only one club, and that they consume its public goods with certainty.

From Tiebout (1956) and Buchanan (1965) a vast assortment of Tiebout-like and club models have evolved, some with many private goods. Most of these retain the linear structure of Lindahl, avoiding the strong interdependencies between private and public goods that are focal in this paper. Ellickson (1979) shows how public goods with asymptotically linear costs can be interpreted as private goods, and then shows existence of an equilibrium with anonymous admission prices to jurisdictions that differ in their public goods. His model does not account for externalities among agents within jurisdictions. It nevertheless has the key feature of a Tiebout model in that consumers sort themselves according to taste, as well as the key feature of a competitive market in that prices are anonymous. Bewley (1981) also restricts attention to one type of anonymous pricing, and shows a similar theorem. He also gives examples to show the difficulties of decentralization when there is crowding in consumption. Wooders (1978, 1981, 1989) provides decentralization theorems for club economies using the linear structure of Lindahl, but the formation of clubs is not decentralized through price-taking. Greenberg (1983), Greenberg and Weber (1986), and Greenberg and Shitovitz (1992) address models with free mobility in which the choice of public goods is governed by voting rather than the profit motive. Guo (1994) stresses that in all these models a complete price system is difficult to observe; he then describes what can be decentralized with more limited information.

2. Complementarities between public and private goods

In regard to pure public goods economies there have been two strands of literature on decentralization: Lindahl equilibrium (Lindahl 1919; Foley 1970) and valuation equilibrium or cost-share equilibrium (Mas-Colell 1980). These two approaches model public goods in ways that are technically different. The technical difference has an economic interpretation, and matters importantly for how one decentralizes an optimum. The technical difference between the two approaches is that for Lindahl equilibrium, one must model public goods as having a linear structure. The level of public goods, say g, is a real number, and more of g is preferred to less. In the Lindahl setup, preferences are typically represented by $U(x,g)$, where $x \in R_+^l$ and $g \in R_+$. If one imposes monotonicity in g, all agents rank levels of g in the same way: more is preferred to less.

This linear structure was avoided by Mas-Colell (1980), who modeled public goods as an unstructured set, say $\mathbf{Y}$, and represented preferences by $U(x,y)$ with $x \in R_+^l$ and $y \in$ Y. The elements $y \in \mathbf{Y}$ can be thought of as different public projects; of course, a special case is when $\mathbf{Y} = R$ as in the Lindahl setup. But, in general, there is no need that all agents rank the elements of $\mathbf{Y}$ in the same way. Further, without a linear structure, one does not impose monotonicity; thus, the ranking of elements $\mathbf{Y}$ can depend on the private goods consumed. It follows that the unstructured set gives more scope for complementarity between public goods and private goods than does the Lindahl setup. For an exhaustive analysis of this approach we refer to Mas-Colell (1980), Diamantaras and Gilles (1994), Diamantaras, Gilles, and Scotchmer (1996), and Hahn and Gilles (1994).

The above technical difference in how one models public goods turns out to have implications both for the nature of preferences that can be modeled and for the price systems required to implement an optimum. This was illustrated by the following example taken from Diamantaras, Gilles, and Scotchmer (1996). In the example, the private good x_1 is complementary with the public good y_1; that is, the marginal rate of substitution between x_1 and x_2 is larger if the public project is y_1 than if it is y_0. Furthermore, according to the preferences, the agent's ranking of y_0 and y_1 depends on the private good x; therefore, even if we impose linear structure on Y and assume $y_0 < y_1$, the example does not exhibit the monotonicity property that is basic to the Lindahl setup. Monotonicity excludes the strong complementarity in this example. Thus, the Mas-Colell setup permits a richer set of preferences, especially regarding complementarity between private goods and public goods.

An important point illustrated by the example is that the prices required for decentralization are fundamentally different than those required by, for example, Foley (1970) for decentralization using the linear structure of Lindahl. In Lindahl equilibrium, there is no need for the consumer to assume that prices for private goods depend on the public goods. This is intuitively so, because the linear structure limits the complementarity between private goods and public goods. Mathematically, this is because the construction of decentralizing prices involves a single bounding hyperplane to a convex set that jointly repesents the preferred consumption of both private and public goods. By contrast, the example shows that decentralization without the linear structure of Lindahl may require conjectural prices.

Example 1 (Diamantaras, Gilles, and Scotchmer 1996). Suppose there are two private goods x_1 and x_2 and two potential public projects, $\mathrm{Y} = \{y_0, y_1\}$, with inputs $c(y_0) = (0,0) = c(y_1)$. There is one consumer with preferences $U(x_1,$

$x_2, y_0) = x_1 + x_2$ and $U(x_1,x_2,y_1) = 4/3x_1 + 1/2x_2$. The consumer's endowment is $w = (1,1)$. It is efficient to produce public goods y_0 so that the consumer gets utility 2. If y_1 is produced, the consumer gets utility 11/6. Equilibrium prices must be $p(y_0) = (.5,.5)$, $V(y_0) = 0$, and $V(y_1) \leq 1$, where p stands for the private goods prices and V for the prices to access the public facilities in the economy. The (in)equalities on the prices V follow from standard perfect competition conditions regarding the provision of public goods, i.e., providers maximize profits and in equilibrium the maximal profits are zero. Suppose that we also impose the condition that $p(y_1) = p(y_0) = (.5,.5)$. After paying $V(y_1) \leq 1$, there remains at least one dollar for the consumer to spend on private goods. This permits a purchase of at least 2 units of x_1, which provide at least 8/3 units of utility. Thus, the consumer prefers y_1 to y_0, and we cannot support the efficient state as an equilibrium.

A solution to the problem of decentralization in the above example is to permit "conjectural prices": If the consumer thinks that the prices for private goods will be (4/3,1) rather than (1,1) for choice y_1 rather than y_0, then the optimum can be decentralized. Following this line of reasoning, Diamantaras, Gilles, and Scotchmer (1996) show that an optimum can be decentralized with such conjectural prices, but not necessarily without them.

We remain agnostic on whether conjectural prices are "reasonable." If not, one must conclude that with strong complementarities between private and public goods, decentralization is impossible. In their favor, one notices that while it might be unreasonable to think that all agents conjecture the same alternative prices for a given alternative to the public goods, it is also unreasonable to conjecture that the prices would not change. This is because the demand for private goods depends on the public goods; therefore, the same price vector will not clear the market for all provisions of public goods.

In the next example we show that the same problem of complementarities carries over to the club context. In this example the complementarity is between the private good x_1 and the size of the club. The marginal rate of substitution between x_1 and x_2 is greater if the club has size 2 rather than 1.

Example 2: Decentralization of an optimum in an unreplicated club economy may require conjectural prices. Consider an economy with two agents of the same type, and with no public goods but with crowding benefits. Initial endowments are given by $w = (1,1)$. Let the utility functions be given by

$$u_a(x,1) = u_b(x,1) = 4/3x_1 + 1/2x_2 \tag{5-1}$$

$$u_a(x,2) = u_b(x,2) = x_1 + x_2 \tag{5-2}$$

An efficient allocation and a core allocation have both agents in one club of size 2, with $u_a + u_b \leq 4$, where a and b are the two agents. If there is an equilibrium, the prices should satisfy $p = (1,1)$, $V_a(2) + V_b(2) = 0$, and $V_a(1) + V_b(1) \leq 0$. Here, V stands for the admission prices to the clubs with the two sizes under the condition of nonpositive profit in club provision. However, such prices cannot decentralize an optimum or core allocation because then the net incomes are, respectively, $2 - V_a(1)$ and $2 - V_b(1)$, and optimal consumption with the two agents in singleton clubs provides utilities

$$\hat{u}_a = 2(4/3) - 4/3 V_a(1) \text{ and } \hat{u}_b = 2(4/3) - 4/3 V_b(1).$$

Since $\hat{u}_a + \hat{u}_b = 4(4/3) - 4/3\,[V_a(1) + V_b(1)] \geq 4(4/3) > 4$, at least one of the agents will be better off choosing a singleton club. Thus, the efficient allocation cannot be decentralized as an equilibrium if the prices for private goods do not depend on the club structure.

3. Replication and optimal size

A central question from the point of view of club theory is how to define the optimal club size, usually referred to as n^*. With homogeneous agents, the optimal size n^* is usually defined as

$$\arg\max U\left[n, y(n), w - \frac{c\,[y(n), n]}{n}\right]$$

where U is the utility function of each agent, n is the number of club members, $y(n)$ is the optimal provision of public goods with n members, w is a real-valued endowment, and c is the cost function for the public goods. The question is how to extend this definition to the case of many private goods. For example, should private goods prices be taken as parametric for purposes of establishing the optimal club size?

Example 3 shows a consequence of the multiplicity of private goods that might be surprising: With multiple private goods, even in the simplest case of homogeneous tastes, there might not be a unique optimal club size. Rather it might be optimal to have clubs of many sizes, among which identical agents trade private goods; furthermore, the optimal size for the economy, which is $N = 14$, bears no simple relationship to the optimal sizes of clubs. This example illustrates three important aspects of club economies when there are many private goods rather than just one:

- It is not necessarily optimal to partition the population into identical clubs, even when all citizens are identical, irrespective of how large the economy is; optimality might require trade among agents of the same type in different clubs.[4]
- Multiples of the economy's optimal scale $N = 14$ are *necessary* for decentralization of the core as a competitive equilibrium. The core is

[4] Wilson (1987) also concluded that identical agents may trade between regions of a Tiebout economy. Our argument relies on complementarities between the size of the region and demands for private goods. His argument was rooted in specialization of production.

nonempty for $N < 14$, but it cannot be decentralized as a competitive equilibrium. If $N > 14$, the core is empty unless N is a multiple of 14.

- Multiples of the optimal scale $N = 14$ are *sufficient* for the core to be decentralizable as a competitive equilibrium. Competitive equilibrium exists only for multiples of $N = 14$.

Example 3: Decentralization requires optimal scale of the economy. Consider an economy with identical agents. To interpret the following utility function, one can either assume that it is a reduced form in which public goods have been provided optimally in each club, or one can consider a club economy without public facilities, but including only membership externalities among agents. There are two private goods, and initial endowments are $w = (1,1)$ for each agent. We will assume that utility depends on the consumption of private goods and the number of agents, n, in an agent's club. Let the utility functions be given by

$$\begin{aligned} U(x,n) &= 0 && \text{for } n > 2, x \in R^2_+ \\ U(x,2) &= x_1 + x_2 && \text{for } x \in R^2_+ \\ U(x,1) &= \tfrac{4}{3}x_1 + \tfrac{1}{2}x_2 && \text{for } x \in R^2_+ \end{aligned} \tag{5-3}$$

where n is the number of members in a club.

Suppose, first, that there are $N = 4$ agents in the population. The efficient allocation is any club structure in which two of the agents are in a club with $n = 2$, and two of the agents are in singleton clubs, $n = 1$. By redistributing private goods such that agents in the singleton clubs consume only the first commodity and agents in the clubs of size $n = 2$ might consume both, all agents can receive the same utility, which is higher in this club structure than in any other club structure in which all agents are in clubs of the same size. The optimal distribution of private goods that equalizes utility is $\tilde{x} = (2/7, 2)$ in clubs of size $n = 2$ and $\hat{x} = (12/7, 0)$ in clubs of size $n = 1$:

$$u = U[(2/7,2),2] = 2\tfrac{2}{7} = U[(12/7,0),1] \tag{5-4}$$

This allocation is a core allocation. However, it is not possible to support this allocation as a competitive equilibrium, as follows.

We define competitive equilibrium such that all agents trade private goods at the same price vector p and, in addition, they pay admission prices V to their individual clubs. There is perfect competition among clubs: The admission prices must be such that every club in equilibrium breaks even and out-of-equilibrium clubs earn nonpositive profit. This implies that $nV(n) \le 0$ for all n, with equality for clubs in the equilibrium club structure. Further, if agents receive utility u in equilibrium, it must be the case that

$$p \cdot x + V(n) > p \cdot w \quad \text{if} \quad U(x,n) > u.$$

That is, a preferred consumption bundle is unaffordable.

To support the optimal allocation, the private goods prices must satisfy $p = (1,1)$ because the members of the club with $n = 2$ must be willing to consume both goods, and the zero-profit condition implies that $V(1) = V(2) = 0$. All agents receive the same income $p \cdot w = 2$. But the private-goods expenditure required for the equal-treatment utility $u = 2\frac{2}{7}$ clubs of size $n = 2$ is $2\frac{2}{7}$ while the expenditure required in clubs of size $n = 1$ is $1\frac{5}{7}$. Thus, to support the efficient allocation as an equilibrium, the admission prices must satisfy $V(1) > 0$ and $V(2) < 0$, a contradiction. Even though the allocation described above is efficient and in the core, it is not a competitive equilibrium.

However, suppose the population is replicated still further, to N=14. With N=14, the optimal allocation is to have 6 agents in clubs of size $n = 2$ (three clubs), with each member consuming $\tilde{x}' = (0,\frac{7}{3})$, and 8 singleton clubs in which each agent consumes $\hat{x}' = (\frac{7}{4},0)$. This allocation is a competitive equilibrium with prices $p' = (\frac{4}{3},1)$, and $V(n) = 0$ for all n. The per-capita utility is $u' = 2\frac{1}{3}$.

It is no coincidence that the utility-maximizing population size coincides with the population size for which equilibrium exists. We have previously shown (1995b) that this coincidence follows in any economy larger than the minimum replicated economy that "exhausts blocking opportunities" (see the discussion beginning with the definition of a club in Section 4).

4. Decentralization and price systems

A lesson learned from Section 2 is that decentralization may require conjectural prices for private goods, both in pure public goods economies and in club economies. The lesson from the example in Section 3 is that conjectural prices may not be required for sufficiently large replicated economies. In this section, we turn to the nature of admission prices to clubs, and to what we mean by "competitive equilibrium" in club economies.

In unreplicated club economies, admission prices are by their nature nonanonymous if every individual confers different externalities. Replicated club economies permit the same admission prices for individuals of the same type – in fact, this restriction is built into much of the previous literature, and we will build it into the following definition of equilibrium. There are, of course, other restrictions that one could put on admission prices. The basic idea is that for decentralization of an optimum, admission prices must reflect all the information that affects crowding externalities. In the bulk of club theory, including our paper (1997), only types matter for crowding effects, hence admission prices are different for different types. However, Engl and Scotchmer (1996) and Scotchmer (1996) show that admission prices can be decomposed as payments for crowding externalities for the special case of transferable utility. Conley and Wooders (1994) make a similar observation, although their prices are not linear on attributes.

The other aspect of competitive equilibrium we would like to emphasize is the manner in which the profit-maximization and utility-maximization conditions are defined. We argue that for "competitive" equilibrium, these conditions must be defined globally: At the specified prices, no *conceivable* club, defined by the types of members and the shared public goods, could provide positive profit or more utility than the equilibrium. The alternative is to require these conditions only for clubs that are *feasible* in the economy. After presenting the basic club model, we point out why the weaker requirement is inconsistent with the usual definition of competitive equilibrium and give a condition on the club economy called "exhaustion of blocking opportunities," which permits the more demanding definition of equilibrium as a decentralization scheme.

We now describe the club economy. Let $\mathbf{T} = \{1, ..., \tau\}$ be an initial type set. (If the initial population has two agents with the same tastes and endowments, they appear as two indices; their similarity is reflected in the definition of costs and preferences.) If we replicate the player set m times, we denote the player set by $m\mathbf{T} = \{1, ..., m\tau\}$, and all agents with indices $t_r \in m\mathbf{T}$, $r \in \{1, ..., m\}$, will have the same tastes and endowments. A player $a \in m\mathbf{T}$ is *type-t* if $a = t_r$ for some $r \in \{1, ..., m\}$ and we refer to the type of player a as $t(a) \in \mathbf{T}$.

A coalition, say E, is a subset of mT. We use

$$n(E) = [n_1(E), ..., n_\tau(E)] \in N^\tau$$

to indicate that the coalition E contains $n_t(E)$ members of type-t, $t \in \mathbf{T}$. A coalition structure is a set of coalitions that partition mT: A finite collection $\mathbf{C} \subset 2^{m\mathbf{T}} \setminus \{\emptyset\}$ is a *coalition structure* if the coalitions in C are pairwise disjoint, and if $\cup_{E \in \mathbf{C}} E = m\mathbf{T}$. The collection of all coalition structures is indicated by C^m.

The main feature of a club economy is that for the purpose of efficiency, the agents must be partitioned into a coalition structure, and the main features of a club are that it provides its members with certain public facilities and that it creates externalities among club members. Following Mas-Colell (1980), Mas-Colell and Silvestre (1989), Diamantaras and Gilles (1994), and Diamantaras, Gilles, and Scotchmer (1996), we model public goods as an unstructured set of provision levels for public facilities Y. Because the set Y is not ordered, one cannot assume monotonicity or convexity of preferences in public goods; hence, we do not assume that an agent ranks the elements of Y the same way for all consumptions of private goods, nor do we assume that agents agree on their rankings.

A *club* is a coalition with a certain level of public facilities Y. A *club structure*, say K, is a collection of clubs that partitions the population; namely, there is some coalition structure $\mathrm{C} \in \mathsf{C}^m$ such that $K = \{(E,y) | E \in \mathrm{C} \text{ and } y \in \mathsf{Y}\}$.

It is assumed that there are $\ell \in \mathsf{N}$ private commodities in the economy, and that endowments are described by a $w = (w_t)_{t \in \mathbf{T}}$, where $w_t \in R_{++}^{\ell}$ denotes the endowment of type t, $t \in \mathbf{T}$. We let $w(n) := \sum_{t \in T} n_t w_t$, and $w(E) \equiv w[n(E)]$ represent the total endowment of a coalition $E \subset m\mathbf{T}$.

The cost of providing facilities could depend on the coalition. We interpret the notion of types to mean that two agents of the same type contribute the same amount to the cost of public facilities and affect other agents' utility in the same way. Therefore, instead of depending on the specific coalition E, cost will depend only on $n(E)$. Costs are therefore introduced as a function c: $\mathcal{N}^{\tau} \times \mathsf{Y} \to \mathcal{R}_+^{\ell}$, where $c[n(E),y] \in \mathcal{R}_+^{\ell}$ denotes the total quantity of private goods required to provide public facilities at a level $y \in \mathsf{Y}$ to all members of a club (E,y).[5]

For every type of agent $t \in \mathrm{T}$, we define preferences over private commodity bundles, the types of agents in the coalition of which the agent is a member, and the public facilities provided by that coalition. These preferences are represented through utility functions U_t: $\mathcal{R}_+^{\ell} \in \mathcal{N} \times \mathcal{N}^{\tau} \times \mathsf{Y} \to \mathcal{R}$. Crowding is nonanonymous in that utility depends on the types, and not just the number, of agents constituting a club.

In what follows, we call the preferences *strictly monotone* if for every $(n,y) \in \mathcal{N}^{\tau} \times \mathsf{Y}$ and all $x', x'', \in \mathcal{R}_{++}^{\ell}$: $x' > x''$ implies that $U_t(x',n,y) > U_t(x'',n,y)$. The collection $\mathcal{E} = \langle \mathbf{T}, U, w, \mathsf{Y}, c \rangle$ is now called a *club type system*. A *club economy* is an m-fold replica of $\mathcal{E}$, indicated by $\mathcal{E}^m$. If the set of agents is comprised of a subset $A \subset m\mathbf{T}$, we refer to the subeconomy of $\mathcal{E}^m$ restricted to A as $\mathcal{E}^m(A)$.

Let $A \subset m\mathbf{T}$. An *allocation* for the economy $\mathcal{E}^m(A)$ is (K,x), where K is a club structure of A and x: $A \to \mathcal{R}_+^{\ell}$ is the allocation of private goods. The allocation is *feasible* if

$$\sum_{a \in A} x(a) + \sum_{(E,y) \in K} c[n(E),y] \leq w(A) \tag{5-5}$$

For $(E,y) \in K$ and every $a \in E$ we define

$$u[a; (K,x)] \equiv U_{t(a)}[x(a), n(E), y] \tag{5-6}$$

and say that an allocation (K,x) *achieves* utilities $u[a;(K,x), a \in \boldsymbol{m}\mathbf{T}]$. Now utilities u: $A \to \mathcal{R}$ are *achievable* by an economy $\mathsf{E}^m(A)$ if there is a feasible allocation in the economy that achieves them. In the case when $A = m\mathrm{T}$, all definitions extend to E^m.

A coalition $A \subset m\mathbf{T}$ is said to *block* an allocation (K,x) in E^m if the subeconomy $\mathcal{E}^m(A)$ achieves utilities $\tilde{u}$: $a \to \mathcal{R}$ such that $\tilde{u}(a) \geq u[a, (K,x)]$, $a \in A$, with strict equality for at least one such a. The *core* of an economy $\mathcal{E}^m$ is a set of feasible allocations, each with the property that no coalition $A \subset m\mathbf{T}$ can block it.

[5] We could also replace the function c by a convex- and closed-valued correspondence that assigns to each level of public facilities a set of input vectors. See Diamantaras, Gilles, and Scotchmer (1996).

An allocation (K,x) is in the *equal-treatment core* of an economy E^m if it is in the core of E^m and there exists $u \in R^T$ such that $u[(a;(K,x)] = u_t$ if agent a is type-t. Equal-treatment payoffs are of interest because in a competitive equilibrium agents of the same type are treated equally. Equal treatment is assumed in how we define an efficient scale for the economy.

As in Example 3, we must define the notion of an efficient scale for the economy. Given $m \in N$, *let* $W(m)$ be the set of equal-treatment utilities that subeconomies in the economy E^m can achieve, i.e.,

$$W(m) = \{ u \in R^T \mid \exists A \subset m\mathbf{T}, A \neq \emptyset,$$

$$\text{such that } u \text{ is achievablein } E^m(A)\}$$

$$W = \bigcup_{m=1}^{\infty} W(m)$$

$$\overline{W} = \{ u \in W \mid \nexists u' \in W \text{ such that } u' >> u \}$$

W is the efficient, or upper boundary of W.

We say that an economy $E^{m'}$ *exhausts blocking opportunities* if $W(m) = W$.[6] If an economy E^m exhausts blocking opportunities, then every u in the interior of W can be blocked. If the equal-treatment core is nonempty, an allocation in the equal-treatment core achieves utilities in $\overline{W}$.

We say that an economy E^m has *efficient scale* if there exists $u \in \overline{W}$ such that u is achievable by E^m. An economy with efficient scale might or might not exhaust blocking opportunities, but every economy that does exhaust blocking opportunities contains a subeconomy of efficient scale.

In Example 3, it holds that $W(14) = W = \{u \in R \mid u \leq 2⅓\}$. Economies larger than $N = 14$ exhaust blocking opportunities, and the only efficient scales are multiples of 14. The equal-treatment utility achieved in the core of any such economy is 2⅓.

The following theorems state, first, that exhaustion of blocking opportunities is a sufficient condition for decentralizing the equal-treatment core as competitive equilibria, and, second, efficient scale is necessary and sufficient for decentralizing the core as competitive equilibria. If an economy has efficient scale, the core is nonempty.

In the following definition private goods prices are in the price simplex

$$\Delta = \{p \in R_+^{\,l} \mid \sum_{i=1}^{l} p_i + 1\} \tag{5-7}$$

Definition 1. *A feasible allocation (K,x) is a competitive equilibrium for E^m if there exists a price vector for private goods $p \in \Delta$ and admission prices V: $N^T \times Y \rightarrow R^T$ such that:*

[6] See also Engl and Scotchmer (1996) and Scotchmer (1994).

(i) *Local budgets are balanced: For each*

$(E,y) \in K, n(E) \cdot V[n(E),y] - p \cdot c[n(E),y] = 0.$

(ii) *No alternative club could make positive profit: For every*

$(n,z) \in N^{\tau} \times Y, \quad n \cdot V(n,z) - p \cdot c(n,z) \leq 0.$

(iii) For every $(E,y) \in K$ *and* $a \in m\mathbf{T}$, $V_{t(a)}[n(E),y] + p \cdot x(a) = p \cdot w_{t(a)}$

For every $(n,z) \in N^{\tau} \times Y, t \in \mathbf{T}$, *if* $a \in m\mathbf{T}$ is of type-t:

$$U_t(x,n,z) > u[a;(K,x)] \text{ implies } V(n,z) + p \cdot x > p \cdot w_t \quad (5\text{-}8)$$

Definition 2. *A feasible allocation (K,x) is a competitive quasi-equilibrium for* E^n *if there exists a price vector for private goods* $p \in \Delta$ *and admission prices* $V: N^{\tau} \times Y \to R^T$ such that (i) and (ii), *above, hold and*

(iv) *For every* $(E,y) \in K$ and $a \in m\mathbf{T}$, $V_{t(a)}[n(E),y] + p \cdot x(a) = p \cdot w_{t(a)}$

For every $(n,z) \in N^{\tau} \times Y, t \in \mathbf{T}$, if $a \in m\mathbf{T}$ *is of type*$-t$:

$$U_t(x,n,z) \geq u[a;(K,x)] \text{ implies } V(n,z) + p \cdot x \geq p \cdot w_t \quad (5\text{-}9)$$

The profit-maximization condition (ii) and the consumers' optimization condition ([iii] or [iv]) apply for any $(n,z) \in N^{\tau} \times Y$; that is, for any conceivable club. Most of the literature gives a less demanding definition of equilibrium in which equilibrium choices only need to be preferred among the clubs for which $n \leq n(m\mathbf{T})$; that is, clubs that are feasible in the economy.[7] We argue that the more demanding conditions (ii), (iii), and (iv) required here are more consistent with the basic idea of competitive equilibrium. A basic premise of price-taking is that in making their choices, agents only consider what is feasible in their budget sets, and not what is feasible in the economy. In an ordinary exchange economy, consumers deciding between two bundles x and y in their budget sets do not ask whether the aggregate endowment permits those trades or whether they can find someone with whom to trade. Similarly here: When an agent chooses between two consumption patterns (x,n,z) and (x',n',z'), it only asks whether they are in its budget set, but not whether the economy contains the agents required to compose such clubs, or whether they would join it.

Our theorems point out that, as is known from private goods economies, more conditions are required for a full equilibrium than for a quasi-equilibrium. At a quasi-equilibrium each agent minimizes the cost of achieving its equilibrium

[7] Because the earliest papers on clubs used concepts of "utility-taking" equilibrium rather than "price-taking" equilibrium, their phrasing does not permit making this distinction. Among later papers with price-taking, the less demanding condition is used by Scotchmer (1994), Conley and Wooders (1994), and Wooders (1993), who only require nonpositive profit for coalitions that are subsets of the economy. The more demanding condition is employed by Scotchmer and Wooders (1987a) for the special case of anonymous crowding; and Scotchmer and Wooders (1987b) and Scotchmer (1993, 1994) for the special case of nonanonymous crowding and transferable utility.

utility level. Full equilibrium imposes the stronger requirement that each agent is maximizing utility subject to the budget constraint. The difference lies in whether preferred bundles exist that cost the same as the equilibrium bundle but provide strictly greater utility. In exchange economies, this is ruled out if private-goods prices are strictly positive.

In club economies, we must also rule out another anomaly, concerning the degree to which utility can be transferred between agents. This is discussed more fully in another paper, Gilles and Scotchmer (1997). Here we report that sufficiently large endowments exclude that anomaly. We say that *endowments are large relative to the value of club goods* if, for each t, $U(w_t e^t, 0) > U(0,n,y)$ for all $(n,y) \in \mathbb{N}_+^T \times \mathsf{Y}$, where e^t is the tth unit vector. This condition means that a consumer would rather be a singleton consuming only his private endowment, than a member of a club in which he consumes no private goods. It should be considered as an assumption on the size of private endowments implying that in a core allocation, every consumer consumes a positive amount of private goods.

We are now in the position to restate the theorems as developed in Gilles and Scotchmer (1997):

Theorem 1: *Suppose that the club economy $\mathcal{E}^m$ exhausts blocking opportunities, and that preferences are strictly monotone and continuous.*

a. *Any allocation in the equal-treatment core of $\mathcal{E}^m$ can be supported as a quasi-equilibrium.*

b. *Suppose in addition that endowments are large relative to the value of club goods. Then any allocation in the equal-treatment core of $\mathcal{E}^m$ such that*

$$\sum_{(E,y) \in K} w(E) >> \sum_{(E,y) \in K} c(E,y)$$

can be supported as a competitive equilibrium.

Theorem 2(a), which follows, states that efficient scale is a *necessary* condition such that any allocation in the core can be decentralized as a competitive equilibrium. Here we use conditions (ii) and (iii) of the definition of competitive equilibrium, namely that they hold for all (n,y), and not just for those that are feasible. Under a less demanding definition of equilibrium, where conditions (ii) and (iii) hold only for (n, y) such that $n \leq \eta\ (m\mathbf{T}) \equiv (m, ..., m)$, the core might be decentralizable as a competitive equilibrium even without efficient scale (Scotchmer 1994, Proposition 4.1).

Theorem 2: *Efficient scale is necessary and sufficient for existence of competitive equilibrium.*

a. *If an allocation (K,x) in the equal-treatment core of the club economy E^m can be supported as a competitive equilibrium, then E^m has efficient scale.*

b. *Suppose that preferences are strictly monotone and continuous and that endowments are large relative to the value of club goods. If E^m has efficient scale, then there exists an equal-treatment allocation (K,x) in the core of E^m that achieves $u \in \overline{W}$. Furthermore, if for (K,x) it holds that*

$$\sum_{(E,y) \in K} w(E) >> \sum_{(E,y) \in K} c(E,y) ,$$

then (K,x) can be decentralized as a competitive equilibrium.

The final theorem completes the core equivalence argument.

Theorem 3: *Every competitive equilibrium in a club economy E^m is an equal-treatment core allocation.*

5. Existence

Existence problems are fundamental to club economies. In this section we exposit three reasons why equilibrium might not exist, and mention how these problems have been treated in the literature, if at all. The three problems are:

- The economy might not have efficient scale.
- With multiple private goods, the efficient scale might not be finite even when returns to scale (feasible per capita utilities) are finite and optimal club sizes are bounded; hence, there is no economy for which existence of equilibria is guaranteed.
- There might not exist an efficient allocation that provides identical utility to identical agents. In such a case, because competitive equilibrium treats identical agents identically, competitive equilibrium does not exist.

An early recognition of the scale problem was made by Pauly (1967, 1970), who discussed the optimal scale of a club rather than the optimal scale of the economy. If an "optimal" club must have ten members, then clubs in the core can have only ten members, and for any economy whose size is not a multiple of ten, the core is empty and competitive equilibrium does not exist. In this chapter we have shifted the focus away from the optimal size of a club toward the optimal scale for the economy, for example, $N = 14$ in Example 3. The optimal scale for the economy accounts for the additional complication that with multiple private goods, the optimal trading community might contain many clubs of many sizes. Although this problem is transparent in Example 3, it is less apparent in Section 4, which refers to an abstract exhaustion hypothesis.

Nevertheless, the problem is present, and equilibrium exists at best for multiples of the economy of efficient scale.

The scale problem for club economies has been dealt with in various ways. It is assumed away in the theorems of Bewley (1981) and Ellickson (1979), where there are no crowding externalities in consumption and no scale effects in producing public goods. Much of the literature simply ignores the existence problem – or the "integer problem" – by implicitly assuming a continuum economy in which any departure from a multiple of the optimal scale is negligible; see, for example, Cole and Prescott (1994). Another approach that may work for a finite economy involves defining equilibrium such that a small percentage of consumers is permitted not to optimize (Scotchmer 1993).

The second problem is most easily seen with an example. In Example 3, the optimal scale $N = 14$ was finite. However, suppose we substitute $\sqrt{2}$ for $4/3$ in the utility function. Then per capita utility is maximized when the fraction of people in clubs of size $n = 2$ is $1/(1+\sqrt{2})$, which is irrational. Hence, there is no finite scale that achieves the maximum utility, and equilibrium does not exist in a finite economy of any scale.

Finally, there is the problem that agents with the same preferences and endowments must receive the same utility in competitive equilibrium since they have the same trading opportunities. By equivalence of competitive allocations and core allocations with the equal-treatment property, competitive equilibrium will not exist if there is no core allocation that treats identical agents identically. The problem is well illustrated by the marriage example of Cole and Prescott (1994), as follows.

Suppose there are two types of agents, males and females, such that for fixed consumption of private goods, utility is higher if the agent is married. Suppose there is only one private good, and that females outnumber males. Suppose further that married females who consume 0 private goods receive utility 2, while unmarried people of either sex consuming their entire endowments receive utility 1. An efficient allocation has as many matches as males, and there are some leftover single females. In any efficient allocation the married females receive at least utility 2, while the unmarried females receive utility 1; hence, there is no efficient allocation and no core allocation with the equal-treatment property. Competitive equilibrium does not exist.

Note, however, that the problem of unequal treatment vanishes if individuals' endowments are sufficiently high. Suppose that endowments are large relative to the value of club goods, as defined above. This means that the endowment of females is increased enough so that the utility to a single female of consuming her endowment is greater than the utility of a married female consuming zero private goods. With such a modification, an efficient allocation with equal treatment exists. The core is nonempty and must treat females equally; competitive equilibrium therefore exists.

References

Berglas, E. (1976) "On the Distribution of Tastes and Skills in the Provision of Local Public Goods." *Journal of Public Economics,* 6, 409-23.

Berglas, E. (1981) "On the Theory of Clubs." *American Economic Review,* 66, 116-121.

Berglas, E. and D. Pines (1980) "Clubs as a Case of Competitive Industry with Goods of Variable Quality." *Economics Letters,* 5, 363-66.

Berglas, E. and D. Pines (1981) "Clubs, Local Public Goods, and Transportation Models: A Synthesis." *Journal of Public Economics,* 15, 141-162.

Bewley, T. (1981) "A Critique of Tiebout's Theory of Local Public Expenditures." *Econometrica,* 49, 713-40.

Boadway, R. (1982) "On the Method of Taxation and the Provision of Local Public Goods: Comment." *American Economic Review,* 72, 846-51.

Brueckner, J. (1994) "Tastes, Skills and Local Public Goods." *Journal of Urban Economics,* 35, 201-20.

Buchanan, J. (1965) "An Economic Theory of Clubs." *Economica,* 33, 1-14.

Cole, H. and E. Prescott (1994) "Valuation Equilibrium with Clubs." Federal Reserve Bank of Minneapolis, Research Department, Staff Report No. 174.

Conley, J.P. and M. Wooders (1994) "Equivalence of the Core and Competitive Equilibrium in a Tiebout Economy with Taste Types." University of Illinois, Department of Economics, Working Paper.

Diamantaras, D. and R.P. Gilles (1994) "The Pure Theory of Public Goods: Efficiency, Decentralization and the Core." VPI&SU, Department of Economics, Working Paper E94-01.

Diamantaras, D., R.P. Gilles, and S. Scotchmer (1996) "Decentralization of Pareto Optima in Economies with Public Projects and Nonessential Private Goods." *Economic Theory,* 8, 555-64.

Ellickson, B. (1979) "Competitive Equilibrium with Local Public Goods." *Journal of Economic Theory,* 21, 46-61.

Engl, G. and S. Scotchmer (1996) "The Core and the Hedonic Core: Equivalence and Comparative Statics." *Journal of Mathematical Economics,* 26, 209-48.

Foley, D. (1970) "Lindahl's Solution and the Core of an Economy with Public Goods." *Econometrica,* 38, 66-72.

Gilles, R.P. and S. Scotchmer (1995) "Decentralization in Club Economies with Non-Samuelsonian Local Public Goods." VPI&SU, Department of Economics, Working Paper E95-04.

Gilles, R.P. and S. Scotchmer (1997) "Decentralization in Replicated Club Economies with Multiple Private Goods." *Journal of Economic Theory,* 72, 363-87.

Greenberg, J. (1983) "Local Public Goods with Mobility: Existence and Optimality of a General Equilibrium." *Journal of Economic Theory,* 30, 17-33.

Greenberg, J. and B. Shitovitz (1992) "Consistent Voting Rules for Competitive Local Public Goods Economies." *Journal of Economic Theory,* 46, 223-36

Greenberg, J. and S. Weber (1986) "Strong Tiebout Equilibrium under Restricted Preferences Domain." *Journal of Economic Theory,* 38, 101-17.

Guo, J. (1994) "A Restricted Efficient Equilibrium in a Competitive Local Public Goods Economy." Mimeograph. Rochester: University of Rochester, Department of Economics.

Hahn, K. and R. P. Gilles (1994) "Economies with Multiple Public Projects." VPI&SU, Department of Economics, Working Paper E94-28.

Lindahl, E. (1919) "Positive Losung, die Gerechtigkeit der Besteurung." Lund.

Manning, J. (1993a) "Efficiency in Economies with Jurisdictions and Public Projects." Mimeo. Philadelphia: University of Pennsylvania, Department of Economics.

Manning, J. (1993b) "Local Public Goods: First Best Allocations and Supporting Prices." Mimeo. Philadelphia: University of Pennsylvania, Department of Economics.

Mas-Colell, A. (1980) "Efficiency and Decentralization in the Pure Theory of Public Goods." *Quarterly Journal of Economics,* 94, 625-41.

Mas-Colell, A. and J. Silvestre (1989) "Cost-Share Equilibria: A Lindahlian Approach." *Journal of Economic Theory,* 47, 239-56.

Pauly, M.V. (1967) "Clubs, Commonality and the Core: An Integration of Game Theory and the Theory of Public Goods." *Economica,* 34, 314-24.

Pauly, M.V. (1970) "Cores and Clubs." *Public Choice,* 9, 53-65.

Scotchmer, S. (1993) "On Price-Taking Equilibrium in Club Economies with Non-anonymous Crowding." *Journal of Public Economics* (forthcoming).

Scotchmer, S. (1994) "Concurrence et Biens Publics." *Annales d'Economie et de Statistique,* 33, 158-86, reprinted as "Public Goods and the Invisible Hand." In J. Quigley and E. Smolensky, eds. *Modern Public Finance,* Cambridge: Harvard University Press.

Scotchmer, S. (1996) "On Externality Pricing in Club Economies," *Ricerche Economiche*, 50, 347-66.

Scotchmer, S. and M. Wooders (1987a) "Competitive Equilibrium and the Core in Club Economies with Anonymous Crowding." *Journal of Public Economics,* 34, 159-74.

Scotchmer, S. and M. Wooders (1987b) "Competitive Equilibrium and the Core in Club Economies with Nonanonymous Crowding." Typescript. Berkeley: University of California, Department of Economics.

Tiebout, C.M. (1956) "A Pure Theory of Local Public Goods." *Journal of Political Economy,* 64, 416-24.

Trockel, W. (1984) *Market Demand.* Lecture Notes in Economics and Mathematical Systems 223, Berlin: Springer Verlag.

Wilson, J. D. (1987) "Trade in a Tiebout Economy." *American Economic Review,* 77, 431-41.

Wooders, M.H. (1978) "Equilibria, the Core and Jurisdiction Structures in Economies with a Local Public Good." *Journal of Economic Theory,* 18, 328-48.

Wooders, M.H. (1981) "Correction." *Journal of Economic Theory,* 25, 144-51.

Wooders, M.H. (1989) "A Tiebout Theorem." *Mathematical Social Sciences,* 18, 33-55.

Wooders, M.H. (1993) "Convergence of the Core to Competitive Outcomes in Economies with Public Goods." University of Toronto, Department of Economics, Discussion Paper 93-01.

CHAPTER 6

Agglomerates and incentives: Some modeling problems

Roger Guesnerie

1. Introduction

Increasing returns to size compete with decreasing returns to size in order to determine the agglomeration of economic agents within firms, cities, regions, or nations.

The relative strength of increasing and decreasing returns that trigger or, on the contrary, reduce agglomeration forces has been analyzed in various problems of local economics, such as the theory of clubs and urban economics. In a sense, the present chapter follows such a line of investigation. The problem under consideration involves the comparison of strong increasing returns to size due to the existence of a pure public good, the per capita cost of which is inversely related to the size of the group that consumes it, and a special form of decreasing returns to size, that could be termed decreasing returns to size due to decision making. The analysis concentrates on the questions of optimal or stable size for the groups involved. Depending on the relative strength of the two effects, optimality and/or stability may or may not require complete agglomeration.

Studies in the somewhat traditional framework that is adopted here (see Guesnerie and Oddou [1979, 1981]; Greenberg and Weber [1986], and Westhoff [1975], generally take for granted the limitations of the tax system that is used for the provision of public goods; hence they do not fully discuss the rationale for the decreasing returns to decision making associated with such limitations. In contrast, attention here is put on the informational basis, from the viewpoint of incentives theory, of the taxation limitations and hence on their theoretical significance. The discussion aims at determining whether basic informational constraints necessarily generate the so-called decreasing returns to size in decision making. The ultimate question goes beyond the analysis of the special tax–public good problem under consideration here: Is it the case that informational asymmetries of the adverse selection type do indeed yield the decreasing returns to size that justify splitting of agents when full information would justify agglomeration?

The analysis will proceed as follows: In the second part of the chapter, a second-best taxation problem will be presented. The simple taxation model considers an economy with one public good that has to be financed through a consumption tax. The investigation of agglomeration forces relies on a number of concepts that are presented here; the results obtained in the literature, and reviewed in Guesnerie (1995), are recalled and their economic meaning is discussed.

The third part examines the objections to the modeling options raised in the previous part and discusses whether these objections might affect the theoretical significance of some of those previous results that have a counterintuitive flavor. The first subsection reinterprets the taxation scheme of the second part as a crude incentives device. In particular, a set of assumptions that would justify, at a more basic informational level, the use of such crude incentives devices (and hence the initial modeling options) is stressed. The second subsection draws upon the preceding development in order to reevaluate the concepts of stability used in the initial analysis. The discussion places major emphasis on the statistical information concerning coalitions that influences the stability analysis. It argues that incomplete information, compared to a context of full information, does indeed make the stability analysis more intricate. Furthermore, the incomplete information may itself be historically dependent rather than "generic." Finally, the fact that informational and incentive problems may affect agglomeration forces within a group in a basic way, seems to be a prevalent phenomenon and not an artifact of our multiple taxation model.

2. Agglomeration forces in a simple taxation model

We will first introduce the model (Section 2.1), then present a number of concepts relevant to the analysis (Section 2.2), and finally state and discuss the results of direct significance to our analysis (Section 2.3).

2.1 *A one-dimensional second-best taxation model*

The model we consider has two private goods, consumption and labor. The transactions bundle of household i is denoted z_i. There are m such households. The public good level is denoted y_o'. The utility function of houshold i can be written as a separable form:

$$U_i(z_i, y_o') = u_i(z_i) + v_i(y_o') \qquad (6\text{-}1)$$

The consumption price vector, an element of R^2_+, *is denoted* π, so that the budget constraint faced by agent i is written:

$$\pi . z_i \leq 0 \qquad (6\text{-}2)$$

Utility maximization under the budget constraint determines a standard demand function $d_i(\pi)$, independent of the public good level under the separability assumption.

In a symmetric way, private firms that produce private goods behave competitively and maximize profit, taking the production price vector p, again an element of R^2_+, as given. The competitive supply is denoted $\eta(p)$.

Finally, the public good is produced from labor with a constant returns-to-scale technology that transforms one unit of labor into one unit of public good.

As the reader has noticed, the model under consideration is nothing else than a special version of the second-best taxation model, first studied systematically by Diamond and Mirrlees (1971). Specifically, in this model, the public good is financed through linear taxation so that the consumption and the production price vectors introduced earlier generally differ. The difference, $T = \pi - p$, is the tax vector. However, without loss of generality, the labor commodity may be chosen as an untaxed numeraire; π, p and T can be identified with numbers, the consumption price, the production price, and the tax on the (unique) consumption good, respectively.

Analyses of the motivation and of the properties of this model nourish segments of the incentives and of the second-best literature respectively. A comprehensive theoretical assessment is proposed in Guesnerie (1995) to whom the interested reader is invited to refer. In fact, a number of relevant aspects of that discussion of motivation, as well as some other useful properties, will be reported in the following.

We are now in a position to define a tax equilibrium as a sequence of three numbers p, π, y_0', which satisfy the following equations:

$$\sum_i d_{i1}(\pi) = \eta_1(p) - y_0' \tag{6-3}$$

$$\sum_i d_{i2}(\pi) = \eta_2(p) \tag{6-4}$$

The first equation describes equilibrium on the labor market when the second describes the goods market-clearing. The set of p, π, y_0', that satisfy the two equations, is identified with the set of tax equilibria.

In fact, it is easy to show that the set of tax equilibria can be parametrized by the number π in the sense that there is a one-to-one correspondence between the numbers $\pi \geq \pi^0$ where π^0 is some given positive price, and the tax equilibria just defined. Indeed, the public-good production associated with the tax equilibrium π is:

$$Y(\pi) = \pi\left[\sum_i d_{i2}(\pi)\right] - g\left[\sum_i d_{i2}(\pi)\right] \tag{6-5}$$

where g is the cost function of the private sector.[1]

Considering the projection of the set of tax equilibria on the public-good level and on the planes of consumption price, and production price, respectively, and

[1] The parametrization property is a very general one as already shown in Fuchs and Guesnerie (1983); see also Guesnerie (1995).

The (easy) proof in the special case under consideration as well as the derivation of the just given formula can be found in Guesnerie and Jerison (1991).

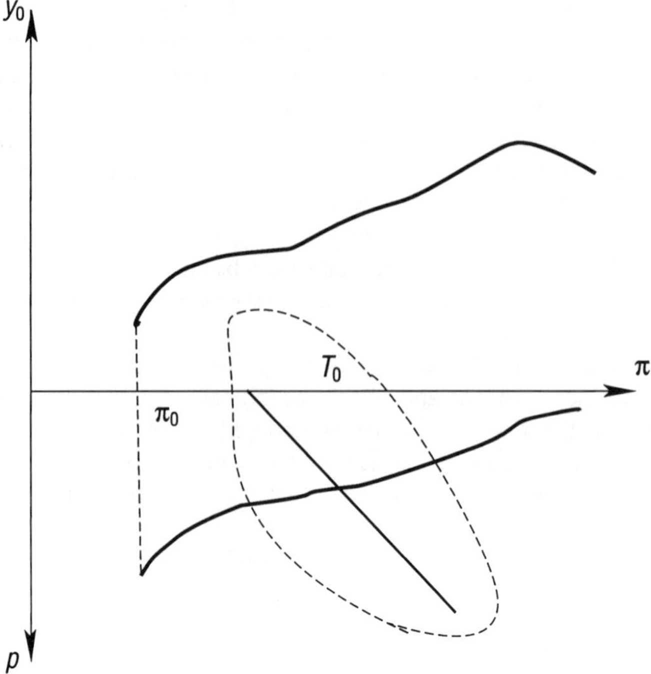

Figure 6-1

visualizing these projections according to the convention of descriptive geometry, yields Fig. 6-1.

Note that Fig. 6-1 visualizes a tax equilibrium associated with the specific tax T_0. Note also that the welfare of every household only depends on what happens in the first orthant, i.e., on the value of π and y_o'. Let us call $V_i\ (\pi, y_0')$ the indirect utility function of household *i*.

The utility frontier of the tax economy under consideration, an economy that consists of the set of all agents, denoted *N*, can be formally described as the frontier of the following set:

$$v(N) = \{(u_1, u_{2,} \dots u_m)/u_i \leq V_i[\pi, Y(\pi)],\ \text{for some}\ \pi \geq \pi_0 \tag{6-6}$$

2.2 *Second-best taxation as a game: Concepts and analysis*

The utility possibility set that has just been introduced depends upon the composition of the "Society" under consideration. In particular, if the "Society" is restricted to the subset *S* of the final agents, even though the same production technologies are available, the feasible utility set is:

$$v(S) = \{(u_1, u_{2,} \dots u_m)/u_i \leq V_i[\pi, Y^S(\pi)],\ \text{for some}\ \pi, \forall\ i \in S\} \tag{6-7}$$

Here, $Y^S(\pi)$ is the quantity of public goods associated with the equilibrium π, in "Society" S, as obtained from the straigthforward transposition of the above formula. The reader will also notice that our notation follows the so-called Shapley convention, according to which the agents not belonging to the "Society" under consideration are given any utility level (from minus infinity to plus infinity); such a notation is particularly convenient for reasons that will become clear below.

Now, if the "Subsociety" (or subset), S is interpreted as a "coalition," the sets of feasible utility $v(S)$ provide a description of a game in characteristic form.

A fcw definitions are in order:

i) The game v is superadditive if:

$$v(S) \cap v(T) \subset v(S \cup T), \forall S, T / S \cap T = \varphi \qquad (6\text{-}8)$$

Superadditivity reflects the standard idea that two disjoint coalitions benefit from uniting.

A structure of coalitions is a partition of N, consisting of $S_1, S_2, \ldots, S_k, \ldots,$ $k \in K$;

This structure is denoted $\Pi = (S_k)_{k \in K}$ and, by definition, is such that:

$$S_i \cap S_j = \varphi, \forall i,j; \text{ and } \cup_{k \in K} S_k = N$$

The set of feasible utilities associated with the partition Π is nothing else (thanks to the Shapley convention!) than:

$$v(\Pi) = \cap_{k \in K} v(S_k)$$

ii) N, the grand coalition, is said to be universally efficient whenever:

$\forall \Pi$, a structure of coalitions, $v(\Pi) \subset v(N)$.

The so-called universal efficiency of the grand coalition is implied by superadditivity; it is a weakened form of superadditivity that applies only to partitions of the grand coalition.

iii) The core utility levels consist of all vectors $u^* = (u_1^*, \ldots, u_m^*)$ such that

$u^* \in v(N)$, and there exists no S and $u' \in v(S)$ such that: $u' \succ u_*$, where $\succ$ designates a component-wise strict inequality.

iv) A stable structure consists of a structure Π and a utility vector $u' \in v(S)$ such that:

$u^* \in v(\Pi)$ and there exists no coalition S and no utility vector u'such that $u' \succ u_*$.

The core is the standard game-theoretical concept: No coalition can object to a core allocation (obtained when the grand coalition forms) by a secession threat beneficial to all its members. The concept of stable structure extends the core concept to the case where the proposed utility vector obtains when a partition, rather than the grand coalition, is formed.[2]

At this stage, it makes sense to supplement the abstract model and definitions by a simplistic story that illustrates them both.

Consider a country with a number of (identical) valleys indexed by the letters of the Greek alphabet. Each valley can accomodate the whole population (there are no congestion effects) but is subject to attack by fierce mosquitos which develop in polluted marshes upstream of the river flowing through it. The public good is the depollution effort, that is well-summarized by an expenditure level (which may be expressed in the number of hours of "efficient" labor). The technology of depollution is the same for each valley. Furthermore, there are as many colonies of mosquitos as there are valleys and these colonies are entirely independent and unconnected so that there are no positive externalities in the depollution effort across valleys. Also, the inconvenience of mosquitos is fairly uniform within a valley, so that the valuation of the public good (depollution) in the utility function does not reflect location but personal sensitivity to the exposure to mosquitos. Finally, public expenditures are financed through a tax on the consumption commodity.

The characteristic function of the game can be fairly simply interpreted: $v(N)$ is the set of utilities attainable if all the agents decide to settle in the same valley when $v(S)$ is the set of utilities accessible to coalition S when this coalition decides to settle in its own valley.

A core utility vector obtains whenever all agents settling in the same valley adopt some well-chosen consumption tax so that no group can be better off by going to another valley and then changing the tax in an adequate manner.

A stable structure obtains when several valleys are occupied and when no group, with members possibly coming from different valleys, can be made better off by a different residence and a different tax law. (Note, in particular, that under the assumption of fixed tax the definition implies that people do not wish to move to another valley: In other words, the stable structure here is compatible with free mobility.)

2.3 *Agglomeration forces in the taxation model: Summary of results and brief discussion*

Are agglomeration forces in the present model sufficient, in some sense, to justify formation of a grand coalition or, in terms of our illustrations will all our agents settle in the same valley?

[2] Indeed, a stable structure coincides with the core of the superadditive cover of the initial game. For a discussion of these relationships, consult Guesnerie and Oddou (1979); for an earlier discussion of similar concepts in the framework of games with transferable utility, see Aumann and Dréze (1975).

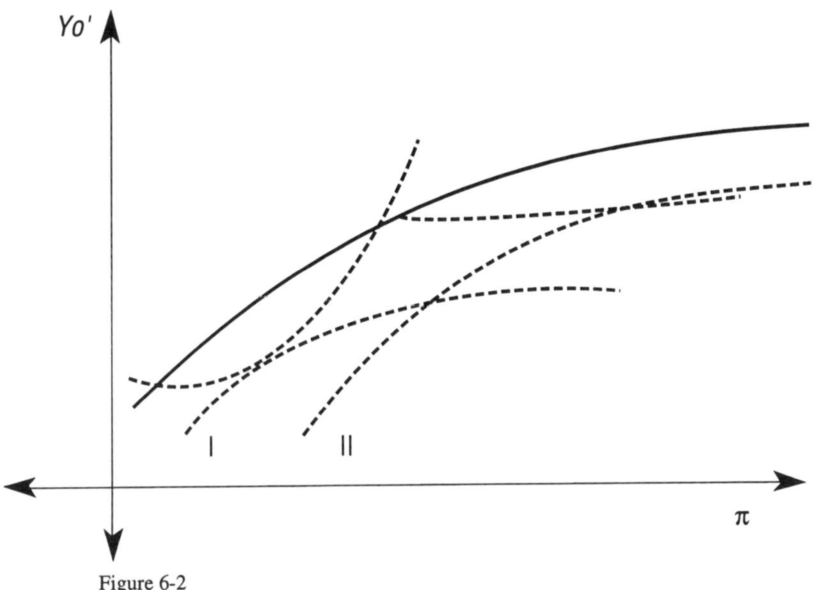

Figure 6-2

Figure 6-2 suggests a negative answer, whatever specific meaning one gives to the question. In the plane of the public-good level, consumption price (that is, the relevant plane for the welfare analysis), the dotted line shows the tax revenue function for a community consisting of (all) the agent(s) of given type 1 (Resp. 2). The same function for the "grand coalition" is the full line which lies, as expected, above both dotted lines. The alternated line features the indifference curve of Agents 1 (Resp. 2), for the maximal utility level obtainable in the homogeneous Community 1 (Resp. 2). Clearly, there is no tax equilibrium in the grand coalition on which agents of Type 1 and 2, coming from their initial homogenous communities, can agree. In the above terminology, the qualitative features of the figure imply first, that the core is empty; second, although this would require additional explanations, that the structure consisting of the two homogeneous communities is stable. The fact that Fig. 6-2 is non-pathological follows from our knowledge of the set of tax equilibria in the model.[3]

This example indicates the fact that the agglomeration forces are overcome by "disagglomeration" forces, a state that is nonpathological. A number of existing results can provide a better insight into the relative strength of the two opposing effects. A summary of such results will now be proposed; the exact statements, as well as the proofs and detailed discussions, can be found in the bibliographical references provided in due course. Four results will be stressed:

[3] In particular, the characterization results found in Guesnerie and Jerison (1991).

i) A first result provides, at least for well-behaved problems of this type, a necessary and sufficient condition for the "universal efficiency" of the grand coalition. This condition asserts the existence of bilateral merging agreements of the following kind: Take a two-partition of the grand coalition; take one "dictator" in each element of the partition; ask them to find a merge agreement beneficial to them both (ignoring the others). Clearly, by definition, they will be able to find such an agreement if the game is superadditive or if the grand coalition is universally efficient. The converse is more surprising, athough true: If such purely bilateral agreements can be found, whatever the partition and whatever the pair of dictators, then the grand coalition is universally efficient.[4]

ii) The fact that the grand coalition is universally efficient justifies its formation from the normative viewpoint, but does not guarantee a priori that it will be stable in a positive sense and, in particular, that it will be immune to the objection of coalitions. Surprisingly, as is the case in the present model, under weak assumptions, universal efficiency implies the nonemptiness of the core.[5]

iii) There exist examples without pathological features in which the game has no stable structure.[6]

iv) A stable structure can be shown to exist, however, when preferences are somewhat restricted in order to meet a Spence-Mirlees-like condition.[7]

At this stage, whose exact statements the interested reader is invited to review in the original contributions, the picture is fairly clear: In spite of the strong increasing returns to size due to the presence of the public good (its per capita cost is inversely proportional to the size of the community), there is still a case, based on efficiency and/or stability arguments, for separation. In terms of our example, the creation of two distinct communities settling in two different valleys, then duplicating instead of adding their efforts to combat mosquitos,

[4] This result – as well as the next one – is proved in Guesnerie (1995) for the present model, following a straightforward adaptation of the original proof of Guesnerie and Oddou (1981) for a very similar context. Greenberg and Weber (1982) proposed calling the property of the existence of bilateral agreements "binary superadditivity." The present necessary and sufficient condition has an n-dimensional equivalent; see Guesnerie and Oddou (1987) for a proof relying on Helly's theorem in convex analysis.

[5] In addition to the references provided in the previous footnote, one should mention the article of Greenberg and Weber (1986) that establishes (stronger) conditions ensuring that the initial Guesnerie-Oddou game is Scarf-balanced. For similar conditions assuring that the present game is Scarf-balanced, see Guesnerie (1995). However, both the direct argument and the indirect one using Scarf-balancedness rely heavily on the one-dimensional aspects of the problem.

[6] Such an example has been produced for the Guesnerie and Oddou game by Weber and Zamir (1985). A minimum of four agents is required.

[7] For a proof that applies to the present taxation model, see Guesnerie (1995).

may be justified. When the grand coalition is not universally efficient, social welfare, at least for some specifications of a social welfare function, does justify splitting. In addition, when the core is empty and there exists a stable structure, the case for the split structure is strong not only on normative but also on positive grounds. Finally, the case where there is both an empty core and no stable structure provides a fuzzy picture in terms of prediction and/or advice.

At this point, it is worthwhile examining the exact theoretical significance of the analysis as well as reviewing a number of objections to our modeling options.

The results stated above go strongly against the intuition of the "first-best" theory of public goods: For example, in the model under scrutiny here,[8] the Lindahl equilibrium would exist and belong to the core of the game in which the possibilities of each coalition are limited only by technological and scarcity constraints; furthermore, the core of such a game is, in some sense, large.[9] However, the "first-best" theory relies on a fiscal system that is more sophisticated than the indirect linear tax system under consideration here. As we shall see later, the issue at stake is informational. If all the information on the preferences of the agents is publicly available and verifiable, then the Lindahl equilibrium can be obtained and provides a stable arrangement (in the sense of the core). Furthermore, no split structure can be stable: Merging, that is, occupying one valley instead of two, creates strong efficiency gains (fighting one source of mosquitos instead of two) that can be transformed into a Pareto-improving change by using appropriate transfers indexed on the actual (and again verifiable) preferences of the agents. On the contrary, in our model, the ensuing gains have to be distributed in a very imperfect way: One post-merge tax rate has to be substituted, for example, for two initial tax rates. Agents may strongly disagree on the post-merge tax law. Such a phenomenon cannot exist in a first–best world where lump sum transfers make possible full compensation of losses. Second-best tax systems, as those considered here, do not permit such a "perfect" compensation. Here is the source of what we called earlier decreasing returns to decision making.

If the phenomenon identified here is clearly of a "second-best" nature, its theoretical significance relies on the validity of the second-best features of the model. As we just argued, our modeling option – using commodity taxes – has to reflect informational constraints: With "perfect" information, "Lindahl" taxes together with lump-sum taxes would provide a more satisfactory solution to the problem of the provision of public goods. Hence, the first question that we have to examine is: Can the modeling options taken here be adequately justified from

[8] In what follows henceforth, most of the comments implicitly refer to an aggregate production set that would be a cone; naturally, the results of the taxation game that has been presented in a different context would not be affected in the modified framework.

[9] A large literature exists on this subject. A survey can be found in Milleron (1976).

more basic informational assumptions? Or, if not, is it the case that the phenomenon stressed is an artifact of an incorrect modeling of the public decision problem?

If we conclude that the modeling options are indeed justified, or at least that they reflect more basic considerations that are plausible in some circumstances, then a second objection will have to be considered: Is the game-theoretical appraisal of the problem satisfactory? To make the question more precise, has the set of concepts mobilized here, the use of which has been well ascertained in games with full information, been appropriately adapted to the context of incomplete information implicit to the present analysis?

The next section attempts to answer these two questions.

3. Assessing the theoretical significance of the results

The first subsection focuses on the examination of the incentives underlying our taxation hypothesis.

3.1 Taxes as incentive devices

Let us consider again the basic economy of Section 2, but with a few modifications. Instead of m agents indexed by $i = 1, \dots m$, with utility functions $u_i(z_i)$, we consider a "mass" of infinitesimally small agents, each having a utility function $u(z,\theta)$ that depends upon an unverifiable characteristic denoted by θ. In order to link this with the previous model, note there are m possible values for these characteristics, $\theta_1, \theta_2, \dots \theta_m$, and a "mass" $1/m$ of the agents has characteristic θ_i. Finally, we complete the link by assuming that

$$d_i(\pi) = d(\pi,\theta_i) \times 1/m \tag{6-9}$$

where d_i is the demand function of agent i in the original model and where $d(.,\theta)$ is the utility-maximizing demand of an agent with characteristic θ, i.e., the solution to the program:

$$\text{Max } u\,(z,\theta),\ \pi.z \leq 0 \tag{6-10}$$

Until now, we have reinterpreted the consumption side of the economy: Our m original agents are now viewed as m groups of equal size – but equality is irrelevant – each group consisting of a large number of identical agents.[10] Indeed, if we keep the production sector as above, the equations determining a tax equilibrium are unchanged.

However, the reinterpretation allows us to face a well-defined incentives problem: Consider a Planner, who controls the production sector but ignores the individual characteristics of the consumers; such a Planner can use incentive devices that simultaneously extract information and allocate goods. Analyzing

[10] The large number ingredient is introduced in order to avoid having agents with monopoly power, i.e., it is a technical ingredient. The information ingredient is, on the contrary, central to the analysis.

the Planner's options is a standard question of the theory of incentives, and one that has attracted much work.[11] Let me mention only a few results that are particularly relevant to our problem.

First, let us consider a mapping, f, that associates a net trade[12] with the announcement of a characteristic and let us say that f defines an Anonymous Revelation Game (ARG) if:

- f is truthful, i.e., $u\,[f(\theta),\theta] \geq u\,[f(\theta'),\theta], \forall \theta, \theta' \in \Theta^2$
- f is admissible, i.e., the sum of individual net trades can be accomodated by the production sector.

An ARG is a special kind of incentives mechanism. It is special in two senses: First, it is, as stated above, truthful, i.e., it induces the agents to truhfully reveal their information. But we know that in many contexts of incentives theory – and especially in the context we have in mind here – such an assumption involves in a sense no restriction (this is the celebrated "revelation" principle). Second, and these are actual restrictions, the game is anonymous in two ways: It is "recipient-anonymous," that is, the allocation does not depend on the "name"[13] of the agent, and it is "influence-anonymous," that is, it depends only (at least implicitly) on the distribution of characteristics of the others.[14]

A first link between the incentives and taxation viewpoints is in the following (straightforward) claim:

Claim 1. Consider any fixed $\pi^* \geq \pi^0$ where π^0 is defined (as in Section 2) and consider $f(\theta) = d\,(\pi^*,\theta)$.

Then f defines an ARG.

Hence, unsurprisingly, a tax system of the kind under consideration here can be viewed in some sense as an incentives device. One can claim that the converse is true, at least under some circumstances: Every incentives mechanism is like a tax system.

Claim 2. Under the following conditions:

- Only the transactions on the consumption good are observable.
- The consumption good can be resold at no cost and without limitation on a "black market."

[11] See for example Hammond (1979), Guesnerie (1981), Dierker and Haller (1990), Mas-Collel and Vives (1993) and Guesnerie (1995), where a more comprehensive bibliography is provided.

[12] Note that for the sake of simplicity, we ignore here the public good dimension of the problem. One may, however, remark that in this large economy, no one agent can have a significant influence on the public good decision (at least for mechanisms that can be termed anonymous).

[13] The name that has not been explicitly introduced here is anything that allows the verification of the agent's identity, given that characteristics are unverifiable.

[14] Indeed, the present ARG is immediately extendable to a broader set of "environments" where the distribution of the characteristics of the agents is variable (see Guesnerie [1995]).

- The characteristic of each agent of the economy has been drawn at random from the same "urn" (with replacement) so that the actual characteristics can be viewed as the realization of a continuum of independently and identically distributed random variables.

Then, there is no "recipient-anonymous" incentives mechanism "better" than mechanisms that are isomorphic to "the affine taxation schemes." "Affine taxation schemes" involve a linear consumption tax together with a uniform (across agents) poll tax.

The claim is voluntarily vague. Both the exact statements and the proof are beyond the scope of this chapter; the intuition, however, is easy to grasp: Because of what J. C. Rochet (1986) called the "taxation principle" (see Guesnerie [1981], Hammond [1979], and Hurwicz [1979]), an incentives mechanism has to be associated with pseudo-budget sets (that depend upon the announced characteristics of the others.) Because of the observability assumption and the no-cost resale of the consumption good, this budget set has to be limited by a line, the slope of which is the same across agents. Because of the stochastic characteristics of the population, the mechanism cannot exploit the correlations between one agent and the rest of the population's characteristics and it is necessarily "influence-anonymous," i.e., dependent only upon the distribution of characteristics of others.

This detailed and more general approach to the comparison between the incentives and the taxation viewpoints is the subject of Chapter 1 of Guesnerie (1995), to which the interested reader is invited to refer. Under the conditions of Claim 2, the most powerful incentive-compatible allocation mechanisms have outcomes that differ from the outcomes of taxation schemes under consideration in Section 2 only in two aspects that are minor, at least for our purpose. First, although a uniform lump-sum transfer might be used, in the present model the public good plays a similar and substitute role. Second, the mechanism might not be "recipient-anonymous." In that case, however, the mechanism would have to be compared (and would indeed compare) to random taxation schemes whose study is ruled out here.

At this stage, two points should be remembered. First, under some assumptions that are strong but theoretically acceptable and empirically not implausible, taxation schemes of the kind under consideration are crude incentive-compatible devices that are, however, not dominated by more sophisticated mechanisms. The results (see Section 1) for the limits to agglomeration forces are theoretically sound. Second, the analysis makes clear that taxation schemes can be viewed as acceptable incentives mechanisms, but only when some informational assumptions hold true; for example, in the absence of correlation between the agents' characteristics as stressed above. In addition, the knowledge of the distribution of characteristics plays a key role in the analysis. This is unsurprising since, for example, the tax equilibria of the model in Section 2.1

could not be defined if the distribution of the agents' characteristics was unknown. However, the informational perspective we have adopted allows us to reassess, hopefully in an improved way, the significance of our stability concepts: the core and the stable structure.

3.2 The significance of the core revisited

Let us return to the game in characteristic form as explicitly defined in the previous section. On the more basic informational grounds just analyzed, the appraisal of the set of feasible utilities by the grand coalition (or by a coalition) requires that this coalition knows the distribution of characteristics of its members in addition to knowing the technology employed. But our definition of the taxation game in characteristic form also assumes that other coalitions have similar knowledge and, in particular, know the distribution of their characteristics. This seems to suggest that the right interpretation of the game is to suppose that each coalition can learn, costlessly and instantaneously, the distribution of its own characteristics. It cannot be true, however, that the distribution of characteristics of each coalition is public information: For example, in an economy with four different types of agents, if the distribution of characteristics of coalitions consisting of agents of a similar type were public information, then the types themselves would be public information and much more powerful mechanisms, such as Lindahl taxes, would be available.

An alternative interpretation, more in line with the standard game-theoretical analysis of incentives problems in a Bayesian setting, is to assume the existence of some initial and generic information on the individuals' characteristics, such as, for example, the fact that the composition of the whole population is generated from some (known) stochastic process. This is basically what we had done when, in Claim 2, above, it was assumed that the agents were drawn at random from some "urn." However, such an alternative interpretation introduces an asymmetry between the grand coalition and other coalitions. In the grand coalition, the distribution of characteristics is known as soon as one knows the law of the stochastic process that generates the population. Indeed, in the case of Claim 2, the distribution is the same as the distribution of the hypothetical urn from which the population is assumed to have been drawn. In other coalitions, the knowledge of the distribution can no longer be derived from the knowledge of the stochastic properties of the whole population. This is to be contrasted with the formulation of the taxation game that assumes that each coalition knows the actual distribution of its characteristics. Hence, the suggested interpretation inspires the first objection to our game-theoretical appraisal of the situation: Coalitions are assumed to know too much.

This objection can be reformulated within the framework of the illustration of the valley(s) with mosquitos. Assume that the whole (large) population has settled in the same valley; in this valley, the distribution of characteristics is appoximately known, so that on theoretical grounds the population can be viewed as drawn from some "urn" (again, let us suppose that the "urn" has only four types). Now, consider a situation in which the consumption tax rate is not in the core (in the sense of the definition of Section 2). Let us suppose, for the sake of simplicity, that the "blocking"coalition consists of all agents, let us say of types 1 and 2, and let us suppose that these agents constitute one-half of the total population. This means that there exists a subset of half the population (here, all agents of types 1 and 2) that can be made better off by going to another valley, setting another tax rate, and using the tax receipts to fight a (different) colony of mosquitos. The question is how such a coalition can be formed.

In principle, when a subset consisting of half of the population meets, they do not have immediate access to the information on the distribution of their characteristics: As argued above, if such information could be immediately inferred from any group, then the individual characteristics could also be inferred and much better incentive devices could be used. Hence in our valley, two somewhat contradictory facts hold true. First, with the non-core tax rate, everybody may know (and thus it may even be "commonly known") the existence of a potential blocking coalition, the size of which is half the population. (In particular, this fact is known from an hypothetical "developer" who could attempt to develop a new settlement.) Second, when half the population meets, they have no reason to a priori discard the (statistically valid) hypothesis according to which they display a distribution of characteristics analogous to the distribution of the whole population! Note that, because of this problem, no coalition consisting of half the population will find an argument to leave the valley – unless the tax rate is too obviously inefficient.

This suggests that at least two different core concepts can be usefully defined for the analysis of the situation.

The first one is the one introduced above. Following Demange and Guesnerie (1995),[15] it could be called the strong (statistical) core since it may be interpreted as implying that the statistical information required for blocking is available when needed (even if such information cannot, for the reasons explained above, be "durable").

The second one might be called the weak (generic) core. It would imply that the blocking coalition have only what we called earlier "generic" information, i.e., in our context, they view their members' characteristics as random variables that reflect the random distribution of characteristics within the whole population.

As noted in the discussion of the valley example, coalitions with generic information have to assume, at least when the number of their members is large

[15] And in the spirit of a similar terminology introduced in a different context by Marquié (1990).

enough to justify the application of the law of large numbers, that they have the same proportion of the different types, or if one prefers, the same composition, as does the grand coalition. Pursuing this idea in a somewhat more general context, Demange and Guesnerie (1995) show that every second-best Pareto-optimal tax schedule belongs to this weak (generic) core.

We believe that both cores have some relevance for the assesment of the stability of our tax or incentives problems. In some sense, the first concept is somewhat too demanding while the second is not demanding enough. This intuition is suggested by the above brief discussion as well as the message conveyed by the analysis of "secession" or "developer" games in Demange and Guesnerie (1996). There, a developer is allowed to challenge the arrangement obtained in the grand coalition by making a proposition that consists of two elements: a "ceiling " on the size of the seceding group, below which secession will not take place; and a tax rate (or more generally, an incentive device) to be implemented after secession. This is a "take it or leave it" offer to which each agent says "yes" or "no," possibly in a two-step process. Secession is successful when the ceiling size is passed. The following illustrates that both solution concepts have some relevance for the analysis of this special "developer" game. When a tax rate does not belong to the weak core, then secession is the common knowledge outcome of the developer game; in other words, secession is a sure outcome of this game. On the contrary, when a tax rate belongs to the strong core, then secession cannot be the outcome of an infinitely iterated process of elimination of weakly dominated strategies; in other words, secession is not, in Guesnerie's (1993) terms, a strongly rational outcome of the game.

3.3 *Stable structures revisited*

The previous subsections have clarified the nature of decreasing returns to size to decision making. They are rooted in basic incentive problems (see Section 3.1) and have analyzed and, in a certain sense, relativized the "disagglomeration forces" they induce (Section 3.2).

The possible existence of a stable structure in the sense defined in Section 2 still remains a challenge to the standard intuition derived from the analysis of public goods problems: It views splitting the grand coalition as a socially desirable and stable outcome of a world with a pure public goods.

The essentials of this phenomenon can be organized about the story previously described in Figure 2.1. In this example, there are two types of agents, 1 and 2. The statistical core is empty; however the structure in which the agents are settled (i.e., in two different valleys) is stable and, as argued above, more satisfactory on welfare grounds.

Four main remarks assist in clarifying the situation:

First, although the statistical core is empty, the so-called weak generic core is nonempty and, according to the above statements, even large. However, whatever the merits of this other core concept[16] this remark does not provide a convincing argument against splitting: The assumption that coalitions only have "generic" information, by weakening the blocking possibilities will in general (if not in this case where there is only one candidate stable structure) increase the size of the core as well as the number of candidate stable structures.

Second, the information that emerges when two valleys are occupied (let us say that agents of type 1 are in valley α when agents of type 2 are in valley β, with different tax rates implemented in each), differ from what was referred to earlier as "generic information": "Generic" information only implies that, let us say, 50 percent of the population belongs to each type. Hence, similar to our definition of what a coalition can do, our definition of the set of feasible utilities accessible to a partition in the taxation game is not innocuous. It assumes that in some sense, a partition of the population yields more information than a grand coalition can retain upon formation.

However, and this will be the third remark, the loss of information when several valleys reunite in the same valley according to our formulation, is somewhat irrelevant to the explanation of the splitting result obtained in the present game. Agents of type 1 are in valley α, agents of type 2 are in valley β; why not put them in the same valley where they would unite their efforts in fighting one (rather than two) colony(ies) of mosquitos? The answer in the context of the model is that the two different tax rates initially implemented cannot be maintained within one valley: The resale possibility prevents the existence of differentiated prices for the consumption good. Hence geographical reunification is incompatible with differential taxation of agents of different origin. In other words, the geographical breakdown, in this case, is a means of *implementing the desirable differentiation that is achievable only through geographical distance.*

This latter remark raises a deeper question, however, and this will be our fourth point. The present model does not incorporate the possibility of using a uniform lump-sum transfer, although this possibility is in line with the basic incentives analysis sketched: If such an enrichment of the tax system was allowed,[17] would it make sense, at least in the present version of the model where each valley has a homogeneous population? That is, is it plausible to merge the inhabitants of the two valleys into a single one where they would be faced with different poll taxes based on their previous geographical location?

[16] In the present context, these merits may not be very great, since the minimal statistical information held by a given coalition may significantly differ from what we earlier called "generic" information: For example, a coalition consisting of 90 percent of agents coming from City 1 will have 90 percent agents of Type 1. The crude character of our illustration makes the story too simplistic; its more complex counterpart indeed relates to our second remark.

[17] More generally, a fully non-linear income tax would have to be envisaged if income were observable.

The answer, again related to the assessment of the validity of possible discrepancies in the information held by the grand coalition versus a partition, is not obvious. On the one hand, previous location is a fact that can be recorded and hence verified. On the other hand, the information acquired from the existence of the partition is non-generic, in the sense used in Section 3. One can argue, for example, that it is a product of history, one related to a more or less accidental formation of the partition, and that it will slowly be forgotten after the conditions of its emergence have disappeared. From such a viewpoint, the creation of a small entity may be a way to generate information that cannot be either created or maintained within a bigger entity. Stories explaining the endogenous creation of information within a group (absent here) might give additional support to such a view.

Clearly, one cannot give a convincing answer to the last question without a more extensive or, if one prefers, historical perspective on our problem. The difficulty behind the concept of stable structure is that its very existence conveys information supplementing generic information, information that may be created permanently or temporarily by successful or unsuccessful secession.[18]

4. Conclusion

Three lessons from the above discussion are recalled.

First, the initial "natural" formulation of the taxation game in its characteristic form clouds a number of delicate informational problems that have to be fully faced for a serious examination of the stability of tax communities in the present context. On the one hand, an analysis of cooperative agreements within a community has to rely upon the utilization of the best available tools; such tools depend upon the information that is verifiable within the community. On the other hand, the way information varies across groups is a key element of the stability analysis.

Second, our taxation game, reinterpreted as an incentives game, relies upon the analysis of information available at the interim phase. The assessment of the information accessible to a subgroup or coalition when it considers blocking, is a rather difficult matter, one that has been confronted in a very different context by Wilson (1978) and Marquié (1990), for example. It has been suggested here that two limiting arguments could be made for blocking: one, based upon the information that is immmediately known, or "commonly known" to the coalition (this is the generic core); the other upon the information that will be learned, at least in the long run, by the coalition (this is the statistical core). Naturally, in

[18] Coming back to our valleys, *our* analysis would be compatible with the following "history": First, there is one valley; then a group secedes; then the offspring, assumed to be similar to their parents, consider reunification; they then reunite using differentiated poll taxes; perhaps later, if similarity of the new offspring to their parents cannot be proven, they will secede again!

the second view, collective arrangements are more fragile and stability more problematic.

Third, the study raises a somewhat novel question concerning the relationship of the solution concepts for games in characteristic form and in the extensive forms of such games. The question is usually approached from the so-called implementation point of view; this is not the viewpoint taken here (although the "developer" game evoked in Section 3.2 may be reminiscent of an implementation game). The specific message conveyed in Section 3.3, which deserves much further investigation, is that beyond the already evoked problems of "interim" assessment, the repartition of information within groups may be difficult to fully evaluate within the characteristic form of the game: Such information will often be a product of history that may be sensitive to the "extensive" succession of events.

References

Aumann, R. and J. Dréze (1975) "Cooperative Game with Coalition Structure." *International Journal of Game Theory,* 3(4), 217-37.

Demange, G. and R. Guesnerie (1996) Interim Design of Core Mechanisms. Mimeo. Paris: Delta.

Diamon, P. A. and J. Mirrlees (1971) "Optimal Taxation and Public Production." *American Economic Review,* 61, 8-27, 261-78.

Dierker, E. and H. Haller (1990) "Tax Systems and Direct Mechanisms in Large Finite Economies." *Journal of Economics,* 52(2), 99-116.

Fuchs, G. and R. Guesnerie (1983) "Structure of Tax Equilibria." *Econometrica,* 51, 403-34.

Greenberg, J. and S. Weber (1982) "The Equivalence between Superadditivity and Balancedness in the Proportional Tax Game." *Economic Letters,* 9, 113-17.

Greenberg, J. and S. Weber (1986) "Strong Tiebout Equilibrium Under Preferences Domain." *Journal of Economic Theory,* 38, 101-10.

Guesnerie, R. (1981) "On Taxation and Incentives: Further Reflections on the Limits to Redistribution." Bonn, Discussion paper.

Guesnerie, R. (1993) "Successes and Failures in Coordinating Expectations." *European Economic Review*, 37, 2-3, 243-68.

Guesnerie, R. (1995) *A Contribution to the Pure Theory of Taxation.* Econometric Society Monographs. New York and London: Cambridge University Press.

Guesnerie, R. and M. Jerison (1991) "Taxation as a Social Choice Problem. The Scope of the Laffer Argument."*Journal of Public Economics*, 44(1), 37-64.

Guesnerie, R. and C. Oddou (1979) "On Economic Games Which Are Not Necessarily Superadditive: Solution Concepts and Application to a Local Public Good Problem with Few Agents." *Economic Letters,* 3, 301-6.

Guesnerie, R. and C. Oddou (1981) "Second-Best Taxation as a Game." *Journal of Economic Theory,* 25, 67-91.

Guesnerie, R. and C. Oddou (1987) "Increasing Returns to Size and Their Limits." *Scandinavian Journal of Economics,* 90(3), 259-73.

Hammond, P. (1979) "Straightforward Incentive Compatibility in Large Eonomies." *Review of Economic Studies,* 46, 263-82.

Hurwicz, L. (1979) "On Allocations Attainable through Nash Equilibria." *Journal of Economic Theory,* 21, 140-65.

Marquié, S. (1991) "Cooperative Game Theory Under Uncertainty." Ph.D. Dissertation. Boston: MIT.

Mas-Colell, A. and X. Vives (1993) "Implementation in Economies with a Continuum of Agents." *Review of Economic Studies,* 60(3), 613-30.

Milleron, J. C. (1972) "Theory of Value with Public Goods: A Survey Article," *Journal of Economic Theory*, 5, 419-77.

Rochet, J. C. (1986) "Le Contrôle des Equations aux Dérivées Partielles Issues de la Théorie des Incitations." *Thèse Université de Paris IX.*

Weber, S. and S. Zamir (1985) "Proportional Taxation: Non-Existence of Stable Structures in an Economy with a Public Good." *Journal of Economic Theory,* 35, 178-85.

Westhoff, F. (1975) "Existence of Equilibria in Economies with a Local Public Good." *Journal of Economic Theory,* 14, 84-112.

Wilson, R. (1978) "Information, Efficiency and the Core of Economy." *Econometrica,* 46, 4, 807-16.

PART III

THE PROVISION OF PUBLIC GOODS

CHAPTER 7

Self-financing of congestible facilities in a growing economy*,**

Richard Arnott and Marvin Kraus

1. Introduction

The basic static *self-financing result* for congestible facilities, following Mohring[1] and Harwitz (1962) and Strotz (1965), is that if the facility exhibits constant long-run average costs, then the revenue from the optimal toll exactly covers the cost of constructing and operating the optimal capacity. More generally, if the user cost function is homogeneous of degree zero in capacity and usage, then the degree of self-financing at the optimum equals the degree of homogeneity of the capacity cost function.[2]

These self-financing results are useful since they indicate, for a first-best environment, the proportion of a congestible facility's capacity costs that should

* The authors would like to thank seminar participants at Australian National University, Boston College, Indiana University, the University of Montreal, the University of Munich, and Princeton University, as well as participants at the Berglas Conference, for helpful discussions. Avinash Dixit, Vesa Kanniainen, Ray Rees, Hans-Werner Sinn, and Oded Hochman, the discussant of the paper at the Berglas Conference, provided particularly insightful comments. Arnott would like to thank the National Science Foundation for financial support under Grant SES-9210319, and the Department of Economics at the University of Melbourne, where the first draft of the paper was written, for its hospitality.

** This paper is dedicated to the memory of Eitan Berglas. Arnott recalls with fondness Eitan Berglas' intellectual enthusiasm and generosity of spirit, which contributed considerably to his enjoyment of visits to the Department of Economics, Tel Aviv University in 1981, 1983, and 1985.

Eitan Berglas, in co-authorship with David Pines, wrote "Clubs, Local Public Goods and Transportation Models: A Synthesis," *Journal of Public Economics*, 15 (1981), 141-62. That paper brought together and synthesized static models of clubs, local public goods, and congestible facilities, and remains one of the most widely-cited papers in each of those literatures. One topic it explored was the relationship between the Henry George Theorem of local public finance and the self-financing result for congestible facilities.

This chapter is a fitting tribute to Eitan Berglas. Not only is it an intellectual descendant of the Berglas-Pines paper, but also the central insight of the Berglas-Pines paper enriches its interpretation – though couched in the language of congestible facilities, the models to be presented can be interpreted as club or local public goods models as well.

1 The result was originally derived by Herbert Mohring.

2 The extent of cost recovery when either pricing or capacity is nonoptimal can be calculated. Cost recovery theorems have stimulated a large number of studies which have attempted to measure the degree of homogeneity of the capacity cost function for various congestible facilities. For example, Kraus (1981) and Keeler and Small (1977) examined the degree of homogeneity of the capacity cost function for highways.

be covered from user fees/tolls and the proportion that should be financed out of general revenues. The results are receiving increased attention in policy circles[3] (especially transportation policy regarding highways, public transit, and airports). In the current fiscal climate, policy makers find the results attractive because they typically justify an increase in cost recovery over current levels. Policy economists, too, find the results attractive – they provide a politically appealing argument in favor of congestion pricing.

The self-financing results were derived and promulgated on the basis of static models. Remarkably, no one seems to have inquired whether they carry over to intertemporal settings.[4] The aim of this paper is to address this oversight. We examine the form of the self-financing results in a variety of intertemporal economic environments – continuous additions to capacity with and without adjustment costs, operating costs, depreciation, and irreversibility – as well as intermittent additions to capacity where the intermittence may be due to fixed costs of capacity additions, increasing returns to the scale of capacity additions, natural discreteness of capacity increments (e.g., airport runways), or the technology of the planning process.

We find, with one exception which is readily explainable, that the self-financing results *do* extend to intertemporal environments *in present value terms*. We also explain why.

Section 2 briefly reviews previous work on the self-financing of congestible facilities in a static environment. Section 3 examines self-financing results in intertemporal environments with *continuous* additions to capacity, and Section 4 treats *intermittent* capacity additions. Section 5 provides a brief *ex post* literature review and Section 6 concludes the discussion.

2. Review of static self-financing results

To set the stage, we provide brief geometric and algebraic derivations of the self-financing results in a static context. To simplify notation, we assume throughout the paper that individuals are identical. The results can be extended to treat heterogeneous users by combining the analysis of this chapter with that of Arnott and Kraus (1995).

[3] For example: Congestion pricing (and political constraints on its implementation) was a central concern of the (Canadian) Royal Commission on National Passenger Transportation (1992); the Transportation Research Board (1994) has recently shown interest in congestion pricing; many countries are considering the feasibility of urban auto congestion pricing as part of the IVHS systems they are experimenting with; and there is increasing discussion of the application of congestion pricing to airports.

[4] Cost recovery in a growing economy has been discussed in the public utilities literature, which is closely related to the literature on congestible facilities. We review the relevant public facilities literature in Section 5. For the moment, suffice it to say that the public utilities literature, while relevant, does not provide as systematic an analysis as we do, and does not consider the central concern of this paper: discounted cost recovery.

Let p denote the price of using the congestible facility (swimming pool, freeway, etc.), which includes both the user cost and any toll; $N(p)$, the demand function; $c(N, K)$, the user cost function ($c_N > 0$, $c_K < 0$, with subscripts denoting partial derivatives) where K is capacity and $c_N > 0$ captures congestion; and $F(K)$ the construction (and operating) cost function. The social surplus associated with the congestible facility equals the consumers' surplus plus toll revenue less construction costs, i.e.:

$$S = \int_p^\infty N(p')dp' + (p - c(N(p), K))N(p) - F(K) \tag{7-1}$$

Maximizing with respect to p and K gives[5]

$$p\colon\ (p - (c + Nc_N))N_p = 0 \tag{7-2a}$$

$$K\colon\ -c_K N - F' = 0 \tag{7-2b}$$

Equation (7-2a) states that price should equal marginal (social) cost, the sum of the user cost plus the marginal congestion externality (Nc_N); Eq. (7-2b) indicates that optimal capacity is such that the marginal benefit of capacity in terms of reduced congestion equals marginal cost.

Now, assume that $\varphi(N, K) \equiv c(N, K)N + F(K)$, the total cost function, is homogeneous of degree h in N and K. Then, by Euler's Theorem,

$$cN + c_N N^2 + c_K KN + F'K = h\varphi \tag{7-3}$$

Multiply Eqs. (7-2a) and (7-2b) by N and K, respectively, add the resulting equations, and substitute Eq. (7-3). This yields

$$R^* = \tau^* N^* = (p^* - c^*)N^* = h\varphi(N^*, K^*) - c^* N^* \tag{7-4}$$

where *'s denote evaluation at the optimum, τ^* is the optimal toll (equal to the marginal congestion externality at the optimum), and R^* is the revenue raised. When $h = 1$, there are constant long-run average costs and $R^* = F(K^*)$.

We illustrate the result graphically in Fig. 7-1 for the case of decreasing long-run average cost. The optimum occurs where the demand curve intersects the long-run marginal cost curve, (N^*, p^*). Associated with this is optimal capacity, K^*, and a corresponding set of short-run cost curves (UC denotes user cost). Toll revenue equals $N^*\tau^* = N^*(\text{SRMC}(N^*, K^*) - UC(N^*, K^*)) = \text{ABFG}$, while construction costs equal total costs less total user costs $= N^*(\text{SRAC}(N^*, K^*) - UC(N^*, K^*)) = \text{ACEG}$.

[5] Throughout the analysis, we ignore second-order conditions. We are interested in the circumstances under which the self-financing results hold at the global optimum; it is of secondary concern whether there are other stationary points where the self-financing results hold as well. In most of our models, corner solutions are not of interest and are ignored. Where they are of interest, notably in the case of irreversible investment, we shall treat them explicitly. Hence, most of our analysis entails a simple examination of the first-order conditions for a series of planning problems.

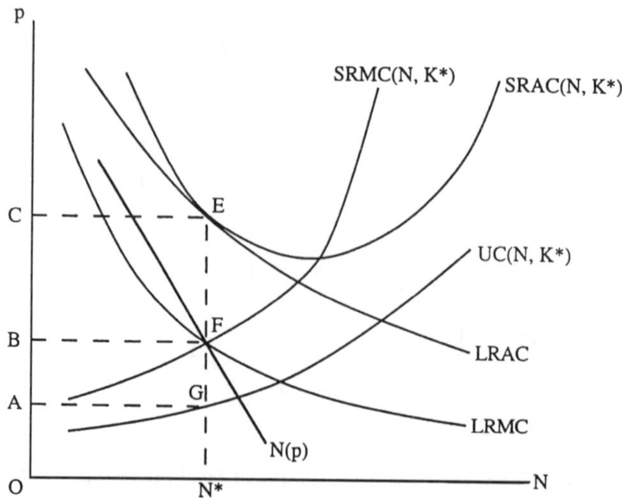

Figure 7-1. The self-financing result with decreasing long-run average cost

In many contexts, it is reasonable to assume that the user cost function is homogeneous of degree zero in N and K. Under this assumption, Eq. (7-4) reduces to

$$R^* = \hat{h}F(K^*) \tag{7-4'}$$

where $\hat{h}$ is the degree of homogeneity of the capacity cost function; this is the result cited in the introduction.

Throughout the rest of the chapter, we assume that the user cost function is homogeneous of degree zero in N and K and that the capacity cost function or its analog is homogeneous of degree one; we then investigate under what circumstances the self-financing result holds in intertemporal environments. More specifically, we ask: Under these assumptions, with first-best pricing and the optimal program of additions to capacity, when will the present value of toll revenues equal the present value of facility construction, operation, and planning costs? In subsequent work, we hope to present a theorem which provides a general answer to this question. This chapter makes a more modest contribution by addressing this question in the context of a series of specific models.

The chapter focuses on exact cost recovery in the first-best optimum because it is the central case of theoretical interest.[6] The analysis can be extended to determine the extent of cost recovery in other circumstances.

[6] One seminar participant (mis-) interpreted our chapter as advocating the market provision of congestible facilities on the grounds that, when the optimum is characterized by exact cost recovery, competition between congestible facilities decentralizes the optimum. We focus on exact cost recovery because it is the central case of theoretical interest, not because we judge constant long-run average costs to be the norm. In fact, many and perhaps most congestible facilities are characterized by decreasing long-run average costs, in which case the optimum cannot be attained through market provision.

3. Continuous additions to capacity

This section investigates a series of models in which the capacity expansion technology is specified such that capacity is adjusted continuously over time. The next section considers an alternative series of models in which the capacity expansion technology is such that capacity is increased intermittently or in increments of fixed size. By proceeding in this manner, we sidestep an important aspect of the problem – whether capacity is added continuously or intermittently should be derived rather than assumed.[7]

3.1 The simplest case

We assume that the economy is continually growing over time; that there are constant costs to adding capacity (no adjustment costs); and that the interest rate, the cost of capital, and the user cost function are fixed over time.[8] We also ignore depreciation, maintenance, and operating costs. Subsequently, we will relax these simplifying assumptions.

We employ the following notation: $p(t)$ – price at time t, $N(p, t)$ – demand at time t, $K(t)$ – capacity at time t, $c(N, K)$ – user cost, $I(t)$ – real investment (= addition to capacity at time t), r – interest rate, ρ – cost of a unit of investment.

Discounted social surplus is

$$S = \int_0^\infty \int_{p(t)}^\infty N(p', t)e^{-rt} dp' dt - \int_0^\infty \rho I(t)e^{-rt} dt - \rho K(0) \\ + \int_0^\infty \{p(t) - c(N(p(t), t), K(t))\} N(p(t), t)e^{-rt} dt \tag{7-5}$$

We assume here and in subsequent models as well that the growth of the economy is such that S is bounded from above. The planner chooses an initial capacity $K(0)$ and investment and price trajectories $I(\cdot)$ and $p(\cdot)$ so as to maximize Eq. (7-5) subject to the state equation $\dot{K}(t) = I(t)$. The associated current-valued Hamiltonian is

$$H = \int_p^\infty N dp' - \rho I + (p - c)N + \varphi I \tag{7-6}$$

where time variables have been dropped to simplify notation, and $\varphi(t)$, the costate variable, is interpreted as the social value of an increment to capacity at time t. The corresponding first-order conditions are:

$$p: \quad (p - (c + Nc_N))N_p = 0 \tag{7-7a}$$

$$I: \quad -\rho + \varphi = 0 \tag{7-7b}$$

[7] We plan to address this issue in subsequent work. The difficulties lie in developing a specification of the capacity expansion technology that is sufficiently general that all the specific models to be treated in this chapter are special cases.

[8] These assumptions, taken together, imply that optimal capacity grows throughout time. Hence, issues associated with irreversibility do not arise.

$$\varphi: \qquad \dot{\varphi} - r\varphi - Nc_K = 0 \tag{7-7c}$$

$$K(0): \qquad -\rho + \varphi(0) = 0 \tag{7-7d}$$

and the infinite-horizon transversality condition[9]

$$\lim_{t\to\infty} \varphi(t)e^{-rt} = 0 \tag{7-7e}$$

Combining Eqs. (7-7a) through (7-7c):

$$\begin{aligned} R^* = \tau^* N^* &= (N^*)^2 c_N^* && \text{(since } \tau^* = N^* c_N^*\text{)} \\ &= -N^* K^* c_K^* && \text{(using homogeneity of degree 0 of } c(\cdot)\text{)} \\ &= (-\dot{\varphi}^* + r\varphi^*)K^* && \text{(using Eq. [7-7c])} \\ R^*(t) &= r\rho K^*(t) && \text{(using Eq. [7-7b])} \end{aligned} \tag{7-8}$$

at each point in time toll revenues equal amortized construction costs. Integration of Eq. (7-8) by parts gives

$$\begin{aligned} \int_0^\infty R^* e^{-rt} dt &= \int_0^\infty r\rho K^* e^{-rt} dt \\ &= -\rho K^* e^{-rt}|_0^\infty + \int_0^\infty \rho I^* e^{-rt} dt \\ &= \rho K^*(0) + \int_0^\infty \rho I^* e^{-rt} dt \quad \text{(see footnote 10)}, \end{aligned} \tag{7-9}$$

[9] It turns out that here and throughout the rest of the chapter, we do not use the infinite-horizon transversality condition. Consequently, in subsequent models, when writing down the first-order conditions we shall omit the infinite-horizon transversality condition.

[10] This step employs the condition $\lim_{t\to\infty} K^*(t)e^{-rt} = 0$. Its derivation goes as follows. From Eq. (7-7b) and Eq. (7-7c), N^*/K^* is the same at all times t. Then from Eq. (7-7a), the optimal toll is constant over time. Thus, at an optimum, discounted toll receipts are given by

$$\tau^* \int_0^\infty N(p^*, t)e^{-rt} dt \tag{7-39}$$

If it were not the case that

$$\lim_{t\to\infty} K^*(t)e^{-rt} = 0, \text{ then } \lim_{t\to\infty} N(p^*, t)e^{-rt} \neq 0$$

and the integral in Eq. (7-39) would diverge, violating our assumption that the objective function is bounded from above. Analogous arguments apply to the analogous step in subsequent models. The proofs will be omitted.

which indicates that discounted toll revenues equal discounted investment expenditures plus the initial cost of capacity – *the self-financing result holds*.

We now provide an explanation of this self-financing result, which suggests its generality. One can regard the planner as producing a continuum of dated products – users or uses of the facility at time t. These outputs are produced employing a continuum of dated inputs – investment at time t and users of the facility at time t. It may seem strange that "users at time t" are both an output and an input, but that is the nature of congestion. Associated with this production function is a cost function. A proportional change in inputs results in the same proportional change in outputs and in costs; construction costs increase proportionally by assumption, and aggregate user costs at t increase proportionally since they are homogeneous of degree one in $N(t)$ and $K(t)$. Since the proportional change in inputs is continuously variable, the multiproduct cost function exhibits constant long-run ray average costs. And it is well known (Baumol, Panzar, and Willig (1982)) that marginal-cost pricing with constant long-run ray average costs results in breakeven operation, which in this context is equivalent to self-financing.

It is sometimes argued that one of the virtues of optimal congestion pricing under constant returns to scale is that if toll revenues are employed to finance additional capacity, optimal capacity is automatically ensured. This argument is typically made for situations where demand is uncertain, which is beyond the scope of the current chapter, but we can check its validity here for the certainty case. The argument has two interpretations. The first is that at each point in time, *investment* should equal toll revenues; the second is that *amortized construction costs* should equal toll revenues. It follows from Eq. (7-8) that the latter interpretation is correct, and not the former. The incorrectness of the former is easily illustrated. Suppose that demand increases, and then remains flat for a period of time. Over that period, toll revenue would be collected although capacity would not be expanded. Thus, the argument that, with optimal congestion pricing under constant returns to scale, investment of toll revenues to finance additional capacity ensures optimal capacity is correct *if construction costs are amortized*, but not otherwise. Thus, an efficient decentralization mechanism (ignoring incentive considerations) for a congestible facility entails instructing the facility operator to congestion price optimally, to borrow to finance capacity expansion, and to expand at that rate for which zero surplus is obtained at each point in time. The planner does not need to know the capacity cost function or the evolution of demand for this decentralization mechanism to work.

The intuition provided above for the self-financing result centered on the constancy of long-run ray average costs. This suggests that the self-financing result should hold for extensions which do not violate this condition. The rest of the section examines this intuition for several extensions.

3.2 Depreciation and maintenance

We now relax some of the simplifying assumptions of the previous subsection's model to incorporate depreciation and maintenance, and to allow for time variation in the interest rate, etc.[11] Time variation is straightforward: Let $\Gamma(t) = \int_0^t r(t')dt'$ be the cumulative interest rate, $\rho(t)$ be the price of a unit of investment, and $c(N, K, t)$ be the user cost function. The treatment of depreciation and maintenance is less straightforward. There might be vintage effects; depreciation might depend on the age-profile of the capital stock; there might be a quality dimension to capital, etc. Rather than treat all these complications, we only consider a simple specification in which

$$\dot{K}(t) = g(K(t), m(t), t) + I(t) \tag{7-10}$$

where $g(\cdot)$ is the depreciation function (with $g_m > 0$ and $g_{mm} < 0$) and $m(t)$ is maintenance (operating expenses at time t).

Discounted social surplus is

$$\begin{aligned} S = & \int_0^\infty \int_{p(t)}^\infty N(p', t)e^{-\Gamma(t)}dp'dt \\ & - \int_0^\infty (\rho(t)I(t) + m(t))e^{-\Gamma(t)}dt - \rho K(0) \\ & + \int_0^\infty \{p(t) - c(N(p(t), t), K(t), t)\}N(p(t), t)e^{-\Gamma(t)}dt \end{aligned} \tag{7-11}$$

The planner chooses an initial capacity $K(0)$ and investment, maintenance and price trajectories $I(\cdot)$, $m(\cdot)$, and $p(\cdot)$ so as to maximize Eq. (7-11) subject to the state Eq. (7-10). The associated current-valued Hamiltonian is

$$H = \int_p^\infty N dp' - \rho I - m + (p - c)N + \varphi(g + I) \tag{7-12}$$

The corresponding first-order conditions are:

$$p\!: \quad (p - (c + Nc_N))N_p = 0 \tag{7-13a}$$

$$I\!: \quad -\rho + \varphi = 0 \tag{7-13b}$$

$$\varphi\!: \quad \dot{\varphi} - r\varphi + \varphi g_K - Nc_K = 0 \tag{7-13c}$$

$$m\!: \quad \varphi g_m - 1 = 0 \tag{7-13d}$$

$$K(0)\!: \quad -\rho + \varphi(0) = 0 \tag{7-13e}$$

[11] With time variation in the interest rate and the price of investment, it may be optimal to disinvest even though the economy is growing. Thus, in this subsection, we assume perfect reversibility of investment. This assumption is relaxed in the next subsection.

Also,

$$
\begin{aligned}
R^* &= \tau^* N^* = (N^*)^2 c_N^* \\
&= -N^* K^* c_K^* \qquad\qquad\qquad\qquad\qquad\qquad \text{(7-14a)} \\
&= -\dot{\rho} K^* + r\rho K^* - \rho g_K^* K^* \quad \text{(using Eqs. [7-13b] and [7-13c]).}
\end{aligned}
$$

If, furthermore, $g(\cdot)$ is homogeneous of degree one in K and m, i.e., the maintenance/depreciation technology exhibits constant returns so that $\rho g_K K = \rho g - \rho g_m m = \rho g - m$ (using Eqs. [7-13b] and [7-13d]), then Eq. (7-14a) reduces to

$$
R^* = -\dot{\rho} K^* + r\rho K^* - \rho g^* + m^* \qquad \text{(7-14b)}
$$

Toll revenues plus capital gains equal the interest cost on capital plus depreciation costs plus maintenance expenditures. Integration of Eq. (7-14b) by parts gives

$$
\begin{aligned}
\int_0^\infty R^* e^{-\Gamma} dt &= -\rho K^* e^{-\Gamma}|_0^\infty + \int_0^\infty \rho(\dot{K}^* e^{-\Gamma} - rK^* e^{-\Gamma}) dt \\
&\quad + \int_0^\infty (r\rho K^* - \rho g^*) e^{-\Gamma} dt + \int_0^\infty m^* e^{-\Gamma} dt \qquad \text{(7-15)} \\
&= \rho K^*(0) + \int_0^\infty \rho I^* e^{-\Gamma} dt + \int_0^\infty m^* e^{-\Gamma} dt
\end{aligned}
$$

Discounted toll revenues equal the initial cost of capacity plus discounted investment and maintenance expenditures; again, the self-financing result holds.

The assumption that the maintenance/depreciation technology exhibits constant returns is crucial in the above derivation. This is consistent with our argument that the essential condition for the self-financing result to hold is that there be constant long-run ray average costs. Accordingly, we conjecture that the self-financing result of this subsection holds for any maintenance/depreciation technology which exhibits constant returns.

In the previous subsection, we discussed a decentralization mechanism that entailed using optimal toll revenues to pay interest on capital costs by the facility operator and showed that capacity expansion will proceed optimally if the operator expands at a rate permitting a zero cash flow surplus. The same decentralization mechanism works here, except that revenues include user fees and capital gains, and costs include debt charges, depreciation, and maintenance/operating costs.

3.3 *Irreversibility and adjustment costs*

We now extend the simplest case of Section 3.1 to treat irreversibility[12] and adjustment costs. Irreversibility is an extreme case of adjustment costs. Even though it is empirically uninteresting (almost all capital equipment has some salvage value), we treat it here because it has been the subject of attention in the literature.

We continue to measure investment in physical terms so that

$$\dot{K}(t) = I(t) \tag{7-16a}$$

We capture adjustment costs via the function

$$Z(I, K), \quad Z_I > 0, Z_{II} > 0 \tag{7-16b}$$

This specification incorporates convex adjustment costs as well as the higher costs of disinvestment than of investment[13] (viz. \$$x$ obtained through disinvestment causes K to fall by more than \$$x$ of investment costs causes K to rise). To allow for the possibility that investment is irreversible, we append the constraint $I(t) \geq 0$, and consider both the situation where it applies and where it does not. We also assume that initial capacity is installed at constant cost.[14]

The corresponding social surplus function is

$$\begin{aligned} S = &\int_0^\infty \int_p^\infty Ne^{-rt} dp' dt - \int_0^\infty Z(I, K)e^{-rt} dt - \rho K(0) \\ &+ \int_0^\infty (p - c)Ne^{-rt} dt \end{aligned} \tag{7-17}$$

The planner maximizes Eq. (7-17) subject to Eq. (7-16a) and the irreversibility constraint, $I(t) \geq 0$. The associated current-valued Hamiltonian is

$$H = \int_p^\infty N dp' - Z(I, K) + (p - c)N + (\varphi + \mu)I \tag{7-18}$$

where μ is the shadow price on the irreversibility constraint. The first-order conditions are:

$$p: \quad (p - (c + Nc_N))N_p = 0 \tag{7-19a}$$

$$I: \quad -Z_I + \varphi + \mu = 0 \tag{7-19b}$$

$$\varphi: \quad \dot{\varphi} - r\varphi - Z_K - Nc_K = 0 \tag{7-19c}$$

$$K(0): \quad -\rho + \varphi(0) = 0 \tag{7-19d}$$

[12] The constraint imposed by irreversibility is binding only if, in its absence, disinvestment is optimal. To allow for this possibility, we drop the assumption made in Section 3.1 that population is continually growing.

[13] Realistically, $Z_I(\cdot)$ would be discontinuous at $I = 0$. To avoid unnecessary complication, we approximate this with a smooth function.

[14] This is consistent with the interpretation of adjustment costs as the costs of adjusting to operating at a different level of capacity but not with the interpretation of adjustment costs as the costs of installing capacity in a hurry.

Thus,

$$R^* = \tau^* N^* = (N^*)^2 c_N^*$$
$$= -N^* K^* c_K^* \qquad (7\text{-}20a)$$
$$= -\dot{\varphi}^* K^* + r\varphi^* K^* + Z_K^* K^* \quad \text{(using Eq. [7-19c])}$$

Now assume that the adjustment cost technology exhibits constant returns in K and I, so that a proportional increase in both results in the same proportional increase in Z. Then $Z_K K = Z - Z_I I$, and Eq. (7-20a) becomes

$$R^* = -\dot{\varphi}^* K^* + r\varphi^* K^* + Z^* - Z_I^* I^*$$
$$= -\dot{\varphi}^* K^* + r\varphi^* K^* + Z^* - (\varphi^* + \mu^*) I^* \quad \text{(using Eq. [7-19b])} \qquad (7\text{-}20b)$$
$$= -\dot{\varphi}^* K^* + r\varphi^* K^* + Z^* - \varphi^* I^* \qquad (\text{since } \mu^* I^* = 0)$$

which states that shadow profits from operating the facility optimally are zero; shadow revenues equal toll revenues plus capital gains plus the shadow profit from investment $(\varphi I - Z)$, while shadow costs equal the opportunity cost of capital. Note that Eq. (7-20b) holds with or without irreversibility.

Integrating Eq. (7-20b) by parts yields

$$\int_0^\infty R^* e^{-rt} dt = -\varphi^* K^* e^{-rt}|_0^\infty + \int_0^\infty (\varphi^* \dot{K}^* - r\varphi^* K^*) e^{-rt} dt$$
$$+ \int_0^\infty (r\varphi^* K^* + Z^* - \varphi^* I^*) e^{-rt} dt \qquad (7\text{-}21)$$
$$= \rho K^*(0) + \int_0^\infty Z^* e^{-rt} dt$$

Thus, again, discounted toll revenues equal discounted investment expenditures plus the cost of initial capacity.

The assumption that the adjustment cost technology exhibits constant returns in I and K is crucial to the self-financing result, which reinforces our earlier argument that exact cost recovery hinges on constant long-run ray average costs. The decentralization procedure with adjustment costs is similar to the decentralization procedures derived earlier, but is complicated by the fact that the facility operator has to continually revalue capital at its shadow price, φ, which presumably would be quoted by the planner.

4. Intermittent capacity additions

When capacity additions are intermittent, it is important to incorporate the cause of intermittence into the model. One possible cause for intermittence is fixed costs in construction and planning; another is technological or planning increasing returns to capacity additions; another is costs to haste in planning; another is natural discreteness to capacity increments such as airport runways; and yet another is a planning cycle. We begin with the simplest case to illustrate basic ideas. We then consider various extensions.

4.1 The simplest case

We suppose that only a single installation of capacity is possible. Perhaps the facility is on a unique site. Once it has been put in place, it cannot be added to, nor can it be demolished with another facility taking its place. A public monument is an example. Let K denote facility size, ρ the cost per unit of facility size, and T construction date. Social surplus is

$$\begin{aligned} S = &\int_T^{\infty}\int_{p(t)}^{\infty} N(p',t)e^{-rt}dp'dt \\ &+ \int_T^{\infty}\{p(t) - c(N(p(t),t),K)\}N(p(t),t)e^{-rt}dt \\ &-\rho K e^{-rT} \end{aligned} \tag{7-22}$$

The first-order conditions are:

$$p(t): \quad e^{-rt}N_p(p - (c + Nc_N)) = 0 \tag{7-23a}$$

$$K: \quad -\int_T^{\infty} Nc_K e^{-rt}dt - \rho e^{-rT} = 0 \tag{7-23b}$$

$$T: \quad \left\{-\int_{p(T)}^{\infty} N(p',T)dp' - ((p-c)N)|_T + r\rho K\right\} e^{-rT} = 0 \tag{7-23c}$$

Equation (7-23a) is familiar. Equation (7-23b) states that capacity should be such that the reduction in the present value of user costs from expanding capacity by one unit equals the cost of the extra unit. Equation (7-23c) is an optimal timing condition. Capacity should be installed when the marginal benefit from postponing installation equals the marginal cost. Here the marginal benefit from postponing installation equals the opportunity cost of construction expenditure, while the marginal cost equals the foregone consumers' surplus plus the foregone toll revenue. We have

$$\begin{aligned} \int_T^{\infty} R^*(t)e^{-rt}dt &= \int_T^{\infty} N^*\tau^* e^{-rt}dt \\ &= \int_T^{\infty} (N^*)^2 c_N^* e^{-rt}dt \\ &= -\int_T^{\infty} N^* K^* c_K^* e^{-rt}dt \\ &= \rho K^* e^{-rT} \quad \text{(using Eq. [7-23b])} \end{aligned} \tag{7-24}$$

Thus, discounted toll revenues equal discounted construction costs – the self-financing result holds. The assumption of constant costs to capital is crucial to the result. Note that Eq. (7-24) was derived without using Eq. (7-23c). Thus, *the self-financing result holds whether or not construction occurs at the optimal time*. The explanation for this result is that with T fixed at any value, there are constant long-run ray average costs.

4.2 Capacity added at fixed time intervals

This case corresponds to a situation where the planner reviews the level of capacity every so often – a planning cycle. Such a policy is commonly pursued with respect to maintenance and upgrading of roads in a network. There are constant costs to investment. Social surplus is

$$\begin{aligned} S = &\sum_{i=1}^{\infty}\int_{T_i}^{T_{i+1}}\int_{p(t)}^{\infty} N(p',t)e^{-rt}dp'dt - \sum_{i=1}^{\infty}\rho I_i e^{-rT_i} \\ &+\sum_{i=1}^{\infty}\int_{T_i}^{T_{i+1}}\{p(t) - c(N(p(t),t),K_i)\}N(p(t),t)e^{-rt}dt \end{aligned} \tag{7-25}$$

where T_i is the fixed time at which the ith capacity increment is added; I_i is the size of the ith capacity increment; and $K_i = \sum_{j=1}^{i} I_j$. After substitution for K_i, the first-order conditions are:

$$p(t):\quad \left[p - \left(c_i + N\frac{\partial c_i}{\partial N}\right)\right] N_p e^{-rt} = 0 \tag{7-26a}$$

$$I_i:\quad -\sum_{j=i}^{\infty}\int_{T_j}^{T_{j+1}}\frac{\partial c_j}{\partial K_j}Ne^{-rt}dt - \rho e^{-rT_i} = 0 \tag{7-26b}$$

Equation (7-26b) states that the size of the ith capacity increment (holding the size of future capacity increments fixed) should be such that the marginal cost equals the discounted marginal benefit, in terms of reduced user costs, from forever increasing capacity by one unit. Subtracting Eq. (7-26b) for I_{i+1} from that for I_i gives

$$\int_{T_i}^{T_{i+1}}\frac{\partial c_i}{\partial K_i}Ne^{-rt}dt + \rho(e^{-rT_i} - e^{-rT_{i+1}}) = 0 \tag{7-27}$$

This corresponds to a perturbation in which capacity is increased by one unit from T_i to T_{i+1}, and held at its original level thereafter. The benefit equals the discounted reduction in user costs over that interval, while the cost equals the increase in discounted construction costs from adding a unit of capacity at T_i rather than at T_{i+1}. Then

$$\begin{aligned} R_i^* &= \int_{T_i}^{T_{i+1}}\tau^* N^* e^{-r(t-T_i)}dt \\ &= \int_{T_i}^{T_{i+1}}\left(N^2\frac{\partial c_i}{\partial N}\right)^* e^{-r(t-T_i)}dt \\ &= \int_{T_i}^{T_{i+1}}\left(-NK_i\frac{\partial c_i}{\partial K_i}\right)^* e^{-r(t-T_i)}dt \\ &= \rho K_i^*(1 - e^{-r(T_{i+1}-T_i)}) \quad \text{(using Eq. [7-27])} \end{aligned} \tag{7-28}$$

where R_i^* is toll revenue obtained between the ith and $(i+1)$st capacity additions, discounted to T_i. Thus, over each construction interval, discounted toll revenues equal discounted amortized construction costs. Summing over intervals yields

$$\begin{aligned}\sum_{i=1}^{\infty} R_i^* e^{-rT_i} &= \sum_{i=2}^{\infty} \rho(K_i^* - K_{i-1}^*)e^{-rT_i} + \rho I_1^* e^{-rT_1} \\ &= \sum_{i=1}^{\infty} \rho I_i^* e^{-rT_i} \quad (\text{since } I_i^* = K_i^* - K_{i-1}^*, \\ &\qquad\qquad\qquad\qquad i = 2, \ldots, \infty)\end{aligned} \tag{7-29}$$

that is, the self-financing result holds.

In the previous section, with continuous additions to capacity, we considered an efficient decentralization mechanism for capacity expansion. At every point in time, the facility operator collects the revenue from the optimal toll and expands capacity at such a rate that the toll revenues exactly cover amortized capacity costs. We now consider how this decentralization procedure needs to be modified when capacity additions are intermittent.

The answer is suggested by Eq. (7-28). If capacity expansions are of optimal size, over each construction interval, discounted optimal toll revenues equal discounted amortized construction costs. Hence, if the facility operator were instructed to finance capacity expansion through debt and were to retain toll revenues, the operator would achieve a zero balance at the *end* of a construction interval. Furthermore, if demand grows continually, the cumulative balance is negative throughout each interval, except at the endpoints. Under this condition, a capacity expansion should occur when and only when the cumulative balance rises to zero. The optimal size of the expansion depends on the future time path of demand, about which the planner, but not the operator, is assumed to be informed. Thus, an efficient decentralization procedure entails the planner saying to the operator: You collect the toll revenue and pay the amortized costs of capacity. When your cumulative balance rises to zero, call me, and I shall decide the size of the next capacity expansion. This decentralization mechanism works but, as the planner is assumed to have perfect information, investment can just as well be controlled directly. The analogous mechanism under uncertainty is, however, nontrivial. Under uncertainty, it is reasonable to assume that the planner, but not the operator, knows the stochastic process generating demand while the operator, but not the planner, observes the realization of demand. Then the planner could choose the size of capacity expansion that would, on average, be appropriate for, say, five years. The next capacity expansion would be initiated when the operator's cumulative surplus rises to zero.

In the context of airport financing, the argument has been made that with constant long-run average costs, investment of toll revenues (net of costs) in capacity expansion ensures optimal capacity. The argument is at best imprecise. One possible interpretation of this statement is that the facility is financed on a cash-as-you-go basis, and that the surplus is channeled to finance capacity expansion. This is obviously incorrect. For one thing, the initial capacity increment cannot be financed on a cash-as-you-go basis; for another, the rule would result in capacity expansion when demand is stationary. A second interpretation is that capacity increments are financed by debt, and that expansions should occur when a sufficient surplus has accumulated. This is too conservative a policy. A capacity expansion should occur whenever the cumulative surplus rises to zero.

4.3 *Capacity replacement*

Suppose that there is only one site at which a bridge can be placed across a river. Periodically, the bridge is torn down and a new bridge with a larger capacity is put up in its place. Social surplus is

$$\begin{aligned} S = & \sum_{i=1}^{\infty} \int_{T_i}^{T_{i+1}} \int_{p(t)}^{\infty} N(p', t)e^{-rt} dp' dt - \sum_{i=1}^{\infty} \rho K_i e^{-rT_i} \\ & + \sum_{i=1}^{\infty} \int_{T_i}^{T_{i+1}} \{p(t) - c(N(p(t), t), K_i)\} N(p(t), t)e^{-rt} dt \end{aligned} \tag{7-30}$$

The timing of capacity replacements can be either endogenous or exogenous. When the timing is exogenous, the first-order conditions are:

$$p(t): \quad \left[p - \left(c_i + N\frac{\partial c_i}{\partial N}\right)\right] N_p e^{-rt} = 0 \tag{7-31a}$$

$$K_i: \quad -\int_{T_i}^{T_{i+1}} \frac{\partial c_i}{\partial K_i} N e^{-rt} dt - \rho e^{-rT_i} = 0 \tag{7-31b}$$

Then

$$\begin{aligned} R_i^* &= \int_{T_i}^{T_{i+1}} \tau^* N^* e^{-r(t-T_i)} dt \\ &= \int_{T_i}^{T_{i+1}} \left(N^2 \frac{\partial c_i}{\partial N}\right)^* e^{-r(t-T_i)} dt \\ &= \rho K_i^* \text{ (using Eq. [7-31b] and homogeneity of degree 0 of } c(\cdot)) \end{aligned} \tag{7-32}$$

where R_i^* is the toll revenue obtained from the ith facility, discounted to the time of its construction. Thus, the self-financing result holds for each of the successive facilities. The result hinges on constant costs to capacity, which ensures constant long-run ray average costs. There is a nice decentralization rule here – replace when the facility has paid for itself. However, it would have to be the planner, rather than the facility operator, who decides on the size of each capacity replacement.

4.4 A more general capacity expansion technology

A commentator on the chapter argued that our analysis of the situations considered in the previous subsections was conceptually flawed because, he claimed, those situations could arise only if there were decreasing costs with respect to the size of capacity additions, which our analysis did not consider. We disagree. With respect to one-shot capacity installations, for example, one can conceive of a putty-diamond technology with constant costs to putting the putty in place; but once the putty has set, it is immutable and indestructible. We concede that, in reality, when capacity is added intermittently, the technology is almost always characterized by decreasing costs with respect to the scale of capacity additions. But our intention in this paper is to examine whether the self-financing result holds for a wide range of constant cost technologies. For any constant cost technology for which the result holds, less than full cost recovery will obtain for the corresponding decreasing cost technology.

We now provide a more general treatment of the capacity expansion technology, one that admits fixed costs and increasing returns to the size of capacity additions. We are interested in determining whether there are any specifications of the technology which simultaneously give rise to intermittent capacity as well as result in self-financing.

We define I_i and K_i as before, such that $K_i = \sum_{j=1}^{i} I_j$. We describe the technology via the cost function for a capacity addition, $A_i = A(I_i, K_i, T_i - T_{i-1})$, $\partial A_i/\partial I_i > 0$, $\partial A_i/\partial K_i \gtreqless 0$, $\partial A_i/\partial(T_i - T_{i-1}) \leq 0$. The idea behind the dependence of costs on $T_i - T_{i-1}$ is that costs are higher if planning for the capacity addition is rushed; thus, $\partial A_i/\partial(T_i - T_{i-1}) \leq 0$ incorporates the costs of haste.

Social surplus is

$$\begin{aligned} S = &\sum_{i=1}^{\infty} \int_{T_i}^{T_{i+1}} \int_{p(t)}^{\infty} N(p', t)e^{-rt} dp' dt \\ &- \sum_{i=1}^{\infty} A(I_i, K_i, T_i - T_{i-1})e^{-rT_i} \\ &+ \sum_{i=1}^{\infty} \int_{T_i}^{T_{i+1}} \{p(t) - c(N(p(t), t), K_i)\} N(p(t), t)e^{-rt} dt \end{aligned} \tag{7-33}$$

Where φ_i is the current-valued Lagrange multiplier on the constraint

$$\sum_{j=1}^{i} I_j - K_i \leq 0$$

the first-order conditions are:

$$p(t): \quad \left[p - \left(c_i + N\frac{\partial c_i}{\partial N}\right)\right] N_p e^{-rt} = 0 \tag{7-34a}$$

$$I_i: \quad -\frac{\partial A_i}{\partial I_i}e^{-rT_i} + \sum_{j=i}^{\infty} \varphi_j e^{-rT_j} = 0 \tag{7-34b}$$

$$K_i: \quad -\int_{T_i}^{T_{i+1}} \frac{\partial c_i}{\partial K_i} N e^{-rt} dt - \frac{\partial A_i}{\partial K_i} e^{-rT_i} - \varphi_i e^{-rT_i} = 0 \tag{7-34c}$$

Then

$$\begin{aligned} R_i^* &= \int_{T_i}^{T_{i+1}} \tau^* N^* e^{-r(t-T_i)} dt \\ &= \int_{T_i}^{T_{i+1}} \left(-NK_i \frac{\partial c_i}{\partial K_i}\right)^* e^{-r(t-T_i)} dt \\ &= \left(\frac{\partial A_i}{\partial K_i} K_i + \varphi_i K_i\right)^* \quad \text{(using Eq. [7-34c])} \qquad (7\text{-}35) \\ &= \left[\frac{\partial A_i}{\partial K_i} K_i + \left(\frac{\partial A_i}{\partial I_i} - \frac{\partial A_{i+1}}{\partial I_{i+1}} e^{-r(T_{i+1}-T_i)}\right) K_i\right]^* \end{aligned}$$

(subtracting Eq. [7-34b] for I_{i+1} from Eq. [7-34b] for I_i).

Equation (7-35) has the following interpretation. Suppose that an extra unit of investment is added to the ith capacity expansion, and a unit of investment subtracted from the $(i+1)$st capacity expansion. This perturbation results in an increase in K_i by one unit, but no increase in capacity in other intervals. The cost of this perturbation is therefore the shadow marginal cost of capital for the period between the ith and $(i+1)$st capacity additions, and equals

$$\frac{\partial A_i}{\partial K_i} + \frac{\partial A_i}{\partial I_i} - \frac{\partial A_{i+1}}{\partial I_{i+1}} e^{-r(T_{i+1}-T_i)}$$

Thus, Eq. (7-35) states that at the optimum, the discounted toll revenue received over a construction interval equals the quantity of capital employed over that interval times the marginal cost of capital over that interval.

From Eq. (7-35),

$$\sum_{i=1}^{\infty} R_i^* e^{-rT_i} = \sum_{i=1}^{\infty} \left(\frac{\partial A_i}{\partial K_i} K_i + \frac{\partial A_i}{\partial I_i} I_i\right) e^{-rT_i} \tag{7-36}$$

Thus, the self-financing result holds if $A(\cdot)$ is homogeneous of degree one in I and K.

There are two interesting situations in which this occurs with intermittent capacity additions being optimal. In the first, there are constant unit costs to the size of each capacity addition, with this constant being independent of the size of the facility but depending negatively on $T_i - T_{i-1}$. Thus, the intermittence of capacity additions can occur even with constant costs to the size of capacity additions if there are costs of haste. The second situation of self-financing occurs when there are decreasing costs with respect to I_i, but increasing costs with respect to K_i, such that an equiproportional increase in I_i and K_i results in an equiproportional increase in capacity expansion costs.[15] Again, the self-financing result holds with constant long-run ray average costs, but not generally otherwise.

A decentralization procedure here is as follows: The planner charges the facility operator a lump sum (equal to the right-hand-side of Eq. [7-35]) at the time each increment of capacity is added, and instructs the operator to charge the optimal toll. When the lump sum is paid off, the next capacity expansion should occur, its size being determined by the planner.

4.5 *Fixed increments to capacity*

In a recent paper, Oum and Zhang (1990) considered the situation where capacity must be added in fixed increments. Their example is airport runways. The practical interest of this case is moot because with a fixed number of airport runways, capacity can be altered by varying the quality of runway maintenance, traffic control, etc. Nevertheless, the situation is of theoretical interest and of practical importance when only one or two runways exist.

The social surplus function is

$$\begin{aligned} S = & \sum_{i=1}^{\infty} \int_{T_i}^{T_{i+1}} \int_{p(t)}^{\infty} N(p', t) e^{-rt} dp' dt - \sum_{i=1}^{\infty} \bar{k} e^{-rT_i} \\ & + \sum_{i=1}^{\infty} \int_{T_i}^{T_{i+1}} \{p(t) - c(N(p(t), t), i\bar{I})\} N(p(t), t) e^{-rt} dt \end{aligned} \tag{7-37}$$

where $\bar{I}$ is the fixed size of each capacity increment, and $\bar{k}$ the fixed cost. The planner chooses $p(t)$ and T_i. The first-order conditions are:

$$p(t): \quad \left[p - \left(c_i + N\frac{\partial c_i}{\partial N}\right)\right] N_p e^{-rt} = 0 \tag{7-38a}$$

$$\begin{aligned} T_i: \quad & \left\{ - \int_{p(T_i^+)}^{p(T_i^-)} N(p', T_i) dp' - [(p - c_i)N]|_{T_i^+} \right. \\ & \left. + [(p - c_{i-1})N]|_{T_i^-} + r\bar{k} \right\} e^{-rT_i} = 0 \end{aligned} \tag{7-38b}$$

[15] In most cases, $A(\bullet)$ is not homogeneous of degree one in I and K. Typically, there are decreasing average costs for each capacity addition due to economies of scale in both planning and construction, which are little affected by the size of existing capacity. If, for example, $A(\bullet)$ is homogeneous of degree .8 in I and K, then with optimal tolling and with capacity additions optimal conditional on timing (which need not be optimal), the discounted cost-recovery ratio is .8.

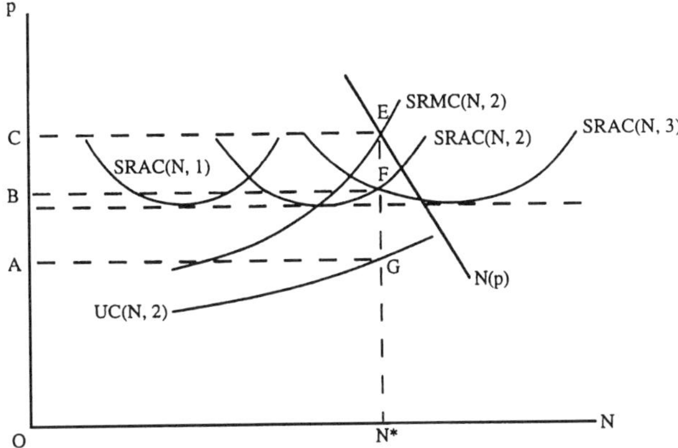

Figure 7-2. Cost curves with fixed capacity increments

where $p(T_i^-) = \infty$ for $i = 1$, and T_i^- and T_i^+ denote just before and just after addition of the ith capacity increment. Equation (7-38b) states that the fixed increment to capacity should be added when the marginal benefit from postponing the capacity addition for a unit of time equals the marginal cost. The marginal benefit equals the interest on the delayed construction costs plus the toll revenue if construction is delayed. The marginal cost equals the toll revenue if construction is undertaken plus the gain in consumers' surplus. Note that this is a local condition: It ignores how demand will grow.

Oum and Zhang pointed out that the self-financing result does *not* generally hold in this situation. They provided the following intuition. Consider an alternative demand path which coincides with $N(p, t)$ at $T_1, \ldots, T_\infty$, but is lower at all points in time between T_1 and T_2, etc. Since this alternative demand path satisfies Eq. (7-38b), capacity additions occur at the same times (assuming that the second-order conditions are satisfied) as with the original demand path. Hence, discounted capacity construction costs are the same for both demand paths. But, because demand is almost everywhere higher with the original demand path, discounted toll revenues are higher. Thus, the self-financing result cannot hold for both cases.

Some intuition concerning this negative result can be gleaned from considering the analogous static problem, displayed in Figure 7-2. Even though the convex hull of the short-run average cost curves is flat, the long-run average cost curve is scalloped-shaped. Since the degree of self-financing depends on the *local* degree of returns to scale, the self-financing result will not hold generally. As drawn, the optimum occurs with two units of capacity, at the point of intersection of the corresponding short-run marginal cost curve and the demand curve. Toll revenue is ACEG, while construction costs are ABFG.

Figure 7-2 can also be interpreted as a snapshot of an intertemporal equilibrium, where the short-run average cost curves are defined to include amortized construction costs. Over time, in a growing economy, the demand curve moves to the right. Losses will be incurred for a period of time after the addition of each capacity increment, followed by a period of profits prior to the addition of the next increment. Between additions of successive capacity increments, the present value of profits will depend on the pattern of demand growth, the elasticity of demand, the congestion technology, and the interest rate.

We have argued that the self-financing result holds when long-run ray average costs are constant, and not otherwise generally. Here, long-run ray average costs are scalloped-shaped, not constant. Thus, the Oum-Zhang result is consistent with our argument.

We have tried, with only partial success, to determine the extent of cost recovery (in present value terms) with fixed capacity increments.[16] We have constructed examples with more-than-full and others with less-than-full cost recovery, and also obtained bounds on the extent of cost recovery for special cases. But general results have eluded us.

5. Literature review

This is an appropriate point at which to review the literature. To our knowledge, there are no papers that examine the self-financing of *congestible* facilities in a growing economy. However, there is a close relationship between the theory of public utilities (e.g., electricity networks and water distribution systems) and the theory of congestible facilities; the self-financing of public facilities in a growing economy *has* been studied. Congestible facilities differ from public facilities in that increased usage results in higher user costs in the former, and in higher production costs in the latter. In the first-best environment that we study, the two classes of problems are isomorphic.[17] To illustrate, consider the

[16] A casual reading of Oum and Zhang might give the false impression that fixity of capacity increments typically results in more-than-full cost recovery.

Oum and Zhang calculated what might be termed *financial* cost recovery between capacity additions, viz. they calculated the ratio of the toll revenue between T_i^* and T_{i+1}^* discounted to T_i^* to the *cost of the capacity increment at* T_i^*. This differs from *economic* cost recovery between capacity additions, the ratio of the toll revenue between T_i^* and T_{i+1}^* discounted to T_i^* to the discounted *amortized costs of capacity over the period.*

Discounted financial costs are, of course, the same as discounted amortized or economic costs. However, their timing is different. Since the financial costs associated with a capacity increment are incurred at the time of construction while the economic costs occur later, financial costs come earlier than economic costs.

Oum and Zhang gave the financial cost-recovery ratio for the second, third, and fourth (p. 369) increments, but not for the first. Since the financial cost-recovery ratio for the first increment is likely to be considerably lower than for subsequent increments, their results are misleading.

[17] We have shown that there are differences between the two classes of problems in second-best environments. See Arnott and Kraus (1993).

simplest problem with continuous additions to capacity we analyzed. Social surplus was

$$S = \int_0^\infty \int_{p(t)}^\infty N(p', t)e^{-rt} dp' dt - \int_0^\infty \rho I(t)e^{-rt} dt - \rho K(0)$$
$$+ \int_0^\infty \{p(t) - c(N(p(t), t), K(t))\} N(p(t), t)e^{-rt} dt$$

The first term is discounted consumer surplus, the second and third discounted investment expenditures, and the fourth discounted toll revenues. Simple rearrangement gives

$$S = \int_0^\infty \left\{ \int_{p(t)}^\infty N(p', t)dp' + p(t)N(p(t), t) \right\} e^{-rt} dt$$
$$- \int_0^\infty \rho I(t)e^{-rt} dt - \rho K(0) - \int_0^\infty C(N(p(t), t), K(t))e^{-rt} dt$$

where $C(N(p(t), t), K(t)) \equiv c(N(p(t), t), K(t))N(t)$. The first term is gross discounted social surplus, the second and third discounted investment expenditures, and the fourth can be interpreted as discounted production costs with output $N(p(t), t)$ at time t. With this rearrangement, we have the isomorphic public utilities problem.

We have not uncovered any references which deal with the self-financing of public utilities in a growing economy when there are continuous additions to capacity. Starrett (1978), however, seemed to consider this problem as solved. Presumably, he was drawing on the result that with constant returns to scale, the cost-recovery theorem holds with dated commodities. Instead, the literature has focused on the optimal management of public utilities in a growing economy when additions to capacity are "lumpy."[18]

The first modern paper on this topic appears to be that of Starrett (1978). The quality of the argument suggests that Starrett had a deep understanding of the problem. Yet he made no mention of discounted cost recovery, and focused instead on the question: If demand growth is exponential and if there are decreasing costs to capacity additions of variable size, will the steady-state revenues generated over an investment cycle be sufficient to finance the *next* capacity increment? His answer is: Normally, yes. He acknowledges that losses will be made over the start-up period, but does not incorporate them into his analysis. It appears his interest was in whether a public utility can be expected to pay for itself (in financial terms) after the government incurs the start-up

[18] The term "lumpy investment" has been used to refer to situations where the size of capacity increments is fixed (see Oum and Zhang [1990] and Rees [1986]) and where the size of capacity increments is a choice variable (see Starrett [1978] and Woroch [1987]). To avoid this ambiguity, we have not used the term.

costs. Woroch (1987) based his work on Starrett's paper, and investigated those circumstances in which revenues generated over an investment cycle were insufficient to finance the next capacity increment.

Rees (1986) examined the case of fixed capacity increments. In his review of the literature, he noted that "(discounted financial) profit (between capacity increments) may or may not be positive, even on the assumption of constant returns to scale – this depends on the precise growth path of demand," (p. 197). Thus, to some extent at least, he anticipated Oum and Zhang (1990). But the focus of his paper is on second-best issues – profit constraints, and pricing constraints to prevent "excessively" high prices immediately prior to capacity expansions.

Surprisingly, therefore, it appears that there has been no systematic analysis of discounted cost recovery in the public utilities literature. Our chapter therefore contributes not only to the literature on congestible facilities, but also to that on public utilities.

6. Conclusion

In this chapter, we investigated the conditions for first-best self-financing of congestible facilities in a variety of intertemporal economic environments. The planner can be viewed as producing a continuum of dated commodities – uses of the facility at different points in time. Associated with this production process is a cost function. If this cost function exhibits constant long-run ray average costs, efficient pricing results in the facility breaking even. This translates into self-financing/cost recovery – with optimal capacity management, the discounted revenue from the optimal toll covers the discounted costs of construction and operating expenses.

We examined the implications of this general result under a wide range of technological specifications. First, we considered specifications which lead to continuous additions to capacity. We showed, for example, that with constant costs to capacity, and depreciation and maintenance, the self-financing result holds if the depreciation function exhibits constant returns to scale (to capacity and investment). If, alternatively, there are convex adjustment costs, cost recovery continues to hold as long as investment costs exhibit constant returns to scale. We then considered a variety of technological specifications which result in intermittent additions to capacity. One surprising implication of the sufficiency of constant long-run ray average costs for self-financing is that the timing of capacity additions need not be optimal because such nonoptimality does not upset the constancy of long-run ray average costs; however, the size of capacity additions must be optimal, conditional on the timing. We examined three exogenous sources of intermittence – a single facility size decision with no additions or replacements, a planning cycle, and a sequence of facility replacements – and then treated a more general specification of capacity addition costs. For the last model, we identified two situations where intermittent capacity additions are consistent with cost recovery. In the first, where constant costs to the scale of capacity additions and costs to haste are involved, unit investment costs fall the longer the period of time elapsed since the last capacity addition; in the second, decreasing costs to investment are offset by increasing costs to capacity.

We also considered the case of fixed increments to capacity, such as airport runways. We showed that self-financing generally does not occur, even when the costs of successive increments to capacity are the same. The reason is that this technology does not exhibit constant long-run ray average costs – the convex hull is flat, but the cost curve itself is scalloped-shaped. Intuitively, due to the discreteness of capacity increments, an incremental change in scale does not induce an equiproportional change in discounted costs.

While we focused on identifying situations in which full discounted cost recovery will occur, our analytics can be applied to determine the extent of first-best discounted cost recovery for congestible facilities under a wide range of technologies. Our analysis can also be extended to treat a variety of second-best situations – to solve for future discounted cost recovery given that current capacity is nonoptimal, and to determine second-best cost recovery under alternative pricing and investment constraints.[19]

We paid some attention to decentralization rules. With continuous additions to capacity, we found that capacity should be expanded at that rate at which toll revenues continually cover amortized capacity costs; with intermittent additions to capacity, the scope for decentralization appears more limited.

We hope, in the near future, to extend our analysis to stochastic dynamic environments. We hypothesize that under conditions of uncertainty, expected discounted cost recovery will occur in similar situations to the cost recovery described in this chapter. The intuition is that if prices are fully flexible, introducing uncertainty will augment the commodity space – facility uses will be both dated and state-contingent – but, with constant returns technologies, long-run ray average costs will remain constant. We also plan to investigate decentralization rules, which are intrinsically more interesting when uncertainty is present.

There is now a sizeable literature that estimates static returns to scale for public utilities and congestible facilities. Our analysis demonstrates that discounted cost recovery in growing economies depends not only on static returns to scale but also on the technological characteristics of facility maintenance and

[19] Some work along these lines has already been done in the public utilities literature. For example, Brock and Dechert (1985) have analyzed dynamic Ramsey pricing, and Rees (1986) has studied the effects of smoothing prices over a construction interval.

capacity expansion. We hope that our chapter will stimulate econometric work along these lines.

Finally, we hope that our extension of the theory of congestion pricing and investment to an intertemporal setting will encourage more sophisticated policy analysis aimed at developing practicable congestion pricing and investment programs.

References

Arnott, R. and M. Kraus (1993) "The Ramsey Problem for Congestible Facilities." *Journal of Public Economics*, 50, 371-96.

Arnott, R. and M. Kraus (1995) "Financing Capacity in the Bottleneck Model." *Journal of Urban Economics*, 38, 272-90.

Baumol, W. J., J. C. Panzar, and R. D. Willig (1982) *Contestable Markets and the Theory of Industry Structure*. New York: Harcourt Brace.

Berglas, E. and D. Pines (1981) "Clubs, Local Public Goods and Transportation Models: A Synthesis." *Journal of Public Economics*, 15, 141-62.

Brock, W. A. and W. D. Dechert (1985) "Dynamic Ramsey Pricing." *International Economic Review*, 26, 569-91.

Keeler, T. E. and K. A. Small (1977) "Optimal Peak-Load Pricing, Investment, and Service Levels on Urban Expressways." *Journal of Political Economy*, 85, 1-25.

Kraus, M. (1981) "Scale Economics Analysis for Urban Highway Networks." *Journal of Urban Economics*, 9, 1-22.

Mohring, H. and M. Harwitz (1962) *Highway Benefits: An Analytical Framework*. Evanston: Northwestern University Press.

Oum, T. and Y. Zhang (1990) "Airport Pricing: Congestion Tolls, Lumpy Investment, and Cost Recovery." *Journal of Public Economics*, 43, 353-71.

Rees, R. (1986) "Indivisibilities, Pricing and Investment: The Case of the Second Best." *Journal of Economics*, 55, 195-210.

Royal Commission on National Passenger Transportation (1992) *Directions: The Final Report of the Royal Commission on National Passenger Transportation*. Ottawa: Minister of Supply and Services.

Starrett, D. (1978) "Marginal Cost Pricing of Recursive Lumpy Investments." *Review of Economic Studies*, 45, 215-27.

Strotz, R. H. (1965) "Urban Transportation Parables." In J. Margolis, ed. *The Public Economy of Urban Communities*. Washington, D.C.: Resources for the Future.

Transportation Research Board (1994) *Curbing Gridlock: Peak-Period Fees to Relieve Traffic Congestion*, Special Report No. 242. Washington, D.C.: National Academy Press.

Woroch, G. (1987) "On Pricing with Lumpy Investment: Two Problems of Boiteux." Economics Working Paper No. 87-2. Waltham, MA: GTE Laboratories.

CHAPTER 8

The monopolistic provision of congested public goods*

William H. Oakland

1. Introduction

This chapter concerns the provision of a congested public good by a single private producer who faces neither a threat of entry nor competition from close substitute goods – that is, the firm is a pure monopolist. While we characterize the general properties of the monopoly outcome, we are particularly interested in the relationship of profit-maximizing price and capacity to their Pareto-efficient counterparts. Do the relationships which apply to monopoly provision of pure private goods or pure public goods carry over to the intermediate case of congested public goods?

The literature has been largely silent on this issue. Other than a special case analyzed by Edelson (1971) and a more general analysis by Buchanan (1969), we only have the cryptic discussion by Knight (1952) as predicates. This apparent neglect is surprising given the obvious empirical relevance of this situation and the heavy attention paid to the competitive case. Solutions to the competitive case have been offered by Berglas (1976) and Berglas and Pines (1981), and are also implicit in the many characterizations of the Tiebout equilibrium for local public goods (see, for example, Hamilton [1975]).

Buchanan (1969) was among the first to point out that the tendency for monopolists to provide a sub-optimal supply of output would be mitigated in the event that the product was associated with negative externalities in consumption or production. In effect, the monopolist's price premium serves as a Pigovian tax on consumption of the product, leading to a decrease in its equilibrium output.[1] In general, however, there is no reason for the monopolist's premium to match the efficient surcharge necessary for complete internalization of the externality. Hence, from an efficiency standpoint, the monopolist's price may be too high or too low.

However, in the event that the product is produced under conditions of free entry where any firm's output is "small" relative to total output, the equilibrium congestion premium would indeed be efficient. No governmental intervention, such as a Pigovian tax, is necessary. This was formalized by Berglas (1976) in

* This paper was prepared for the 10th Pinhas Sapir Conference in memory of Eitan Berglas, Tel Aviv, Israel, January 11-12, 1995.

[1] If the externality involves the use of some input in particular, the efficient Paretian tax should not be imposed upon consumption but be imposed upon the use of the offending input. Thus, the argument only applies to production when the externality applies to all inputs "equally."

the context of the Theory of Clubs. The key mechanism here, however, is not a conscious price policy on the part of the participating firms but, rather the result of the free-entry condition. For as long as it is possible for a new firm to offer the consumer a combination of price and congestion that would increase utility, profits would be possible and entry would occur.[2] By definition, such a mechanism is not available under conditions of monopoly supply.

Knight (1952) argued that the same efficiency properties would characterize monopoly provision. His reasoning was that congestion itself amounts to a "tax" upon the consumption of the product. Unlike the monopoly premium, however, this tax would involve a consumer "outlay" which does not accrue to the firm. By increasing price, consumption, and hence congestion, would be reduced. In effect, this enables the firm to substitute a money price for the "congestion" price. This would continue, according to Knight, until consumers were indifferent between a small increase in money price and the concomitant reduction in congestion price.

As we show below, this line of reasoning, while correct for the special case analyzed by Knight, generally fails for two reasons: (1) The monopolist can exploit any imperfect substitutability between the congested good and other goods; (2) because the tradeoff between the money price and the congestion price, which would hold total *consumption* constant, is not identical to the tradeoff to keep consumer *utility* constant. While the former is widely recognized as a source of market imperfection, the latter has to be considered as well. Indeed, as Buchanan conjectured, these two effects may be offsetting.

We first establish these results under the assumption of identical consumers and then relax this important assumption.

2. Identical consumers

The model under consideration is quite simple. We assume there are but two goods, x and y, and n identical consumers. Good y is a pure private good produced under conditions of constant costs with free entry. Good x, by contrast, is produced and provided by a single firm with a cost function of $C = C(X)$, where X denotes "capacity." We assume marginal capacity costs to be positive; i.e., $C'(X) > 0$. Consumers have the utility function $u(x,c,y)$, where x and y represent consumption levels, and c represents the degree of congestion associated with x. The latter is defined by $c = c(nx,X)$, with $c_1 > 0$ and $c_2 < 0$.

Consumers maximize utility subject to the budget constraint $I = tx + y$ where, for convenience, the price of y is normalized at 1. Since n is large, consumers

[2] The reader will recognize the parallels between this argument and that advanced by Tiebout (1956) and his followers. As long as new communities could be costlessly introduced, the equilibrium configuration of communities would be that where the cost savings from spreading public service costs over a larger population are just offset by the increase in the unit costs of producing public services. The latter costs can clearly be given an interpretation as congestion costs.

treat congestion as a parameter when making their consumption choices. Hence, consumer demand and indirect utility functions are given by

$$x = D(t,c,I) = \arg\max_x u(x,c,I - nx) \quad (8\text{-}1)$$

and

$$u = V(t,c,I) = u[D(t,c,I),c,I - D(t,c,I)\,] \quad (8\text{-}2)$$

2.1 The monopoly solution

Firms maximize profit, $\pi = tnx - C\,(X)$, subject to the demand and congestion functions. This yields the first order conditions.

$$nx + ntD_t - \frac{c_1 n^2 D_c D_t t}{(c_1 nD_c - 1)} = 0 \quad (8\text{-}3a)$$

$$C'\,(X) + \frac{c_2 D_c nx}{D_t} = 0 \quad (8\text{-}3b)$$

Given capacity, the first condition determines the profit-maximizing price, t. The first two terms are those associated with an ordinary private good, representing direct revenue impact of the price change. The third term, which is always positive, involves the favorable indirect revenue impact of raising the price; by reducing congestion, it increases the price the firm can charge consumers. The second equation, Eq. (8-3b), establishes profit-maximizing capacity, given total demand nx. An increase in capacity lowers congestion, enabling the firm to increase its price to existing users.

The preceding remarks can be given greater clarity by introducing the following definition. Let

$$w = -\left(\frac{\partial t}{\partial c}\right)\Big|_x = \frac{D_c}{D_t} \quad (8\text{-}4)$$

represent the price reduction required to offset a small increase in congestion so as to keep market demand constant. Hereafter, we refer to this as "demand compensation." Using this definition, we can rewrite Eq. (8-3a) and Eq. (8-3b) as follows:

$$t = -\frac{D}{D_t} + c_1 nxw \quad (8\text{-}5a)$$

$$C'\,(x) = c_2 nxw \quad (8\text{-}5b)$$

The monopolist's price is seen to be made up of two parts: The first (D/D_t), is the monopoly rent component which is equal to the direct gain in revenue by selling one less unit of output; the second, $c_1 nxw$, is the congestion component which reflects the increased revenues derived by the reduction in congestion obtained by selling one less unit of output. The profit-maximizing capacity level is equal to that for which the marginal cost of capacity is equal to the added revenues obtained by selling a less congested product.

2.2 The efficient solution

To determine the efficient combination of price and capacity, we choose t^*, X^* and I so as to maximize the indirect utility function Eq. (8-2) subject to the congestion function and the following budget constraint:

$$t^* nx + n(I_o - I) = C(X^*) \tag{8-6}$$

where I_o is the fixed individual endowment. The choice of I should be viewed as setting the lump-sum tax $I_o - I$.[3] This yields the following conditions for price and capacity:

$$tV_I + nc_1 V_c = 0 \tag{8-7a}$$

$$C'(X)V_t + c_2 V_c nx = 0 \tag{8-7b}$$

As before, these conditions can be given greater clarity by defining v:

$$v = -\left(\frac{\partial t}{\partial c}\right)_u = \frac{V_c}{V_t} \tag{8-8}$$

to represent the price reduction required to offset a small increase in congestion so as to keep utility constant. In effect, v is the consumer's "willingness to pay" for a reduction in congestion. Making use of Shephard's Lemma, the efficiency conditions Eq. (8-7a) and Eq. (8-7b) can then be reexpressed as:

$$t^* = c_1 nxv \tag{8-9a}$$

$$C'(X^*) + c_2 nxv \tag{8-9b}$$

The efficient price is seen to be equal to the aggregate value of the congestion externality created by an additional unit of consumption. Unlike the monopoly solution, there is no marginal revenue term in the optimal price equation. The rule for efficient capacity is seen to closely resemble that for the monopolist with willingness to pay, v, replacing demand compensation, w, as the measure of the decongesting benefit of new capacity.

Comparing equation sets Eqs. (8-5a), (8-5b) and Eqs. (8-9a), (8-9b), it is apparent that for a given price, the relationship of the monopolist's capacity choice to the efficient level will depend only on the relative size of w and v. In particular, if $w > v$, then the monopolist will choose "too much" capacity, and vice versa for $w < v$. It is only if $w = v$ that the monopolist will choose the efficient capacity level.[4,5]

[3] The reader may wonder why the monopolist could not avail itself of this lump-sum charge. Indeed, it is easy to see that if such a charge were available, the monopolist's problem would be identical to the efficiency problem. We choose not to allow the monopolist this instrument because, for the more general case of consumer heterogeneity, a simple two-part tariff would not be sufficient for the monopolist to achieve the efficient solution. The analysis of identical consumers should be viewed as suggestive of the problems posed by monopoly provision rather than as a definitive statement of a likely outcome in real economies with identical agents.

[4] Capacity is efficient for the particular price behavior employed by the monopolist. For the case under discussion, $w = v$, the monopoly price will be above the efficient price. The benefits of added capacity are only considered for those units actually consumed.

Comparison of the monopolist's with the efficient price rule is more complicated, since the former's rule includes a marginal revenue effect. To facilitate the comparison, we can add and subtract the efficient price from the monopolist's optimal condition for price,

$$t - t^* = -\frac{D}{D_t} + c_1 nx(w - v) \tag{8-10}$$

Since the first term is unambiguously positive, a sufficient condition for $t > t^*$ is that $w \geq v$.

Proposition 1. *If consumer willingness to pay for reduced congestion (v) is less than demand compensation (w), the monopolist's price (t) will be above the efficient level (t^*) and it will choose too much capacity ($X > X^*$).*[6]

The example discussed by Knight (1952) amounted to $w = v$. However, Knight also assumed that there exists a non-congested alternative which is a perfect substitute; hence the first term in Eq. (8-5a) vanishes. If other goods are imperfect substitutes for the congested good, however, the monopolist can exploit this to its advantage. Thus, even when congestion costs take the form of monetary outlays, a monopolist would charge an excessive price.

2.3 A comparison of willingness to pay and demand compensation

The above analysis makes clear the critical importance of the relative size of w and v to the question at hand. Unfortunately, in general, little can be said about the comparative size of these magnitudes. Willingness to pay depends upon the first derivatives of the utility function and, in particular, upon the non-observable u_C. Demand compensation, on the other hand, is potentially observable, but depends upon the higher order derivatives of the utility function. Without more specific assumptions, therefore, it is impossible to make comparisons between the two magnitudes.

Fortunately, without a tremendous loss of generality, the two parameters can be compared. What is necessary is to assume weak separability in the utility function between the congested good and other goods:

$$u = u\,[\psi(c,x),y] \tag{8-11a}$$

$$\psi_c < 0 \quad \psi_x > 0 \tag{8-11b}$$

Consumer maximization requires

[5] Strictly speaking, these are only local conditions. Whether or not the monopolist's actual capacity exceeds the efficient level will also depend upon its choice of price. Throughout this and the ensuing discussion of comparative prices, we will be comparing only one choice variable at a time. Insufficient structure has been imposed to make global comparisons.

[6] Once again, the local nature of these comparisons must be emphasized. Given the capacity and price choices of the monopolist, efficiency gains would be realized by lowering capacity. Similarly, efficiency gains would be realized by reducing price.

$$\varphi = \frac{du}{dx} = u_1\psi_x - u_2 t = 0 \tag{8-12}$$

In the Appendix, it is shown that

$$w - v = \frac{\psi_c \varphi_x}{\psi_x \varphi_t} - \frac{u_1}{\varphi_t}\mu \tag{8-13a}$$

$$\mu = \frac{\psi_c}{\psi_x}\psi_{xx} + \frac{\psi_c}{x} - \psi_{xc} \tag{8-13b}$$

The second-order conditions for consumer maximization require that $\varphi_x < 0$. Normality of the demand for x also insures that $\varphi_t < 0$. Hence, the first term in Eq. (8-13a) is negative. It follows that if $\mu \leq 0$, $w < v$.

Substituting from Eqs. (8-13a), (8-13b) into Eq. (8-10) and using the definitions of t and t^* yields

$$t - t^* = \frac{u_1\mu}{\varphi_c} \tag{8-14}$$

An increase in congestion can be expected to reduce the demand for x. Hence, $\varphi_c < 0$. Thus, the sign of $t - t^*$ will assume the sign of μ. It follows:

Proposition 2. *If the utility function is separable in the congested good,*

1. a monopolist that charges the efficient price, i.e., t = t*, *will choose a sub-optimal level of capacity, i.e.,*

   $X < X^*$.

2. *a monopolist that chooses the efficient capacity will choose a price above the efficient price.*
3. *a monopolist can never choose both an efficient price and an efficient capacity.*

These results follow directly from Eqs. (8-13a), (8-13b) and (8-14). Thus, even if Knight were correct and the monopolist correctly priced its product, it would continue to underprovide capacity. And, if it chooses the appropriate capacity, it will tend to unduly restrict access to its good. This suggests that the proclivity of monopolists to underprovide may not be mitigated by congestion externalities. Before we can make any definitive statements, however, we have to explore the sign of μ.

If the congestion function is of the constant elasticity form, i.e.,

$$\psi(c,x) = Ac^{\alpha}x^{\beta}$$
$$\alpha < 0 \quad \beta > 0 \tag{8-15}$$

then $\mu = 0$. More generally, consider the following problem. Suppose consumers are confronted by a price congestion spectrum: $t = t(c)$, $t'(c) > 0$, $t''(c) < 0$. As part of their optimization process, for fixed expenditure (E) on the congested good, they must choose (c, x) so as to maximize

$$\max_{x,c} \psi(c,x) \quad \text{s.t. } t(c)x = E \tag{8-16}$$

The first-order condition for this problem is

$$\Theta = -\psi_x E \frac{t'(c)}{t^2} + \psi_c = 0 \tag{8-17}$$

Also,

$$\frac{\partial c}{\partial E} = -\frac{\theta_E}{\theta_c}$$

$$\theta_E = -\frac{\mu}{t} \tag{8-18}$$

$$\theta_c < 0$$

The latter inequality follows from the second-order conditions of the optimization problem.

Proposition 3. *If the utility function is separable in the congested good and other goods:*

1. *A monopolist will charge a lower price ($t < t^*$) and choose a smaller capacity ($X < X^*$) than socially efficient if congestion is an inferior good; that is, as income increases, consumers choose a less congested alternative on the price congestion spectrum. Moreover, under the same conditions, willingness to pay will be greater than demand compensation.*
2. *If congestion is a normal good, a monopolist will charge a price above the efficient price. However, the monopolist's choice of capacity could be greater than or less than the efficient capacity.*

Thus, the relationship between the monopolist's price and the efficient price turns squarely upon whether utilization of more congested modes increases or decreases with household income. In the former event, the monopolist price would lie *below* the efficient price – a truly novel outcome. At first blush, however, it may seem unlikely that income and congestion are positively associated; richer consumers are able to afford higher quality consumption. On second thought, however, there are reasons for the relationship to go the other way. Because they are likely to consume more, high-income households have more to save by consuming more congested modes. Thus, introspection cannot guide us to a definitive conclusion: The relationship between monopoly price and the efficient price could go either way. On the other hand, as Proposition 2 indicates, there is a bias towards underprovision of capacity under monopoly; even if $\mu = 0$, the monopolist would choose too little capacity. Thus, for values of μ near zero, the classical result would obtain. Only if there were a sharp drop-off of congestion with income would this relationship be reversed.

These results are to be contrasted with those for pure private and pure public goods. That monopolists tend to set prices above efficient levels is well known for private goods and has also been established for pure public goods (Brito and Oakland, 1980). However, under plausible conditions, a monopolist would actually price *below* efficient levels. This might seem counterintuitive since congestion encourages the firm to charge more so as to increase the quality of its product. This would only seem to exacerbate the tendency for the monopolist to charge in excess of marginal cost. However, the relevant base point for the congestion charge is not zero, but the efficient congestion charge which is itself based upon the consumer's willingness to pay. In the normal case, the monopolist's profit-maximizing congestion charge is below the efficient congestion charge. This, in turn, offsets the monopoly rent component of price. Indeed, the offset is sufficiently strong so as to reverse the usual relation between monopoly price and efficient price. Monopoly provision of congested public goods would thus be characterized by super-optimal congestion. The latter is further intensified by the tendency of the monopolist to provide too little capacity. This raises a potential dilemma for policy officials who would attempt to correct for the inefficient price and capacity behavior. On the price front, a Pigovian tax could induce a more efficient utilization of capacity. However, such a charge would induce further reductions in capacity, which is already sub-optimal. Without other policy instruments, therefore, the relative merits of efficient pricing and efficient capacity investment need to be weighed.

3. Heterogeneous consumers

We turn now to the situation where consumers are diverse, meaning that willingness to pay and demand compensation may differ among groups of consumers. For simplicity, we analyze two groups of individuals which, for concreteness, we shall label "rich" (R) and "poor" (P). However, it should be noted that the following analysis can be generalized to any number of diverse consumer groups, including a world where each individual consumer has unique income and/or tastes. The monopolist's problem becomes

$$\max_{tX} \pi = t(n_r D^r + n_p D^p) - C(X) \tag{8-19}$$
$$\text{s.t. } c = c(n_r D^r + n_p D^p, X)$$

where the demand function and indirect utility function for each group is defined as before. The first-order conditions for this problem can be written

$$t = -\frac{Q}{Q_t} + c_1 Q\hat{w} \tag{8-20a}$$

$$C'(X) = c_2 Q\hat{w} \tag{8-20b}$$

where $Q = n_r x_r + n_p x_p$, $Q_t = (\partial Q/\partial t)$, and

$$\hat{w} = \beta w_r + (1 - \beta)w_p \tag{8-21a}$$

$$\beta = \frac{n_r D_t^r}{Q_t} \tag{8-21b}$$

The similarity of these conditions to the identical consumer case should be clear. It is important to note that while w is a weighted average of individual group w's, the weights are shares of *changes* in demand induced by a change in price.

The conditions for Pareto-efficiency are also similar.

$$\begin{aligned} t^* &= c_1 Q\bar{v} \\ C'(X^*) &= c_2 Q\bar{v} \\ \bar{v} &= \rho v_r + (1 - \rho)v_p \\ \rho &= \frac{n_r x_r}{Q} \end{aligned} \tag{8-22}$$

Here, however, the consumers' average willingness to pay is based upon *demand* weights. Adding and subtracting several terms from the profit condition for price yields:

$$t - t^* = -\frac{Q}{Q_t} + c_1 Q\,(\bar{w} - \bar{v}) + c_1 Q\,(\hat{w} - \bar{w}) \tag{8-23}$$

This appears as it did in the homogeneous case with the addition of a third term: the difference between the two weighted averages of demand compensation. The first term, the monopoly rent term, is exactly as it was before. If the utility functions are separable, the second term can be written

$$\bar{w} - \bar{v} = \left(\frac{\rho v_r}{\varepsilon_r} + \frac{(1 - \rho)v_p}{\varepsilon_p}\right) + \tilde{\mu} \tag{8-24a}$$

$$\tilde{\mu} = -\left(\frac{\beta_r u_1^r \mu^r}{\varphi_t^r} + \frac{(1 - \beta)u_1^p u^p \mu^p}{\varphi_t^p}\right) \tag{8-24b}$$

Hence, as with identical individuals, $\bar{w} - \bar{v}$ will be negative if $\mu^i < 0$. *If* $\bar{w} - \hat{w} = 0$, *then our analysis continues as before. With some manipulation, we obtain*

$$\hat{w} - \bar{w} = \frac{1}{\varepsilon}[(w_r - \bar{w})(\varepsilon_r - \varepsilon) + (w_p - \bar{w})(\varepsilon_p - \varepsilon)] \tag{8-25}$$

where ε_i and ε correspond to the price elasticity of demand of group i and the overall market, respectively. This condition may be represented more succinctly by

$$\hat{w} - \bar{w} = \frac{1}{-\varepsilon}\text{cov}\,(-\varepsilon, w) \tag{8-26}$$

Thus, the sign of $\hat{w} - \bar{w}$ turns on the covariance between the absolute value of price elasticity and demand compensation. If the covariance is positive, $\hat{w} - \bar{w}$

is negative and vice versa. In the two-group case under discussion, only if demand compensation and/or demand price elasticity are equal will this term vanish. But this is tantamount to having identical individuals. In the event that the number of groups is large, it is sufficient that price elasticity and demand compensation be uncorrelated. Otherwise, diversity in consumer tastes will modify the conclusions drawn for the homogeneous case.

Proposition 4. *If consumers are heterogeneous, and the utility function is weakly separable:*

1. *The monopolist will charge a lower price ($t < t^*$) and choose a smaller capacity ($X < X^*$) than socially efficient under the following conditions:*

   (a) Congestion is an inferior good.

   (b) Demand compensation and absolute value of price elasticity of demand are negatively correlated.

   Moreover, under such circumstances, average willingness to pay will be greater than average demand compensation when demand quantities are used as weights in computing the averages.

2. *If congestion is a normal good and demand compensation and price elasticity of demand are positively correlated, the monopolist will set its price above the efficient level.*

While the covariance between demand compensation and demand price elasticity could be of either sign, for the case at hand involving rich and poor consumer groups, one could presume that it is negative. Rich consumers are likely to require higher demand compensation because of greater opportunity costs of congestion and because they can more afford to pay to avoid congestion. At the same time, because of their greater resources, they will tend to respond less to price increases. Under these circumstances, the monopolist's tendency to charge too little and to underinvest in capacity will be reinforced.

However, consumers may differ in tastes as well as income. Moreover, the relationship may vary from one congested commodity to another. In such cases, there are no prior expectations for the sign of the covariance. If sensitivity to price and to congestion tend to run together, consumer diversity will mitigate underpricing and underproduction when congestion is an inferior good. Such cases may well exist in practice. Undoubtedly, a major factor influencing the outcome will be intergroup accessibility to substitute commodities or services. Such accessibility may well influence price and congestion sensitivity in the same direction. Since accessibility may also be positively correlated with income, this may serve to mute the influence of pure income differences, as outlined in the previous paragraph.

4. Concluding comments

The properties of monopoly provision of a congested public good have received scant treatment in the literature on public economics. Instead, analysis of congested public goods has been restricted to the competitive case. While competitive provision is of theoretical interest, especially as it pertains to the provision of local public goods and club goods, monopoly provision would seem more empirically relevant. Moreover, because a monopolist will attempt to incorporate congestion externalities into the market price, it is important to determine whether such behavior will be sufficient to provide an efficient price outcome. The present paper offers a modest first step in this direction by analyzing the behavior of a simple nondiscriminating monopolist. We show that, under broad conditions, monopoly provision is inefficient. However, the form of inefficiency, whether non-optimal price or non-optimal capacity, cannot be generalized. In the event that demand compensation and price elasticity of demand are uncorrelated across consuming agents, there may be situations where the monopolist's price is too *low* – a novel result. Moreover, it is even more likely that the monopolist's capacity will be sub-optimal. Indeed, even if it chooses the efficient price, it will still choose too little capacity. On the other hand, if it chooses the efficient capacity, it chooses a super-optimal price. Hence, its policies are similar to the findings for the monopolistic provision of private and public goods in this important respect.

Appendix

Consumers are assumed to maximize

$$u = u[\psi(c,x),y] \quad \text{s.t. } tx + y = I \tag{8A-1}$$

The first order condition for this problem is

$$\varphi = \frac{du}{dx} = u_1\psi_x - u_2 t = 0 \tag{8A-2}$$

It is assumed that $\psi_i < 0$, $i = c,t$. Moreover, $\psi_x < 0$ by the second-order conditions for Eq. (8A-1). Furthermore,

$$w = \frac{\varphi_c}{\varphi_t}$$

$$v = \frac{V_c}{V_t} = -\frac{u_1\psi_c}{u_2 x} \tag{8A-3}$$

with

$$w - v = \frac{1}{\varphi_t u_2 x}[\varphi_c u_2 x + \varphi_t u_1 \psi_c] \tag{8A-4}$$

From Eq. (8A-2) we compute

$$\varphi_c = u_{11}\psi_c\psi_x - tu_{21}\psi_c + u_1\psi_{xc} \tag{8A-5a}$$

$$\varphi_t = -x\psi_x u_{12} - u_2 + xu_{22}t \tag{8A-5b}$$

Substituting Eq. (8A-5) into (8A-4) and rearranging terms yields:

$$w - v = \frac{\psi_c x u_1}{t}\left(\varphi_x - \frac{\psi_x}{\psi_c}u_1\mu\right) \tag{8A-6a}$$

$$\mu = \frac{\psi_c}{\psi_x}\psi_{xx} + \frac{\psi_c}{x} + \psi_{xc} \tag{8A-6b}$$

which simplifies to Eq. (8-13a) in the text.

References

Berglas, E. (1976) "On the Theory of Club Goods." *American Economic Review,* 66, 1976, 116-21.

Berglas, E. and D. Pines (1981) "Clubs, Local Public Goods and Transportation Models: A Synthesis." *Journal of Public Economics,* 15, 141-62.

Brito, D. L. and W. H. Oakland (1980) "On the Monopolistic Provision of Excludable Public Goods." *American Economic Review,* 70, 691-704.

Buchanan, J. M. (1969) "External Diseconomies, Corrective Taxation, and Market Structure." *American Economic Review,* 59, 174-77.

Edelson, N. M. (1971) "Congestion Tolls under Monopoly." *American Economic Review,* 57, 873-82.

Hamilton, B. W. (1975) "Zoning and Property Taxes in a System of Local Governments." *Urban Studies,* 12, 205-11.

Knight, F. (1952) "Some Fallacies in the Interpretation of Social Cost." In G. Stigler and K. Boulding, eds. *Readings in Price Theory,* Vol. VI, Homewood, 160-79.

Tiebout, C. M. (1956) "A Pure Theory of Local Expenditures." *Journal of Political Economy,* 64: 416-24.

CHAPTER 9

Imperfect solutions to the musical-suburbs problem*

John Douglas Wilson

1. Introduction

It is well-known that efficient pricing in a system of jurisdictions requires that each resident pay a head tax equal to the cost of being provided with the jurisdiction's public goods and services. In other words, residents should be taxed according to their "marginal congestion costs" (MCC). Any shortfall in the government budget is then balanced by taxing the jurisdiction's land. In standard Tiebout models, this type of tax system is easily implemented, since individuals efficiently sort themselves across jurisdictions according to taste and income differences, leaving each jurisdiction with a homogeneous residential population. Tax policy becomes more complicated, however, when jurisdictions contain heterogeneous populations. The pioneering work of Eitan Berglas (1976) specifies one such model, in which complementarities between the labor supplied by two types of individuals cause them to reside within the same jurisdiction.[1] Under his simplifying assumption that the MCCs are identical across residents, efficiency can be achieved by levying a uniform head tax on all residents. If the model is generalized to allow for cost differences, however, these taxes must differ across residents.

Many models in the literature recognize the difficulties involved in matching a resident's tax payments with his or her MCC. In Schwab and Oates (1991) and de Bartolome (1990), local governments are constrained to collect the same tax payments from each resident, although the existence of "peer-group effects" causes the residents' MCCs to effectively differ. This constraint might be explained by difficulties in obtaining the information on how the MCCs differ.[2] Alternatively, the MCCs may all be identical but only "second-best" taxes are available, under which tax payments necessarily differ across residents with

* I am grateful for the comments from participants at the 10th Pinhas Sapir Conference, in Memory of Professor Eitan Berglas, at Tel Aviv University. Funding for this research was provided by the National Science Foundation, grant no. SES-9209168.

[1] Brueckner (1994) extends the Berglas analysis by allowing labor types to be complementary but not essential for production. In this case, the issue of whether clubs are homogeneous or heterogeneous is endogenously determined within the model.

[2] For example, de Bartolome (1990:117) writes, "This assumption [of equal tax payments] can be motivated either by the positive observation that educational taxes are not levied according to the child's ability or by information constraints: individual ability is private information but mean ability is observable."

different incomes or tastes. The residential property tax is a good example. As modeled by Epple et al. (1984) and others, this tax is essentially an excise tax on the consumption of housing.[3] High-income individuals tend to consume larger amounts of housing and therefore have higher property tax payments than low-income individuals. If MCCs do not rise significantly with income, high-income individuals then subsidize the public good consumption of low-income individuals. Sales and income taxes also possess this problem.

This failure to match tax payments with MCCs has been said to produce problems for the existence of an equilibrium with free migration. This is the "musical-suburbs problem" cited in the title of this chapter. Under a residential property tax, for example, low-income individuals may continuously attempt to move into high-income jurisdictions in an effort to obtain subsidized public good supplies. The high-income individuals respond by moving, and the process continues without ever converging to an equilibrium. Epple et al. (1984) formulate a model with voting over tax-expenditure packages and use it to identify conditions on consumer preferences that eliminate the musical-suburbs problem. But these assumptions are much stronger than those normally imposed on preferences in general equilibrium models. In the Schwab-Oates model, an equilibrium often fails to exist, and it always fails to exist in Wheaton (1975).[4] Thus, attempts by local governments to achieve a Tiebout equilibrium, with perfect sorting of different types of individuals across jurisdictions, may be most damaging.

One characteristic of models that generate a musical-suburbs problem is that local governments are typically assumed to ignore the problem when choosing their tax and expenditure policies. Specifically, they behave *myopically* by choosing the tax and expenditure policies that are optimal in some sense for the *existing* residential population. In the voting models used by Epple et al. (1984) and Westhoff (1977), for example, the chosen tax-expenditure package is that which is optimal for the median voter, given the existing population.[5] In

[3] In contrast, the tax competition literature models the property tax as a tax on the capital used in all production activities.

[4] I refer here to two of Wheaton's (1975) models, one with an income tax and the other with a Lindahl tax. In both cases, he assumes a pure public good, implying no congestion costs. More recently, Wheaton (1993) adds land to the model and assumes a publicly provided private good financed with property taxation. In this case, the existence of an equilibrium is possible. The current paper concentrates solely on cases where the type of equilibrium described in the latter paper does not exist.

[5] An alternative interpretation is that individuals choose where to reside only once, prior to voting for public goods. If they possess perfect foresight about voting outcomes, they will not have an incentive to move again. However, the assumption that individuals do not have an option to move again is restrictive because allowing for this option would change the set of feasible tax and expenditure policies and, consequently, affect voting outcomes.

Wheaton's model, where jurisdictions are homogeneous, governments choose the public good level that satisfies the Samuelson condition for the *existing* population. Epple and Romer (1991) and Cassidy and Epple (1994) do assume perfect foresight of migration responses, but their property tax is used only for income redistribution, rather than for the financing of productive public goods. Epple and Romer (1991) explain that the assumption of voter myopia would necessarily lead to nonexistence of a voting equilibrium in their model.

The purpose of the present chapter is twofold. First, I describe how local governments can "imperfectly solve" the musical-suburbs problem if they possess perfect foresight of the migration responses to changes in their tax and expenditure policies, allowing them to take actions that control these responses. The solution is "imperfect" because the actions of local governments produce an equilibrium that is not efficient. The other purpose of the chapter is to investigate forms of central-government intervention that increase the efficiency of the equilibrium, i.e., policies that produce Pareto improvements. I consider only those policies that are consistent with the constraints placed on local governments. In other words, if a local government is unable to distinguish between two types of residents, then the central government also faces this restriction. I concentrate on the use of interjurisdictional transfers, which satisfy this criteria. Perhaps the most surprising result of the paper is that such transfers may make all jurisdictions better off by reducing the musical-suburbs problem.

I stay within the confines of the Tiebout literature by assuming that individuals are mobile across a large number of competitive jurisdictions, each possessing a fixed amount of some immobile factor ("land"). My model also includes the property that it is efficient for each jurisdiction to be populated by only one type of resident, i.e., there is perfect Tiebout sorting. Nevertheless, the model produces a musical-suburbs problem precisely because jurisdictions are constrained to use a second-best tax policy under which different types of individuals would be treated identically by the tax system were they to reside in the same jurisdiction. The equilibrium that emerges from this model is one in which some jurisdictions respond to the need to prevent entry of particular types of individuals by choosing levels of public goods that are sufficiently unattractive to these outsiders.

Section 2 describes the basic model, in which residents possess different MCCs, and Section 3 examines the equilibrium properties of the model. Interjurisdictional transfers are investigated in Section 4, and Section 5 extends the analysis by allowing jurisdictions to restrict entry, but only at a cost. The basic model contains two types of workers, but Section 6 argues that the extension to many types is straightforward. Section 7 investigates an alternative model in which the use of a distortionary property tax is responsible for the musical-suburbs problem. Changes in the condition for beneficial interjurisdictional transfers are highlighted. Section 8 provides some concluding remarks.

2. The model

Consider a system of a large number of identical "jurisdictions," each containing a given amount of a fixed factor called "land." This factor is combined with mobile labor to produce "output" via a constant-returns-to-scale production function. This output is either consumed as a final consumption good or transformed into a public good available to all residents in equal amounts. To produce a musical-suburbs problem, I assume that there exist two types of individuals, "high-cost workers" and "low-cost workers," who are freely mobile between jurisdictions. These workers are distinguished by the marginal cost of providing them with the public good (i.e., different "marginal congestion costs," or "MCCs"). They each supply one unit of homogeneous labor and are indistinguishable for tax purposes, forcing the local government to collect identical head taxes from all residents.[6] Thus, one type's tax payments will necessarily differ from that type's MCC, if both types reside in the same jurisdiction.

The two types of workers possess different preferences for the public good. In particular, high-cost workers are assumed to have a greater willingness to pay for this good. This assumption may be interpreted as meaning that high-cost workers make greater use of the public good. Similar results would be obtained if the preference ordering were reversed.

Tax and expenditure policies within each jurisdiction are controlled by competitive "developers," who seek to maximize the value of land. The present model satisfies the conditions under which this assumption is justified. In particular, workers are freely mobile between many competing jurisdictions, each of which is unable to directly block the entry of new workers. The assumption of many jurisdictions implies that each jurisdiction is a "utility-taker" on national factor markets. In other words, type-i workers can receive utility level u^{i*} by residing elsewhere, and the given jurisdiction has no influence over u^{i*}. Thus, only landowners care about policy choices. For workers, any policy change would be met by a migration response that re-equated their utilities with those available elsewhere.

Free entry exists in the developer market. Thus jurisdictions are "developed" until the maximum after-tax value of land drops to the opportunity cost of land, which is set at zero. Similar results could be obtained from a model with constraints on the number of jurisdictions, the added complication being that the value of land would be endogenously determined by the equilibrium conditions.

To formally state the developer's problem, I first define the utility function for a type-i worker (i = 1 for high-cost, 2 for low-cost) as $u^i(x^i, g)$, where g is

[6] In contrast to the current chapter, Conley and Wooders (1994) consider the case where the "crowding characteristics," but not "taste characteristics," of individuals are observable. They demonstrate that this informational assumption is enough to ensure efficiency.

the public good level and x^i is private consumption. All residents within a given jurisdiction receive identical amounts of the public good, and the cost of producing this good is denoted $C(g, n^1, n^2)$, where n^i is the number of type-i residents. I have assumed that

$$\frac{\partial C}{\partial n^1} > \frac{\partial C}{\partial N^2} \tag{9-1}$$

An example is the peer-group effects model of Schwab and Oates, where the cost function effectively takes the form $C(g,n^1,n^2) = c^1(n^2/n^1)\, n^1 + c^2(n^2/n^1)\, n^2$, with "peer-group effects" modeled by assuming that the unit cost functions, c^1 and c^2, are decreasing in the ratio of low- to high-cost residents.

The after-tax value of land in a jurisdiction equals the total value of output produced in that jurisdiction, $f(n)$ for $n = n^1 + n^2$, minus public good costs and after-tax wage payments to workers:

$$\pi = f(n) - C(g,n^1,n^2) - \omega n \tag{9-2}$$

where ω denotes the single after-tax wage provided to all workers, reflecting the assumption that the government is unable to distinguish between different types of workers. To simplify the notation, I choose units so that each worker provides one unit of labor and each jurisdiction contains one unit of land.

The land-value maximization problem may now be stated as follows:

Problem 1. $\underset{n^1,\, n^2,\, g,\, \omega}{\textit{Maximize}}\; f(n) - C(g, n^1, n^2) - \omega n.$

$$\textit{subject to:}\quad u^k(\omega,g) = u^{k*} \text{ for } n^k > 0 \tag{9-3}$$

$$u^k(\omega,g) \leq u^{k*} \text{ for } n^k = 0 \tag{9-4}$$

The constraints in Eqs. (9-3) and (9-4) reflect the requirement that residents obtain at least the utilities they could get elsewhere, and that workers residing elsewhere not be able to raise their utilities by moving into the given jurisdiction. Equation (9-3), which allows the developer to choose only those population compositions under which each resident is indifferent about where to reside, follows from these requirements because the assumption of many small "utility-taking" jurisdictions implies that no single jurisdiction can possess all of the workers of a given type; if some type-k residents reside in the jurisdiction, then other type-k residents reside elsewhere. If resident utilities were required only to be at least as great as those available elsewhere, then we would be effectively assuming the jurisdiction could erect costless barriers to the entry of whichever workers it wished to exclude. The absence of such barriers will be an important consideration in the subsequent analysis, precisely because there is a musical-suburbs problem.

As already noted, the absence of constraints on community development implies that developers earn zero "profits." In other words, the maximized net value of land equals zero in equilibrium. Stiglitz (1983) takes advantage of this fact and models government decision making using the "dual" problem of maximizing the utilities for a given type of resident, subject to migration constraints for the other types, and a zero-profit constraint. For a jurisdiction containing, say, low-cost residents, this dual problem may be stated as follows for the current model:[7]

Problem 2. *Maximize* $u^2(\omega, g)$
n^1, n^2, g, ω

$$\textit{subject to:}\quad u^1(\omega,g) = u^{1*} \text{ for } n^1 > 0 \tag{9-5}$$

$$u^1(\omega,g) \le u^{1*} \text{ for } n^1 = 0 \tag{9-6}$$

$$f(n) - C(g,n^1,n^2) - \omega n = 0 \tag{9-7}$$

A similar problem can then be stated for high-cost residents, if they also reside in the jurisdiction. Stiglitz explains that the migration constraints force all types of residents to agree on the same tax and expenditure policies. In other words, there is complete unanimity, with each type's maximized utility level equal to the level available elsewhere in equilibrium. However, Stiglitz does not consider constraints on the tax treatment of different individuals. The next section shows that these constraints lead to completely homogeneous jurisdictions.

Finally, it is interesting to note that Rothschild and Stiglitz (1976) work with a similar model to investigate competitive insurance markets. In their paper, insurance companies replace the competitive developers modeled here, and different types of insurance demanders, high-risk and low-risk, replace the high-cost and low-cost residents.

3. Properties of the equilibrium

This section first demonstrates that each jurisdiction is occupied by only one type of worker in equilibrium. I then show that jurisdictions with low-cost residents essentially "solve" the musical-suburbs problem by choosing public good levels that eliminate the high-cost workers' incentives to reside with low-cost workers. Given this policy goal, the equilibrium public good levels are inefficient in the sense that they fail to satisfy the familiar Samuelson rule.

The conclusion that jurisdictions contain homogeneous populations is obtained from the first-order condition for n^i in Problem 1:

$$f' - C_i - \omega = 0 \tag{9-8}$$

[7] Stiglitz (1983) uses a weak inequality, rather than an equality, in the constraint corresponding to my Eqs. (9-3) and (9-5). As previously explained, the equality must hold here because if type-*k* workers reside in the jurisdiction, then type-*k* workers also exist elsewhere, and the latter workers must not be able to increase their utilities by migrating.

where subscripts denote partial derivatives and a prime denotes a total derivative. Because the marginal product of labor equals the before-tax wage in equilibrium, w, Eq. (9-8) implies that each resident's tax payments equal the marginal congestion cost: $w - \omega = C_i$. The basic argument here is that if both types of workers reside in the same jurisdiction, then an increase in the ratio of low- to high-cost workers, holding fixed their total number (n), would lower the cost of public good provision without changing wages or total tax payments. The government budget surplus could then be used to tax land less heavily, thereby raising after-tax land values.

Thus, heterogeneous jurisdictions cannot exist in equilibrium, given that all workers pay identical head taxes but generate different MCCs. There must then exist two types of jurisdictions, those containing high-cost workers ("high-cost jurisdictions") and those with low-cost workers ("low-cost jurisdictions"). With free entry, developers are indifferent about which type of worker to attract, and they earn zero "profits" in either case:

$$f(n^1) - C(g,n^1,0) - \omega n^1 = f(n^2) - C(g,0,n^2) - \omega n^2 = 0 \tag{9-9}$$

Schwab and Oates (1991) argue on similar grounds that jurisdictions cannot be heterogeneous. But unlike the current paper, they use this result to argue that an equilibrium will often fail to exist. By examining the first-order condition for g, I next demonstrate how an equilibrium can be achieved.

Because each jurisdiction contains only one type of worker, I may investigate Problem 1 for the case where each of the two migration constraints applies to only one type of worker (i.e., one value of k). Attach Lagrange multipliers λ^1 and λ^2 to these two constraints, where the superscript represents the labor-type to which they apply. Differentiating the Lagrangian then gives the remaining first-order conditions for a type-k jurisdiction (where $j \neq k$):

$$\omega\text{:}\ \ n^k = \lambda^k u^k_x + \lambda^j u^j_x \tag{9-10}$$

$$g\text{:}\ \ C_g = \lambda^k u^k_g + \lambda^j u^j_g \tag{9-11}$$

By combining Eqs. (9-10) and (9-11), the first-order condition for g may be rewritten in terms of marginal rates of substitution between the public good and private consumption, $MRS^{ik} = u^{ik}_g / u^{ik}_x$ for a type-i worker in a type-k jurisdiction ($i, k = 1, 2$):

$$n^k[\beta^k MRS^{kk} + (1 - \beta^k)\, MRS^{jk}] = C^k_g \tag{9-12}$$

where

$$\beta^k = \frac{\lambda^{kk} u^{kk}_x}{\lambda^{kk} u^{kk}_x + \lambda^{jk} u^{jk}_x} \tag{9-13}$$

This condition departs from the familiar Samuelson rule, which requires that the sum of marginal rates of substitutions (MRS) across all residents equal the marginal cost of public good provision. Instead, each resident's MRS in this sum is replaced by a weighted average of the MRSs for residents and nonresidents.

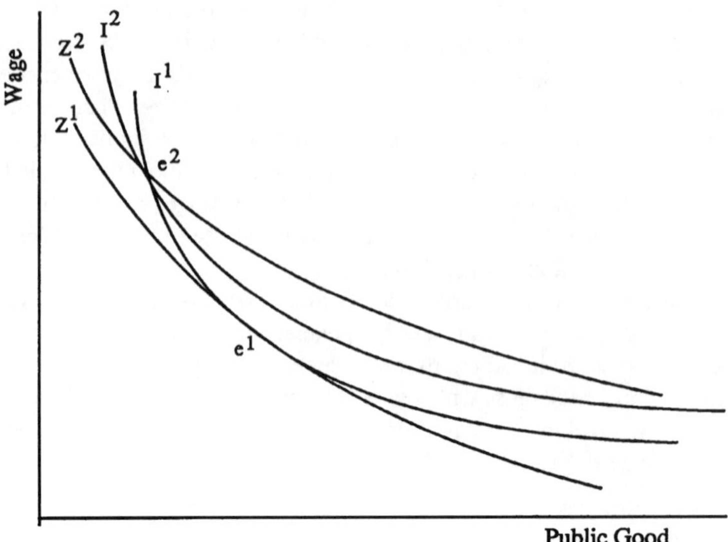

Figure 9-1

Whether the weight for nonresidents is nonzero depends on whether the migration constraint for these workers is binding, i.e., whether the jurisdiction faces a musical-suburbs problem. The situation is illustrated in Fig. 9-1. Curves Z^1 and Z^2 represent zero-profit curves for high-cost and low-cost jurisdictions, respectively, defined over public good levels and after-tax wages. Along each of these curves, worker population levels are chosen to maximize the net value of land. Algebraically, we may describe these curves as follows:

$$\max_{n^1} f(n^1) - C(g,n^1,0) - \omega n^1 = 0 \tag{9-14}$$

and

$$\max_{n^2} f(n^2) - C(g,0,n^2) - \omega n^2 = 0 \tag{9-15}$$

These curves normally will not be everywhere concave, but I will assume a unique profit-maximizing (g, ω) for each jurisdiction.[8] A critical property of the two curves is that the one for the low-cost jurisdiction lies above that for the high-cost jurisdiction, reflecting the condition in Eq. (9-1). The remaining curves in Fig. 9-1, I^1 and I^2, represent indifference curves for high- and low-cost workers.

As illustrated by point e^1 in Fig. 9-1, a high-cost jurisdiction locates where its zero-profit curve is tangent to a worker indifference curve. The tangency implies the Samuelson rule for efficient public good provision:

[8] For a pure public good, the zero-profit curves would be convex. See Atkinson and Stiglitz (1980), especially their Figure 17-3 and the corresponding discussion.

$$n^1 MRS^{11} = C_g^1 \tag{9-16}$$

The Samuelson rule holds because the migration constraint for nonresidents [Eq. (9-4) in Problem 1] does not bind for a high-cost jurisdiction. In terms of the weighted-average rule given by Eqs. (9-12) and (9-13) for $k = 1$, the Lagrange multiplier λ^{21} equals zero, making them coincide with Eq. (9-16).

For low-cost jurisdictions, however, it is clear from Fig. 9-1 that similarly locating at a tangency between the zero-profit curve and a low-cost indifference curve would produce a "ruinous" influx of high-cost workers because these latter workers could raise their utilities by moving out of their high-cost jurisdictions. The critical assumption behind this result is that this tangency is located above I^1, a condition that I maintain throughout the chapter to generate a musical-suburbs problem. Thus, the equilibrium utility level for low-cost residents must be located elsewhere. With high-cost jurisdictions located at point e^1 in Fig. 9-1, low-cost jurisdictions choose a (g, ω) where the zero-profit curve intersects indifference curves for *both* types of workers, which is at point e^2. As with e^1, this point satisfies the migration constraints and, by construction, produces zero developer profits. The relatively steep indifference curve for high-cost workers at e^2 reflects the assumption made earlier that these individuals also possess a relatively high demand for the public good. Referring to the weighted-average rule, the weight assigned to nonresidents is actually negative, because the inequality on the nonresident migration constraint, $u^1(\omega,g) \le u^{1*}$, implies a negative Lagrange multiplier. In contrast, a positive Lagrange multiplier is assigned to the resident migration constraint, $u^2(\omega,g) = u^{2*}$, which could be rewritten as $u^2(\omega,g) \ge u^{2*}$ without changing the solution. As shown in Fig. 9-1, the MRSs in the weighted-average rule satisfy,

$$n^2 MRS^{12} > n^2 MRS^{22} > C_g^2 \tag{9-17}$$

Thus, the musical-suburbs problem is "solved" under natural assumptions about indifference curves. The critical property here is that the indifference curves for the two types of workers cross only once; without it, there would be no two values of (g, ω), one for each type of jurisdiction, under which developer profits would be maximized in all jurisdictions, given the migration constraints. A similar property arises in Epple et al.'s (1984) analysis of property taxation and voting, where the existence of many more types of individuals than jurisdictions implies heterogeneous jurisdictions. On the other hand, no such assumption about preferences rescues the nonexistence results in Wheaton (1975), which shares the property of homogeneous jurisdictions with the current model. Again, it is the assumption of perfect foresight that makes possible the existence of an equilibrium.

Rothschild and Stiglitz (1976), in their analysis of insurance markets, provide an additional reason for nonexistence, which has not been allowed here. They show that if an equilibrium does exist, then it must involve a perfect sorting of different risk types across insurance companies, with some companies specializing in high-risk buyers and others in low-risk buyers. This finding corresponds to the homogeneous jurisdictions of the current model. However, their equilibrium may fail to exist if a company can increase profits by offering a policy that is preferred by both types.[9] This will be the case if the percentage of all workers who are the high-risk type is small. In terms of Fig. 9-1, the corresponding policy for the current model would lie above indifference curves I^1 and I^2 but below Z^2. But this policy is not sustainable in the current model because it requires that some workers be prevented from entering the low-cost jurisdiction, where they would receive higher utilities than elsewhere. Otherwise, they would enter freely, driving the marginal product of labor to zero, which is certainly not profit-maximizing for developers. Such considerations do not enter into the Rothschild-Stiglitz model because they assume constant returns to scale in the production of insurance policies. Stiglitz (1983) appears to recognize this distinction by imposing a migration constraint on nonresident utilities of the form given by Eq. (9-6), above, which requires that nonresidents are unable to increase their utilities by moving to the given jurisdiction.

One alteration of the model that would produce the Rothschild-Stiglitz existence problem would allow a jurisdiction to costlessly restrict the number of migrants in a way that does not distinguish between types. This is rather paradoxical in light of the common characterization of the musical-suburbs problem as the result of an inability of jurisdictions to restrict entry. It remains the case, however, that the inability of jurisdictions to distinguish between different types of workers is the underlying cause of existence problems. In Section 5, I relax this assumption somewhat by allowing low-cost jurisdictions to impose entry barriers on nonresidents, but only at a cost.

Finally, the presence of the Rothschild-Stiglitz existence problem points to a beneficial form of central government intervention. Suppose, in particular, that a central government requires all jurisdictions to choose identical public good levels, thereby forcing jurisdictions into a pooling equilibrium with heterogeneous populations. Then ω adjusts so that developer profits equal zero, and the migration constraints are trivially satisfied because migrant utilities are identical across all jurisdictions. High- and low-cost workers locate randomly across these jurisdictions, so that each jurisdiction attracts a ratio of high- to low-cost workers equal to the ratio of these types for the entire population. Given this ratio, a new zero-profit curve can be defined in (g,ω)-space, denoted Z^3 in Fig. 9-2. This curve will lie somewhere between the original high- and low-cost zero-profit curves, with the exact location depending on the relative numbers of high- and low-cost workers. If high-cost workers make up a sufficiently small share of the world economy's worker population, Z^3 will lie sufficiently close

[9] Rothschild and Stiglitz (1976) discuss an alternative equilibrium concept that does not lead to the existence problem discussed here.

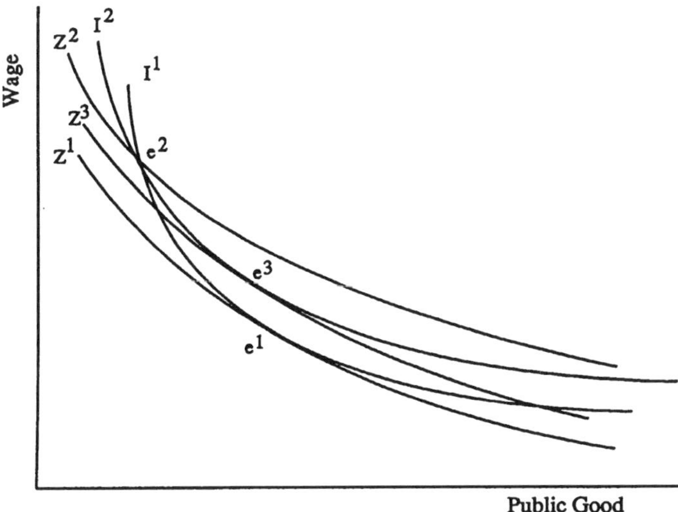

Figure 9-2

to Z^2 to realize a Pareto improvement over the separating equilibrium depicted in Fig. 9-2 by points e^1 and e^2. In the pooling equilibrium illustrated in this figure, each local government sets its (g, ω) at a point e^3 on Z^3 where low-cost workers are as well off as before, whereas high-cost workers are better off.

To conclude, I have shown that a pooling equilibrium obtained through central government intervention may be Pareto superior to the separating equilibrium described above. The following section discusses an alternative means of obtaining Pareto improvements.

4. Interjurisdictional transfers

This section investigates the use of interjurisdictional transfers to achieve Pareto improvements. Specifically, I derive a condition under which a positive transfer of income to high-cost jurisdictions leaves all workers better off. This transfer may be financed by a uniform head tax on all workers, or by a tax collected from only low-tax jurisdictions. The results are the same in both cases, because they each represent a means of transferring income out of low-cost jurisdictions and into high-cost jurisdictions. This transfer effectively lessens the musical-suburbs problem by making high-cost jurisdictions more attractive. As a result, low-cost jurisdictions are able to choose a public good level closer to that dictated by the Samuelson rule for efficient public good provision, thereby creating the possibility of a Pareto improvement. In terms of Fig. 9-1, Z^1 shifts up and Z^2 shifts down. However, the intersection of the two indifference curves at e^2 moves closer to the utility-maximizing level of g for low-cost workers. Unlike the Schwab-Oates analysis of "equalizing grants," it is not possible to use these transfers to achieve a first-best optimum. The equalizing grants can be implemented only if different types of workers are distinguishable from each other, an assumption that would allow local governments to achieve the first-best optimum without any need for central government intervention.

The method of analysis consists of considering the first-order effects of a small transfer. Giving a dollar to each resident of a high-cost jurisdiction raises utility there by u_x^{11}, *where the second superscript again indicates the arguments of the utility function,* (g^1, ω^1) or (g^2, w^2). Letting μ denote the fraction of all workers of the high-cost type, the transfer may be financed by collecting a poll tax equal to μ from both types of workers. Thus, the net change in utility within the high-cost jurisdiction equals $u_x^{11}(1-\mu)$. Since high-cost workers are indifferent between the two types of jurisdictions in equilibrium, the utility they could receive in the low-cost jurisdiction must rise by the same amount. In other words, the equilibrium change in (g^2, ω^2) satisfies

$$u_x^{11}(1-\mu) = u_x^{12}(d\omega^2 - \mu) + u_g^{12} dg^2 \tag{9-18}$$

Notice that μ appears on both sides of this equality because workers pay the poll tax regardless of where they reside.

To satisfy a low-cost jurisdiction's zero-profit condition, the transfer-induced change in the equilibrium (g^2, ω^2) must not alter the value of wage and public good costs:

$$n^2 d\omega^2 + C_g^2 dg^2 = 0 \tag{9-19}$$

Solving Eqs. (9-18) and (9-19) then gives

$$dg^2 = \frac{n^2\left[\dfrac{u_x^{11}}{u_x^{12}}(1-\mu) + \mu\right]}{n^2 MRS^{12} - C_g^2} \tag{9-20}$$

and

$$d\omega^2 = \frac{-C_g^2\left[\dfrac{u_x^{11}}{u_x^{12}}(1-\mu) + \mu\right]}{n^2 MRS^{12} - C_g^2} \tag{9-21}$$

For these changes to make low-cost workers better off, we must have

$$du^{22} = u_x^{22}(d\omega^2 - \mu) + u_g^{22} dg^2 > 0 \tag{9-22}$$

By substituting Eqs. (9-20) and (9-21) into (9-22) and rearranging, I obtain:

Proposition 1. *An income transfer from low-cost to high-cost jurisdictions is Pareto-improving if and only if*

$$\frac{n^2MRS^{22} - C_g^2}{n^2MRS^{12} - C_g^2} > \frac{\mu}{\frac{u_x^{11}}{u_x^{12}}(1-\mu) + \mu} \tag{9-23}$$

The numerator and denominator on the left side of Eq. (9-23) are both positive, and their ratio is less than one. This follows from Eq. (9-17) and is reflected in the differences in the slopes of the three curves passing through point e^2 in Fig. 9-1. The right side of Eq. (9-23) would exactly equal μ if the marginal utilities of consumption for high-cost workers were identical in the two types of jurisdictions. It is reasonable to assume that the diminishing marginal utility of income gives $(u_x^{11}/u_x^{12}) > 1$, as low-cost workers receive less income and higher public good levels in high-cost jurisdictions. In this case, the right side is less than μ. We can conclude that Pareto improvements are possible if low-cost workers represent a sufficiently small percentage of the entire population, or if public good preferences are sufficiently similar, as measured by the difference between MRS^{22} and MRS^{12} at e^2.

There exist parallels between Proposition 1 and the Rothschild-Stiglitz analysis of insurance. In particular, their analysis of the cross-subsidization of low- and high-risk insurance contracts produces a condition for beneficial cross-subsidies that depends on the percentage of the population in the high-risk category. In contrast to Proposition 1, differences in accident probabilities are a key concern for their condition. It is interesting to note, however, that buried in the Rothschild-Stiglitiz article is a theory of interjurisdictional grants that has previously not been exploited by the local public economics literature.

5. Costly entry barriers

Thus far, local governments have not been given the power to control migration, other than through the incentives created by their choice of public good levels. In practice, local governments do provide a variety of methods to limit entry. This section examines the use of interjurisdictional transfers when local governments employ "entry barriers," but only at a cost.

Returning to the profit-maximizing decisions of developers, I modify Problem 1 for a low-cost jurisdiction by subtracting an "entry cost," b, from the incomes of high-cost workers who choose to reside there. To capture the idea that it is not possible to perfectly discriminate between the two types of workers, I further assume that each low-cost worker faces a cost given by $k(b)$, assumed to be an increasing and convex function.[10] The modified problem then includes b as a control variable:

[10] There is no loss of generality from not including an entry cost directly in the expression for developer profits because such a cost could be transferred back to workers through a reduction in the wage rate.

Problem 3. *Maximize* $f(n) - C(g,0,n^2) - \omega n^2$
n^2, g, b, ω

$$\textit{subject to:} \quad u^2[\omega - k(b), g] = u^{2*} \tag{9-24}$$

$$u^1(\omega - b, g) \leq u^{1*} \tag{9-25}$$

Attaching Lagrange multipliers λ^1 and λ^2 to constraints Eqs. (9-25) and (9-24), respectively, the first-order condition for b may be written as:

$$-\lambda^1 u^1_x = \lambda^2 u^2_x k'(b) \tag{9-26}$$

where, as previously discussed, λ^1 is negative and λ^2 is positive. Substitution of this first-order condition into Eq. (9-13) allows us to express the weights in Eq. (9-12) in terms of $k'(b)$ and rewrite this rule for optimal public good provision as follows:

$$n^2\left[\left(\frac{1}{1-k'(b)}\right)MRS^{22} + \left(\frac{-k'(b)}{1-k'(b)}\right)MRS^{12}\right] = C^2_g \tag{9-27}$$

As one should expect, a costless entry barrier $[k'(b) = 0]$ eliminates any weights on the preferences of nonresidents, but as entry barriers become more costly, an increasingly negative weight is given to nonresident preferences.

By solving the new rule for $k'(b)$, we can relate the optimal entry barrier to differences between marginal rates of substitution and marginal costs:

$$k'(b) = \frac{n^2 MRS^{22} - C^2_g}{n^2 MRS^{12} - C^2_g} \tag{9-28}$$

Equation (9-28) and Proposition 1 imply:

Proposition 2. *Assuming that low-cost jurisdictions employ costly entry barriers, an income transfer from low-cost to high-cost jurisdictions is Pareto-improving if and only if*

$$k'(b) > \frac{\mu}{\dfrac{u^{11}_x}{u^{12}_x}(1-\mu) + \mu} \tag{9-29}$$

Equation (9-29) provides a criterion for the superiority of transfers over entry barriers. To understand this condition, note that the provision of a dollar of income to a resident of a high-cost jurisdiction is equivalent to an entry barrier equal to u^{11}_x/u^{12}_x in the low-cost jurisdiction. To finance this effective entry barrier, each resident of a low-cost jurisdiction would need to pay $\mu/(1-\mu)$. Taking this tax into account, the transfer becomes equivalent to an entry barrier equal to $u^{11}_x/u^{12}_x + \mu/(1-\mu)$, in terms of the disincentives it creates for the migration of high-cost workers to low-cost jurisdictions. The average cost of this effective entry barrier to low-cost residents equals

$$\frac{\dfrac{\mu}{1-\mu}}{\dfrac{u_x^{11}}{u_x^{12}}+\dfrac{\mu}{1-\mu}} \tag{9-30}$$

which is equal to the right side of Eq. (9-29). Proposition 2 then states that transfers are superior to entry barriers in cases where the marginal cost of the latter, $k'(b)$, exceeds the "barrier-equivalent" cost of the transfer, given by Eq. (9-30). If a high-cost worker's marginal utility of consumption is identical between the two types of jurisdictions, this condition becomes particularly simple: $k'(b) > \mu$, i.e., the marginal cost of the transfer exceeds the portion of workers who are of the high-cost type.

Note that it may be possible to use Pareto-improving transfers to entirely eliminate entry barriers. As transfers are increased, thereby raising the utility received by high-cost nonresidents, the equilibrium level of entry barriers can be expected to fall. If Eq. (9-29) continues to hold when transfers are substituted for entry barriers, then Pareto improvements will continue to occur as b falls to zero. At $b = 0$, Eqs. (9-28) and (9-29) are no longer valid because they assume an interior solution. Rather, Eq. (9-23) in Proposition 1 becomes the relevant

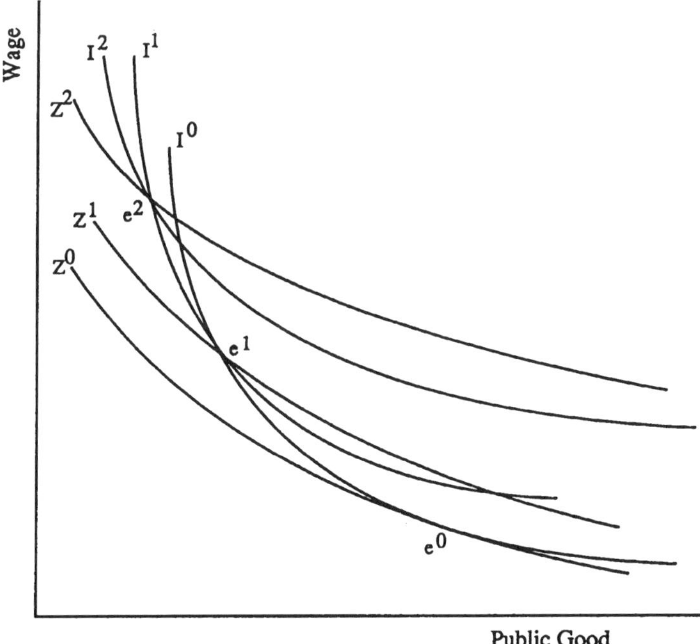

Figure 9-3

condition for determining whether further increases in the transfer produce Pareto improvements.

Stated another way, the existence of entry barriers may be inefficient in the sense that the use of interjurisdictional transfers might produce Pareto improvements while eliminating entry barriers. Taken as a whole, the analysis suggests that the decentralized use of entry barriers by local governments can often be improved upon by central government intervention.

6. Many types

The ideas developed in the previous sections can be extended to a model with many types of workers. I illustrate the equilibrium for three types in Fig. 9-3. Here, the zero-profit curve for a type-0, or "highest-cost," jurisdiction has been added. Its presence anchors the equilibrium in the sense that it determines the indifference curve on which the (g, ω) obtained by type-0 workers lies (indifference curve I^0), and this indifference curve is then used to determine e^1 and, finally, e^2. Again, there may exist a system of interjurisdictional transfers that produces Pareto improvements. Such a system will necessarily involve the transfer of income to the highest-cost jurisdiction, but the amount of this transfer that comes from each of the other two types of jurisdictions is indeterminate, given that the only criterion is achievement of a Pareto improvement. I have found no sense in which one can say that Pareto improvements become more or less easy to achieve as the number of different types of workers increases.

7. Property taxation

The musical-suburbs problem is often associated with the use of property taxation, given the prevalence of this tax instrument as a revenue source for local governments. As described in the introduction, property taxes create the same central problem dealt with in my previous model: a failure to match tax payments with marginal congestion costs. In the present case, this failure results from differences in property tax payments between residents with different housing demands, rather than differences in marginal congestion costs. The analysis is similar, except that the distortionary effects of the property tax on the housing market must now be taken into account. The main issue addressed in this section is how the use of property taxation affects the desirability of interjurisdictional transfers. I begin by sketching the model.

7.1 The model

Consider, again, the system of many jurisdictions but assume that the land in each jurisdiction is used for "housing." There exist two types of individuals, low-income and high-income, as distinguished by endowments of a single numeraire commodity, $y^2 > y^1$. The numeraire commodity may be consumed directly as a private consumption good, combined with land to produce housing, or purchased by the government to produce the public good. Public good production is described by the cost function $C(g,n)$, and profit-maximizing developers continue to choose the tax and expenditure policies.

Each individual's utility is a function of housing, h, the composite private good, x, and a public good, g: $u(x, h, g)$. With q denoting the consumer price of housing, the solution to the individual's utility maximization problem defines a housing demand function, $h(q, g, y^i)$, a consumption demand function, $x(q,g,y^i)$, and an indirect utility function, $v(q, g, y^i)$. Profit maximization by private housing producers yields a housing supply function for the jurisdiction, $H = H(p)$, where p is the producer price of housing (which will differ from q bccause of taxes). Letting n^i represent the number of type-i residents in the jurisdiction, the housing market equilibrium requires that

$$H(p) = n^1 h(q,g,y^1) + n^2 h(q,g,y^2) \tag{9-31}$$

Each local government finances its public good expenditures with a property tax and a land tax. The property tax is modeled as an excise tax on housing, which is equivalent to identical ad valorem tax rates on land and housing capital. The existence of a separate land tax therefore effectively allows the government to tax land and housing capital at different rates. Consequently, the second-best problem considered here arises from the inability of the government to use nondistortionary head taxes rather than from constraints on its ability to tax land. Hoyt (1991) and Krelove (1993) analyze the behavior of a single jurisdiction under a similar set of assumptions, but only for the case of a publicly-provided private good and a homogeneous population.

The government's land-value maximization problem may be stated by using the following control variables: the revenue collected from land taxation, T, the consumer and producer prices of housing, q and p (which determine the property tax rate, $q-p$), and the population levels, n^1 and n^2. These variables must satisfy the market-clearing condition for housing, a government budget constraint, and the same types of migration constraints described previously. The producer price, p, determines the jurisdiction's gross land rents, $r(p)$, via the requirement that profits in the housing market equal zero.[11] With $r(p) - T$ denoting the after-tax value of land, the government's problem may be stated as follows:

Problem 4. *Maximize* $\underset{p,\, g,\, T,\, n^1,\, n^2}{} r(p) - \mathrm{T}$

subject to:
$$H(p) = n^1 h(q,g,y^1) + n^2 h(q,g,y^2) \tag{9-31}$$

$$C(g,n^1 + n^2) = (q-p)[n^1 h(q,g,y^1) + n^2 h(q,g,y^2)] + T \tag{9-32}$$

[11] The other price entering the zero-profit condition is the price of the "numeraire commodity" used with land to construct housing. Here, this price has been fixed at one.

$$v(q,g,y^i) = u^{i*} \text{ for all } i \text{ where } n^i > 0 \qquad (9\text{-}33)$$

$$v(q,g,y^i) \leq u^{i*} \text{ for all } i \text{ where } n^i = 0 \qquad (9\text{-}34)$$

In equilibrium, maximum land values equal zero.

7.2 *Equilibrium*

Property taxes are set according to the same rule employed in the previous sections for head taxation: each resident's property tax payments should equal the resident's marginal congestion cost (MCC):

$$C_n = (q-p)h^i \quad \text{if } n^i > 0 \qquad (9\text{-}35)$$

This result follows from the first-order conditions for n^1 and n^2 in problem 4. Because housing demands differ across the two types of individuals, it is impossible to employ "marginal-cost pricing" with both types of individuals residing in the same jurisdiction. Thus, there are two types of jurisdictions in equilibrium, low-income and high-income. I consider those cases where the latter face the problem of preventing the entry of low-income individuals.

To graphically depict the resolution of this musical-suburbs problem, solve the market-clearing condition for housing, Eq. (9-31), to obtain the population demand function for a type-*i* jurisdiction:

$$n^i = n^i(q,p,g) \qquad (9\text{-}36)$$

The government budget constraint may then be written as

$$C[g,n^i(q,p,g)] = (q-p)H(p) + T \qquad (9\text{-}37)$$

Finally, the land tax can be eliminated from the problem by substituting the government budget constraint into the government objective function:

Problem 5. *Maximize* $\underset{q,\,p,\,g}{} \; r(p) - C[g,n^i(q,p,g)] + (q-p)H(p)$

subject to: $v(q,g,y^i) = u^{i*}$ (9-33)

$v(q,g,y^j) \leq u^{j*}$ for $j \neq i$ (9-34)

As developers receive zero profits in equilibrium, Problem 5 may be rewritten in terms of its dual as follows:

Problem 6. *Maximize* $\underset{q,\,g}{} \; v(q, g, y^i)$

subject to: $\pi(q,g) = \underset{p}{\text{Maximize}} \; r(p) - C[g,n^i(q,p,g)]$ (9-38)

$+ (q-p)H(p) = 0$

$v(q,g,y^j) \leq u^{j*}$ for $j \neq i$ (9-34)

Figure 9-4 illustrates the equilibrium. The horizontal axis measures the public good level, and the vertical axis gives the consumer price of housing.

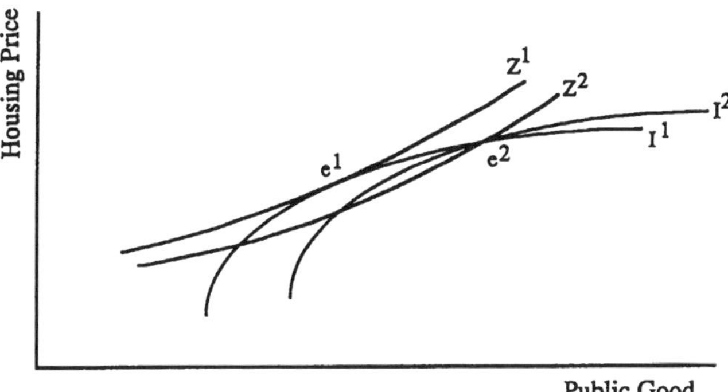

Figure 9-4

Curve Z^i is the zero-profit curve for a type-i jurisdiction, giving the consumer price q that solves Eq. (9-38) at each public good level. It is easy to show that the zero-profit curve for a high-income jurisdiction lies below that for a low-income jurisdiction, as illustrated.

The solution to a low-income jurisdiction's problem ($i = 1$ in Problems 5 and 6) is represented by point e^1, where the zero-profit curve Z^1 is tangent to an indifference curve for low-income individuals, I^1. Exactly where high-income jurisdictions locate depends on the relative preferences of high- and low-income individuals. Following Epple et al. (1984), I assume that high-income individuals possess more steeply sloped indifference curves than do low-income individuals. Given that high-income jurisdictions face a musical-suburbs problem, these jurisdictions are constrained to locate at a g above the tangency between Z^2 and a high-income indifference curve. Specifically, developer profits are maximized at e^2, where the indifference curves for both types of individuals intersect curve Z^2. Individual developers are indifferent between e^1 and e^2, as both yield zero profits, but the equilibrium division of jurisdictions between the low-income and high-income types depends on the relative numbers of the two types of individuals. As in the previous model, an assumption required to achieve this equilibrium is that indifference curves for high- and low-income individuals cross only once.

7.3 Interjurisdictional transfers

Consider an income transfer from the governments of high-income jurisdictions to the governments of low-income jurisdictions.[12] The desirability of such a

[12] In the present case, whether the central government transfers income directly between the local governments or between residents of the jurisdictions is important, as these two methods have different implications for housing-market distortions. The interjurisdictional transfers considered here are "intergovernmental." In this way, I maintain the assumption that individuals receive no lump-sum transfers.

transfer depends, again, on the extent to which marginal rates of substitution diverge from the marginal cost of public good provision, but now this cost reflects the distortionary effects of property taxation on housing demands. For simplicity, I assume that these demands are independent of public good provision levels. To understand the condition for a desirable transfer, I first state the equilibrium conditions for public good provision.[13] For a low-income jurisdiction, the tangency condition illustrated in Fig. 9-4 implies the following familiar rule for optimal public good provision under distortionary taxation:

$$n^1 MRS^{11} = \frac{C_g^1}{1 + \tau^1 \varepsilon^{11}} \tag{9-39}$$

where MRS^{ij} again denotes a marginal rate of substitution between the public good and private consumption for a type-i individual in a type-j jurisdiction, ε^{ij} is the elasticity of demand for housing for this individual (which is negative), and τ^j is the ad valorem tax rate on property in a type-j jurisdiction. The elasticity reflects the distortionary effects of the property tax, which raise the effective marginal cost of public good provision. For high-income jurisdictions, the musical-suburbs problem gives rise to the same type of weighted-average rule that appeared in the previous problem, amended now to take into account both housing market distortions and variable tax payments. Specifically, the first-order conditions for Problem 5 and Problem 6 yield

$$n^2 \left[\beta^2 MRS^{22} + (1 - \beta^2)\, MRS^{12} \left(\frac{h^{22}}{h^{12}} \right) \right] = \frac{C_g^2}{1 + \tau^2 \varepsilon^{22}} \tag{9-40}$$

where

$$\beta^2 = \frac{\lambda^{22} v_q^{22}}{\lambda^{22} v_q^{22} + \lambda^{12} v_q^{12}} \tag{9-41}$$

with λ^{ik} again representing the Lagrange multiplier on the migration constraint corresponding to a type-i individual residing in a type-k jurisdiction. As before, the high-income residents receive a positive weight, whereas a negative weight is given to low-income nonresidents. Thus, Eq. (9-40) holds with

$$\frac{C_g^2}{1 + \tau^2 \varepsilon^{22}} > n^2 MRS^{22} > n^2 MRS^{12} \left(\frac{h^{22}}{h^{12}} \right) \tag{9-42}$$

Dividing Eq. (9-42) by $n^2 h^{22}$ gives the slopes of Z^2, I^2, and I^1 at the point e^2 in Fig. 9-4.

With this condition in mind, I now amend the previous condition for positive transfers as follows:

Proposition 3. *In the property tax model, an income transfer from high-income governments to low-income governments is Pareto-improving if and only if*

[13] The proofs of the results in this section are available upon request.

$$\frac{\dfrac{C_g^2}{1+\tau^2\varepsilon^{22}} - n^2 MRS^{22}}{\left(\dfrac{C_g^2}{(1+\tau^2\varepsilon^{22})}\right)\left(\dfrac{h^{12}}{h^{22}}\right) - n^2 MRS^{12}} > \frac{\mu}{\left(\dfrac{v_y^{11}/(1+\tau^1\varepsilon^{11})}{v_y^{12}/(1+\tau^2\varepsilon^{22})}\right)(1-\mu) + \left(\dfrac{h^{12}}{h^{22}}\right)\mu} \tag{9-43}$$

Housing market distortions now enter this condition on both sides of the inequality. Note also that the condition depends directly on the ratio of housing demands in the high-income jurisdiction, which determine the relative tax payments collected from the low- and high-income residents that choose to reside there. Specifically, a fall in h^{12}/h^{22} lowers the denominator on the left side of Eq. (9-43) by a greater percentage than on the right side. Holding the other terms fixed, we can then say that a fall in h^{12}/h^{22} makes it more likely that an efficiency-enhancing role exists for transfers. This conclusion should not be entirely surprising – it is the shortfall of h^{12} below h^{22} that is responsible for the musical-suburbs problem and, therefore, for the possible role of transfers in lessening the resulting inefficiencies.

8. Conclusion

This study has shown that musical-suburbs problems may not be as severe as portrayed in previous models of the problem. These models typically assume that public good levels are set without regard to their implications for migration, in which case local governments are denied the opportunity to take steps to prevent entry. By working with perfect foresight models, I have shown how entry is prevented through the choice of public good levels, even in the absence of other barriers to entry. The analysis explains why musical-suburbs problems such as "the poor chasing the rich" are not typically observed in practice; once local governments recognize such problems, they can easily correct them, even if their policy instruments for doing so are severely limited. However, the decentralized choice of such "corrections" has been shown to create efficiency problems. In particular, I have derived conditions under which a central government can achieve Pareto improvements by means of interjurisdictional income transfers.

As an extension of the basic model, I have also analyzed the local governments' use of costly barriers to the entry of new residents. The main finding here is that these barriers may represent an inefficient means of "solving" the musical-suburbs problem. Specifically, interjurisdictional income transfers may produce Pareto improvements while inducing local governments to reduce or eliminate entry barriers. This result has been demonstrated for the model with cost differences between residents, but similar results could be obtained by extending the property tax model to include costly entry barriers.

One topic for future research would be to explicitly model how individuals are prevented from entering a jurisdiction and consuming its public goods. The issue of costly exclusion in the theory of club goods has recently received attention in the literature. See, in particular, Helsley and Strange (1991, 1994) and Silva and Kahn (1993). But none of these papers considers the matching problems associated with the provision of public goods by many independent providers to several types of consumers. One approach would be to add costly zoning policies to the property tax model considered in Section 7. Such costs might arise from the inability of high-income jurisdictions to costlessly target zoning policies in a way that prevents the entry of low-income residents. In particular, high-income residents may be indirectly harmed by such policies through constraints on their own housing choices. To adequately model this consideration, housing should be specified as a multi-dimensional choice variable, in contrast to the one-dimensional choice of the present model. Such a model might produce further insights into the importance of musical-suburbs problems and the role of central government intervention.

It would also be useful to extend the analysis to a dynamic framework. Such a framework might produce a musical-suburbs problem in the form of equilibrium cycles of migration, by which the tendency of low-income individuals to attempt to live with high-income individuals causes the residential composition of individual jurisdictions to oscillate between low and high incomes over time. The extent to which local governments attempt to eliminate this migration through the use of either second-best public expenditure policies or more direct entry barriers could then be explored. Another role for a dynamic framework would be to investigate the extent to which costly mobility reduces the importance of the musical-suburbs problem. Wildasin and Wilson (1996) demonstrate that the existence of moving costs produces too much migration, because local governments have an incentive to heavily tax those residents who are relatively immobile. A model with potential musical-suburbs problems might produce very different efficiency implications for moving costs.

References

Atkinson, A. B. and J. E. Stiglitz (1980) *Lectures on Public Economics.* New York: McGraw-Hill.

Berglas, E. (1976) "Distribution of Tastes and Skills and the Provision of Local Public Goods." *Journal of Public Economics,* 6, 409-23.

Brueckner, J. K. (1994) "Tastes, Skills, and Local Public Goods." *Journal of Urban Economics,* 35, 201-20.

Cassidy, G. and D. Epple (1994) "Property Ownership and Tax Structure." Unpublished manuscript.

Conley, J. P. and M. Wooders (1994) "Equivalence of the Core and Competitive Equilibrium in a Tiebout Economy When Tastes Are Not Publicly Observable." Unpublished manuscript.

de Bartolome, C.A.M. (1990) "Equilibrium and Inefficiency in a Community Model with Peer Group Effects." *Journal of Political Economy,* 98, 110-33.

Epple, D., R. Filimon, and T. Romer (1984) "Equilibrium Among Local Jurisdictions: Toward an Integrated Treatment of Voting and Residential Choice." *Journal of Public Economics,* 24, 281-308.

Epple, D. and T. Romer (1991) "Mobility and Redistribution." *Journal of Political Economy,* 99, 828-58.

Helsley, R. W. and W. C. Strange (1991) "Exclusion and the Theory of Clubs," *Canadian Journal of Economics,* 24, 888-99.

Helsley, R. W. and W. C. Strange (1994) "Exclusion and the Private Enforcement of Property Rights." *Journal of Public Economics,* 53, 291-308.

Hoyt, W.H. (1991) "Competitive Jurisdictions, Congestion, and the Henry George Theorem: When Should Property be Taxed Instead of Land?" *Regional Science and Urban Economics,* 21, 351-70.

Krelove, R. (1993) "The Persistencc and Inefficiency of Property Tax Finance of Local Public Expenditures." *Journal of Public Economics,* 51, 415-35.

Rothschild, M. and J. E. Stiglitz (1976) "Equilibrium in Competitive Insurance Markets: An Essay on the Economics of Imperfect Information." *Quarterly Journal of Economics,* 90, 629-60.

Schwab, R. M. and W. E. Oates (1991) "Community Composition and the Provision of Local Public Goods: A Normative Analysis." *Journal of Public Economics,* 44, 217-38.

Silva, E. and C. Kahn (1993) "Exclusion and Moral Hazard: The Case of Identical Demand." *Journal of Public Economics,* 52, 217-35.

Stiglitz, J. E. (1983) "Public Goods in Open Economies with Heterogeneous Individuals." In J.-F. Thisse and H.G. Zoller, eds. *Locational Analysis of Public Facilities.* Amsterdam: North-Holland.

Westhoff, F. (1977) "Existence of Equilibria in Economies with a Local Public Good." *Journal of Economic Theory,* 14, 84-112.

Wheaton, W. C. (1975) "Consumer Mobility and Community Tax Bases." *Journal of Public Economics,* 4, 377-84.

Wheaton, W. C. (1993) "Land Capitalization, Tiebout Mobility, and the Role of Zoning Regulations." *Journal of Urban Economics,* 34, 102-17.

Wildasin, D. E. and J. D. Wilson (1996) "Imperfect Mobility and Local Government Behavior in an Overlapping-Generations Model." *Journal of Public Economics,* 60(2), 177-98.

CHAPTER 10

Nationalism and secession*

Daniel H. Berkowitz

1. Introduction

In a fiscal federation, each region pays taxes to a federal government. In turn, the federal government finances public goods such as defense, internal security, a monetary system, interregional transport systems, and enforcement of free trade between regions. Several papers have addressed the question of when a would region tend to secede from such an arrangement. Austin (1994), Berkowitz (1996), Bos (1979)[1] and Buchanan and Faith (1987) analyze how voting procedures, changes in regional income, patterns of intraregional income distribution, and the self-interested behavior of federal bureaucrats might cause a region to secede. In this chapter, the following question is posed: When is a fiscal federation likely to break up even though it is in the economic interest of all the members to keep it intact? More specifically, what noneconomic factors might drive a region to secede from an economically viable fiscal federation?

This chapter studies how nationalism can destabilize an economically viable fiscal federation. Nationalism is defined as a situation in which a group of regional leaders chooses to secede even though such an action depresses regional income. This loss in regional income is the price that nationalists are willing to pay for independence.[2] Modern examples of this kind of nationalism include the separatist movement in Slovakia that led to the breakup of the former Czechoslovak Federal Republic and the secessionist movements that currently threaten the stability of Canada as well as some of the new countries of the former Soviet Union. A model is developed of an economically viable fiscal federation which, for simplicity, is comprised of two regions. The leadership in one region is non-nationalistic and always makes decisions on the basis of

* I wish to thank Jozef Danco (former Finance Minister of the Slovak Republic), Bogdan Heyduk, Jan Kinst, Lubomir Klimo, Gordon Meyers, Enrico Perotti, Tessa Van der Willigan, and participants at the 1994 ISPE Conference on Fiscal Aspects of Evolving Federations and at the 10th Sapir Conference in Memory of Eitan Berglas. This research was partially supported by the National Council for Soviet and East European Research.

[1] Bos (1979) examines conditions under which a region would decide to finance a good that the federal government had initially provided. While he does not call this a secession, this action is consistent with the definition of secession used in this chapter.

[2] According to Breton's (1964) analysis of nationalism, the regional income lost in a secession is an example of an investment in nationality which is justified by the "alteration of the inter-national or inter-ethnic distribution of ownership" (p. 377). In this chapter, nationalism is assumed to be a noneconomic objective and, therefore, the precuniary returns to secession are ignored.

economic criteria. However, the leadership in the other region is divided between nationalists and non-nationalists. The probability that the nationalists will succeed in implementing a secession is exogenous and known to the leadership of both regions. The following questions are asked: (1) When, if ever, does the possibility of a secession due to nationalism drive the non-nationalistic region to secede? (2) How much nationalism will the non-nationalistic region tolerate? (3) What is the impact of federal tax policy and regional income levels on the non-nationalistic region's tolerance of nationalism? (4) What is the impact of nationalism on resource allocation within the federation?

This chapter is organized in the following manner: The next section develops a simple model of an economically viable fiscal federation; Sections 3 and 4 study the impact of nationalism on the non-nationalistic region's decision to remain within the federation and on resource allocation within the federation. Section 5 concludes.

2. An economically viable fiscal federation[3]

This section models an economically viable fiscal federation in which the federal government coordinates the provision of public goods so that all regions, acting on the basis of economic criteria, choose to remain within it.

The fiscal federation is comprised of two regions, denoted i = 1,2. Each region is endowed with wealth, ω_i, and has collective preferences defined over a private and a public good, $\{x_i, G\}$, represented by a utility function, $u^i(x^i, G)$. Preferences are continuous and strictly convex. The federation is intact when each region pays its mandatory federal taxes, τ_i, and divides its after-tax wealth, $\omega_i - \tau_i$, between private goods and voluntary payments to the federation, $g_i - \tau_i \geq 0$. The federal government converts regional payments into a public good: $G = g_1 + g_2$.

Let g_{-i} denote the other region's payment to the federation. If the leadership in Region i is non-nationalistic, it acts on the basis of economic criteria and maximizes welfare within its region. Therefore, Region i's total payment to the federation, g_i, is computed by solving the program:

$$\text{choose } \{x_i, G\} \geq 0\text{: } \max u^i(x_i, G) \tag{10-1}$$

$$\text{s.t. } x_i + g_i = \omega_1 \tag{10-1a}$$

$$g_i \geq \tau_i \tag{10-1b}$$

[3] The model used in this section is based upon the work of Bergstrom, Blume and Varian (1986). See Wildasin (1991) for a discussion of how this basic model can be applied to fiscal federalism problems. For important applications, see Boadway, Pestieau and Wildasin (1989), Boskin (1973), Pauly (1970), Steinberg (1987), Wildasin (1991), and Williams (1966). A basic inspiration for this literature is Olson (1965). All these papers, however, ignore the possibility of secession. Guesnerie and Oddou (1981) and Westhoff (1977) incorporate an exit option. However, regions (agents) either pay mandatory taxes or secede. Bergstrom, Blume and Varian (1986) allow regions (agents) to make payments to the federation exceeding mandatory obligations.

$$g_i + g_{-i} = G \tag{10-1c}$$

where Eq. (10-1a) is the region's federal budget constraint and Eq. (10-1b) is the mandatory federal tax constraint. Using the Nash equilibrium assumption, g_{-i} is exogenous. Substituting Eq. (10-1c) into Eq. (10-1b) and substituting Eq. (10-1a) into the utility function, Region *i*'s maximization problem in Eqs. (10-1), (10-1a), (10-1b), and (10-1c) is equivalent to:

$$\text{choose } G \geq 0\text{: max } u^i(\omega_1 + g_{-i} - G, G) \tag{10-2}$$

$$\text{s.t. } G \geq g_{-i} + \tau_i \tag{10-2a}$$

where Eq. (10-2a) is Region *i*'s federal public good constraint (floor). Differentiating with respect to *G*, the demand for public goods is a function of Region i's exogenous parameters:

$$G = \max\{f_i(\omega_i + g_{-i}), g_{-i} + \tau_i\} \tag{10-3a}$$

or

$$g_i = \max\{f_i(\omega_i + g_{-i}), g_{-i} + \tau_i\} - g_{-i} \tag{10-3b}$$

where the public and private goods are assumed to be normal goods:

$$0 < f_i(\omega_i + g_{-i}) < 1, \quad \text{for } i = 1,2^4 \tag{10-3c}$$

When the demand for public goods is $g_{-i} + \tau_i$, the federal public good constraint is nonbinding. Otherwise, Region *i*'s federal taxes exceed what it would voluntarily pay. Substituting Eq. (10-3a) into Eq. (10-2), Region *i*'s welfare level as a member of the federation is

$$F^i = u^i(\omega_i + g_{-i} - \max\{\ldots\}, \max\{\ldots\}) \tag{10-4}$$

A non-nationalistic region tries to secede from a fiscal federation if, and only if, this improves its welfare.[5] A region engages in the act of secession when it withholds all mandatory taxes and allocates its wealth between a private good and a regionally provided public good, G_1^s. A secessionist region excludes itself from consuming the federally provided public good and excludes the other region from the benefits of its regionally provided public good.[6] Regional provision is most desirable for such public goods as internal security or reform

[4] As shown in Andreoni and Bergstrom (1995), Theorem 1, if preferences are continuous and strictly convex, and if the public and private goods are normal, then a unique Nash equilibrium exists.

[5] In many cases, secession is illegal and a region will be forced to remain in the federation. In the former Soviet Union, every republic had the legal right to secede from the Union; but, in fact, this right could not be exercised. The model in this chapter is relevant to fiscal federations in which secession is an option. One such case is the contemporary Russian federation in which many regions have been withholding taxes and making formal declarations of sovereignty (see Wallich [1994]).

[6] Clearly, a region that secedes may be able to free-ride off of federally provided public goods, such as interregional transport systems. Benefits from spending on regional public goods within the secessionist region may also spill over to the federation. For simplicity, this chapter ignores these issues.

programs because regional politicians are more sensitive to local tastes than is a federal government. Federal provision is more desirable for such goods as money and defense, in which there are gains to standardization and returns to scale. For simplicity, it is assumed that regionally provided and federally provided public goods are perfect substitutes and that regional politicians can convert a unit of regional wealth into a unit of a public good. Therefore, a region which secedes solves the problem:

$$\text{choose } \{x_i, G_i\} \geq 0\text{: } \max u^i(x_i, G_i) \tag{10-5}$$

$$\text{s.t. } x_i + G_i = \omega_i \tag{10-5a}$$

where Eg. (10-5a) is the region's independent budget constraint.

Substituting in the independent budget constraint, a region that secedes chooses G_i in order to maximize $u^i(\omega_i - G_i, G_i)$, s.t. $G \geq 0$. Denoting the solution to this problem $G_i^s = f_i(\omega_i) \geq 0$ utility in a secession is

$$S^i \equiv u^i(\omega_i - G_i^s, G_i^s) \tag{10-6}$$

Therefore, a fiscal federation is economically viable if, and only if, $F^i > S^i$ for $i = 1,2$. Note that $F^i = u^i(\omega_i - g_i, g_i + g_{-i}) \geq u_i(\omega_i - \tau_i, \tau_i + \tau_{-i})$ since Region 1 freely chooses $g_i \geq \tau_i$ and $g_{-i} \geq \tau_{-i}$. Therefore, a fiscal federation is economically viable when the following assumptions hold:

$$u^1(w_1 - \tau_1, \tau_1 + \tau_2) > S^1 \tag{A1}$$

$$u^2(w_2 - \tau_2, \tau_1 + \tau_2) > S^2 \tag{A2}$$

The next two sections analyze conditions in which a non-nationalistic region secedes from an economically viable fiscal federation.

3. Secession from an economically viable fiscal federation

Suppose that the leadership in Region 1 is non-nationalistic. However, there are two types of decision makers in Region 2. One type is non-nationalistic and decides to remain in the federation as long as Region 1 remains in the federation. The other type is nationalistic and always decides to secede. Thus, the nationalists always secede despite the economic costs.[7] The leadership in both regions know that the nationalists in Region 2 will succeed in pushing through a secession with probability π^2.[8] This raises the following questions: When, if ever, does nationalism cause the non-nationalistic Region 1 to secede? How much nationalism will Region 1 tolerate? What is the impact of changes in taxation and regional wealth on Region 1's tolerance of nationalism? Finally, what is the impact of nationalism on resource allocation within the federation?

7 Using an expenditure function, denoted E, it is possible to compute this cost as regional income foregone, $E(F^2)–E(S^2)$, which is clearly positive since $F^2 > S^2$ by assumption.

8 It is possible to incorporate a nationalistic leadership in both regions. This would not, however, alter the results. For a remarkably lucid analysis of deviations from rationality in two-person games with complete information, see Reny (1992).

If Region 1 remains in the federation, there are two possible outcomes. Region 2 stays in with probability $1 - \pi_2$ and Region 1's utility is $u^1(\omega_1 - g_1^r, g_1^r + g_2^r)$ w.r.t. $g_1^r \geq \tau_1, g_2^r \geq \tau_2$. Region 2 secedes with probability π_2. In this outcome, Region 1 bears the cost of committing resources to a dissolving federation. One way to capture this cost is to assume that Region 1 is able to withdraw its initial payments to the federation, g_1, and that its utility is the max of $(1 - \alpha_1) u^1(\omega_1 - g_1, g_1)$ w.r.t. $g_1 \geq 0$. The parameter $\alpha_1 \varepsilon (0,1)$ is Region 1's cost of committing resources to a dissolving federation. Another way to capture this cost is to assume that Region 1 cannot reallocate the resources that it commits to the federation in the event of a secession. In this case, Region 1's utility is the max of $u_1(\omega_1 - g_1, g_1)$ w.r.t. $g_1 \geq \tau_1$. This chapter uses the latter case. Therefore, if Region 1 is risk-neutral, its expected utility within the federation is

$$\pi_2 u^1(\omega_1 - g_1^r, g_1^r) + (1 - \pi_2) u^1(\omega_1 - g_1^r, g_1^r + g_2^r) \quad \text{w.r.t. } g_1^r \geq \tau_{1,}\ g_2^r >\!- \tau_2 \tag{10-7}$$

When differentiating with respect to g_1^r, Region *1*'s payment to the federation is a function of exogenous parameters ω_1, g_2^r, τ_1 and π_2:

$$g_1^r{*} = \max\{f_1(\omega_1 + g_2^r, \pi_2), g_2^r + \tau_1\} - g_2^r \tag{10-8}$$

Therefore, Region 1 remains in the federation if, and only if, its expected utility, EF^1, exceeds its utility from seceding:

$$EF^1 = \pi_2 u^1(\omega_1 - g_1^{r*}, g_1^{r*}) + (1 - \pi_2)\, u^1(\omega_1 - g_1^r{*}, g_1^r{*}, + g_2^r{*}) > S^1 \equiv u^i(\omega_i - G_i^s, G_i^s), \text{ w.r.t. } g_1^{r*} \geq \tau_1, g_2^{r*} \geq \tau_2 \tag{10-9}$$

There are several relationships in the model. First, Region 1's welfare from seceding is no less than its welfare from remaining in the federation when Region 2 secedes:

$$S^1 \equiv u^i(\omega_i - G_i^s, G_i^s) \geq u^i(\omega_1 - g_1^{r*}, g_1^{r*}) \tag{10-10}$$

Furthermore, Eq. (10-10) is an equality if, and only if, federal taxation is nonbinding and Region 2 always secedes:

$$S^1 \equiv u^1(\omega_1 - G_1^s G_1^s) \Leftrightarrow \tau_1 \leq G_1^s, \pi_1 = 1 \tag{10-11}$$

This equation holds since G_1^s is the unrestricted best choice when $\pi_2 = 1$ and Region 2 secedes with certainty, while g_1^{r*} is restricted (i.e., $g_1^{r*} \geq \tau_1$) and allows for the possibility that $\pi_2 < 1$. Finally, if the leadership in Region 2 is non-nationalistic, then Region 1's expected utility when the federation is certain is no less than its utility when each region pays at least its mandatory taxes:

$$EF^1(\pi_2 = 0) \equiv u^1(\omega_1 - \tau_{1,} \tau_1 + \tau_2) \geq u^1(\omega_1 - \tau_1, \tau_1 + \tau_2) \tag{10-12}$$

Since the fiscal federation is economically viable, then Eqs. (10-10), (10-11), and (10-12) and the viability assumption (A1) imply that

$$EF^1(\pi 2 = 0) > S^1 \equiv u^1(\omega 1 - G_1^s G_1^s) \geq u^1(\omega 1 - g_1^r{*}, g_1^{r*}) \tag{10-13}$$

where $S^1 = u^1(\omega_1 - g_1^{r*}, g_1^{r*}) \Leftrightarrow \tau_1 \leq G_1^s, \pi_1 = 1$

To solve for non-nationalistic Region 1's response to nationalism in Region 2, suppose that Region 1's mandatory federal taxes are no less than its consumption of public goods if it secedes: $\tau_1 \geq G_1^s$. In this case, Region 1 pays only its mandatory taxes should it decide to remain in the federation. The reason for this is that if the nationalists win with certainty, then Region 1's best choice would be to consume the level of public goods that is optimal at the time that it secedes: $g_1^{r*} = G_1^s$. However, if Region 1 is forced to remain in the federation, then it would pay only its mandatory taxes, since

$$\frac{\delta EF^1}{\delta g_1\ (\pi_1 = 1)} = \frac{\delta u^1\ (\omega_1 - g_{1,} g_1)}{\delta g_1} \leq 0 \tag{10-14}$$

Equation (10-14) implies Region 1 pays only its mandatory taxes when the leadership in Region 2 is completely non-nationalistic since

$$\frac{\delta EF^1(\pi_1 = 1)}{\delta g_1} = \delta u^1(\omega_1 - g_{1,} g_1 + g_1^{r*}) < \tag{10-15}$$

$$\frac{\delta EF^1(\pi_1 = 1)}{\delta g_1} = \frac{\delta u^1(\omega_1 - g_{1,} g_1)}{\delta g_1} \leq 0$$

Equations (10-14) and (10-15) imply that when $\tau_1 \geq G_1^s$, Region 1 pays only its mandatory taxes if it remains in the federation.

The following proposition characterizes the critical probability level at which Region 1 secedes.

Proposition 1. *If* $\tau_1 \geq G_1^s$, *then there exists a unique* $\pi_2^* \in (0,1,)$:

Region 1 remains in the federation and pays $g_1^{r*} = \tau_1$; *the non-nationalist leadership in Region 2 also chooses to stay in the federation when* $\pi_2 < \pi_2^*$;

Region 1 secedes and the non-nationalist leadership in Region 2 also chooses to secede when $\pi_2 \geq \pi_2^*$ *and*

$\pi_2^* = 1$ *when* $\tau_1 = G_1^s$, *and* $\pi_2^* < 1$ *when* $\tau_1 > G_1^s$.

Proof. The basis of the proof is Eq. (10-13). Differentiating EF^1 (Eq. [10-9]) with respect to π_2, then Eq. (10-13) and the envelope theorem imply that,

$$\frac{\delta EF^1}{\delta \pi_2} = u^1\ (\omega_1 - g_1^{r*}, g_1^{r*}) - u^1\ (\omega_1 - g_1^{r*}, g_1^{r*} + g_2^{r*}) < 0 \tag{10-16}$$

when $\pi_2 < 1$, since $g_2^{r*} \geq \tau_2 > 0$.

When $\pi_2 = 0$, Region 1 does not secede according to the former inequality in Eq. (10-13). When $\pi_2 = 1$ and $\tau_1 > G_1^s$, the latter weak inequality is a strict inequality and Region 1 secedes. Therefore, there exists a unique $\pi_2^* \in (0,1,)$: $EF^1\ (\pi_2^*) = S^1$ for all $\tau_1 > G_1^s$. When $\tau_1 = G_1^s$, the latter weak inequality is an equality, so that $\pi_2^* = 1$.

Assumption (A2) implies that the non-nationalists in Region 2 choose to remain within the federation when $\pi_2 \leq \pi_2^*$. Otherwise, they would always choose to secede. ■

Proposition 1 captures Region 1's benefit and cost of remaining in the federation when $\tau_1 > G_1^s$ and there are nationalists in Region 2. The benefit consists of Region 2's contribution to the federal budget if it remains. Since $\tau_1 > G_1^s$, the cost is the disutility of overconsuming public goods if Region 2 secedes. When π_2 is sufficiently high, the expected cost of overconsuming public goods when Region 2 secedes is no less than the expected benefit of Region 2's federal payment. Thus, Region 1 secedes.

The next proposition analyzes Region 1's tolerance of nationalism and the impact nationalism has on resource allocation within the federation.

Proposition 2. *If* $\tau_1 \geq G_1^s$ *and* $\pi < \pi_2^*$, *then*

$$\frac{\delta g_1^{r*}}{\delta \pi_2} = \frac{\delta g_2^{r*}}{\delta \pi_2} = \frac{\delta G}{\delta \pi_2} = 0 \qquad \text{(10-17a)}$$

when the federation remains intact.

Furthermore,

$$\frac{\delta \pi_2}{\delta \tau_1} < 0, \ \frac{\delta \pi_2^*}{\delta \omega_1} > 0, \text{ and} \qquad \text{(10-17b)}$$

$$\frac{\delta \pi_2^*}{\delta \omega_2} = 0, \ \frac{\delta \pi_2}{\delta \tau_2} > 0, \text{ when } g_2^{r*} = \tau_2 \qquad \text{(10-17c)}$$

$$\frac{\delta \pi_2^*}{\delta \omega_2} > 0, \ \frac{\delta \pi_2^*}{\delta \tau_2} = 0, \text{ when } g_2^{r*} > \tau_2 \qquad \text{(10-17d)}$$

Sketch of Proof. When $\tau_1 \geq G_1^s$, $g_1^{r*} = \tau_1$. Therefore, when $\pi_2 < \pi_2^*$, the non-nationalist leadership in Region 2 solves the program:

Choose g_2^r: max $u_2\,(\omega_2 - g_2^r, \tau_1 + g_2^r)$, w.r.t. $g_2 \geq \tau_2$ where the solution is independent of π_2:

$$g_2^{r*} = \max\{f_1[\omega_1 + g_2^r, \pi_2], g_2^r + \tau_1\} - g_2^r = \tau_1 \qquad \text{(10-18)}$$

This implies that

$$\frac{\delta g_1^{r*}}{\delta \pi_2} = \frac{\delta g_2^{r*}}{\delta \pi_2} = \frac{\delta G}{\delta \pi_2} = 0$$

(The comparative static results are included in the Appendix.)

In order to understand Region 1's response to nationalism in Region 2, it is useful to compute its federal consumption bundle:

$$x_1 = \omega_1 - \tau_1, \ G = \max\{\tau_1 + \tau_{2,} f_2\,[\omega_2 + \tau_1]\} \qquad \text{(10-19)}$$

A small increase in τ_1 increases the equilibrium supply of federal public goods and lowers Region 1's consumption of private goods. Thus, higher federal taxes force Region 1 to increase its overconsumption of public goods and lower its tolerance of nationalism: $\delta\pi_2^*/\delta\tau_1 < 0$. Because Region 1 overconsumes public goods, its marginal utility of income in the federation exceeds its marginal utility of income when it secedes. Therefore, an increase in w_1 induces Region 1 to be more tolerant of Region 2's nationalism: $\delta\pi_2^*/\delta\omega_1 > 0$.

Small increases in ω_2 and t_2 have no impact on Region 1's consumption of private goods. However, such increases may change the federal supply of public goods. When Region 2 pays only its mandatory taxes, then $G = \tau_1 + \tau_2$ and the equilibrium supply of federal public goods is increasing in τ_2 and constant in ω_2. Thus, Region 1's tolerance of nationalism is increasing (constant) in τ_2 (ω_2). When $g_2^{r*} > \tau_2$, then $G = f_2(\omega_2 + \tau_1)$ and the equilibrium supply of federal public goods is constant (increasing) in τ_2 (ω_2). This implies that small changes in $\tau 2$ have no impact on Region 1's tolerance of nationalism, while a marginal increase in ω_2 induces Region 1 to be more tolerant.

4. Tolerating nationalism

The last section argued that, if Region 1's taxes are high, then it then secedes for all $\pi_2 \geq \pi_2^*$. This section analyzes the case in which Region 1's taxes are low: $\tau_1 < G_1^s$. It is shown that Region 1 secedes only when the leadership in Region 2 is completely nationalistic. Furthermore, in contrast to the previous case, growing nationalism in Region 2 may lead Region 1 to increase its payments to the federation and increase the supply of federal public goods. These results are analyzed in the following propositions.

Proposition 3. *If $\tau_1 < G_1^s$ and $\pi_2 \in (0,1)$, then Region 1 does not secede and the non-nationalists in Region 2 always remain in the federation.*

Proof. Using Eq. (10-13) and the analysis in Proposition 1, $EF^1 > S^1$ when $\pi^2 < 1$ and $EF^1 = S^1$ when $\pi^2 = 1$. Since EF^1 and S^1 are decreasing and constant in π^2, the non-nationalists in Region 2 stay in the federation as long as Region 1 remains in.

The next proposition analyzes the impact of growing nationalism on resource allocation. In order to simplify the proof, the following assumption on preferences is employed:

$$\frac{\delta^2 u^i(x_i,G)}{\delta x_i \delta x_i} < 0, \frac{\delta^2 u^i(x_i,G)}{\delta G \delta G} < 0 \tag{A3}$$

$$\frac{\delta^2 u^i(x_i,G)}{\delta x_i \delta G} \geq 0: \quad i = 1,2$$

Proposition 4. *If $\tau_1 < G_1^s$ and $\pi_2 \in (0,1,)$, then a small increase in π_2 has no impact on federal resource allocation when $g_1^{r*} = \tau_1$. However, when $g_1^{r*} > \tau_1$, then g_1^{r*} and G are both increasing in π_2, while g_2^{r*} is non-increasing.*

Sketch of Proof. When $\tau_1 < G_1^s$, Region 1 pays at least its mandatory taxes to the federation. If $g_1^{r*} = \tau_1$, then by Proposition 2, a small increase in π_2 has no impact on resource allocation in the federation.

There are two other cases: $g_1^{r*} > \tau_1, g_2^{r*} = \tau_2$ and $g_1^{r*} > \tau_1, g_2^{r*} > \tau_2$.

Suppose that $g_1^{r*} > \tau_1, g_2^{r*} = \tau_2$. Then the federal equilibrium satisfies the following Eq. (10-20) and inequality (10-21):

$$\frac{\delta EF^1}{\delta g_1^{r*}} = \pi_2 \left[\left(\frac{-\delta u^1(\omega_1 - g_1^{r*}, g_1^{r*})}{\delta x_1} \right) + \left(\frac{\delta u^1(\omega_1 - g_1^{r*}, g_1^{r*})}{\delta G} \right) \right] \tag{10-20}$$

$$+ (1-\pi_2) \left[\left(\frac{-\delta u^1(\omega_1 - g_1^{r*}, g_1^{r*} + \tau_2)}{\delta x_1} \right) + \left(\frac{\delta u^1(\omega_1 - g_1^{r*}, g_1^{r*} + \tau_2)}{\delta G} \right) \right] = 0$$

The restriction on preferences in assumption (A3) and Eq. (10-20) imply

$$\frac{\delta u^2}{\delta g_2^{r*}} = \frac{-\delta u^2(\omega_2 - \tau_2, g_1^{r*} + \tau_2)}{\delta x_2} + \frac{\delta u^2(\omega_2 - \tau_2, g_1^{r*} + \tau_2)}{\delta G} \leq 0 \tag{10-21}$$

$$\frac{-\delta u^1(\omega_1 - g_1^{r*}, g_1^{r*})}{\delta x_1} + \frac{\delta u^1(\omega_1 - g_1^{r*}, g_1^{r*})}{\delta G} > 0$$

$$\frac{-\delta u^1(\omega_1 - g_1^{r*}, g_1^{r*} + \tau_{2)}}{\delta x_1} + \frac{\delta u^1(\omega_1 - g_1^{r*}, g_1^{r*} + \tau_2)}{\delta G} < 0$$

and

$$\delta^2 Eu^1 B(x_{1,} G)/\delta g_1^{r*} \delta\pi_2 > 0$$

By the implicit function theorem, it follows that

$$\frac{\delta g_1^{r*}}{\delta \pi_2} > 0$$

Since Eq. (10-21) is independent of π_2, then,

$$\frac{\delta g_2^{r*}}{\delta \pi_2} = 0$$

Since $G = g_1^{r*} + \tau_{2,}$ $\delta G/\delta\pi_2 > 0$.

Suppose that $g_1^{r*} > \tau_{1,}$ $g_2^{r*} > \tau_2$. Then the federal equilibrium satisfies the following two equalities:

$$\frac{\delta EF^1}{\delta g_1^{r*}} = \pi_2 \left[\left(\frac{-\delta u^1(\omega_1 - g_1^{r*}, g_1^{r*})}{\delta x_1} \right) + \left(\frac{\delta u^1(\omega_1 - g_1^{r*}, g_1^{r*})}{\delta G} \right) \right] \tag{10-22}$$

$$+ (1-\pi_2) \left[\left(\frac{-\delta u^1(\omega_1 - g_1^{r*}, g_1^{r*} + g_2^{r*})}{\delta x_1} \right) + \left(\frac{\delta u^1(\omega_1 - g_1^{r*}, g_1^{r*} + g_2^{r*})}{\delta G} \right) \right] = 0$$

and

$$\frac{\delta u^2}{\delta g_2^{r*}} = \left[\frac{-\delta u^2(\omega_2 - g_2^{r*}, g_1^{r*} + g_2^{r*})}{\delta x_2} \right] + \left[\frac{\delta u^2(\omega_2 - g_2^{r*}, g_1^{r*} + g_2^{r*})}{\delta G} \right] = 0 \tag{10-23}$$

Differentiating Eqs. (10-22) and (10-23) and using (A3), it follows that

$$\frac{\delta g_1^{r*}}{\delta \pi_2} > 0, \frac{\delta g_2^{r*}}{\delta \pi_2} < 0, \frac{\delta G}{\delta \pi_2} > 0 \qquad (10\text{-}24)$$

(The details are in the Appendix.)

When $\tau_1 < G_1^s$ and $g_1^{r*} = \tau 1$, an increase in nationalism has no impact on federal resource allocation. When Region 1 pays more than its mandatory taxes to the federal government, it overconsumes public goods when the federation is intact and underconsumes public goods when Region 2 secedes. Therefore, an increase in nationalism induces Region 1 to make additional payments to the federation since the likelihood of a secession increases. This also implies that the supply of federal public goods increases when, with probability $1 - \pi_2$, the federation survives.

5. Conclusions

This chapter poses four questions about nationalism and secession using a two-region model of an economically viable fiscal federation. The first question is: When, if ever, does the threat of secession from a nationalist movement in Region 2 drive the non-nationalistic Region 1 to secede? The model predicts that Region 1 secedes when its taxes are high and the secessionist movement in Region 2 is strong: $\tau_1 > G_1^s$ and π_2 is high.

The second question raised is: How much nationalism will non-nationalistic Region 1 tolerate? The answer is that Region 1 tolerates a great deal of nationalism when its taxes are low: $\tau_1 < G_1^s$.

The third question is: What is the impact of changes in federal taxation and regional wealth on Region 1's tolerance of nationalism? Since Region 1 tolerates nationalism when its taxes are low, the answer is limited to the case in which its taxes are high: $\tau_1 > G_1^s$ and when Region 1, if it chooses to stay in the federation, pays only its mandatory taxes. An increase in Region 1's mandatory federal taxes increases its consumption of public goods, decreases its consumption of private goods in the federation, and decreases its tolerance of nationalism. Region 1's tolerance of nationalism is increasing its own income, since its marginal utility of income is higher in the federation. Region 1's tolerance of nationalism is non-decreasing in Region 2's income and federal taxes, since the federal supply of public goods is non-decreasing in these parameters.

The fourth question is: What is the impact of nationalism on resource allocation within the federation? The answer is limited to situations in which Regions 1 and 2 remain in the federation. When Region 1's taxes are high ($\tau_1 \geq G_1^s$), an increase in nationalism in Region 2 has no impact on Region 1's payments to the federation and no impact on the federal supply of public goods. The same result holds when Region 1's taxes are low and it pays only its mandatory taxes to the federation. However, when Region 1 pays more than its mandatory federal taxes, its payments to the federation and the overall supply of federal public goods both increase in response to a growth in nationalism in Region 2.

The results have been generated in a highly stylized model. Future research will try to incorporate the kind of sophisticated federal tax systems used in Andreoni and Bergstrom (1995) and Boadway, Pestieau and Wildasin (1989). Furthermore, it would be important to consider how policies in Region 1 might be able to change the probability that the nationalists in Region 2 can force a secession.

Appendix

Proposition 2. *Proof of comparative static results*
Let $\psi\ (\pi_2^*, \omega_1, \omega_2, \tau_1, \tau_{2,} \ldots) = 0$ be an implicit function defining the critical level of nationalism, π_2^*:

$$\psi = EF^1 - S^1 = 0 \qquad \text{(10A-1)}$$

where

$$EF^1 = \pi_2^* u^1\ (\omega_1 - \tau_1, \tau_1) + (1 - \tau_2^*) u^2\ [\omega_1 - \tau_{1,}\ \max\left\{f_2\ (\omega_2 + \tau_1),\ \tau_1 + \tau_2\right\}] \qquad \text{(10A-2)}$$

$$S^1 = u^1\ [\omega_1 - f_1\ (\omega_1) , f_1\ (\omega_1)\ ] \qquad \text{(10A-3)}$$

Let η denote an exogenous fiscal parameter, such as $\tau_{1,}$ τ_2, ω_1, or ω_2. By the implicit function theorem,

$$\frac{\delta\pi_2^*)}{\delta\eta} = \frac{-(\delta\psi/\delta\eta)}{\delta\psi/\delta\eta} \qquad \text{(10A-4)}$$

Since $\dfrac{sgn\ \delta\psi}{\delta\pi_2^*} = \dfrac{sgn\ \delta EF^1}{\delta\pi_2^*} < 0$ for $\pi_2 < 1$, then

$$\frac{sgn\ \delta\pi_2^*}{\delta\eta} = \frac{sgn\ \delta\psi}{\delta\eta} \qquad \text{(10A-5)}$$

Therefore, the impact of an increase in τ_2 is

$$\frac{sgn\ \delta\pi_2^*}{\delta\tau_2} = \frac{sgn\ \delta\psi}{\delta\tau_2} = \frac{\delta EF^1}{\delta\tau_2} > 0 \qquad \text{(10A-6)}$$

where

$$\frac{sgn\ \delta\pi_2^*}{\delta\tau_2} = \frac{sgn\ \delta u^1\ (\omega_1 - \tau_1, \tau_1 + \tau_2\ )}{\delta\tau_2} =$$

$$\frac{sgn\ \delta u^1\ (\omega_1 - \tau_{1,} \tau_1 + \tau_2)}{\delta G} > 0$$

when

$$g_2^{r*} = \tau_2:$$

and

$$\frac{sgn\ \delta\pi_1^*}{\delta\tau_2} = \frac{sgn\ \delta u^1\ [\omega_1 - \tau_{1,} f_2(\omega_2 + \tau_1)]}{\delta\tau_2} = 0$$

when

$$g_2^{r*} > \tau_2:$$

The impact of an increase in w_2 is

$$\frac{sgn\ \delta\pi_2^*}{\delta\omega_2} = \frac{sgn\ \delta\psi}{\delta\omega_2} = \frac{\delta EF^1}{\delta\omega_2} \geq 0 \qquad \text{(10A-7)}$$

where

$$\frac{sgn\ \delta\pi_2^*}{\delta\omega_2} = \frac{sgn\ \delta u^1(\omega_1 - \tau_{1,}\tau_1 + \tau_2)}{\delta\omega_2} = 0$$

when

$$g_2^{r*} = \tau_2:$$

$$sgn\ \frac{\delta\pi_2^*}{\delta\tau_2} = sgn\left[\frac{[\delta u^1(\omega_1 - \tau_{1,} f_2(\omega_2 + \tau_1))}{\delta G}\right] f_2{}' > 0$$

when

$$g_2^{r*} > \tau_2:$$

The impact of a increase in τ_1 is

$$sgn\ \frac{\delta\pi_2^*}{\delta\tau_1} = sgn\ \frac{\delta\psi}{\delta\tau_1} = \frac{\delta EF^1}{\delta\tau_1}$$

$$\pi_2^*\left[\frac{\delta u^1\ (\omega_1 - \tau_{1,}\tau_1)}{\delta G} - \frac{\delta u^1\ (\omega_1 - \tau_{1,}\tau_1)}{\delta x_1}\right] \qquad \text{(10A-8)}$$

$$+ (1 - \pi_2^*)\left[\frac{\delta u^1(\omega_1 - \tau_1, \max\{.,.\})}{\delta G} - \frac{\delta u^1(\omega_1 - \tau_{1,} \max\{.,.\})}{\delta x_1}\right] < 0$$

The above expression is negative because $\delta u^1/\delta x_1 > \delta u^1/\delta G$ in both outcomes, since $\tau_1 > G_1^s$. Therefore, $\delta\pi_2^*/\delta\tau_1 < 0$.

The impact of an increase in ω_1 is

$$sgn\ \frac{\delta\pi_2^*}{\delta\omega_1} = sgn\ \frac{\delta\psi}{\delta\tau_1} = \frac{\delta Eu^1}{\delta\omega_1} - \frac{\delta S^1}{\delta\omega_1} = \qquad \text{(10A-9)}$$

$$\frac{\pi_2^*\delta u^1(\omega_1-\tau_1,\tau_1)}{\delta x_1}+\frac{(1-\pi_2^*)\delta u^1(\omega_1-\tau_{1,}\max\{.,.\})}{\delta x_1}$$
$$-[\delta u^1(\omega_1-f_1(\omega_1),f_1(\omega_1))/\delta x_1](1\varphi-f_1')$$
$$-[\delta u^1(\omega_1-f_1(\omega_1),f_1(\omega_1))/\delta G]f_1'$$

When Region 1 secedes, then $G = G_1^s$, which implies that

$$sgn\frac{\delta\pi_2^*}{\delta\omega_1}=\pi_2^*\frac{\delta u^1(\omega_1-\tau_{1,}\tau_1)}{\delta x_1}+\frac{(1-\pi_2^*)\delta u^1(\omega_1-\tau_1,\max\{.,.\})}{\delta x_1}-\frac{\delta u^1[\omega_1-f_1(\omega_1),f_1(\omega_1)]}{\delta x_1} \tag{10A-10}$$

To sign Eq. (A10), note that

$$\frac{\delta u^1(\omega_1-\tau_{1,}\max\{.,.\})}{\delta x_1}>\frac{\delta u^1(\omega_1-\tau_1,\tau_1)}{\delta x_1}>\frac{\delta u^1(\omega_1-f_1(\omega_1),f_1(\omega_1))}{\delta x_1} \tag{10A-11}$$

since $\max\{f_2[\omega_2+\tau_1],\tau_1+\tau_2\}>\tau_1>f_1(\omega_1)=G_1^s$.

Since $\pi_2^*\in(0,1)$, Eq. (10A-11) implies that $\delta\pi_2^*/\delta\omega_1>0$.

Proposition 4. *Proof for the case in which $g_1^{r*}>\tau_1$, $g_2^{r*}>\tau_2$. Differentiating (A3) and (A4) with respect to π_2 yields*

$$\begin{vmatrix}\delta^2EF^1/\delta g_1^{r*} & \delta^2EF^1/\delta g_1^{r*}\delta g_2^{r*}\\ \delta^2u^2/\delta g_2^{r*}\delta g_1^{r*} & \delta^2u^2/\delta g_2^{r*}\delta g_2^{r*}\end{vmatrix}\begin{vmatrix}\delta g_1^{r*}/\delta\pi_2\\ \delta g_2^{r*}/\delta\pi_2\end{vmatrix}\begin{vmatrix}-\delta^2EF^1/\delta g_1^{r*}\delta\pi_2\\ 0\end{vmatrix}$$

Denoting the system matrix D, assumption (10-A3) implies that all of the components of D can be signed:

$$D=\begin{vmatrix}- & -\\ - & -\end{vmatrix},\quad\text{and}\quad sgn-\frac{\delta^2EF^1}{\delta g_1^{r*}\delta\pi_2}<0$$

Furthermore, it follows from (A3) that sgn D>0, since

$$\frac{\delta^2EF^1}{\delta g_1^{r*}\delta g_1^{r*}}<\frac{\delta^2EF^1}{\delta g_1^{r*}\delta g_2^{r*}}<0$$

$$\frac{\delta^2u^2}{\delta g_2^{r*}\delta g_2^{r*}}<\frac{\delta^2u^2}{\delta g_2^{r*}\delta g_1^{r*}}<0$$

since

$$sgn \frac{\delta^2 EF^1}{\delta g_1^{r*} \delta g_2^{r*}} - \frac{\delta^2 EF^1}{\delta g_1^{r*} \delta g_1^{r*}}$$

$$= \pi_2^2 \left[\frac{\delta^2 u^1(\omega_1 - g_1^{r*}, g_1^{r*})}{\delta x_1 \delta G} \right] - \frac{\delta^2 u^1(\omega_1 - g_1^{r*}, g_1^{r*})}{\delta x_1 \delta x_1}$$

$$+ (1 - \pi_2^*) \left[\frac{\delta^2 u^1(\omega_1 - g_1^r *, g_1^{r*} + g_2^{r*})}{\delta x_1 \delta G} - \frac{\delta^2 u^1(\omega_1\ g_1^{r*}, g_1^{r*} + g_2^{r*})}{\delta x_1 \delta x_1} \right] > 0$$

$$sgn \frac{\delta^2 u^2}{\delta g_1^{r*} \delta g_2^{r*}} - \frac{\partial^2 u^2}{\delta g_1^{r*} \delta g_1^{r*}} =$$

$$\left[\frac{\delta^2 u^2(\omega_2 - G_2^s)}{\delta x_2 \delta G} - \frac{\delta^2 u^2(\omega_2 - G_2^s, G_2^s)}{\delta x_2 \delta x_2} \right] > 0$$

Therefore, by Cramer's rule, it follows that

$$sgn \frac{\delta g_1^{r*}}{\delta \pi_2} = sgn - \left(\frac{\delta^2 EF^1}{\delta g_1^{r*} \delta \pi_2} \right) \left(\frac{\delta^2 u^2}{\delta g_2^{r*} \delta g_2^{r*}} \right) > 0$$

$$sgn \frac{\delta g_2^{r*}}{\delta \pi_2} = sgn - \left(\frac{\delta^2 EF^1}{\delta g_1^{r*} \delta \pi_2} \right) \left(\frac{\delta^2 u^2}{\delta g_2^{r*} \delta g_2^{r*}} \right) < 0$$

Furthermore, Eq. (10-A3) implies that

$$sgn \frac{\delta G}{\delta \pi_2} = sgn \left(\frac{\delta g_1^{r*}}{\delta \pi_2} + \frac{\delta g_2^{r*}}{\delta \pi_2} \right)$$

$$= sgn \left(\frac{\delta^2 u^2}{\delta g_2^{r*} \delta g_1^{r*}} \right) - \left(\frac{\delta^2 u^2}{\delta g_2^{r*} \delta g_2^{r*}} \right) > 0.$$

References

Andreoni, J. and T. Bergstrom (1995) "Do Government Subsidies Increase the Private Supply of Public Goods?" Manuscript. Madison: University of Wisconsin. *Public Choice* (Forthcoming).

Austin, A.D. (1994) "Coordinated Action in Local Public Goods Models: The Case of Secession Without Exclusion." *Journal of Public Economics,* 58, 235-56.

Bergstrom, T., L. Blume, and H. Varian (1986) "On the Private Provision of Public Goods." *Journal of Public Economics,* 29, 25-50.

Berkowitz, D. (1996) "Regional Income and Secession: Center-Periphery Relations in Emerging Market Economies." Forthcoming, *Regional Science and Urban Economies*, 26, December.

Boadway, R.W., P. Pestieau, and D. Wildasin (1989) "Tax Transfer Policies and the Voluntary Provision of Public Goods." *Journal of Public Economics,* 39, 157-76.

Bos, D. (1979) "A Voting Paradox of Fiscal Federalism." *Journal of Public Economics,* 11, 369-82.

Boskin, M.J. (1973) "Local Government Tax and Product Competition and the Optimal Provision of Public Goods." *Journal of Political Economy,* 81, 203-210.

Breton, A. (1964) "The Economics of Nationalism." *Journal of Poltical Economy,* 72(4), 376-86.

Buchanan J. and R. L. Faith (1987) "Secession and the Limits of Taxation: Towards a Theory of Internal Exit." *American Economic Review,* 77(5), 1023-1031.

Guesnerie, R. and C. Oddou (1981) "Second-best Taxation As a Game." *Journal of Economic Theory,* 25, 67-91.

Olson, M. (1965) *The Logic of Collective Action.* Cambridge: Harvard University Press.

Pauly, M.V. (1970) "Optimality, 'Public Goods', and Local Government: A General Theoretical Analysis." *Journal of Political Economy,* 78, 572-85.

Reny, P.J. (1992) "Rationality in Extensive Form Games." *Journal of Economic Perspectives,* 6(4), 103-118.

Steinberg, R. (1987) "Voluntary Donations and Public Expenditures in a Federalist System." *American Economic Review,* 77, 24-36.

Wallich, C.I., ed. (1994) *Russia and the Challenge of Fiscal Federalism.* Washington, DC: World Bank, Regional and Sectoral Studies Section.

Westhoff, F. (1977) "Existence of Equilibria in Economies With a Local Public Good." *Journal of Economic Theory,* 14, 84-112.

Wildasin, D.E. (1991) "Some Rudimentary 'Duopolity' Theory." *Regional Science & Urban Economics,* 21 (3), 393-422.

Williams, A. (1966) "The Optimal Provision of Public Goods in a System of Local Government." *Journal of Political Economy,* 74, 18-33.

PART IV

TAXATION AND DISTRIBUTION

CHAPTER 11

Why is there corporate taxation in a small open economy? The role of transfer pricing and income shifting*

Roger H. Gordon and Jeffrey K. MacKie-Mason

1. Introduction

The role of the corporate income tax in distorting capital investment and savings decisions has been investigated at length in the academic literature.[1] While much progress has been made in understanding the behavioral implications of the tax, the recent literature has increasingly raised questions regarding why such taxes continue to exist. For example, Gordon (1986) and Razin and Sadka (1991) argued that a small open economy should not impose a source-based tax such as a corporate income tax on capital income. If capital is mobile and the country is a price-taker in the world capital market, then capital cannot bear the incidence of the tax. Firms would continue to locate in the country only if other factor prices (primarily for land and labor) drop by enough to compensate firms for the higher amount they have to generate pretax so as to be able to provide capital owners the going rate of return after tax. But if these other factors bear the tax anyway, then it would be better to tax them directly, thereby eliminating a distortion that discourages capital investment in the country.

While the theory forecasts that small open economies should not impose source-based taxes on capital income, in fact, essentially all developed economies do impose corporate income taxes. Not only are corporate tax rates nonzero, but in recent years they tend to be roughly comparable with the top personal tax rate imposed in each country. Are countries systematically using a tax that is dominated by other available instruments? Or has something important been omitted from the existing theories?[2]

* We would very much like to thank Scott Newlon for comments on an earlier draft, and Yong Yang for most able research assistance. The views expressed in this paper are those of the authors, and not necessarily those of the NBER. Jeffrey MacKie-Mason was a visitor at the Department of Economics, University of Oslo, while this paper was written. Financial support for this paper was provided in part through N.S.F. Grant No. SES 9122240.

[1] See Auerbach (1983), for example, for a recent survey of the effects of the tax on corporate investment.

[2] A more extended discussion of alternative explanations for corporate taxation, and their limitations, can be found in Gordon (1992).

The problem with the existing theories cannot be simply that they assume economies are small and open. If economies are large, then they certainly have an incentive to take advantage of their market power in world capital markets. Capital importers would want to reduce their capital imports to drive down the interest rate they pay on these imports, so would want to tax domestic investment and encourage domestic savings. Conversely, capital exporters would want to reduce their capital exports by taxing domestic savings and subsidizing domestic investment. But we do not see opposite patterns of taxation in capital-importing and capital-exporting countries, nor do we see sign changes when countries change from exporting to importing capital (as the U.S. did in the 1980s).

What if countries are not that open? Feldstein and Horioka (1980) provided striking empirical evidence suggesting that capital is quite immobile internationally. If economies are relatively closed, then it might appear that pressures due to capital mobility would be much abated, allowing capital income taxes to survive. But any conclusions here will depend critically on what factors limit capital mobility. Gordon and Bovenberg (forthcoming) explore the policy implications of various possible explanations for the observed capital immobility and find little prospect for rationalizing existing corporate taxes by this route.

The puzzles are not confined to government behavior. Firm behavior is also puzzling. Existing theories forecast, for example, that multinationals based in high-tax-rate countries are at a distinct tax disadvantage when investing in low-tax-rate countries. As do all firms located there, they pay corporate income taxes to the local government. However, they pay additional taxes to their home government when profits are repatriated. This surtax should put the multinational at a disadvantage. Yet US multinationals, for example, invest heavily even in the lowest-tax-rate countries (see Hines and Rice [1990], among others).

Reported rates of return also contradict the theoretical predictions. Domestic surtaxes on foreign earnings are postponed until repatriation, so multinationals face lower effective rates in countries with lower statutory rates. This implies that the pre-tax competitive rate of return should be lower in low-tax countries. But Hines and Hubbard (1990) and Grubert and Mutti (1987) find that pre-tax profit rates are *higher* in low-tax countries.

Observed investment and profit rates in low-tax countries are almost certainly explained by the ease with which a multinational can shift its accounting profits from high-tax to low-tax jurisdictions. For example, a subsidiary in a high-tax country can charge artificially low prices for outputs and pay artificially high prices for inputs that it exchanges with a subsidiary in a low-tax country. This lowers higher-taxed income and raises lower-taxed income, reducing the firm's global tax liabilities. Locating subsidiaries in tax havens facilitates this process, and it is not surprising that these subsidiaries consequently report a high pre-tax rate of return. Confirming evidence of the prevalence of income shifting is provided by Harris et al. (1993). They find that firms with subsidiaries in low-tax countries pay lower U.S. taxes, and firms with subsidiaries in high-tax countries pay higher U.S. taxes, suggesting income shifting from high-tax to low-tax locations.

Cross-border income shifting alone cannot explain the puzzling aspects of government behavior, however. If we take account of not only the mobility of real capital but also the mobility of accounting profits, the pressures to reduce corporate tax rates are only increased. The forecast is still that corporate tax rates should equal zero.

Transfer pricing is not, however, the only important type of income shifting that is likely to occur. Musgrave (1959), for example, argued that a primary role for the corporate income tax is to close off opportunities for individuals to shift labor income to an otherwise untaxed corporate tax base. Without a corporate tax, for example, owner/managers of closely held firms could incorporate, retain earnings rather than pay them out as wages, then sell some of their shares, making their earnings subject to capital gains tax rates rather than labor income tax rates. A corporate tax would offset this tax incentive as well as reduce the efficiency costs that such income shifting might induce.

In this chapter, we explicitly model the effects of both forms of income shifting on behavior and on optimal tax policy. In Section 2, we introduce only domestic income shifting (between personal and corporate income) and explore its effects on optimal tax design. We find that optimal source-based taxation on corporations is positive, with a tax rate equal to the labor income tax rate. The optimal tax is a pure profits or cash-flow tax.

In Section 3, we add cross-border income shifting (transfer pricing) to the model. In response to transfer pricing, countries face incentives to tax elements of reported income that are most subject to transfer pricing at a reduced rate, or to make them only partially deductible. The optimal corporate tax rate is then somewhat less than the rate on labor, which is consistent with most tax systems in developed countries (at least for the top tax rates on labor, which presumably apply to those people best able to shift income to the corporate sector).

We explore a variety of other seemingly puzzling aspects of existing corporate tax codes in Section 4. Why, for example, do many countries allow multinationals to receive credits rather than deductions for taxes they paid abroad? Why are they taxed only when profits are repatriated? Why do host countries tax the income of foreign subsidiaries? We argue that these aspects of the law make sense if the primary pressure affecting the design of the law is the need to prevent income shifting.

2. Tax policy with domestic income shifting

We first explore two approaches to modeling tax policy in the face of domestic income shifting. In the first, the model we will ultimately use for the host countries, individuals can shift the form of payment of their labor income from cash wages to nonwage forms, taxed in practice at the corporate tax rate. For example, a closely held firm in which the shares are owned by the manager and employees can retain what would otherwise have been wage payments, generating capital gains for the shareholder/employees.[3] Eliminating wage deductions generates income subject to corporate taxes, while we assume for simplicity that the capital gains received by employees on their shares are free of personal taxes.[4] Such income shifting presumably imposes real costs on the firm, however, because these alternative forms of compensation affect employees' liquidity and risk-bearing and may create complications due to asymmetric information about the value of these shares.

The second model, which we apply to home countries, assumes that only corporate entrepreneurs are in a position to shift their form of pay at a reasonable cost. When individuals make a career choice between becoming an entrepreneur or an employee, and between incorporating or not, they take into account that income earned as an employee (or noncorporate entrepreneur) would be taxed under the personal income tax whereas income earned as a corporate entrepreneur could, in practice, be taxed under the corporate tax but exempt from personal taxes. The choices of entrepreneurship and incorporation both involve a variety of nontax considerations, however, that must be traded off against any tax factors.[5]

In each model, a corporate income tax can be used to reduce the tax incentives that would otherwise exist to shift one's form of pay or one's career path. This role for the corporate income tax was mentioned at least as far back as Musgrave (1959). To focus on this role of the corporate tax, we will not introduce capital into the model. Our objective is not to rationalize the existence of *capital* income taxes, but of *corporate* income taxes. While existing corporate taxes do distort capital investment decisions, much of the revenue seems to be collected from the taxation of pure profits, which we interpret to represent the return to entrepreneurial ideas and effort.[6] We are able to introduce a distortionary tax

[3] Alternatively, the firm can pay employees in the form of stock transfers or qualified stock options rather than wages, generating extra taxable income for the firm (due to the lost wage deductions) and normally generating only capital gains income for the employees.

[4] In most countries personal capital income in at least some forms is taxed more lightly than labor income. Examples include a zero tax on capital gains that are passed on to heirs at death; a lower tax rate on dividends; and favorable treatment of pension savings.

[5] See Gravelle and Kotlikoff (1989), MacKie-Mason and Gordon (forthcoming), and Gordon and MacKie-Mason (1994) for more detailed analyses of the decision whether to incorporate.

[6] Gordon and Slemrod (1988) and Shoven (1991) have calculated that although the U.S. corporate income tax generates substantial revenues, capital income taxes in the U.S. in toto have generated *negative* revenues in recent years.

that captures the essential features of a corporate income tax without explicitly modeling capital.

2.1 *Optimal tax policy in home countries*

Consider first a situation in which corporate entrepreneurs but not other individuals can shift their income from the personal to the corporate tax base. In particular, assume that the population consists of a composite individual. This individual spends some fraction $1-h$ of total work effort as an employee, earning a wage w that is taxed at the personal tax rate t. The remaining work effort is spent running corporations. Here, the net return per unit of effort before tax equals π; this income is taxable at rate t leaving $\pi_n \equiv (1-\tau)\pi$ net of tax.[7] Setting up a new corporation requires an outlay of resources, however, and we assume that there are diminishing returns to these expenditures. These start-up costs are assumed to be deductible against the profits tax. On net, we therefore describe the individual's net wage rate, w_n, by

$$w_n = (1-h)\, w(1-t) + h(1-\tau)\, \pi - (1-\tau)\, c(h) \qquad (11\text{-}1)$$

where $c(h)$ measures the cost of setting up a new corporation of sufficient size to absorb the fraction h of one's work time. The individual's resulting utility can be expressed by the indirect utility function $V(w_n)$.

Individuals decide how much to work, and how to split this time between being an employee vs. being an entrepreneur. The first-order condition for h simply implies that $w(1-t) = (1-\tau)\,(\pi - c')$, so that the net returns from the two career paths are equalized at the margin, after taking into account the costs of becoming an entrepreneur.

Consider the optimal tax policy in this country. The government's objective is to choose the tax rates t and τ so as to maximize the objective

$$W = V(w_n) + \lambda L \left\{ (1-h)\, tw + h\tau\pi - \tau c\,(h) \right\} \qquad (11\text{-}2)$$

where L represents total hours of work, and λ measures the marginal utility received from extra government expenditures. Consider the effect of increasing t and cutting τ simultaneously so as to leave w_n unaffected. To keep w_n unaffected, we need that $\delta t/\delta\tau = -\,[(h\pi - c(h)]/[(1-h)\, w]$. With w_n fixed, L also remains unchanged. Since $\delta W/\delta t = \delta W/\delta\tau = 0$ under the optimal policies, this combined tax change should leave welfare unaffected at the margin. The

[7] In general, τ includes both corporate and personal taxes due on corporate income. For simplicity of discussion, we will refer to τ as the corporate tax rate, as if no personal taxes are due on this income, whether paid out as dividends or realized as capital gains. Because the entrepreneur has the option to pay all income out as wages, the maximum effective tax rate on corporate income is t.

resulting first-order condition for this proposed tax change, after some simplification, equals

$$\frac{dW}{\delta h}\left(\frac{\delta h}{\delta \tau}+\frac{\delta h}{\delta t}\frac{\delta t}{\delta \tau}\right)=0 \tag{11-3}$$

Raising corporate taxes (τ) and lowering labor taxes (t) lead to an unambiguous decrease in h, lowering the time spent as an entrepreneur and increasing time spent as an employee. Therefore, this first-order condition implies that $\delta W/\delta h = 0$, implying that $\tau(\pi - c') = tw$ under the optimal tax policy – the same taxes are paid regardless of career choice, so as not to distort the individual's choice of h. Substituting for $\pi - c'$ from the individual's first-order condition, we find that $\tau = t$ under the optimal policy.

In addition, we can show that the government would not want to introduce a distorting tax on corporate activity. Consider, for example, some distorting tax σ on the firm, leaving it with net profits $(1 - \tau)\,[\pi - S(\sigma,X)]$, where X represents the real decisions made by the firm which have been distorted by σ. The government's policy objective would now equal

$$W = V(w_n) + \lambda L\left\{(1-h)tw + h[\tau\pi + (1-\tau)S] - \tau c(h)\right\} \tag{11-4}$$

In order to show that the optimal value of σ is zero, consider the effects of raising σ and simultaneously lowering τ so as to leave w_n, and thus L, unchanged. This requires that $\delta\tau/\delta\sigma = -\,[(1-\tau)\,h/(h(\pi - S) - c)]\,\delta S/\delta\sigma$. The resulting first-order condition for W is[8]

$$\frac{\delta W}{\delta h}\left(\frac{\delta h}{\delta \sigma}+\frac{\delta h}{\delta \tau}\frac{\delta \tau}{\delta \sigma}\right)+\lambda Lh\left(\tau\frac{\delta \pi}{\delta X}+(1-\tau)\frac{\delta S}{\delta X}\right)\frac{\delta X}{\delta \sigma} \tag{11-5}$$

By Eq. (11-1), $\delta W/\delta h = 0$ under the optimal tax policy, so that the first term in Eq. (11-5) is zero. Because the firm's first-order condition for X implies that $\delta\pi/\delta X = \delta S/\delta X$, Eq. (11-5) implies that $\delta S/\delta X = 0$ under the optimal policy. By assumption σ distorts the firm's choice of X. Therefore, $\delta S/\delta X$ can equal zero only when $\sigma = 0$. The optimal tax policy then consists of a wage tax plus a nondistortionary cash-flow corporate tax at equal rates.

2.2 *Optimal tax policy in host countries*

Consider next a slightly different model, in which all employees are in a position to shift the tax treatment of their labor income. In particular, assume that there is only one source of employment, working to produce some good X. This good is produced using a constant returns technology subject to free entry, so that there are no pure profits in equilibrium. Normally, we would assume that all

[8] Because a pure profits tax rate is nondistorting, changing τ cannot change the firm's choice of X.

earnings are paid out as wages, taxed at the personal rate t^*. Now add the complication that if the tax rate on a firm's income, denoted by τ^*, is lower than that on labor income, then the firm can pay individuals in a form that is taxed at the firm's rate rather than at the individual's rate. This income shifting is not costless, however. If the individual receives the fraction s of her labor income w^* in a form taxable at the firm's tax rate, we assume that the labor costs to the firm equal $w^*[1 + b(s)]$. Here, $b(s)$ represents the real costs of shifting the tax treatment of labor income where, by assumption, $b(s)$ is convex, $b' > 0$, and $b(0) = 0$. In equilibrium, firms continue to break even, so that $p = w^*(1 + b)$.

The net wage rate, w_n^*, of the representative individual therefore equals

$$w^*[(1 - s)(1 - t^*) + s(1 - \tau^*)] \tag{11-6}$$

The individual chooses s so as to maximize her after-tax wage, holding fixed the wage costs of the firms, giving as a first-order condition for s:

$$\frac{b'}{1 + b} = \frac{t^* - \tau^*}{(1 - t^*) + s(t^* - \tau^*)} \tag{11-7}$$

It is straightforward to show that s is increasing in $t^* - \tau^*$. This individual's utility equals $V^*(w_n^*)$. Denote the individual's labor supply by L^*.

Consider next the optimal policy of a host-country government. The objective function of this government is

$$W^* = V^*(w_n^*) + \lambda^* L^*[\tau^* p - \tau^* w^*[1 + b(s)] + t^* w^*(1 - s) + \tau^* s w^*] \tag{11-8}$$

where λ^* once again represents the marginal utility received from extra government expenditures. What happens if the government raises τ^* and simultaneously lowers t^* by an amount chosen so as to leave w_n^*, and therefore L^*, unchanged? Note that given the lack of pure profits, changes in τ^* leave firms unaffected as well. However, these changes make income shifting less attractive, so s falls, causing w^* to rise. The resulting change in social welfare equals

$$\left[\frac{\tau^* - t^*}{(1 - t^*) + s(t^* - \tau^*)}\right]\left(\frac{\delta s}{\delta \tau^*} + \frac{\delta t^*}{\delta \tau^*}\frac{\delta s}{\delta t^*}\right) = 0 \tag{11-9}$$

Given that this policy change leads to a drop in income shifting, the term in the brackets should equal zero, implying that $\tau^* = t^*$. Again, the optimal tax system consists of a wage tax plus a cash-flow corporate tax at equal rates.

An alternative to this wage tax, combined with a cash-flow tax on firms to prevent income shifting, would have been simply to tax output of firms at some rate σ^*. Given our assumptions, raising σ^* is equivalent to raising τ^* and t^* simultaneously – both simply tax labor income and distort only the labor supply decision. This is simply the equivalence of a uniform value-added tax and a labor income tax.

3. Tax policy with cross-border income shifting

With domestic income shifting alone, we find that countries face an incentive to supplement a labor income tax with a cash-flow tax on corporate income at the same rate. How does this optimal tax structure change if we now take into account that each economy is open, that multinationals can set up subsidiaries abroad, and that transfer pricing allows these firms to shift accounting income easily between the parent firm and the subsidiary? Many types of situations could be examined. We focus on the effects of possible transfer pricing between the parent firm and its subsidiaries, and ignore other forms of mobility across borders.

To capture these ideas formally, we develop a model with two types of countries, home countries and host countries. We allow for multiple countries of each type, and assume that each is a price taker in international markets. We will examine policies for some representative home country j or representative host country i.

Multinationals are based in countries of type j, and use an imported good X to produce a good Q. If the representative individual in a country j allocates time h to producing Q, we assume that the resulting output equals $hf(X) - c(h)$, produced using inputs hX, where $f(0) = 0, f' > 0$ and $f'' < 0$.[9] The firm takes as given the price for Q in the output market, and this price is the numeraire. The input X can be purchased on the international market at price p or, alternatively, the firm can acquire a subsidiary in some country i, produce X there, then sell this good to the parent firm for some accounting price p^*. We assume that the same accounting price, p^*, must be used for tax purposes in the host country.

In any country i, X can be produced by either domestic firms or foreign subsidiaries. Labor is the only input used to produce X; the production function is simply $X = L^*$. For simplicity, we assume that multinationals have no technological advantage in producing X – the only reason for a multinational to open up a foreign subsidiary is to take advantage of transfer pricing. The going net-of-tax wage rate is w_n^*. As described above, the firm can either pay workers cash wages or, at a cost, pay them in a form taxed at the corporate rate rather than the personal rate. If the fraction s of labor income is paid in a form taxed at the corporate rate, then the pre-tax wage rate faced by the firm equals $w^*[1+b(s)]$, where w^* adjusts so as to leave workers with the going net-of-tax wage, w_n^*.

Each country is assumed to tax pure profits, with a rate τ in country j and a rate τ^* in country i. In addition, we assume that country j (country i) imposes a surtax on sales revenue at rate $\sigma(\sigma^*)$. Surtax payments are assumed to be deductible under the pure profits part of the tax. For example, a firm in country

[9] The rest of the individual's time is still spent as an employee earning a wage w taxable at rate t.

j buying inputs on the open market would pay taxes of $[\tau(1-\sigma) + \sigma] f(X) - \tau pX$.[10,11]

For convenience of notation, we let $T = \tau(1-\sigma) + \sigma$ represent the effective tax rate on gross sales revenue for operations in country j, so that a firm in country j pays $Tf(X) - \tau pX$ in taxes. We define T^* analogously.

Consider the incentive faced by firms in country j to acquire subsidiaries in country i. If a multinational acquires a subsidiary in country i, then it must pay taxes on its operations there to the host country; it may also owe some surtax to home country j on the income generated in i.[12] Denote the resulting effective gross tax rate on subsidiary revenues by T_r. Due to the home-country surtax, $T_r \geq T^*$, but because the tax is deferred until the income is repatriated, $T_r \leq T$.[13] Similarly, denote the effective tax rate on subsidiary wage deductions by τ_r, where $\tau^* \leq \tau_r \leq \tau$. Given T_r and τ_r, we define σ_r implicitly by the relation $(1-\tau_r)(1-\sigma_r) = (1-T_r)$. In order to parameterize the degree to which surtaxes are due on foreign-source income, we assume that $T_r = \rho T + (1-\rho)T^*$ and that $\tau_r = \rho\tau + (1-\rho)\tau^*$ for some ρ, where $0 \leq \rho \leq 1$.[14]

We focus on tax systems that give multinationals an incentive to shift profits out of the home country. With a subsidiary that provides an input, profits can be shifted by paying a higher price for the input. The increased factor cost in the home country is deducted at rate τ, while the increased revenue for the subsidiary is taxed at an effective rate of T_r. Therefore, to make transfer pricing attractive, we assume for purposes of discussion that $\tau > T_r$.

If the firm can set its own factor transfer price by choosing some arbitrary accounting price p^* for the input X, and if $\tau > T_r$, then we would forecast, without

10 We capture the difference in existing corporate taxes from a pure profits tax by this surtax on output. For example, if X represents capital equipment, then this rate difference can capture the fact that revenues are taxable immediately, whereas the amount spent buying capital is deductible only gradually over time. If, instead, X represents materials, then inventory accounting rules can also lead to a postponed deduction.

11 In country j, the entrepreneur's start-up costs are also deductible at the corporate tax rate, so total corporate taxes are reduced by $\tau c(h)$. However, as this deduction affects only the individual's time allocation, not the firm's optimal choices of p^* and X, we suppress this tax term when studying firm behavior.

12 Many countries, including the U.S., tax foreign-source income when it is repatriated, with a credit given for foreign taxes paid on this income. Firms may or may not have sufficient foreign tax credits to eliminate all home country taxes on the subsidiary's income.

13 Deferral is a gain only to the extent to which funds kept abroad can be invested there and earn a higher after-local-tax rate of return than the individual's after-home-tax discount rate. If there were full capital mobility and no taxation of capital income, then $T_r = T$ in spite of deferral.

14 If the firm repatriates profits every year, and does not have excess credits, then $\rho = 1$; if the firm systematically has excess credits, then $\rho = 0$. In general, the value of ρ depends on the length of time repatriation is deferred, the gain from deferral given the rate of return abroad relative to the discount rate, and the likelihood that the firm has excess credits. It is worth noting that σ_r, which is defined implicitly by $(1-\sigma_r) = (1-T_r)/(1-\tau_r)$, does not satisfy $\sigma_r = \rho\sigma + (1-\rho)\sigma^*$.

other additions to the model, that all taxable profits would be shifted to the subsidiary. That rarely seems to be the case.[15] To rationalize this, we assume that the tax authorities expend resources trying to prevent use of transfer pricing and that the threat of being caught and fined limits a firm's use of transfer pricing.[16]

In particular, in order to limit use of transfer pricing, the government is assumed to expend resources trying to detect use of transfer pricing. Due to these enforcement efforts, the government would have some probability θ of documenting the use of transfer prices, where θ should be an increasing function of p^*. If the firm is caught using transfer prices, then it would need to pay an amount $\tau(p^* - p)FX$ in additional taxes on domestic earnings, where F reflects any fines that are imposed (and perhaps any systematic deviation of the corrected price from p). If the corrected price is then used in assessing the tax on foreign-source income at repatriation, then the firm also receives back an amount $\rho T(p^* - p)FX$ on the taxes paid on repatriated foreign earnings if caught using transfer pricing,[17] implying an expected net penalty of $(\tau - \rho T)(p^* - p)FX\theta$. We explore the concrete example where $\theta = a[(p^* - p)/p]^{\beta}$, with $\beta > 0$, and assume risk-neutrality for simplicity.

3.1 Behavior of multinationals with cross-border shifting

For any given h, a multinational chooses X and p^* to maximize its net profits of

$$\pi_n = (1 - T) f(X) - (1 - \tau) p^* X + (1 - T_r) p^* X - (1 - \tau_r) w^* (1 + b) X - (\tau - \rho T)(p^* - p) FX\theta \tag{11-10}$$

Given this objective function, the first-order condition for p^* can easily be solved to show that

$$p^* = p\left[1 + \left(\frac{\tau - T_r}{(\beta + 1) aF (\tau - \rho T)}\right)^{1/\beta}\right] \tag{11-11}$$

15 U.S. firms taking advantage of the "possessions tax credit" by manufacturing in Puerto Rico apparently come close to total income shifting; see Grubert and Slemrod (1993).

16 In an earlier version of this chapter, we also constructed a model in which the accounting price, p^*, is used by the parent firm's manager in deciding how much X to purchase, creating an inefficiency because the transfer price is artificially high. Such inefficiencies might arise within a firm due to principal-agent problems, or due to the high transactions costs of keeping one set of books for tax reporting and another set for management operations. (Transfer-price accounting is at a much finer level of detail and complexity than the separate tax and financial reporting income statements and balance sheets that firms in many countries are required to maintain.) The results of this model were qualitatively similar to those we present here. Therefore, we do not report the details here.

17 We assume here that the fine is assessed on the net change in overall tax liability, and that foreign tax payments are unaffected by these recalculations of domestic tax liabilities.

The optimal value of p^* decreases with the severity of enforcement, as measured here by aF.[18] In addition, p^* increases with τ, but decreases with T^* and T. Increasing τ raises the value of deducting a high input cost, p^*. Increasing T^* or T (and thus T_r) reduces the value of reporting a high foreign unit revenue, p^*. Also, $p^* > p$ as long as $\tau > T_r$.

It will prove convenient to note that at this optimal value of p^*, the value of $F\theta$ equals[19]

$$F\theta = \frac{\tau - T_r}{(\beta + 1)\,(\tau - \rho T)} \tag{11-12}$$

If wc substitute this expression for $F\theta$ into the profit measure, we find that net profits equal[20]

$$\begin{aligned}\pi_n = {} & (1 - T)\,f(X) - (1 - \tau)pX + \frac{\beta}{\beta + 1}(\tau - T_r)\,(p^* - p)\,X \\ & - \rho(1 - \tau_r)(\sigma - \sigma^*)pX\end{aligned} \tag{11-13}$$

Here, the first two terms measure what profits would have been had the firm simply purchased X on the open market. The third term measures the net gain from use of transfer pricing, after taking into account the effects of tax enforcement – tax enforcement not only lowers p^* but also recaptures the fraction $1/(1+\beta)$ of the tax savings from transfer pricing. This term in itself raises profits. The last term reflects the fact that, without use of transfer pricing, the subsidiary operates at a competitive disadvantage because of the surtaxes due when profits are repatriated.

The first-order condition for X can be written, after substituting for the value of $F\theta$, as

$$\begin{aligned}(1 - T)f' = {} & (1 - \tau)p - \frac{\beta}{\beta + 1}(\tau - T_r)(p^* - p) \\ & + \rho(1 - \tau_r)(\sigma - \sigma^*)p\end{aligned} \tag{11-14}$$

Here, the left side equals the value of the extra output whereas the right side equals the net-of-tax cost of the extra input. Only the first term on the right side appears if the firm does not set up a subsidiary. As the second term on the right side is negative whereas the third term is positive, it would appear that the change in X due to use of transfer pricing is ambiguous. However, we show next that X must increase whenever the subsidiary is worth acquiring.

When is the subsidiary worth acquiring? The answer depends on the extent of enforcement in the home country. Comparing profits with or without the

[18] In general, the direction of effect of β on p^* is ambiguous.

[19] Note that the equilibrium probability of being caught is independent of a and a decreasing function of β.

[20] In simplifying this expression, we have assumed that competitive firms survive in the host country, so that $(1 - \sigma^*)p = w^*(1 + b)$.

subsidiary, and simplifying using a second-order approximation to output around the output level without the subsidiary, the change in profits from opening the subsidiary equals

$$\Delta\pi_n \approx .5(1-T)f''(X_s - X)^2 + X_s\left[\frac{\beta}{\beta+1}(\tau - T_r)(p^* - p) - \rho(1-\tau_r)(\sigma - \sigma^*)p\right] \tag{11-15}$$

where X_s is the chosen output level with the subsidiary, and X is the chosen output level without it. For the subsidiary to be worth opening, the sum of the terms inside the brackets must be positive, because the first term is necessarily negative. Equation (11-14) then implies that $X_s > X$. Therefore, a necessary but not sufficient condition for the subsidiary to be worth opening is that desired output increases with the subsidiary. As tax enforcement (measured by aF) increases, the first term inside the brackets becomes smaller, due to the fall in p^*, and is eventually dominated by the second term.[21] Therefore, subsidiaries and transfer pricing would no longer be attractive if there were sufficient tax enforcement. Similarly, as ρ rises, increasing the importance of the surtax at repatriation, then T_r increases and p^* falls. Both these changes cause the first term inside the brackets to fall. In addition, the rise in ρ causes the second term to become more negative, again making the subsidiary less attractive.

If X is produced in various countries, each with its own tax structure, where will the multinational prefer to invest? Assume that w^* has been set so that competitive firms break even in all countries where X is produced, implying that $p(1-\sigma^*) = w^*(1+b)$. To judge the locational preferences of a multinational, we examine how the firm's aggregate profits, as measured in Eq. (11-10), change as we vary the tax rates faced in country i. The derivative of the firm's profits with respect to τ^*, taking into account the forecast that wages will not vary, equals $-(1-\rho)X[(1-\sigma^*)p^* - w^*(1+b)]$. This expression equals zero when $p^* = p$, hence it is necessarily negative given that $p^* > p$, yielding the expected conclusion that multinationals prefer to invest in countries with lower τ^*.[22] Put differently, they would be willing to pay somewhat higher wage rates in countries with lower τ^*, potentially leading to production where real resource costs are not minimized.

Similarly, if we differentiate Eq. (11-10) with respect to σ^*, taking into account the forecasted change in w^*, we get

$$X[(1-\tau_r)p - (1-\rho)(1-\tau^*)p^*] \tag{11-16}$$

The first term in this equation reflects the fact that countries with a higher σ^* have lower wage rates, making them more attractive locations, everything else

[21] In general, however, increasing β has ambiguous effects on the net gain from transfer pricing.

[22] As expected, introducing transfer pricing enables us to rationalize the substantial activity by multinationals in tax havens.

being equal. However, the higher σ^* also means higher local tax payments, which are only partly offset by the credit received against home-country taxes when profits are repatriated. If repatriation of profits can be deferred for a long time, so that $\rho \approx 0$, then the second term dominates and the firm would prefer to invest in countries with a low value of σ^*. But this is not generally true.

3.2 *Optimal tax policy in the host country*

Consider next the optimal tax policy in the host country, now allowing for the possible set-up of subsidiaries and the resulting use of transfer pricing. The objective of the government now equals

$$W^* = V(w_n^*) + \lambda^* L^*[T^* p^* - \tau^* w^*(1 + b(s)) + t^* w^*(1 - s) + \tau^* s w^*] \tag{11-17}$$

In analyzing this case, we assume that multinationals own all production facilities and that the wage is set so that these firms are indifferent to locating in this rather than in some other country. If the country is small, then at the margin, the domestic wage must adjust in response to any given tax change so as to leave the net profits of multinationals unaffected. (If the wage falls far enough, domestic ownership will replace foreign ownership.)

Consider then what happens if the government raises σ^* while simultaneously lowering τ^* so as to leave the profits of multinationals unaffected at the existing wage rate. Under these simultaneous tax changes, T^* falls to compensate for the fall in the rate that applies to tax deductions, leading to a rise in p^*. In addition, assume that the government simultaneously raises τ^* to compensate for the fall in τ^* so as to leave w_n^*, and therefore L^*, unaffected. These tax changes cause s to rise, leading to a compensating fall in w^* so as to leave $w^*(1 + b)$ unchanged. The resulting change in social welfare must equal zero, implying

$$T^*\left(\frac{\delta p^*}{\delta \sigma^*} + \frac{\delta p^*}{\delta \tau^*}\frac{\delta \tau^*}{\delta \sigma^*}\right) = \frac{w^*(t^* - \tau^*)}{(1 - t^*) + s(t^* - \tau^*)}\left(\frac{\delta s}{\delta t^*}\frac{\delta t^*}{\delta \sigma^*} + \frac{\delta s}{\delta \tau^*}\frac{\delta \tau^*}{\delta \sigma^*}\right) \tag{11-18}$$

We conclude from Eq. (11-18) that sign(T^*) = sign($t^* - \tau^*$). Given the need for government revenue, the sign of each must be positive, implying that $T^*>0$ and $t^* > \tau^*$. Not only is there a positive corporate tax but, in general, this tax will be distorting – there is nothing in Eq. (11-18) causing T^* to equal τ^*.

Simply taxing labor income directly leads to efficiency losses due to income shifting, whereas the alternative of taxing output creates an efficiency loss by making the country a less attractive location for multinationals. These two sources of efficiency loss are traded off under the optimal tax system.

Note that if domestic income shifting is not a problem, so that s is not responsive to tax policy, then the right side of Eq. (11-18) equals zero. We then infer that $T^* = 0$ under the optimal policy, making the country a very attractive location for multinationals, a tax haven in effect. Given the lack of domestic income shifting, taxes are simply collected on labor income. If all labor income is paid out as wages, this can be done either through a personal tax on labor income, a payroll tax at the firm level, or a refundable VAT.[23]

If, instead, domestic income shifting is responsive enough to tax policy, so that the optimal value of T^* is high, then multinationals would be outbidden for workers by domestic firms. But with only domestic operations surviving, output prices would no longer be responsive to tax policy. This implies, as in the original model, that the tax system simply consists of a tax on labor income, taking the form either of a personal wage tax supplemented by a cash-flow corporate tax at an equal rate, or of a value-added tax.

In general, there are two local optima for tax policy. One has a low T^* satisfying Eq. (11-18), leading foreign multinationals to set up local subsidiaries. The second has a high T^*, no activity by multinationals, but no domestic income shifting. Which local optimum dominates would depend on the country's circumstances. In choosing between the two local optima, a country would be making a conscious decision whether or not to become a tax haven and thereby attract foreign multinationals at the expense of undermining its domestic tax system.

Another result worth noting is that the host country does not attempt to take advantage of the credits offered to multinationals when they repatriate profits – as seen in Eq. (11-18), the size of any credit, which is captured by ρ, does not affect the host country's optimal tax policy. This result holds as long as $\rho < 1$, which stands in contrast to the results in Gordon (1992), derived assuming $\rho = 1$. Even though the net cost of a host country tax may be small to a multinational, competition among host countries drives this tax to zero.

3.3 *Optimal tax policy in the home country*

What can be said about optimal tax policy in the home country, once we take into account the ability of multinationals to shift their profits abroad? The government's objective function now becomes

$$\begin{aligned} W = V(w_n) + \lambda L\{ & (1-h)tw - e(a) - \tau c(h) + \\ & h[Tf(X) - \tau p^* X + \rho(T-T^*)p^* X - \rho(\tau - \tau^*)w^*(1+b)X \\ & + (\tau - \rho T)(p^* - \rho)XF\theta] \} \end{aligned} \tag{11-19}$$

Here, $e(a)$ measures the real costs of monitoring the use of transfer pricing at an intensity level a.

We first consider the optimal revenue surtax, σ. We showed above that with no cross-border shifting, $\sigma = 0$, and that the optimal corporate tax was a

[23] Note that if the VAT is not refundable, and adjustment occurs, instead, through changes in the exchange rate, then the tax still distorts the transfer pricing decisions of foreign subsidiaries.

non-distortionary cash-flow tax. Such a result no longer holds when firms can use transfer pricing to shift income across borders.

In the appendix we show that $\delta W/\delta X > 0$ when tax rates are optimized. To use this result, first differentiate W with respect to X to find that

$$Tf' - \tau p^* + \rho(T - T^*)p^* - \rho(\tau - \tau^*)w^*(1 + b) + (\tau - \rho T)(p^* - p)F\theta > 0 \tag{11-20}$$

We can rewrite Eq. (11-14), the first-order condition for X, as

$$(1 - T)f' - (1 - \tau)p + (\tau - T^*)(p^* - \rho) - \rho(T - T^*)p^* + \rho(\tau - \tau^*)w^* - (\tau - \rho T)(p^* - p)F\theta = 0 \tag{11-21}$$

Since we have shown that $(1 - T)f' < (1 - \tau)p$ (i.e., X is greater with a subsidiary than without), the sum of the last four terms of Eq. (11-21) must be positive when opening a subsidiary is profitable. Multiplying Eq. (11-21) by $\tau/(1 - \tau)$ and subtracting from Eq. (11-20) yields

$$\sigma f' - T^*(p^* - p) - \frac{1}{1-\tau}[(\tau - T^*)(p^* - p) - \rho(T - T^*)p^* + \rho(\tau - \tau^*)w^* - (\tau - \rho T)(p^* - p)F\theta] > 0 \tag{11-22}$$

In Eq. (11-21), we showed that the sum of the terms in the brackets is positive. Therefore, $\sigma > 0$ under the optimal policy, which means that a distortionary corporate tax is used. Taxing entrepreneurs using τ is now more costly because it induces transfer pricing. As a result, entrepreneurs are taxed at least in part by a distorting tax, σ, on gross revenue. This tax also prevents an excessive shift into entrepreneurial activity and *lessens* the firm's use of transfer pricing, but at the cost of distorting the firm's internal decisions.

We now characterize the relationship between the optimal t, τ, and T. To do so, we make use of another result proved in the appendix: that $\delta W/\delta h < 0$ (holding w_n constant) when policies are at their optimal values. Since, by utility maximization, $\delta w_n/\delta h = 0$, this result implies that at the optimal policy, tax revenue – the other component of social welfare – falls at the margin as h increases. As a result, the labor income tax must exceed the effective tax rate on time spent as an entrepreneur, another distortion appearing only with transfer pricing. The opportunity for transfer pricing makes it more difficult to tax entrepreneurial activity. Under an optimal policy, there is a tradeoff between cutting the distortion favoring entrepreneurial activity and increasing the distortion encouraging transfer pricing.

To show this more formally, take the derivative of W with respect to h, holding w_n constant, to get

$$Tf - X[\tau p^* - \rho(T - T^*)p^* + \rho(\tau - \tau^*)w^*(1 + b) - (\tau - \rho T)(p^* - p)F\theta] - tw - \tau c' < 0 \tag{11-23}$$

Multiplying Eq. (11-20), $\delta W/\delta X$, by X and subtracting from Eq. (11-23) yields

$$T(f - Xf') - tw - \tau c' < 0 \tag{11-24}$$

Multiply the individual's first-order condition for h by $\tau/(1-\tau)$ and subtract, to find that

$$T(f-f'X)-\frac{(t-\tau)}{1-\tau}w-\frac{\tau}{1-\tau}\pi_n<0 \tag{11-25}$$

Now multiply the firm's first-order condition for X by X and rearrange to find

$$\frac{\pi_n}{1-\tau}=(1-\sigma)\,(f-f'X) \tag{11-26}$$

Substituting and rearranging terms yields

$$\sigma(f-f'X)-\frac{(t-\tau)}{1-\tau}w<0 \tag{11-27}$$

Because the concavity of $f(X)$ ensures that the first term is positive, we learn that $t>\tau$ under the optimal policy.

Finally, we can also show that $T<t$ under the optimal policy. To see this, first combine the first-order conditions for X and for h to get $(1-T)\,(f-Xf')-(1-\tau)c'=w(1-t)$. Similarly, combine the inequalities characterizing $\delta W/\delta h$ and $\delta W/\delta X$, to get $T(f-Xf')-\tau c'<tw$. If we multiply the first equation by t and the second equation by $1-t$, then subtract the first equation from the second, we find that

$$(t-T)(f-Xf')>(t-\tau)c' \tag{11-28}$$

Since $\tau<$ t, we therefore learn, in addition, that $T<$ t. Since $\sigma>0$, we find that $t>T>\tau$ under the optimal policies. In contrast, without transfer pricing, $t=T=\tau$ under the optimal policies.

3.4 Discussion

U.S. tax policy appears to have responded to these pressures to some degree. Excluding the period 1986–93, corporate tax rates have been below the top personal tax rate, the rate probably most applicable when considering the behavior of potential entrepreneurs. In addition, the U.S. has introduced some special provisions to reduce incentives to use transfer pricing. For example, in 1986 the U.S. introduced new rules for allocating interest expenses among the various countries in which a multinational operates. Previously, a firm could shift income by locating its interest expense where it was most advantageous. The new rules require U.S. multinationals to allocate a fixed fraction of the parent's interest expense to foreign-source income,[24] which reduces the deductibility of the parent's interest payments and thereby reduces the incentive for

[24] Usually, the allocation fraction is equal to the ratio of foreign to worldwide assets. This allocation rule is itself vulnerable to shifting; for example, firms could reduce the allocation by leasing foreign assets and buying assets used in domestic operations.

intracorporate borrowing.[25] A similar allocation procedure is used for R&D expenses.

One change in enforcement policy now under discussion is to judge the plausibility of a multinational's domestic profits as a whole, rather than the plausibility of each of the prices used in calculating profits. This would be done presumably by comparing a ratio of the firm's profits to sales or capital, to an equivalent ratio for purely domestic firms operating in the same industry. In the limit, the firm would simply be assigned profits for tax purposes equal to the profits-to-sales ratio observed for domestic firms times the subsidiary's reported sales. As a result, the tax becomes a tax on sales rather than a tax on income, with the rate varying by industry. Transfer pricing would no longer affect a firm's tax liabilities, except to the degree to which it affected reported sales revenue, or reported capital values. In terms of the notation used in our model, this policy has a positive σ but a zero value of τ, a policy not directly consistent with the results from the model but arguably not a distant approximation.

Note that we have assumed in this model that only inputs are subject to transfer pricing, so that a tax tied to sales revenue is not vulnerable to transfer pricing. It could equally well be the case, however, that outputs are subject to transfer pricing, for example, intermediate goods could be sent abroad for assembly. Some of our specific results certainly change if we allow for the export of outputs. But the main conclusion should be robust: Countries face pressure to keep corporate rates low, to discourage transfer pricing, at the expense of distorting individual career choices.[26]

So far, we have taken the value of ρ as given. What happens as ρ is changed? If ρ is raised, use of transfer pricing drops. For high enough values of ρ, multinationals will choose not to set up subsidiaries abroad, eliminating any problems from transfer pricing. The tax system would then revert to a wage tax supplemented by an equal rate cash-flow corporate tax, given the assumptions of the model. Within the model, there is no efficiency loss from taxing more heavily the pure profits earned by foreign subsidiaries since, transfer pricing aside, they earn no pure profits; therefore, this would be the optimal policy.

One way to raise the value of ρ is to force more rapid repatriation of profits from abroad, in the limit, by taxing foreign-source income at accrual. Such a policy may be costly to enforce. Another method would be to decrease the tax on domestic-source capital income, thereby reducing the gain from having funds accumulate abroad free of this domestic tax. In the limit, if there were no

[25] Gordon and MacKie-Mason (1991) examine the theoretical implications of the new U.S. interest allocation rule for borrowing location, while Froot and Hines (1994) and Collins and Shackelford (1992) provide empirical evidence regarding its impact on firm behavior.

[26] The policy proposal to base taxes on sales is obviously very vulnerable to transfer pricing on exported outputs.

domestic tax on capital income, then there would be no gain from deferral until repatriation of the tax due on foreign-source income.[27]

We can also solve for the optimal values of a versus F. Here, the result is immediate and clear. Holding aF fixed, and thereby holding p^* fixed, the government would want to lower a in order to save on resource costs, and to increase fines to compensate. Fines can equally well discourage transfer pricing, but they involve a redistribution from the firm to the government rather than a loss of real resources. This is simply a replication of the results in Becker (1968).

Imposing large fines on those caught using transfer pricing results in firms facing sizable risks, however, as it is uncertain whether or not use of transfer prices will be detected by the government. Polinsky and Shavell (1979) have argued against such aggressive use of fines because of the risk-bearing costs this policy imposes. But idiosyncratic risk faced by publicly traded firms should impose little or no risk-bearing costs on diversified shareholders. Large fines can well lead to heavy litigation costs, however, and these litigation costs must be traded off with the real costs of greater enforcement efforts. Another problem with high fines is that the government's assessment of the market price may be systematically in error. Hence, the high potential fines force the firm to make use of distorted prices for tax purposes, thereby distorting its real decisions. Considering that the government may be in a poor position to determine the appropriate market price for each of the thousands of specific items transferred within a firm, large fines could well lead to substantial distortions of internal allocation decisions within firms.

Rather than the government expending resources on enforcement, it could require firms to expend resources (for example, by documenting more carefully the criteria used in setting their transfer prices) to aid the government in its enforcement efforts. Simply shifting resource costs to the firm, however, does not eliminate the loss of real resources.[28] Furthermore, note that this approach may be more effective at raising β than at raising a; yet increases in β have ambiguous effects on the firm's net gain from using transfer pricing.

4. Other tax implications of income shifting

The above model helps explain the existence of cash-flow corporate taxes in small open economies, and justifies some deviations from a cash-flow tax in order to lessen the amount of transfer pricing that occurs. The mere existence

[27] This is equivalent to arguing that the current tax treatment of pensions would not affect the return to labor in a setting with a proportional wage tax and no capital income taxes.

[28] It is certainly possible that resources expended by firms gathering internal information may improve enforcement more than equivalent resources expended by the government attempting to acquire the same information from a distance.

of corporate income taxes is not the only puzzle raised in recent theoretical analyses of optimal tax policy in an open economy, however. Many details of existing taxes have also seemed puzzling. In particular, the past literature argues that residence-based taxes on the return to savings can be appropriate for a small open economy, but that source-based taxes would not be. Yet existing corporate taxes deviate in a variety of ways from a residence-based tax. To begin with, existing taxes equally apply to all firms operating in a country, whereas a residence-based tax would not tax the return earned by foreign-owned firms operating in the country – doing so prevents the country from taking full advantage of the gains from trade in the world capital market. Second, when domestic-owned subsidiaries operating abroad face local taxes, a number of authors (for example, Hamada [1966]) have argued that these taxes should be treated as a deductible expense rather than credited against domestic taxes, as under U.S. law. The idea is that a tax system should be designed to equate the return to the country on domestic investments with the return on foreign investments measured net of any taxes paid abroad. Third, under a pure residence-based tax, domestic-owned subsidiaries operating abroad would be taxed on their income at accrual (so that income from domestic and foreign sources is taxed at the same rate) rather than at repatriation as under existing tax systems.

Each of these aspects of existing corporate taxes would be puzzling if corporate taxes were in fact being designed to tax the return to savings of domestic residents. As argued above, however, another important use of a corporate tax is that of a backstop to the tax on the labor income of domestic residents. If this is the sole role for the corporate tax, that is, if it does not represent an attempt to tax the return to savings by domestic residents, then the above features of the corporate tax can be rationalized easily.

Consider the first puzzle: Why do countries impose a source-based tax on foreign firms at the same rate as the residence-based tax on domestic firms? We will treat the case of a host country. We showed above that host countries would have an incentive to impose at least some taxes on foreign subsidiaries located in the country if domestic income-shifting is a problem. However, in that model, domestic firms are not competitive with multinationals; therefore, all ownership is foreign and we cannot determine the optimal tax rules for domestic firms. If we alter our assumptions to allow some domestic firms to survive in equilibrium (perhaps in a different industry), what would be the appropriate policy? If these firms were not multinationals, they would not be able to shift income across borders. Then, by our arguments in Section 2, the optimal policy would be a cash-flow tax at rate t^*, so as to avoid domestic income shifting. This suggests that domestic-owned and foreign-owned firms would face different tax rates, and only employees of foreign-owned firms would engage in domestic income shifting. But if tax rates differed by ownership, then a new form of income shifting becomes possible: Domestic owners can transfer their firms to foreign owners – the foreign owners receive nothing in return since the firms continue to break even. However, the domestic employees of these firms gain because they can now shift part of their labor income into corporate form, making it subject to the lower corporate tax rate faced by foreign-owned firms. If this nominal transfer of ownership to foreigners is simple enough, no rate differential between domestic-owned and foreign-owned firms can survive. A similar argument would achieve this same result for foreign and domestic firms both operating in a home country.

Consider next the second puzzle: Why do countries give credits for foreign taxes paid? To begin with, we have already shown that a government would want to tax income earned abroad, and that the tax on foreign-source income should be designed to limit the incentives for cross-border income shifting. In the model above, this is most directly accomplished by setting $\rho = 1$, so that foreign income is taxed at the same rate as domestic income. In fact, international income shifting can take a variety of forms in addition to transfer pricing, increasing the pressure to keep ρ high. For example, if the tax rate on foreign earnings is less than the domestic tax rate on labor income, then domestic entrepreneurs have the incentive to set up subsidiaries abroad, rather than at home, to make use of their ideas. (In this case, the subsidiary embodies the ideas of the home-country entrepreneur; in the previous case, it embodied the ideas of the host-country entrepreneur.) Following the logic of Section 2, the optimal tax treatment would again involve taxing this foreign-source income at the same rate as domestic-source income.

Together, these pressures would lead us to expect a subsidiary to be taxed at the maximum of the corporate tax rates prevailing in the host and the home countries in order to prevent tax avoidance by either domestic or foreign residents. This is precisely what happens under existing crediting schemes (assuming deferral has no effect on the net tax rate). Does crediting introduce other distortions due to the differential tax treatment of foreign and domestic firms operating in the same country? Suppose a group of domestic entrepreneurs is considering selling their firm to foreigners. If they retain the firm, they face the domestic tax rate; but if they sell it to foreigners, the firm would face the maximum of the domestic and the foreign rates, which would seem to discourage such a sale even though there might be good economic grounds for it. The foreign firm can avoid this surtax, however, simply by making royalty or wage payments to the original entrepreneurs equal to the profits earned from their ideas. The return to the entrepreneurs' ideas would still be taxed at the labor income tax rate. Net of these royalty/wage payments, the firm would break even, so that any cash-flow surtax on the firm would collect no revenue and be nondistorting.[29] Therefore, existing crediting schemes can readily be rationalized.[30]

The third puzzle we discuss is why countries tax foreign-source income upon repatriation rather than at time of accrual. In fact, the deferral of taxes on foreign-source income creates no problems as long as the after-local-tax rate of return earned abroad equals the firm's discount rate.[31] If the rate of return earned abroad were lower, then the domestic owner could simply repatriate earnings as they accrue. Deferral is only a problem if the rate of return earned on funds kept abroad exceeds that available at home. If the domestic government does not tax the return to savings, then capital mobility leads to an equalization of net rates of return. Deferral remains a puzzle, however, to the extent to which there is a domestic tax on the return to savings, unless the costs of enforcing a tax at accrual are too high.

While we have provided a rationale for a variety of aspects of existing corporate income taxes, some other puzzles remain. For one, we have not addressed the question raised in prior literature concerning why existing corporate taxes include the return to capital in the tax base.[32] In addition, while we have argued that countries have an incentive to tax foreign-source income at the same effective rate as domestic-source income, some countries (such as France and the Netherlands) exempt foreign-source income from tax. This also seems puzzling, unless their domestic tax rates are low enough so that residents would not gain by shifting income abroad. An intermediate position is taken by Norway, which exempts foreign-source income earned in countries with tax rates at least two-thirds as high as Norway's rate, while taxing income from low-tax countries.

Several further complications could be added to the model, changing the results. For example, given the set-up of the model, the optimal tax scheme ignoring transfer pricing would impose equal tax rates on employees and entrepreneurs in order to avoid distorting career choices. But a major activity

[29] If the foreign corporate tax is distorting, then the sale can increase tax payments. However, if the foreign tax applies uniformly to firms owned by foreign residents, regardless of where these firms are located, then it simply reduces the return to labor in the foreign countries rather than affecting the attractiveness of acquiring such a firm, leaving the above results unchanged.

[30] This theory rationalizes the use of credits, but does not preclude the use of deductions. If taxes paid abroad were allowed as a deduction rather than credited against domestic tax liabilities, as recommended in Hamada (1966), the tax rate on foreign-source income would be yet higher. It would certainly be high enough to prevent income shifting; yet without income shifting, it would still apply to a zero tax base and so impose no distortions.

[31] See Footnote 13.

[32] While the above model could rationalize limiting the deductions for capital purchases if physical capital inputs were particularly subject to transfer pricing, this explanation does not seem very plausible.

of entrepreneurs is to develop new ideas for profitable business activities. The return earned by entrepreneurs on these new ideas can differ from the social return to the ideas for a variety of reasons, justifying a differential tax treatment to correct for these distorted incentives. For example, others can learn an entrepreneur's ideas from observation and set up competing firms using the same ideas, diluting the profits of the original entrepreneur.[33] In addition, the original entrepreneur can use any new information to profit from trading on the securities market. As argued by Hirshleifer (1971), the resulting profits from trade can well exceed the social return to the idea. If returns to the entrepreneur's ideas result from acquired monopoly rents, from successful rent-seeking behavior for instance, then the social return to the effort will again be less than the private return. Therefore, a variety of questions can be raised about the appropriate relative tax rates on employees versus entrepreneurs.

One response to transfer pricing by states in the U.S. is to shift from separate accounting to formula apportionment. Under separate accounting, transfer prices are needed for all goods and services traded across state lines, raising severe enforcement problems. In contrast, under formula apportionment, national rather than state profits are calculated. These national profits are then apportioned among the various states based on the fraction of the firm's capital, payroll, and sales located in each state. This approach effectively eliminates any gains from transfer pricing among domestic operations of firms, at least as long as the factors in the formula are not themselves subject to transfer pricing. Would this approach also make sense for taxation at an international level? Not if income shifting is the primary consideration justifying the presence of a corporate income tax. To prevent income shifting, a country would want an entrepreneur to face the same tax rate on corporate income as on personal income. But under formula apportionment, the effective tax rate faced by an entrepreneur would be a weighted average of the tax rates prevailing in all the jurisdictions in which he does business. The entrepreneur would therefore have an incentive to invest in low-tax jurisdictions, thereby raising the return to being an entrepreneur.

5. Conclusions

Several recent papers, such as Gordon (1986) and Razin and Sadka (1991), show that standard theoretical models forecast that a small open economy will not impose source-based taxes on capital income. Unless residence-based taxes on income from capital can, in practice, include foreign-source as well as domestic-source income (which in practice is unlikely given the difficulties a government faces in monitoring foreign-source income), as argued by Razin and Sadka (1991), residence-based taxes would not be feasible. Optimal taxes would

[33] Patents provide some limited protection for certain types of ideas, but many profitable ideas are not patentable.

simply consist of taxes on immobile domestic factors, presumably labor and land. But this theoretical forecast stands in stark contrast to the tax laws observed in essentially all developed countries, where corporate taxes not only exist but where corporate rates are roughly comparable to the top personal tax rates.

In this paper, we argue that many aspects of the existing corporate tax law would seem quite sensible if the primary role of the corporate tax is to discourage income shifting between personal and corporate tax bases, or between domestic and foreign subsidiaries. Unless corporate tax rates are roughly comparable to personal tax rates, business owners would be able to avoid taxes by retaining earnings within their firms, and later selling shares in the firm, so that the earnings would be taxed at capital gains rates rather than at personal rates. Unless foreign-owned firms operating in the country are subject to domestic taxes at the same rate, then domestic business owners would be able to avoid taxes on the returns to their ideas by selling their firms to foreigners. Similarly, a country would need to tax the income of domestic-owned subsidiaries operating abroad to prevent entrepreneurs from facing a tax incentive to make use of their ideas abroad rather than in the home country.

If the tax rate on domestic-owned subsidiaries abroad were lower than the domestic corporate tax rate, then an additional distortion would be created because multinationals could avoid domestic taxes by shifting their profits abroad through transfer prices even if the firms embodying their profitable ideas remain at home. While taxing foreign-source income at the same rate as domestic-source income eliminates this pressure, a second-best response is to lower the domestic tax on elements of income that are most amenable to transfer pricing. For example, the U.S. has reduced the effective tax rate applying to interest deductions of multinationals through its Section 482 rules.

Viewing the corporate tax as primarily a backstop to the personal tax on labor income, rather than as primarily a tax on capital income, requires an important change in focus from that of the recent academic literature. Given the ease with which existing tax policy can be rationalized based on this role for the corporate tax, such a change in focus appears warranted. How great are the pressures from income shifting between the personal and the corporate tax bases? We have presented some evidence in Gordon and MacKie-Mason (1994) and MacKie-Mason and Gordon (forthcoming) on the degree to which firms shift between corporate and noncorporate status in response to tax incentives. There has been virtually no attempt in the tax literature to date, however, to measure the degree to which individuals shift their form of pay in response to tax differences. Since our model suggests that this form of income shifting appears to be a major consideration in the design of existing tax structures, measuring the degree to which such income shifting occurs in response to tax differences is an important topic for future research.

Appendix

Proof that $\delta W/\delta h < 0$ when w_n is held constant

In the model with both domestic and cross-border income shifting, consider the effects in the home country of raising τ, and in addition raising T by enough to keep firms' choice for X unchanged, given p^*. Assume in addition that t is simultaneously cut by enough so as to keep w_n unchanged.[34] Under the optimal tax policy, the resulting marginal change in welfare should be zero. The resulting change in welfare equals

$$\frac{\delta W}{\delta p^*}\left(\frac{\delta p^*}{\delta \tau}+\frac{\delta p^*}{\delta T}\frac{\delta T}{\delta \tau}\right)+\frac{\delta W}{\delta h}\left(\frac{\delta h}{\delta \tau}+\frac{\delta h}{\delta T}\frac{\delta T}{\delta \tau}+\frac{\delta h}{\delta t}\frac{\delta t}{\delta \tau}\right)=0 \qquad \text{(11A-1)}$$

It is straightforward to demonstrate that the combined increases in τ and T cause p^* to rise, and that this rise in p^* lowers welfare. Therefore, the second term in Eq. (11-A1) must be positive. But the increase in business taxes and the drop in labor taxes will cause h to fall, implying that $\delta W/\delta h$ must be negative when evaluated at the optimal policies.

Proof that $\delta W/\delta X > 0$ when w_n is held constant.

In the model with both domestic and cross-border income shifting, consider the effects of raising σ, while cutting t so as to leave w_n unchanged. The first-order condition is

$$\frac{\delta W}{\delta h}\left(\frac{\delta h}{\delta \sigma}+\frac{\delta h}{\delta t}\frac{\delta t}{\delta \sigma}\right)+\frac{\delta W}{\delta p^*}\frac{\delta p^*}{\delta \sigma}+\frac{\delta W}{\delta X}\frac{\delta X}{\delta \sigma}=0 \qquad \text{(11A-2)}$$

This tax policy raises corporate taxes and cuts personal taxes. As a result, h will fall, implying that the first term in Eq. (11-A2) is positive. In addition, raising the surtax on repatriated profits by raising σ makes transfer pricing relatively less attractive. Hence, p^* decreases, implying that the second term is also positive. Therefore, the third term must be negative. But the increase in the surtax on revenues leads to a reduction in X, implying that $\delta W/\delta X > 0$ under the optimal policies.

References

Auerbach, A. (1983) "Taxation, Corporate Financial Policy, and the Cost of Capital." *Journal of Economic Literature,* 21, 905-40.

Becker, G. S. (1968) "Crime and Punishment: An Economic Approach." *Journal of Political Economy,* 76, 169-217.

Collins, J. H. and D. A. Shackelford (1992) "Foreign Tax Credit Limitations and Preferred Stock Issuances." Chapel Hill: University of North Carolina Business School, Working Paper.

Feldstein, M. S. and C. Horioka (1980) "Domestic Savings and International Capital Flows." *The Economic Journal,* 90, 314-29.

[34] That the required change in t is negative is straightforward but tedious to demonstrate.

Froot, K. and J. Hines (1994) "Interest Allocation Rules, Financing Patterns, and the Operations of U.S. Multinationals." In M. Feldstein, J. R. Hines, Jr., and R. G. Hubbard, eds. *The Effects of Taxation on Multinational Corporations*. Chicago: University of Chicago Press.

Gordon, R. H. (1992) "Can Capital Income Taxes Survive in Open Economies?" *Journal of Finance*, 47, 1159-80.

Gordon, R. H. (1986) "Taxation of Investment and Savings in a World Economy." *American Economic Review*, 76, 1086-1102.

Gordon, R. H. and A. L. Bovenberg (forthcoming) "Why Is Capital So Immobile Internationally: Possible Explanations and Implications for Capital Income Taxation." *American Economic Review*.

Gordon, R. H. and J. K. MacKie-Mason (1994) "Tax Distortions to the Choice of Organizational Form." *Journal of Public Economics*, 55, 279-306.

Gordon, R. H. and J. K. MacKie-Mason (1991) "Effects of the Tax Reform Act of 1986 on Corporate Financial Policy and Organizational Form." In J. Slemrod, ed. *Do Taxes Matter?: The Impact of the Tax Reform Act of 1986*. Cambridge, MA: MIT Press.

Gordon, R. H. and J. Slemrod (1988) "Do We Collect Any Revenue from Taxing Capital Income?" *Tax Policy and the Economy*, 2, 89-130.

Gravelle, J. G. and L. J. Kotlikoff (1989) "The Incidence and Efficiency Costs of Corporate Taxation When Corporate and Noncorporate Firms Produce the Same Good." *Journal of Political Economy*, 97, 749-81.

Grubert, H. and J. Mutti (1987) "The Impact of the Tax Reform Act of 1986 on Trade and Capital Flows." In *Compendium of Tax Research 1987*. Washington, D.C.: U.S. Treasury Department.

Grubert, H. and J. Slemrod (1993) "The Effects of Taxes on Investment and Income Shifting to Puerto Rico." Mimeo. Ann Arbor: University of Michigan.

Hamada, K. (1966) "Strategic Aspects of Taxation on Foreign Investment Income." *Quarterly Journal of Economics*, 80, 361-75.

Harris, D., R. Morck, J. Slemrod, and B. Yeung (1993) "Income Shifting in U.S. Multinational Corporations." In A. Giovannini, R. G. Hubbard, and J. Slemrod, eds. *Studies in International Taxation*. Chicago: University of Chicago Press.

Hines, J., Jr. and R. G. Hubbard (1990) "Coming Home to America: Dividend Repatriations by U.S. Multinationals." In A. Razin and J. Slemrod, eds. *Taxation in a Global Economy*. Chicago: University of Chicago Press.

Hines, J. R., Jr. and E. M. Rice (1990) "Fiscal Paradise: Foreign Tax Havens and American Business." Cambridge, MA: NBER, Working Paper No. 3477.

Hirshleifer, J. (1971) "The Private and Social Value of Information and the Reward to Inventive Activity." *American Economic Review*, 61, 561-74.

MacKie-Mason, J. K. and R. H. Gordon (forthcoming) "How Much Do Taxes Discourage Incorporation?" *Journal of Finance*.

Musgrave, R. (1959) *The Theory of Public Finance*. New York: McGraw-Hill.

Polinsky, A. M. and S. Shavell (1979) "The Optimal Tradeoff between the Probability and Magnitude of Fines." *American Economic Review*, 69, 880-91.

Razin, A. and E. Sadka (1991) "International Tax Competition and Gains from Tax Harmonization." *Economics Letters*, 37, 69-76.

Shoven, J. (1991) "Using the Corporate Cash Flow Tax to Integrate Corporate and Personal Taxes." *Proceedings of the 83rd Annual Conference of the National Tax Association*, 83, 19-26.

CHAPTER 12

Patterns of tax arbitrage and decentralized tax autonomy*

Bernd Genser

1. Introduction

The assignment of tax competencies in a multi-stage fiscal system is a traditional issue to be faced in fiscal federalism. Nevertheless, a clear-cut answer does not exist to the question of which governmental level should be responsible for the determination of key tax parameters to cover its financial needs in the pluralistic tax system of the modern welfare state. Public economic theory provides a series of arguments in favor of a centralization of tax policy, viz., economies of scale in tax administration, distributional equity, and avoidance of welfare losses from fiscal externalities through tax competition. Economic arguments which support decentralized tax policy decisions are based on fiscal equivalence in order to meet the heterogeneous preferences of citizens as well as on the inherent subsidiarity principle of market economies as adapted for a governmental hierarchy. In addition, the political economy view of fiscal policy has stressed tax competition among territorial authorities as a necessary measure against the exploitation of citizens by an unconstrained Leviathan government.

Empirical evidence shows that the power to tax is assigned predominantly to the central government, even in federal states where subfederal authorities are installed and empowered with fiscal autonomy by the constitution, such as in Germany, Austria, and Australia. Central taxes are the major source of government finance in most developed economies and there is little room for tax autonomy at subfederal levels (Lamfalussy 1989). From the standpoint of a positive theory of federalism, we might conclude that the centralization arguments have outweighed the subsidiarity arguments.

But there is a striking difference when we include the supranational level as the top layer in governmental hierarchy. EU member states have revealed an extremely limited readiness to give up national tax competencies and to pass them on to a supranational EU tax authority. This rigidity appears to be even stronger than the resistance to giving up subfederal tax competencies in the US, Canada, or Switzerland, all of them federal states with remarkable subfederal

* Paper presented at the 10th Pinhas Sapir Center Conference in memoriam of Eitan Berglas, Tel Aviv University, January 11-12, 1995. I owe thanks to Andreas Haufler (University of Konstanz), Joram Mayshar (Hebrew University), and Günther Schulze (University of Konstanz) for helpful comments and remarks on a prior draft of the paper.

tax autonomy. With respect to indirect taxes only the US is operating a purely decentralized system which is firmly founded in the US Constitution, whereas Canada has chosen a mixed commodity tax system with a federal VAT and separate provincial sales taxes, and Switzerland switched from a purely federal turnover tax to a federal VAT in 1995.[1]

Although indirect taxes have been a major issue for EC-wide regulation from the very beginning, tax harmonization measures left unfettered member competence in setting the commodity tax rates. Each national government therefore had the right to decide the fiscal scope of commodity taxes independently of other member countries. Effects of commodity tax differentials on liberalized trade were neutralized by the strict application of the destination principle through border tax adjustments. Border controls served the objective of consumer-restricting tax arbitrage activities, although touristic cross-border shopping for commodities was tolerated up to small free quota thresholds and the right to tax services in the country of origin somewhat expanded the scope for tax arbitrage to EC citizens. Basically, the EC tax order adopted GATT recommendations for the taxation of international commodity trade.

Since 1985, the new EU tax order for the internal market has been a contentious and still unresolved problem. Abolition of controls at internal borders was recognized as an indispensable hallmark of the completion of the internal market. As the scope of VAT and excise tax arbitrage was extended, in the face of severe trade distortions expected if large scale consumer purchases in low-tax countries could not be controlled, the Commission has suggested further restrictions in national VAT and excise tax autonomy (cf. Smith 1993). Besides constraining the number and the feasible range of tax rates, the extension of the VAT credit method to all intra-EU purchases of intermediate goods should be supplemented by a supranational clearing mechanism in the Commission's original proposals. Based on national notifications, a clearing house should ship back VAT charged on intermediate goods in the country of origin to the destination country in order to compensate for the revenue lost through transnational VAT credits. Nevertheless, clearing was not supposed to compensate for VAT revenue losses due to cross-border shopping by consumers (apart from vehicles and mail-order purchases) or to national VAT rate changes required to meet the harmonization constraints. As none of the various proposals toward a more centralized EU commodity tax system was approved by the Council, a "Deferred Payment System" was implemented in 1993 as a provisional system for a period of four years. In addition, the number of VAT rates was reduced, a minimum floor of 15% was decreed for the regular VAT rate, and the application of border tax adjustment according to the destination system

[1] A first look at tax policy targets under discussion and at tax policy measures implemented in federal states and in the EU indicates that tax harmonization policy concentrates on commodity taxes rather than on factor income taxes (cf. Genser 1992).

was restricted to trade between enterprises, to mail-order purchases, and to purchases of new vehicles. Since 1993, consumers and nonregistered enterprises have been free to purchase goods in any EU country at final prices including the going VAT rate of the country of purchase.

This transitory system would perfectly correspond to the old destination-based VAT system if consumers only shopped domestically. The decisive difference of this VAT system from that in effect prior to 1993 is the scope for legal cross-border tax arbitrage, which introduces elements of an origin-based VAT and therefore creates a mixed system. The second important difference is the restriction in national tax autonomy by reducing the feasible range for national VAT rates.

Economic analyses of alternatives to the traditional VAT regime basically come to the conclusion that the only economically equivalent solution would be a change to a general origin-based system. But it is also recognized that this solution has little political support within the EU due to the fact that EU countries are not willing to give up the credit method in order to operate their domestic VAT system. A less frequently raised argument hints at potential distortions if trade with non-EU countries was still to be taxed according to the GATT-conforming destination principle because it contains no motivation for the rest of the world to change their tax systems in order to support internal EU policy objectives.

In a recent paper, Lockwood, de Meza, and Myles (1994a) show, however, that a switch from a global destination regime to a mixed VAT regime which simultaneously applies destination- and origin-based elements on a nonreciprocal basis does not create any changes in real economic variables. In particular, the authors prove that a basic equivalence result holding between a VAT system based on a worldwide destination principle and one based on a worldwide origin principle (Lockwood et al. 1994b) carries over to a mixed regime, where all EU countries would charge an origin-based VAT on all their worldwide trade, whereas all non-EU countries would keep their destination-based VAT. This result seems to contradict earlier nonequivalence results derived by Whalley (1979, 1981) and Berglas (1981) for "restricted origin-based VAT systems" but is in line with economic intuition when two basic features of the "nonreciprocal restricted origin VAT" are recognized. First, a fall in flexible commodity prices is able to neutralize simultaneously the double taxation of EU exports to the rest of the world as well as the VAT free import to the EU from the rest of the world. Second, dispensing with border tax adjustment eliminates one important source for VAT revenue shifts between the member states of a tax union. On the other hand, Lockwood et al. (1994a) themselves question whether the equivalence property of their mixed system might convince policy makers faced with the accusation that the formal tax incidence pattern is a major discriminator against EU entrerprises, particularly those in high-tax member countries.

The main objective of the chapter is to show that the abolition of border controls and the extended scope for tax arbitrage still leaves room for a unilateral switch of EU countries to an origin-based VAT among EU member countries. A mixed origin/destination system with a uniform EU border tax is also shown to be equivalent to the pre-1993 global destination regime. A switch to the new system induces neither real effects nor revenue shifts among EU members and it preserves national tax rate autonomy in the sense that tax rates need not be harmonized when the system is introduced. This result can be regarded as a delayed rehabilitation of Shibata's (1967) proposal to switch to a "restricted origin principle" that is supplemented by a common external tax rate on imports and export tax rebates at the external EU borders. Lockwood's nonreciprocal origin-based VAT system turns out as a special case for a common external tax of zero (Shibata 1967: 237).

The remainder of the chapter is organized as follows. Section 2 presents a three-country model to identify the benchmark case of a universal destination-based VAT regime with border controls. In Section 3, a restricted destination-based system is modeled, where the abolition of border controls between two countries allows for cross-border shopping. Such a tax regime, which corresponds to the transitory EU system (deferred-payment system) as well as to the final EU system proposed by the Commission (international credit/invoice system with clearing), is shown to generate a deviation from the benchmark case, although it must be recognized that distributional effects rather than allocative distortions are responsible for the nonequivalence result. In particular, it is shown that distributional inequities are exacerbated rather than reduced by the clearing mechanism. In Section 4 we show that there are various reasons why the equivalence property of the origin principle ceases to hold if the EU's external trade is subject to the destination principle. In Section 5 we sketch the basic features of the nonreciprocal restricted origin principle and in Section 6 the origin principle for internal EU trade is supplemented by a uniform, external supranational EU border tax adjustment. It is shown that this "mixed common border tax VAT regime with a common border tax" is equivalent to the benchmark case of a pure destination VAT with border controls. Section 7 discusses the pros and cons of decentralized VAT systems in the EU as well as in federal countries.

2. The benchmark case of a global destination-based VAT regime with border controls

2.1 The model

The model used to illustrate the equivalence results is that of a competitive three-country world. Each country, D (domestic), F (foreign) and R (rest of the world), operates a VAT system with one uniform rate t^i ($i = D,F,R$). Technology allows the production of n consumer goods $x^i_j (j = 1, \ldots, n)$ and one intermediate good x^i_0 according to a country-specific production function $x^i = f^i(l^i, x^i_0)$ $(i = D,F,R)$ by means of a vector of primary input factors l^i, which are immobile across countries.[2] Goods can be traded on the world market, transaction costs for trade are assumed to be zero.

Production in each country is performed by a representative, profit-maximizing firm which sells its consumer goods and supplies ($x^i_0 > 0$) or demands ($x^i_0 < 0$) intermediate goods at VAT-inclusive prices $q^i = p^i(1 + t^i)$, employs the primary factors l_i at the going factor prices w^i, and pays its VAT liability to the domestic tax authority. The VAT liability is calculated by applying the uniform ad valorem rate t_i on the net of tax value of output (producer prices p^i) minus the tax credit on intermediate inputs. For a pure destination-based VAT, the profit of the representative firm in country i is

$$P^i(p^i,w^i) = q^i x^i - t^i p^i x^i - w^i l^i = p^i x^i - w^i l^i \tag{12-1}$$

Maximizing P^i subject to the given technology yields the factor demand functions $l^i(p^i,w^i)$ and the commodity supply functions $x^i(p^i,w^i)$. Under constant returns to scale, the firm's profit is zero and factor income $w^i l^i$ is the only source of income for the representative household in country i.

Representative consumers in the three countries are each endowed with one unit of each factor. They demand consumer goods c^i and supply immobile factors y^i in order to maximize their utility $u^i(c^i, 1 - y^i, g^i)$, subject to their budget constraints

$$q^i c^i = w^i y^i \tag{12-2}$$

where g^i is a public good produced by means of immobile factors and financed out of VAT revenue in country i. For a specified utility function, we derive the Marshallian demand functions for commodities $c^i(q^i,w^i,g^i)$ and factor supply functions $y^i(q^i,w^i,g^i)$.

VAT revenue depends on the VAT regime in operation. Under the benchmark case of the global destination principle, the VAT base is domestic consumption. Tax revenue $T^i = t^i p^i c^i$ is used to pay the factor costs associated with public goods production

$$T^i = w^i l^i_g = p^i_g g^i \tag{12-3}$$

with p^i_g being the shadow price of the public good.

The global equilibrium is characterized by zero global excess demand for traded goods on the world markets and zero excess demand for immobile factors in the three national factor markets.

$$\Sigma\,[c^i_j(q^i,w^i g^i) - x^i_j(p^i,w^i)] = 0 \quad \text{for } j = 0,1,2,\ldots,n \tag{12-4}$$

[2] In order to facilitate the interpretation of the arbitrage conditions derived below we assume a Ricardo-Viner-world, where sector-specific factors allow for domestic production of all commodities in the trade equilibrium.

$$l^i(p^i,w^i) + l^i_g - y^i(q^i,w^i,g^i) = 0 \quad \text{for } i = D,F,R \tag{12-5}$$

Given the VAT regime and the VAT rates in the three countries, equilibrium prices for commodities and factors must solve the two sets of excess demand conditions given above. National excess demand functions for commodities and factors are homogeneous of degree zero in their price arguments, so we are free to choose a suitable numeraire commodity, e.g., $w^i_1 = 1$. The equilibrium prices take rational behavior of economic agents into account, particularly regarding arbitrage possibilities offered through trade. These arbitrage conditions, which depend on the tax regime in operation, allow for a characterization of the equilibrium price vectors and the resulting quantity levels without solving the whole system of equations.

2.2 *The benchmark case of a global destination regime*

If a pure destination-based VAT can be enforced by border tax adjustments, the representative consumer in country i pays the domestic tax rate t^i on any consumer good purchased, irrespective of whether this good was produced domestically or imported. Consumers in any country i are therefore offered an opportunity of consumer price arbitrage, as illustrated in the three columns of Table 12-1. If commodity j is domestically produced as well as imported, in the equilibrium, the consumer prices for commodity j must be equal in the equilibrium. For a destination-based VAT regime, this requires that producer prices for this good must be equal across countries. The tradable intermediate good does not enter the household utility function but is supplied and demanded by producers at prices net of VAT under the credit method. Cost arbitrage (if x_0 is demanded) or profit arbitrage (if x_0 is supplied) imply that producer prices for the intermediate good must also be equal across countries.

Taking account of these arbitrage conditions, the equilibrium prices of commodities and factors are related across countries. In Table 12-2, we use a common producer price vector p_d to represent the consequences of price arbitrage. We choose the first primary factor input in country R as the numeraire, viz. $w^R_1 = 1$. The zero homogeneity property of the excess demand functions further allows for a country-specific normalization of commodity and factor prices by an arbitrary suitable factor e^i_d $(i = D,R)$. We can then characterize the class of equivalent equilibrium price vectors for consumers and producers according to Table 12-2. VAT is charged at an ad valorem rate t^i on net of tax prices p^i. The normalization of prices influences tax revenue in nominal terms but does not violate the government budget constraint as long as private consumption c^i and public consumption g^i remain unchanged.

Equilibrium prices for the global destination regime with given VAT rates are used as the benchmark case for the comparison with alternative tax regimes which apply the same tax rates.

Table 12-1. Consumer prices under a global destination regime (subscript d)

	Country of destination		
Country of production	*D*	*F*	*R*
D	$p_d^D(1+t^D)$	$p_d^D(1+t^D)\frac{1+t^F}{1+t^D}$	$p_d^D(1+t^D)\frac{1+t^R}{1+t^D}$
F	$p_d^F(1+t^F)\frac{1+t^D}{1+t^F}$	$p_d^F(1+t^F)$	$p_d^F(1+t^F)\frac{1+t^R}{1+t^F}$
R	$p_d^R(1+t^R)\frac{1+t^D}{1+t^R}$	$p_d^R(1+t^R)\frac{1+t^D}{1+t^R}$	$p_d^R(1+t^R)$

3. The implementation of a destination-based VAT without border controls

The switch to a deferred-payment system in our three-country world implies that border controls have been abolished between countries D and F, which form a tax union but still apply a destination-based VAT with border adjustment for trade among registered traders. Consumer prices thus remain the same as in Table 12-1, but the switch in tax regimes extends the scope for consumer price arbitrage. Without border controls, consumer goods may be purchased across

Table 12-2. Equilibrium prices and tax revenue under a pure destination regime

	Country D	*Country F*	*Country R*
Consumer prices	$\frac{p_d(1+t^D)}{e_d^D}, \frac{w_d^D}{e_d^D}$	$\frac{p_d(1+t^F)}{e_d^F}, \frac{w_d^F}{e_d^F}$	$p_d(1+t^R),\ w_d^R$
Producer prices	$\frac{p_d}{e_d^D}, \frac{w_d^D}{e_d^D}$	$\frac{p_d}{e_d^F}, \frac{w_d^F}{e_d^F}$	$p_d,\ w_d^R$
Tax revenue	$\frac{t^D p_d c_d^D}{e_d^D}$	$\frac{t^F p_d c_d^F}{e_d^F}$	$t^R p_d c_d^R$

the border, where they are subject to the VAT rate of the country of purchase rather than the consumer's country of residence. If transaction costs for cross-border purchases are assumed to be zero, analogous to transaction costs of trade, rational consumers in D and F will choose the location of their purchases according to consumer prices in the two first columns of Table 12-3.

If the VAT rates in D and F differ, e.g. $t^D < t^F$, then consumer price arbitrage implies that the representative consumer in the low-tax country D has no incentive to shop across the border, because goods even produced in F are less expensive in country D. Price arbitrage will cause this consumer to buy all consumer goods at home at prices given in the first column of Table 12-3. The representative consumer in the high-tax country F faces the same bundle of consumer prices; price arbitrage makes this consumer concentrate all purchases across the border in the low-tax country D. Finally, the scope for price arbitrage open to the representative consumer in R is unchanged since border controls prevent this consumer from utilizing lower tax rates abroad. We therefore arrive at a situation where producer prices are equal across countries as under the pure destination principle with border adjustment. Producer price arbitrage leads to equal producer prices for the intermediate good as well, since deferring border adjustment to the importing firm has no consequence on the firm's VAT credit claims.

The class of equivalent price vectors for consumers and producers after allowing for a normalization procedure analogous to Table 12-2 is given in Table 12-4. Row 2 shows that relative producer prices are the same in each country, indicating that no distortion arises from VAT differentials within the tax union. This result contradicts a widely quoted statement by Sinn (1990), who argues

Table 12-3. Consumer prices under a destination regime without border control between D and F (subscript w)

	Country of purchase		
Country of production	*D*	*F*	*R*
D	$p_w^D(1+t^D)$	$p_w^D(1+t^F)$	$p_w^D(1+t^R)$
F	$p_w^F(1+t^D)$	$p_w^F(1+t^F)$	$p_w^F(1+t^R)$
R	$p_w^R(1+t^D)$	$p_w^R(1+t^F)$	$p_w^R(1+t^R)$

Table 12-4. Equilibrium prices and tax revenue under a destination regime without border control between D and F

	Country D	*Country F*	*Country R*
Consumer prices	$\frac{p_w(1+t^D)}{e_w^D}, \frac{w_w^D}{e_w^D}$	$\frac{p_w(1+t^F)}{e_w^F}, \frac{w_w^F}{e_w^F}$	$p_w(1+t^R),\ w_w^R$
Producer prices	$\frac{p_w}{e_w^D}, \frac{w_w^D}{e_w^D}$	$\frac{p_w}{e_w^F}, \frac{w_w^F}{e_w^F}$	$p_{w,}\ w_w^R$
Tax revenue	$\frac{t^D p_w(c_w^D + c_w^F)}{e_w^D}$	0	$t^R p_w c_w^R$

that cross-border consumer shopping within a destination system creates distortions of the price ratios of consumer goods and intermediate goods between high-tax and low-tax countries[3]. Comparing Sinn's arbitrage condition for consumers, $p^D(1+t^D) = p^F(1+t^F)$, with our arbitrage schedule (see Table 12-3) reveals that he rules out consumer price arbitrage open to a resident of the low-tax country D, who gains by purchasing final goods produced in F from a domestic retailer in D. On the other hand, he also excludes consumer price arbitrage for residents of the high-tax country F through cross-hauling, namely purchasing commodities produced in F through cross-border reimports from the low-tax country D. Whereas Sinn does not comment on these assumptions in his model, a transport cost argument is frequently raised in other, related studies.[4] While it is true that transaction costs affect cross-border shopping in practice, the transportation cost argument seems poor in the trade framework sketched. It cannot support Sinn's arbitrage condition for the low-tax country D and it is also rather weak regarding the exclusion of reimports. Since reimports

[3] Sinn argues that if the distortion arises because trade between member countries includes consumer goods as well as intermediate goods. While VAT rate differentials do not affect trade in intermediates when, due to the destination principle, foreign VAT on imports is either rebated to the exporter (border adjustment) or credited to the importer (international credit system), they induce tax arbitrage for consumers, who avoid high domestic taxes by purchasing in the low-tax country. Whereas price arbitrage for intermediates equates producer prices, price arbitrage for final goods equates consumer prices in the high- and the low-tax countries, which leads to higher producer prices for consumer goods in the low VAT country as well as production inefficiencies.

[4] Haufler (1996), for example, analyzes the effects of tax competition and tax coordination in a model where cross-hauling of a single private good occurs. In this framework, all arbitrage opportunities are exhausted but cross-border shopping is limited by convex transaction costs.

in our model are purchases of commodities produced in country F by consumers in country F, no physical transport of goods across the border is required when exports and reimports can be reduced to an operation in the books. With respect to our three country world, we might add that the transport cost argument is able to explain limited trade deflection, since arbitrage activities which channel imports from the rest of the world R to the high-tax country F through the tax haven D require costly cross-border shopping to bring those commodities from D to F.

While Sinn's results are based on an incomplete model which excludes an important strand of tax arbitrage, we are going to show that the abolition of border controls within a destination-based VAT is nonetheless a nonequivalent and unattractive change in the tax regime.

A comparison of equilibrium prices in Tables 12-2 and 12-4 shows that given the normalization chosen for country R, equality of consumer and producer prices requires $p_d = p_w$ and $w_d^R = w_w^R$. Equality of consumer and producer prices in country D, given $p_d = p_w$, can always be attained by choosing $e_d^D = e_w^D$. But a consistent adjustment factor e_w^F to equate consumer and producer prices in country F does not exist. Such a factor would allow for a replication of the equilibrium producer and consumer price vector under the two regimes. Since it always pays for residents in F to earn the VAT differential by reimporting any domestically produced consumer goods from D[5], the equilibrium under the new tax regime will not yield any tax revenue in the high-tax country F. Therefore, abolishing border controls and allowing for tax arbitrage by cross-border shopping will not lead to an equilibrium which replicates the demand, supply, and trade flows of the initial equilibrium under the destination regime. While the price structure in the "no border control"-equilibrium does not distort relative prices, since an indirect harmonization of commodity taxes for consumers is implied by shifting all consumption activities to the low-tax country D, the revenue effects associated with this consumption deflection cannot be absorbed by price changes. Hence, nonequivalence prevails.

Sinn (1990) offers two proposals to escape the undesirable consequences associated with an abolition of border controls, a switch to the origin principle or a harmonization of VAT rates prior to the switch in the tax regimes. It is trivial to show that equivalence can be attained if the tax rates in the tax union countries coincide. The shift to an origin-based VAT will be shown to need some further qualification as long as trading partners exist outside the tax union.

It must be emphasized that the transitional "deferred payment system" is not the only administrative variant of a destination-based VAT without border adjustment. The Commission's proposal of a "EU-wide VAT credit system with

5 Finally, the no-revenue equilibrium in the high-tax country is not an equilibrium in the tax competition game because a strategic change of its VAT rate will allow country F to regain tax revenue by equating or undercutting the VAT rate of country D.

subsequent clearing" operating without border controls is also characterized by the same tax arbitrage pattern summarized in Table 12-3. Producer prices for intermediate goods are equalized as well, since the VAT credit fully compensates for VAT payments to the domestic and to the foreign tax authority. As before, we cannot expect equivalency with the pure destination principle, thus the incentive for tax arbitrage will prevail. As the clearing house uses VAT revenue collected in the high-tax country *F* to compensate for VAT credits in the low-tax country D, we end up in the same no-revenue situation as with the transitional system.

If the Commission abandons its preference for a clearing mechanism and implements a general intra-EU credit system without border controls in the EU, the basic features for VAT arbitrage will remain unchanged, the equilibrium prices of Table 12-3 will hold, and a switch in the tax regimes will be nonequivalent as well. However, the distribution of tax revenues among EU countries will be affected. Without clearing, the country of origin keeps the VAT revenue levied on its output x^i as well as on net imports from the rest of the world m^{iR}, $i = F, D$. Therefore, the tax base of the high-tax country will no longer be zero . The low-tax country D collects VAT on domestic (C_c^D)and cross-border (C_c^{DF}) consumption activities, but has to credit VAT on regular as well as deflected imports from F (see Table 12-5).

For a comparison of the tax bases in the last rows of Tables 12-2 and 12-5, we can make use of the balance of trade conditions and get

$$T_c^D = t^D p_c c_c^D - (t^F - t^D)\, p_c c_c^{DF} - t^F p_c m_c^{FR} \quad \text{and} \tag{12-6}$$

$$T_c^F = t^F p_c c_c^{DF} + t^F p_c m_c^{FR} \tag{12-7}$$

Consumer tax arbitrage induces two characteristic differences in the tax bases of the tax union countries. The low-tax country loses tax revenue by covering the tax rate differential through VAT credits and is affected (positively or negatively) by the trade flows to the rest of the world. While this latter effect vanishes when trade is bilaterally balanced, a tax shifting effect remains due to the exploitation of tax arbitrage.

While it is frequently argued that an abolition of border controls will only harm high-tax countries, which lose clients and VAT revenue to low-tax countries, and consequently force them to adjust their VAT rates, we can identify an opposite incentive effect for the intra-EU credit system without clearing. Since a high-tax country's VAT can be neutralized for its resident domestic consumers through reimports from the low-tax country, whose tax authority is obliged to credit VAT on imported goods, a further increase of the VAT rate allows raising domestic tax revenue at the cost of the low-tax country's tax authority (see Table 12-5). In such a tax regime, we would expect tax competition to put an upward pressure on tax rates, which would require fixing an upper bound on VAT rates within the EU in order to limit ruinous tax exporting within the tax union.

Table 12-5. Equilibrium prices and tax revenue under an intra-union VAT credit system without border control (subscript c)

	Country D	*Country F*	*Country R*
Consumer prices	$\frac{p_c(1+t^D)}{e_c^D}, \frac{w_c^D}{e_c^D}$	$\frac{p_c(1+t^D)}{e_c^F}, \frac{w_c^F}{e_c^F}$	$p_c(1+t^R),\ w_c^R$
Producer prices	$\frac{p_c}{e_c^D}, \frac{w_c^D}{e_c^D}$	$\frac{p_c}{e_c^F}, \frac{w_c^F}{e_c^F}$	$p_c,\ w_c^R$
Tax revenue	$\frac{t^D p_c(c_c^D + c_c^{DF}) - t^F p_c(x_c^F + m_c^{FR})}{e_c^D}$	$\frac{t^F p_c(x_c^F + m_c^{FR})}{e_c^F}$	$t^R p_c c_c^R$

We can thus conclude that the costs of switching from a pure destination system to a destination-based tax regime without border controls turn out to be pretty high. The unpleasant trade-off between violating subsidiarity and distorting historical, presumably efficient national revenue patterns on the one hand, and the lasting incentive for distortionary tax arbitrage and strategic VAT rate competition on the other, has renewed the interest in a switch to an origin-based VAT system in the EU.

4. The implementation of a restricted origin principle with country specific border adjustment for trade with third countries

It is well known that a pure destination regime and a pure origin system are equivalent (Grossman 1980, Lockwood et al. 1994b), provided that the destination principle is enforceable through border controls and that VAT arbitrage through cross-border shopping of consumers is avoided. A switch from a global destination-based VAT-regime to an origin-based VAT regime is neutral in the sense that the national adjustment of flexible prices prevents any changes in quantity variables and production, consumption, and trade are not affected by a change in VAT regimes.

Shibata's (1967) restricted origin principle follows a rule of international reciprocity and requires that bilateral trade should be taxed under to the same VAT principle by both trading partners viz. the origin principle for trade with another tax union member country and the destination principle for trade with any country outside the tax union. Such a mixed VAT system has been shown to be nonequivalent to the two pure global tax principles (Berglas 1981, Haufler 1993, Whalley 1979).

The economic reaction patterns associated with the introduction of the restricted origin principle are manifold and give rise to different views, depending on the arbitrage mechanisms included in the model. Nevertheless, non-equivalence is the final result, although in varying facets.[6] Within our three-country world, the basic features of the restricted origin principle can be illustrated in Table 12-6. Consumer price arbitrage based on final commodity trade and cross-border shopping requires equal prices for consumer goods in the relevant markets. For the tax union countries D and F, this implies an equalization of consumer prices along the first column of Table 12-6. Evidently, there exists an incentive for country F's consumers to refuse direct imports from the rest of the world but to buy these goods across the border in the low-tax country D. Consumer price arbitrage in country R implies equal consumer prices along the third column. Since equivalence with the pure destination principle only allows for proportional price adjustment in the three countries, the relations between relative producer prices in F and R required cannot be met simultaneously, and the equilibrium price vectors cannot be equivalent as long as the VAT rates in the tax union differ (Shibata 1967, Berglas 1981). But even if tax rates were identical, non-equivalence follows from VAT revenue changes, since after the switch to the origin in tax regime VAT on commodities exported to the other tax union country is no longer rebated; instead, domestic tax revenues increase in the exporting country. Even with full tax rate harmonization equivalence would only be attained for bilaterally balanced trade within the tax union.

The arbitrage pattern in Table 12-6, however, does not include all arbitrage possibilities, which are viable in a free-trade world with zero transaction costs. Consumers in the low-tax country D would realize a double benefit if they do not import commodities from tax union partner F directly, but via imports from the rest of the world. First, the VAT rate would be reduced to t^D due to the double border adjustment. Second, VAT revenue would be directed from country F to country D. The same arbitrage opportunity is open to consumers in high-tax country F if they purchase their domestically produced goods charged with the lower VAT rate t^D after they have been shipped back to F via countries R and D. The high-tax country F will therefore again be faced with a zero revenue situation, and it will be forced to react by equating or undercutting the neighbor's VAT rate. Whereas trade deflection caused by tax arbitrage eliminates allocative distortions (Georgakopoulos and Hitiris 1992), VAT revenue shifts are responsible for nonequivalence.

[6] Nonequivalence must be regarded as an important argument against the introduction of the origin principle in the EU. Another objection against the origin principle is the widespread conjecture that operating the origin principle requires a switch from the credit/invoice method to the subtraction method (e.g. Sinn 1990).

Table 12-6. Consumer prices under the restricted origin principle (subscript r)

	Country of purchase		
Country of production	*D*	*F*	*R*
D	$p_r^D(1+t^D)$	$p_r^D(1+t^D)$	$p_r^D(1+t^R)$
F	$p_r^F(1+t^F)$	$p_r^F(1+t^F)$	$p_r^F(1+t^R)$
R	$p_r^R(1+t^D)$	$p_r^R(1+t^F)$	$p_r^R(1+t^R)$

Finally, we must emphasize that the trade deflection pattern sketched above need not come to an end after the first cycle. If commodities produced in F are shipped back to F via R and D in order to reduce their consumer price, a circular trade pattern emerges which continuously provides an arbitrage gain and consequently never ends (Haufler 1994). Nonequivalence and incentives for trade deflection must therefore be regarded as serious warnings against a unilateral step toward an origin-based VAT in the EU.

5. The implementation of a nonreciprocal restricted origin principle

Lockwood, de Meza and Myles (1994a) have recently shown that the basic equivalence result between VAT systems based either on a worldwide destination principle or on a worldwide origin principle carries over to a mixed regime, where each member country i of the tax union U applies an origin-based VAT in its trade with all trading partners. Outside U, each country k would apply a destination-based VAT including border tax adjustment with all its trading partners. Lockwood et al. (1994a) tagged their mixed regime a "nonreciprocal restricted origin principle" to differentiate it from the "restricted origin principle," addressed in Section 4.

Table 12-7 contains the consumer price formulas implied by the mixed tax regime. Consumer price arbitrage leads to an equalization of consumer prices in the tax union, which implies that producer prices must differ across countries because the regime charges different tax burdens on domestically produced versus imported goods. Commodities traded between tax union countries bear the VAT rate of the country of origin. Tax union imports from the rest of the world remain untaxed in the importing country. Consumer prices in the rest of the world bear the VAT rate t^R; imports from the tax union receive no rebate and are double taxed. Although this VAT scheme seems to discriminate against the tax union's exports, it is evident that tax arbitrage gives rise to an unchanged pattern of relative producer prices across countries. It can also be deduced immediately from Table 12-7 that the tax regime does not provide an incentive for tax arbitrage. Cross-border shopping does not pay since commodity prices are the same everywhere in the tax union while commodity prices outside the union are higher due to the additional border tax. Cross-border shopping incentives do only exist for citizens outside the tax union. Therefore border controls have to be maintained by the rest of the world.

Following Lockwood et al. (1994a), it can be shown that the nonreciprocal restricted origin principle is equivalent to a global destination principle with border controls. Finally, equivalence requires that under both regimes the VAT revenue collected suffices to finance the same level of the collective good supply. For country D we get

$$T_n^D = \frac{t^D q_n x_n^D}{(1+t^D)e_n^D} = \frac{t^D q_n x_n^D}{e_d^D} = \frac{t^D w_d^D l_d^D}{e_d^D} = \frac{t^D p_d c_d^D}{e_d^D} = T_d^D \tag{12-8}$$

after substitution of the price adjustment and the household budget constraints, and the VAT revenues in Tables 12-2 and 12-8 coincide. The equilibrium prices in Tables 12-2 and 12-8 coincide if we select $p_d = q_n$ and $e_n^i / e_d^i = 1/(1+t^i)$ for $i = D,F$ respectively.

Trade in intermediate goods leads to an arbitrage equilibrium analogous to that for consumer goods as shown in Table 12-7. An origin-based VAT can be administered either by the international subtraction method or by the notional

Table 12-7. Consumer prices under the nonreciprocal restricted origin principle (subscript n)

	Country of purchase		
Country of production	*D*	*F*	*R*
D	$p_n^D(1+t^D)$	$p_n^D(1+t^D)$	$p_n^D(1+t^D)(1+t^R)$
F	$p_n^F(1+t^F)$	$p_n^F(1+t^F)$	$p_n^F(1+t^F)(1+t^R)$
R	p_n^R	p_n^R	$p_n^R(1+t^R)$

VAT credit method.[7] Under the latter, the notional VAT credit granted to a firm in country D for an intermediate good 0 imported from country F or R amounts to

$$TC^F = \left[\frac{t^D}{(1+t^D)}\right] p_0^F(1+t^F) \quad \text{or} \quad TC^R = \left[\frac{t^D}{(1+t^D)}\right] p_0^R \tag{12-9}$$

respectively, whereas the tax credit on a domestically produced intermediate good is

$$TC^D = t^D p_0^D \tag{12-10}$$

Price arbitrage for intermediate goods in net-of-credit prices requires

$$p_0^D(1+t^D) - TC^D = p_0^F(1+t^F) = p_0^R - TC^R \tag{12-11}$$

based on which we get

$$p_0^D = \frac{p_0^F(1+t^F)}{(1+t^D)} = \frac{p_0^R}{(1+t^D)} \tag{12-12}$$

in perfect correspondence to the producer price pattern of traded consumer goods.[8]

Basically, equivalence under the nonreciprocal restricted origin principle is attained because flexible producer prices in each tax union country fall by the full amount of the domestic tax, which is no longer rebated after the switch in the tax regimes and which ensures that domestic products are competitive in all markets. Lockwood et al. (1994a) have shown that the equivalence result also holds for trade environments with transport costs and imperfectly competitive markets. Based on this equivalence result, Lockwood et al. (1994a) consider their nonreciprocal restricted origin principle as an attractive VAT regime for the EU since it would permit dispensing with border controls at internal borders without creating allocative distortions, trade deflection, or fiscal imbalances through displacement of VAT revenues when national VAT rates differ.

[7] Under an origin-based, stage-of-processing VAT, a commodity whose production stages are carried out in different countries should bear a total tax burden which reflects the different countries' VAT rates on their shares of value-added. The subtraction method and the notional credit method are equivalent in avoiding the recouping effect of the conventional VAT credit, which creates a tax burden that always corresponds to the VAT rate of the last processing step. The notional VAT credit can be calculated by applying the "gross" stage-of-processing VAT rate (e.g., for country D: $t^D/[1 + t^D]$) to the gross price of an intermediate input good (e.g., for an Iimported good from country F: $p_0[1 + t^F]$). In contrast to the notional credit method, an internationally applied conventional credit method leads to a destination-based VAT.

[8] In country R, the credit method is applied under the destination principle, which is neutral with respect to gross versus net-of-tax price arbitrage.

Table 12-8. Equilibrium prices and tax revenue under the nonreciprocal restricted origin regime (subscript n)

	Country D	Country F	Country R
Consumer prices	$\frac{q_n}{e_n^D}, \frac{w_n^D}{e_n^D}$	$\frac{q_n}{e_n^F}, \frac{w_n^F}{e_n^F}$	$q_n(1+t^R),\ w_n^R$
Producer prices	$\frac{q_n}{(1+t^D)e_n^D}, \frac{w_n^D}{e_n^D}$	$\frac{q_n}{(1+t^F)e_n^F}, \frac{w_n^F}{e_n^F}$	$q_n,\ w_n^R$
Tax revenue	$\frac{t^D q_n x_n^D}{(1+t^D)e_n^D}$	$\frac{t^F q_n x_n^F}{(1+t^F)e_n^F}$	$t^R q_n c_n^R$

6. The implementation of a mixed origin/destination principle with a common border tax adjustment

The nonreciprocal restricted origin principle can be regarded as a special representative of a class of mixed VAT regimes which supplements a tax union's origin-based VAT with a common border tax adjustment at the tax union's external border.[9] Exports to the rest of the world receive a VAT rebate of t^U irrespective of the VAT rate charged in the country of origin while imports from the rest of the world are subject to the import VAT rate t^U, irrespective of the going VAT rate in the country of destination. Mixed VAT regimes with a common border tax can be shown to be equivalent to either of the pure VAT regimes (cf. Genser 1996). Within this class of mixed regimes, the nonreciprocal restricted origin principle is a special case, having a common external tax of zero.

Switching to a mixed origin/destination regime with a common border tax adjustment t^U brings about the consumer prices presented in Table 12-9. Again, consumer price arbitrage creates equal prices for imported or domestically produced commodities. Since the tax factors differ, producer prices are no longer equalized across countries.

The equilibrium prices which generate excess demands of zero on the global commodity markets and on the domestic factor markets are summarized in Table 12-10. To show the equivalence with our global destination benchmark scheme, we first concentrate on the rest of the world R and conclude that the commodity and factor prices under the new mixed system would replicate the benchmark

[9] Such a common external tax to avoid trade deflection by tax arbitrage has been suggested by Shibata (1967). Genser (1996) has coined the notion Unified Restricted Origin Principle (UROP) for this mixed VAT regime.

Table 12-9. Consumer prices under the mixed origin destination regime with a common border (subscript F)

	Country of puchase		
Country of production	*D*	*F*	*R*
D	$p_m^D(1+t^D)$	$p_m^D(1+t^D)$	$p_m^D\frac{(1+t^D)(1+t^R)}{1+t^U}$
F	$p_m^F(1+t^F)$	$p_d^F(1+t^F)$	$p_m^F\frac{(1+t^F)(1+t^R)}{1+t^U}$
R	$p_m^R(1+t^U)$	$p_m^R(1+t^U)$	$p_m^R(1+t^R)$

price structure of Table 12-2 only if $p_d = q_m/(1+t^U)$ and $w_d^R = w_m^R$. It can easily be confirmed that choosing $e_m^D/e_d^D = (1+t^U)/(1+t^D)$ and correspondingly $e_m^F/e_d^F = (1+t^U)/(1+t^F)$ generates a price vector under the mixed VAT regime, which perfectly replicates the equilibrium prices under the global destination principle.

The switch from one tax regime to the other can be completely neutralized by adjusting flexible prices without changing either consumers' or producers' decisions in the countries involved. Trade in intermediate goods in country D is governed by notional VAT credits $TC^D = t^D p_0^D$, $TC^F = t_p^D p_0^F(1+t^F)/(1+t^D)$ and

Table 12-10. Equilibrium prices and tax revenue under the mixed origin/destination regime with a common border tax

	Country D	*Country F*	*Country R*
Consumer prices	$\frac{q_m}{e_m^D}, \frac{w_m^D}{e_m^D}$	$\frac{q_m}{e_m^F}, \frac{w_m^F}{e_m^F}$	$\frac{q_m(1+t^R)}{1+t^U}, w_m^R$
Producer prices	$\frac{q_m}{(1+t^D)e_m^D}, \frac{w_m^D}{e_m^D}$	$\frac{q_m}{(1+t^F)e_m^F}, \frac{w_m^F}{e_m^F}$	$\frac{q_m}{(1+t^U)}, w_m^R$
Tax revenue	$\frac{t^D q_m x_m^D}{(1+t^D)e_m^D}$	$\frac{t^F q_m x_m^F}{(1+t^F)e_m^F}$	$t^R q_m c_m^R$

$TC^R = t^D p_0^R(1 + t^U) / (1 + t^D)$, and price arbitrage for the intermediate good again replicates the price pattern for consumer goods found in Table 12-9; viz. $p_0^D = p_0^F(1 + t^F) / (1 + t^D) = p_0^R(1 + t^U) / (1 + t^D)$. The equivalence property must also include the government sector to ensure that no real effects are triggered due to changes in national tax revenues.

VAT revenue for country D under the destination regime is given by $T_d^D = t^D p_d^D c^D$, if we fix $e_d^D = 1$ (see Table 12-2). Under the mixed system with common border tax adjustment, VAT revenue from two different sources can be distinguished. VAT revenue from taxing domestic production amounts to

$$T_m^D = t^D p_m^D x^D \tag{12-13}$$

and is assumed to accrue to the national tax authority of country D. The second source of VAT revenue stems from operating the border tax adjustment for country D's exports to, and imports from, the rest of the world. Import VAT is levied on net import prices from the rest of the world, p^R. Export VAT rebate is granted on gross domestic prices $p^D(1 + t^D)$ scaled down by the border tax factor $1 / (1 + t^U)$. For the unit rebate rate we obtain $t^U p^D(1 + t^D) / (1 + t^U) = t^U p^R$ according to Table 12-9. Net VAT revenue therefore is given by

$$T_m^{DU} = t^U p_m^R \beta^D (c^R - x^R) \tag{12-14}$$

where $c^R - x^R$ is the vector of country R's excess demand and β^D is the diagonal matrix containing the share of excess demand covered by trade with country D. T_m^{DU} may turn out positive or negative, depending on the trade flow between countries D and R. We assume that T_m^{DU} does not accrue to country D's tax authority but increases or decreases the revenue of a supranational border tax authority. Revenue T_m^{FU} from border tax adjustment for exports and imports by country F, which covers the complementary share of the excess demand for country R, $\beta^D + \beta^F = I$ (with I representing the identity matrix), is calculated analogously. The fiscal revenue from border tax adjustment collected by the supranational authority is

$$\begin{aligned} T_m^{DU} + T_m^{FU} &= t^U[p_m^R \beta^D (c^R - x^R) + p_m^R \beta^F (c^R - x^R)] \\ &= t^u p_m^R (c^R - x^R) = 0 \end{aligned} \tag{12-15}$$

and adds up to zero if trade is balanced between the tax union and the rest of the world R. Note that the zero revenue result is based primarily on the common border tax rate t^U, whereas the trade balance requirement for the tax union, standard in static trade models, carries over to an intertemporal trade balance in dynamic trade models. From Table 12-10 and the national budget constraints it follows that

$$T_m^D = \frac{t^D q_m x^D}{(1+t^D)} e_m^D = \frac{t^D q_m x^D}{(1+t^U)} = t^D p_d x^D = t^D p_d c^D = T_d^D \tag{12-16}$$

Since a suitable adjustment of producer prices keeps all quantity levels unchanged after the switch in tax regimes, equivalence prevails.

Extensions of the equivalence results proved by Lockwood et al. (1994a) for their nonreciprocal restricted origin principle, viz. the introduction of transaction costs and of imperfect competition, also carry over to the mixed VAT regime with a common border tax. Furthermore, the equivalence property also holds in a world with nontradable commodities. Since demand and supply are not affected by a switch in the tax regime, VAT revenue from nontradables is not changed. If nontradable intermediate goods are used in domestic production of final commodities, these intermediates can be treated much in the same way as immobile primary input factors. As long as the VAT on imported intermediate goods is notionally credited to the importing firm in the tax union under the mixed VAT regime, intermediates are treated in a nondiscriminatory way under both regimes and the switch in regimes does not change production patterns and trade flows.

7. The scope for a decentralized VAT regime

When the first two VAT directives passed the Council of the six founding EEC members in 1967, they decided in favor of a VAT regime which complied with basic political and economic objectives: tax rate autonomy for the national governments, avoidance of international fiscal spill-over effects through border tax adjustment, and conformity with efficiency requirements. The completion of the European Internal Market in 1993 required the abolition of one of the most important buttresses of the traditional EU tax order, viz. the border controls used as a safeguard for the general border tax adjustment mechanism.

Recognizing the necessity for a new VAT order, the Commission offered a number of VAT proposals, which might be characterized as minimal deviation scenarios from the traditional VAT system. The continuation of the conventional VAT credit method has evidently received the highest priority, and the Commission seems to have been willing to sacrifice a significant degree of national tax autonomy and avoidance of fiscal spill-overs.

We have shown in this chapter that all the Commission's proposals are essentially attempts to retain a destination-based VAT system without border controls and these regimes will create severe conflicts with the subsidiarity principle and the neutrality principle. Harmonizing VAT rates completely might avoid allocative distortions through tax arbitrage but will do so at the costs of a loss of VAT autonomy, of major welfare losses to countries which have to redesign their fiscal systems, and of a critical violation of the subsidiarity principle guaranteed in the EU treaty. Dispersed VAT rates, on the other hand, provide a permanent incentive for tax arbitrage, cause high adjustment costs, and will presumably lead to harmonization measures in order to end undesirable tax competition.

A switch to an origin-based VAT within the EU while maintaining the destination-based VAT with third countries will create even worse results, unless the rest of the world can be convinced to switch to the origin principle as well. A revision of the GATT, favoring the destination principle and border tax adjustment, would be an important step on this way.

In view of the economic and political problems associated with the existing VAT proposals, a broad discussion of the mixed origin/destination-based VAT system with common border adjustment seems desirable. The equivalence property shows that this VAT system is able to perfectly reproduce any economic situation resulting from a destination-based VAT with dispersed tax rates and border controls, given uniform national VAT rates and sufficiently flexible prices. Moreover, an investment neutrality property between destination- and origin-based VAT systems can be shown to hold if capital mobility is introduced (Genser, Haufler, and Sørensen 1995). Since no harmonization of tax rates is required to support the replacement of the old VAT system after the abolition of border controls, fiscal autonomy is preserved at the national level. Given the importance of VAT for feeding national budgets, the subsidiarity principle of the EU treaty must be regarded as the most powerful argument in favor of the common border tax system.

A widely accepted argument against switching to an origin-based VAT within the EU is the conjecture that such an act would require a major change in VAT administration by replacing the credit method with the subtraction method.[10] While it is true that a general switch to the subtraction method will impose a high burden on tax administration and tax compliance and that a partial introduction of the subtraction method for cross-border trade flows only will create major problems of keeping track of the tax burden, it is not sufficiently appreciated that the notional credit method complies with the origin principle. Switching to the notional credit system would be fully in line with the Commission's objective of extending the VAT credit method to all intra-community transactions. A similar administrative procedure is required for border tax adjustment at external borders, where VAT rebates to exporters are calculated according to the common border tax t^U instead of the going VAT rate of the exporting country t^i.

The equivalence property ceases to hold if countries levy multiple instead of uniform VAT rates. Nonequivalence occurs since price level adjustments are unable to equalize two different price changes at the same time. In such a case,

[10] Sinn (1990: 497) argues that "it seems that the EC has made an irrevocable decision against the subtraction method and for the invoice method. Given this decision, only a harmonization of VAT rates can prevent the distortion."

equivalence can be regained under two restrictive conditions. First, if the reduced tax rate applies to nontradables only, then neither trade nor tax revenue would be distorted and equivalence would prevail. While this assumption might certainly hold for agricultural products and print media having local importance, it is not true for the bulk of low-taxed commodities traded within the EU. Second, a harmonization measure exists which secures undisturbed prices for two-tier VAT systems (Fratianni and Christie 1981). If the relation between the regular and the reduced rate is characterized by the same tax factor for all EU members $(1 + t^i_r = \mu(1 + t^i), i = D,F)$, then a simultaneous adjustment of all relative prices is viable after the switch to an origin-based VAT. Equivalence, however, could only be reached if EU members were to agree on harmonizing their VAT rate structures, rather than their VAT rate levels, prior to the introduction of the common border tax system as well as a compensation mechanism for income effects triggered by the trade pattern.

Finally, we must ask what might be gained by introducing the common border tax $t^U > 0$ instead of switching directly to the nonreciprocal restricted origin principle and abandoning border tax adjustment altogether. While it is true that a border tax system which creates zero revenue by definition is not very appealing, it should be recognized that an experienced authority capable of administering an external EU border tax already exists and will continue to do so as long as the EU collects external tariffs. Hence, the fixed costs of administering external border taxes should be close to zero. In addition, one has to concede that the price adjustment process required to ensure equivalence after the switch to the mixed system entails risks. Inadequate and therefore nonequivalent adjustment is more likely if the required fall in factor prices or exchange rates is large. Consequently, the political acceptability of introducing a new VAT regime for the EU will certainly be higher if the necessary price adjustment vis-à-vis the rest of the world can be reduced.[11] Basically, the introduction of a common border tax permits a leveling of the monetary shock. Also, an optimal selection of t^U, leading to a minimal price movement for the EU as a whole, does not prevent a piecemeal reduction of the common border tax in subsequent periods.

A renewed interest in the common border tax system as blueprint for the future VAT system in the EU is a rehabilitation of Hirofumi Shibata (1967), whose proposals have been reduced to the reciprocal restricted origin principle without a common external tax. Note, however, that a common border tax

[11] The introduction of a mixed VAT regime with a common border tax requires an adjustment of price levels of $(1 + t^U)/(1 + t^i)$ in country *i*. Ignoring the reduced tax rates in the EU, the nonreciprocal restricted origin principle ($t^U = 0$) requires a fall in price levels between 13% (in Germany and Spain, $t^i = 15\%$) and 20% (in Denmark $t^i = 25\%$). This is, of course, a dramatic change compared to an adjustment requirement of zero in Germany and Spain and –8% in Denmark when the common border tax is $t^U = 15\%$.

system is not only applicable to the EU. It might become an attractive device also in countries with a federal constitution and a strong preference for decentralized tax autonomy, as the US, Canada, or Switzerland. But federal states inside the EU might also consider assigning VAT rate competencies to regions, provinces, or Länder, once a common border tax adjustment for external trade is adopted by the EU.

References

Berglas, E. (1981) "Harmonization of Commodity Taxes: Destination, Origin and Restricted Origin Principles." *Journal of Public Economics,* 16, 377-87.

Fratianni, M. and Christie, H. (1981) "Abolishing Fiscal Frontiers Within the EEC." *Public Finance,* 36, 411-29.

Genser, B. (1992) "Tax Competition and Harmonization in Federal Economies." In H.J. Vosgerau, ed. *European Integration in the World Economy.* Berlin: Springer.

Genser, B. (1996) "A Generalized Equivalence Property of Mixed International VAT Regimes." *Scandinavian Journal of Economics,* 98(2). 253-62.

Genser, B., A. Haufler, and P. Sørensen. (1995) "Indirect Taxation in an Integrated Europe: Is There a Way of Avoiding Tax Distortions without Sacrificing National Tax Autonomy?" *Journal of Economic Integration,* 9, 178-205.

Georgakopoulos, T. (1992) "Trade Deflection, Trade Distortions, and Pareto Inefficiencies under the Restricted Origin Principle." *Journal of Public Economics,* 47, 381-90.

Georgakopoulos, T. and T. Hitiris. (1992) "On the Superiority of the Destination over the Origin Principle of Taxation for Intra-Union Trade." *Economic Journal,* 102, 117-26.

Grossman, G. (1980) "Border Tax Adjustments: Do They Distort Trade?" *Journal of International Economics,* 10, 117-128.

Haufler, A. (1993) *"Commodity Tax Harmonization in the European Community."* Heidelberg: Physica.

Haufler, A. (1994) "Trade Deflection with Transaction Costs: The Case of the Restricted Origin Principle." University of Konstanz, Discussion Papers of the SFB 178, Series II, Nr. 234.

Haufler, A. (1996) "Tax Coordination with Different Preferences for Public Goods: Conflict or Harmony of Interest?" *International Tax and Public Finance,* 3, 5-28.

Lamfalussy, A. (1989) "Macro-coordination of Fiscal Policy in an Economic and Monetary Union in Europe." In Committee for the Study of Economic and Monetary Union, ed. *Report on Economic and Monetary Union in the European Communitiy.* Luxembourg: EC Commission, 91-125.

Lockwood, B., D. de Meza, and G. Myles (1994a) "The Equivalence Between the Destination and Non-Reciprocal Restricted Origin Tax Regimes." *Scandinavian Journal of Economics,* 96 (3), 311-328.

Lockwood, B., D. de Meza, and G. Myles (1994b) "Are Origin and Destination Regimes Equivalent?" *International Tax and Public Finance,* 1, 5-24.

Shibata, H. (1967) "The Theory of Economic Unions: A Comparative Analysis of Customs Unions, Free Trade Areas, and Tax Unions." In C. Shoup, ed. *Fiscal Harmonization in Common Markets. Vol. 1: Theory.* New York: Columbia University Press.

Sinn, H.-W. (1990) "Tax Harmonization and Tax Competition in Europe." *European Economic Review,* 34, 489-504.

Smith, S. (1993) "Subsidiarity and the Coordination of Indirect Taxes in the European Community." *Oxford Review of Economic Policy*, 9, 67-96.

Whalley, J. (1979) "Uniform Domestic Tax Rates, Trade Distortions and Economic Integration." *Journal of Public Economics*, 11, 213-21.

Whalley, J. (1981) "Border Adjustment and Tax Harmonization: Comment on Berglas." *Journal of Public Economics*, 16, 389-90.

CHAPTER 13

Destination- and origin-based taxation under international capital mobility*

A. Lans Bovenberg

1. Introduction

Recent discussions about tax harmonization in the European Community as well as the wider processes of economic integration worldwide have rejuvenated interest in the macroeconomic implications of commodity taxation, including its effects on the international allocation of resources, international trade, and external accounts. Commodity taxes can be levied according to two alternative principles. Under the origin principle, the country of production collects the tax. In contrast, under the destination principle, commodities are taxed where they are consumed. Assuming that production factors are internationally immobile and external trade is balanced, the literature has demonstrated that a uniform origin-based tax is equivalent to a uniform destination-based tax, as long as factor and commodity prices are fully flexible (see for example Whalley [1979], Berglas [1981], and Lockwood, de Meza, and Myles [1994]). In recent years, however, the growing international integration of financial markets has increased international capital mobility and has facilitated the widening of external trade imbalances among the major industrial countries. In view of these developments, it is important to reexamine the macroeconomic effects of destination- and origin-based taxes in a framework that allows for international mobility of capital and for external trade imbalances.

This chapter uses a simple intertemporal equilibrium model, which incorporates international capital mobility, to investigate analytically the differential macroeconomic effects of the two alternative principles of commodity taxation. It focuses on the macroeconomic consequences for consumption, saving, investment, and external accounts. Given the importance of saving and investment behavior in an intertemporal setting with capital mobility, the model incorporates nontrivial saving and investment behavior.

To analyze effects on economy-wide saving, the chapter adopts a version of the overlapping-generations models developed by Blanchard (1985) and Weil (1989). This model allows for a meaningful role of intergenerational transfers and, therefore, does not exhibit debt-neutrality. Whereas the model has been

* This paper was published earlier in *International Tax and Public Finance*, Vol. 1, pp. 247-73 (1994). The author would like to thank Mick Keen and two anonymous referees for helpful comments on an earlier draft.

used to explore the effects of intergenerational transfers associated with budget deficits, this paper applies the model to show how the intergenerational distributional effects of alternative tax systems impact on aggregate saving and, therefore, external accounts. In this framework, taxes that do not impose any distortions may still impact on aggregate saving due to their effect on the intergenerational distribution of wealth. The overlapping generations model also allows the chapter to explore the sensitivity of macroeconomic effects with respect to the birth rate of new households which, in effect, provides a measure for the length of the planning horizon of households.

As regards investment behavior, the chapter incorporates adjustment costs. Hence, unanticipated policy shocks give rise to capitalization effects impacting on intergenerational incidence and saving. Employing a two-period overlapping generations model with a fixed factor, Chamley and Wright (1987) demonstrated how the capitalization effects associated with unanticipated fiscal policies could affect the intergenerational distribution of welfare. This chapter extends their analysis to a continuous-time model of an open economy with capital accumulation while emphasizing the macroeconomic impact of the intergenerational incidence effects.

Adjustment costs may also affect saving through changes on the international distribution of welfare. In particular, the government can use unanticipated fiscal policies to affect the international distribution of wealth by changing the value of the domestic capital stock owned by foreigners. Hence, distortionary taxes can raise domestic welfare if the international redistribution in favor of domestic residents more than offsets the losses in overall efficiency. As regards nondistortionary taxes, these policy instruments can exert effects on saving through their impact not only on the intergenerational but also on the international distribution.

There is a growing body of literature adopting intertemporal equilibrium models that allow for international capital mobility (see for example Frenkel and Razin [1987]). In contrast to previous analytical studies, the present study combines adjustment costs affecting investment with overlapping generations determining saving behavior. The results reveal that the interaction between, on the one hand, adjustment costs in investment and, on the other, overlapping generations, plays an important role in determining the macroeconomic effects of fiscal policies. The model differs from numerical studies (see for example Keuschnigg [1991]) in presenting analytical solutions with an intuitive interpretation. These solutions explicitly reveal how several major structural parameters affect transmission of commodity taxation to savings, investment, and external accounts. In particular, the model identifies the roles of, among others, adjustment costs in investment, the birth rate of new households, initial foreign ownership of domestic capital, the substitution elasticity between labor and capital in domestic production, and initial tax rates.

In incorporating both adjustment costs and overlapping generations in an analytical intertemporal equilibrium model of a small open economy, this study is closely related to that of Nielsen and Sørensen (1991). The latter paper, however, focuses on capital income taxation. Furthermore, it assumes that both foreign ownership and the initial tax rate on capital income are zero. Therefore, it does not investigate the macroeconomic implications of effects on the international distribution and intertemporal efficiency. Moreover, compared to Nielsen and Sørensen (1991), the present chapter pays greater attention to the interpretation of the adjustment dynamics.

Furthermore, Genser, Haufler and Sørensen (1993) have explored the equivalence between origin and destination principles in the presence of international capital mobility. They establish equivalence in an intertemporal model with a representative agent who owns all equity in domestic firms. The present chapter extends their analysis by introducing both overlapping generations and foreign ownership of domestic equity. Similar to Genser, Haufner, and Sørensen (1993), I find that neither the origin nor the destination principle distorts the international allocation of capital. Nevertheless, both principles are not equivalent as a rule because they tend to exert different impacts on the intergenerational and international distribution of income and wealth.

Two important issues involving the switch from destination-based to origin-based taxation are outside the scope of the current chapter, which takes a macroeconomic approach. First, in the tradition of most of the literature on the equivalence between origin-based and destination-based commodity taxes, this chapter assumes the existence of a uniform consumption tax covering all goods and services. However, governments may not be able to implement such a comprehensive tax due to administrative obstacles. For example, goods produced in the home and in the black economy cannot be included in the tax net. Another subject outside the scope of the current chapter is regional economic integration, where several countries decide to substitute the origin principle for the destination principle without the rest of the world doing the same.[1]

The chapter proceeds as follows. After presentation of the model in Section 2, Section 3 explores the impact of a destination-based tax levied on consumption. This tax is nondistortionary because the labor supply is exogenous and the tax rate is constant over time. Nevertheless, it generates macroeconomic implications because it redistributes resources across generations. The consequences of an origin-based production tax are analyzed in Section 4. This tax generally affects not only the distribution of resources across domestic generations but also the international distribution of welfare and intertemporal efficiency. Section 5 combines this production tax with an investment subsidy to produce an origin-based consumption tax, which can in fact be interpreted as a cash-flow

[1] For an analysis of this issue, see Lockwood, de Meza, and Myles (1994).

tax. Whereas this tax does not cause any intertemporal distortions, it does impact on the intergenerational and the international distribution of wealth. Section 6 compares destination- and origin-based consumption taxes. The conclusions are presented in Section 7. Four appendices describe how the results in the main text were derived. Appendices containing full details of the mathematical manipulations are available upon request from the author.

2. The model

2.1 Production and investment

Let a neoclassical net production function represent a constant-returns-to-scale technology:

$$y = f(k) \tag{13-1}$$

where y corresponds to output per capita (net of depreciation) of the single tradable commodity and k stands for the capital-labor ratio.[2] In addition to the production technology, the production sector faces a second technological constraint describing the accumulation of capital – the installation function. With the labor force growing at the rate n and labor being immobile internationally, the linear homogeneous installation function can be written as (see for example Bovenberg [1986])[3]

$$\dot{k} = k[g(x) - n] \quad g'(x) > 0 \quad g''(x) < 0 \tag{13-2}$$

where x is the ratio of net investment to the capital stock and $g'(x) = dg(x)/dx$. Marginal installation costs rise with the rate of investment, which is reflected in the concavity of the installation function in investment. How rapidly costs increase is mirrored by the elasticity of the marginal productivity of investment σ_x, defined as

$$\sigma_x = -\frac{xg''(x)}{g'(x)} \tag{13-3}$$

For any given capital stock, the faster the capital stock expands, the more capital goods per additional unit of capital are required.

Shares and bonds are perfect substitutes and thus must pay the same after-tax return. The arbitrage condition is thus given by (see also Nielsen and Sørensen [1991])

$$rV = \dot{V} + [(1 - t_f)(1 - t_p)f(k) - w - (1 - t_f)nk]e^{nt} \tag{13-4}$$

[2] In the rest of this paper, unless indicated otherwise, variables are to be understood as dated at time t.

[3] The installation function is given by $\dot{K} = G(K,I)$ where K and I denote the capital stock and net investment, respectively. The function $G(K,I)$ is homogeneous of degree one in its arguments.

where V stands for the market value of shares, w denotes the wage rate, t_p stands for the rate of origin-based production tax (see Section 4), and t_f represents the origin-based tax rate on consumption (see Section 5).[4] The term between square brackets on the right-hand side of (4) represents after-tax dividends, as the firm is assumed to be equity-financed. Integrating the arbitrage condition, one obtains the following expression for the market value of the firm's equity capital:

$$V = \int_0^\infty [(1 - t_f)(1 - t_p) f(k) - w - (1 - t_f)xk]e^{-(r-n)t}dt \tag{13-5}$$

Firms maximize this market value subject to the installation function. This gives rise to the optimal path for the shadow price of capital q,

$$\frac{\dot{q}}{q} = r - g(x) - \frac{(1 - t_f)(1 - t_p)f'(k)}{q} + \frac{(1 - t_f)x}{q} \tag{13-6}$$

and the implicit demand function for investment,

$$qq'(x) = (1 - t_f) \tag{13-7}$$

The marginal productivity condition for labor yields wages:

$$w = (1 - t_f)(1 - t_p)[f(k) - kf'(k)] \tag{13-8}$$

Following Hayashi (1982), one can show that, given the assumption of a linear homogeneous installation function, the shadow price of capital (i.e., marginal Q) q measures the per unit market value of the firm's capital stock (i.e., average Q), V/K:

$$V = qK \tag{13-9}$$

2.2 *Consumption and saving behavior*

The saving and consumption side of the model consists of an overlapping generations model described in Buiter (1988), which is a combination of a version developed by Yaari (1965) and Blanchard (1985) and a version developed by Weil (1989). Following the Yaari-Blanchard model, each household faces a constant probability of passing away, θ.[5] In the absence of an operative bequest motive and the presence of efficient annuity markets, households conclude the following contract with insurance companies: When households die, the insurance company collects the entire estate. In return, the insurance company pays a return contingent on being alive. Given free entry and a zero

[4] The production tax applies to output net of depreciation. The origin-based consumption tax applies to output net of not only depreciation but also net investment (i.e., to output net of gross investment).

[5] One can also interpret this constant probability of death as the probability that a dynasty expires. By allowing for $q < 0$, one can allow for intra-dynasty growth.

profit condition for insurance companies, this return equals the probability of death. The domestic economy is assumed to be small relative to the rest of the world so that the real rate of return, r, is fixed by world capital markets. Accordingly, the real rate of return earned by a household on its financial wealth is the sum of the real rate of return on world capital markets, r, and the probability of death, θ.

New households that are *not* linked through operative intergenerational transfers to older households are born at a constant rate, $n + \theta$.[6] This birth rate measures the heterogeneity, or economic disconnectedness, of the population (see Weil [1989]).[7] In particular, if the birth rate is zero, household behavior is described by a single representative individual. At time $t \geq v$, the representative household of the generation born at time v maximizes the expected value of additive separable utility, adopting a subjective rate of time preference, δ:

$$U(v,t) = \int_t^\infty u[c(v,s)]e^{-\delta(s-t)}e^{-\theta(s-t)}ds \tag{13-10}$$

subject to a budget constraint:

$$\dot{a}(v,t) = (r+\theta)a(v,t) + l(t) + w(t) - c(v,t)[1 + t_c(t)] \tag{13-11}$$

where $c(v,t)$ and $a(v,t)$ represent, respectively, consumption and financial wealth per capita at time $t \geq v$ of the generation born at time v. A dot above a variable denotes a time derivative. The rate of destination-based tax on consumption (see Section 3) is denoted by $t_c(t)$. Every living household supplies one unit of homogeneous labor per capita, which pays a wage of $w(t)$, and receives the same lump-sum transfer per capita $l(t)$. Hence, per capita non-capital disposable income (i.e., the sum of wages and per capita lump-sum transfers) is age-independent. This income can be interpreted as the return to human capital and is denoted by $\omega(t) = w(t) + l(t)$.

The optimal path for individual consumption is described by

$$\frac{\dot{c}(v,t)}{c(v,t)} = \frac{1}{\sigma}(r - \sigma) \tag{13-12}$$

The intertemporal substitution elasticity of consumption is constant and given by the reciprocal of the elasticity of marginal felicity, $\sigma = -cu''(c)/u'(c)$. In the overlapping generations model, the world rate of return is assumed to exceed the rate of time preference, δ.[8] Accordingly, individual consumption is rising

[6] Weil (1989) interprets this birth rate as the rate at which new dynasties enter the domestic economy. This rate depends on the proportion of newly-born children who are not "loved."

[7] Hence, the birth rate, $n + \theta$, and the death rate, σ, are distinct in this model. Blanchard (1985), in contrast, assumes that the birth rate equals the death rate (i.e., $n = 0$), while Weil (1989) abstracts from death (i.e., $\theta = 0$).

[8] In a representative agent model (i.e., $n + \theta = 0$), r should equal δ for a balanced growth path to exist (see below).

over time. Substituting Eq. (13-12) into the budget constraint Eq. (13-11), one arrives at the following individual consumption function:

$$[1 + t_c(t)]\, c(v,t) = \Delta[a(v,t) + \bar{h}(t)] \tag{13-13}$$

$\bar{h}(t)$ represents per capita human wealth at time t, which is identical for all agents alive at that time because noncapital income does not depend on age:

$$\bar{h}(t) = \int_t^{\infty} [\omega(s)]\, e^{-(r+\theta)(s-t)} ds \tag{13-14}$$

Also, the propensity to consume out of total wealth, Δ, is age-independent because all agents display the same time horizon:

$$\Delta = r + \theta - \frac{r-\sigma}{\sigma} \tag{13-15}$$

With rising individual consumption (i.e., $r > \delta$), this propensity to consume is less than the discount rate on human wealth, $r + \theta$.

Following Blanchard (1985), one can aggregate across generations to arrive at expressions in terms of per capita aggregate variables:

$$[1 + t_c(t)]\, C(t) = \Delta[A(t) + H(t)] = \Delta W(t) \tag{13-16}$$

$$\dot{A}(t) = (r - n)A(t) + \omega(t) - C(t)[1 + t_c(t)] \tag{13-17}$$

where the per capita aggregate variables are derived from the per capita generation-specific variables as follows:

$$X(t) = \int_{-\infty}^{t} x(v,s,)(n+\theta)e^{-(n+\theta)(t-v)} dv \quad X = C,A \tag{13-18}$$

and $H(t) = \bar{h}(t)$. $W(t) = A(t) + H(t)$ corresponds to per capita aggregate wealth at time t.

A dynamic equation for consumption is found by differentiating Eq. (13-16) with respect to time and substituting both Eq. (13-17) and the differentiated version of Eq. (13-14). This yields

$$\dot{C}(t) = \left(\frac{r-\sigma}{\sigma}\right) C(t) - \frac{\Delta(n+\theta)A(t)}{1 + t_c} \tag{13-19}$$

Rising individual consumption can be consistent with balanced growth and, hence, constant consumption per capita because newly born individuals enter the economy without any financial wealth and thus feature lower levels of consumption than those born earlier. If the birth rate is zero, however, a well-defined steady state requires that individual consumption is constant. Accordingly, the rate of return should equal the rate of time preference (see Eq. [13-12]).

2.3 Government

Ricardian equivalence fails under the overlapping generations model. Accordingly, how the government disposes of tax revenues importantly affects the intertemporal equilibrium. The government distributes the additional tax revenues in a way that is distributionally neutral. In particular, the additional public revenues are used to supply a constant and uniform lump-sum transfer per capita to every (living) household. The lump-sum transfer can also be interpreted as a subsidy to labor (or a reduction in the tax on labor income) because labor supply is inelastic. The remainder of this chapter adopts this latter interpretation. Hence, labor earnings, ω, include the labor subsidy.

The magnitude of the constant lump-sum transfer is determined by the intertemporal budget constraint faced by the government:

$$\dot{B} = (r-n)B + l - t_c C - t_p f(k) - t_f[(1-t_p)f(k) - xk] \tag{13-20}$$

where B stands for per capita public debt. The government uses public debt to smooth fluctuations in the tax base.[9] In the initial steady state, public debt is assumed to be zero. Accordingly, on the initial balanced-growth path, the after-tax return to human capital, ω, is given by

$$\omega = f(k) - (1-t_p)kf'(k) + t_c C + t_f[(1-t_p)kf'(k) - xk] \tag{13-21}$$

If one combines the public budget constraint Eq. (13-20) with the aggregate budget constraint of private households Eq.(13-17) and the accumulation equations for the value of the physical capital stock (from Eqs. [13-2] and [13-4]), one arrives at the budget constraint for the country as a whole:

$$\dot{F} = (r-n)\,F + TB \tag{13-22}$$

where F denotes net foreign assets per capita,

$$F = A - B - V \tag{13-23}$$

and TB represents the external trade balance, which amounts to the difference between domestic supply of and aggregate domestic demand for commodities:

$$TB = f(k) - xk - C \tag{13-24}$$

Equation (13-22) can be interpreted as the definition of the growth-adjusted external current account. It states that the accumulation of net foreign assets per capita is equal to the sum of growth-adjusted net capital income received from abroad, $(r-n)F$, and the external trade balance, TB. In the initial steady state, the trade account does not necessarily balance. For example, a positive net asset position allows the country to run a trade deficit.

[9] If the public budget were balanced at each moment, the tax rate would vary over time. Anticipating these changes, agents would substitute intertemporally. These intertemporal substitution effects would complicate the adjustment process and distract from the intergenerational and international distributional impacts that are the focus of this chapter.

2.4 The model's solution

This chapter explores the local behavior of the small open economy around the initial steady state by log-linearizing the model around the initial balanced growth path.[10] Unless otherwise indicated, a tilde (~) above a variable stands for the change in this variable relative to its initial steady-state value. As regards the three tax rates, tildes are defined as follows:

$$\tilde{t}_i = \frac{d(1-t_i)}{(1-t_i)} < 0 \quad i = p,f \tag{13-25}$$

$$\tilde{t}_c = \frac{d(1+t_c)}{1+t_c} > 0 \tag{13-26}$$

Hence, *increases* in the production tax and the origin-based consumption imply that $\tilde{t}_p$ and $\tilde{t}_f$ are *negative*. Changes in the tax rates are unanticipated and permanent. They are implemented at time $t = 0$ and normalized so that they yield the same rise in lump-sum transfers.

3. A destination-based consumption tax

This section examines the effects of a commodity tax on consumption goods that are purchased by domestic households. This time-independent tax can be interpreted as a broad-based value-added tax of the consumption type, which is levied according to the destination principle. The consumption tax distorts neither saving nor the labor-leisure margin because the tax rate is constant over time while labor supply is exogenous. Nevertheless, it does affect aggregate consumption and saving by redistributing income across generations at home. In particular, the saving system yields the following solution for the effect of a destination-based consumption tax on the time path of economy-wide consumption (see Appendix C):

$$\tilde{C}(t) = \tilde{C}(0)e^{-h^* t} + \tilde{C}(\infty)(1 - e^{-h^* t}) \tag{13-27}$$

where $\tilde{C}(0)$ and $\tilde{C}(\infty)$ represent, respectively, the short-run and long-run effects on aggregate consumption:

$$\tilde{C}(0) = -\left(\frac{\frac{r-\sigma}{\sigma}}{r+\theta}\right)\tilde{t}_c < 0 \tag{13-28}$$

$$\tilde{C}(\infty) = \left(\frac{r-n}{h^*}\right)\left(\frac{\frac{r-\delta}{\sigma}}{r+\theta}\right)\tilde{t}_c < 0 \tag{13-29}$$

[10] For a similar approach, see, for example, Judd (1985).

and h^* corresponds to the rate of convergence of aggregate consumption to its new steady-state value (see Appendix C)[11]:

$$h^* = n + \theta - \frac{r - \delta}{\sigma} \tag{13-30}$$

Accordingly, the adjustment speed h^* is closely related to the birthrate $n + \theta$.

The destination-based tax affects the trade balance Eq. (13-24) only through changes in economy-wide consumption, as it impacts upon neither investment demand nor domestic capital accumulation. The corresponding solution for net foreign assets is given by

$$\tilde{F}(t) = \tilde{F}(\infty)(1 - e^{-h^* t}) \tag{13-31}$$

where $\tilde{F}(t) = (r - n)(dF(t)/y)$. Accordingly, two elements characterize the time path of net foreign assets, namely the rate at which the stock of net foreign assets converges to this new steady-state equilibrium, h^*, and the long-run change, $\tilde{F}(\infty)$:

$$\tilde{F}(\infty) = a_c \tilde{C}(\infty) = a_c \frac{r - n}{h^*} \left(\frac{\frac{r - \delta}{\sigma}}{r + \theta} \right) \tilde{t}_c \tag{13-32}$$

where a_c denotes the net income share of consumption in the initial steady state. These two elements determine the short-run effect on national saving:

$$\dot{\tilde{F}}(0) = h^* \tilde{F}(\infty) \tag{13-33}$$

The destination-based tax initially reduces consumption and boosts national saving if the birth rate is positive (as $r > \delta$ if $n + \theta > 0$). With unchanged investment behavior, both the external current account and the net foreign asset position improve. The destination-based consumption tax raises national saving because it redistributes wealth across generations.

The intergenerational redistribution from older towards younger generations operates as follows. The consumption tax-cum-redistribution scheme favors the less wealthy at the expense of the wealthy. In particular, every household receives the same transfer. However, the wealthy contribute a relatively large share to the financing of this transfer because the tax base (consumption) is proportional to wealth (see Eq. [13-13]). Since wealth increases with age (human wealth is constant across cohorts but financial wealth increases as cohorts become older), the policy shock implies a transfer of resources from older towards younger households. In particular, those alive at the time of the unanticipated policy shock lose because, at any future point in time, they will be wealthier; therefore, they will consume more than the then-living younger generations not yet born when the policy shock occurs. The reduced wealth of

11 Saddle point stability requires that $h^* > 0$.

current generations causes consumption to fall, saving to rise, and external accounts to improve when the unanticipated shock occurs.

On a new balanced growth path, aggregate consumption exceeds its initial steady-state value (see Eq. [13-29]). This reflects the improved wealth position of the generations born on the new balanced growth path: They benefit from a net transfer from the older generations because the discounted value of transfers collected by the young exceeds the discounted value of the consumption taxes they pay.

Another interpretation of the macroeconomic effect of the policy experiment is that it subsidizes human wealth at the expense of financial wealth. The tax on financial wealth is fully capitalized by those who are currently alive, as the stock of tangible wealth is owned entirely by current generations. The subsidy on human wealth, in contrast, is partly shifted to those generations not yet born.

The macroeconomic effects of the destination-based consumption tax originate in the impact of the tax on the intergenerational distribution of resources.[12] The government can use public debt policy to neutralize these effects on the intergenerational distribution. In particular, it should provide a one-time subsidy to tangible wealth at the time the unanticipated policy shock occurs. This subsidy should be debt-financed and should offset the windfall loss suffered by capitalists. Accordingly, the initial jump in public debt, ~$B(0) = (r - n)(dB(0)/y)$, corresponds to the deteriorating real-wealth position of the owners of financial capital (see Appendix A):

$$\tilde{B}(0) = a_{\omega}(r - n)\frac{A}{\omega}\tilde{t}_c \tag{13-34}$$

where a_w represents the initial share of noncapital disposable income in net income. In order to ensure that all generations share equally in the burden of servicing the stock of public debt, the government chooses a constant path of transfers that meets the public budget constraint:

$$\tilde{l}^* = -\tilde{B}(0) \tag{13-35}$$

where $\tilde{l}^*$ represents the change in per capita transfers (relative to initial net domestic income) aimed at neutralizing the intergenerational impact of the destination-based tax. These transfers are additions to the constant path of transfers generated by the revenues from the consumption tax. Hence, total transfers amount to the revenues from the consumption tax net of the funds that are required to compensate older generations for the loss in the real value of their financial wealth.

[12] Without overlapping generations, consumption is not affected (see Eqs. [13-28] and [13-29]; note that $r = \delta$ if $n + \theta = 0$).

4. An origin-based production tax

This section examines the effects of a tax on all commodities produced in a small open economy. In the absence of intermediary goods, this production tax is equivalent to a value-added tax of the income type, which is levied according to the origin principle.[13] Unlike the destination-based consumption tax, the origin-based production tax does affect domestic capital accumulation. In the small open economy model, the investment side is separable from the saving side and yields the following solution for the time path of the capital-labor ratio (see Appendix A):

$$\tilde{k}(t) = \tilde{k}(\infty)\,(1 - e^{-ht}) \tag{13-36}$$

Accordingly, two elements characterize the time path of the capital-labor ratio, namely the long-run effect, $\tilde{k}(\infty)$, and the adjustment speed, h. The steady-state reduction in the capital intensity of production depends on the substitution elasticity between labor and capital in production, σ_k:

$$\tilde{k}(\infty) = -\frac{\sigma_k}{1-\alpha_k}(-\tilde{t}_p) \tag{13-37}$$

where a_k represents the net income share of net capital income in the initial steady state. The adjustment speed h (see Appendix A) is given by

$$\frac{h}{r-n} = -\tfrac{1}{2} + \sqrt{\tfrac{1}{4} + \frac{(1-t_p)\,\alpha_k a_I\,(1-\alpha_k)}{\sigma_x \sigma_k z^2}} \tag{13-38}$$

where a_1 denotes the initial income share of net investment and $z = (1-t_p)\alpha_k - a_I$ stands for the net income share of the cash flow net of the (origin-based) production tax but gross of the origin-based consumption tax, t_f. The elasticity σ_x, which reflects the concavity of the installation function, is an important determinant of the adjustment speed. The economy approaches the new steady rate more rapidly if the installation function is less concave, which implies that adjustment costs in investment rise only slowly with the rate of investment. In the absence of any adjustment costs (i.e., $\sigma_x = 0$), adjustment occurs instantaneously and investment becomes infinitely large on impact.

How the unanticipated policy shock affects short-run investment is particularly dependent on both the speed of adjustment and the steady-state effect on the capital-labor ratio (see Appendix A):

$$\tilde{x}(0) = \frac{z}{a_I}\frac{\tilde{k}(o)}{r-n} = \frac{h}{r-n}\frac{z}{a_I}\tilde{k}(\infty) \tag{13-39}$$

[13] Origin-based value-added taxes are typically of the income type if they are levied according to the additive method because tax authorities using the additive method rarely allow investors to expense capital inputs (see Tait [1988]). Given exogenous age-independent labor supply, the production tax-cum-redistribution experiment can be interpreted as replacing a tax on labor income by a capital income tax levied according to the source principle; capital income originating within the country is taxed at the same rate, irrespective of whether it accrues to domestic or foreign households, and the revenue accrues to labor.

The origin-based production tax affects domestic saving through two channels: the time path for the return to human capital (i.e., the sum of after-tax wages and lump-sum transfers), $\tilde{\omega}(t)$, and the jump in the initial value of domestically owned tangible wealth, $\tilde{A}(0)$. The investment side of the model yields the following solution for the initial jump in the per-unit value of the domestic capital stock q (see Appendix A):

$$z^*\tilde{q}(0) = -(1-t_f)(1-t_p)\,\alpha_k\left(\frac{r-n}{h+r-n}\right)(-\tilde{t}_p) \tag{13-40}$$

where $z^* = (1-t_f)\,[(1-t_p)\,\alpha_k - a_I]$ represents the initial share of the after-tax cash flow in net income. The owners of the domestic capital stock lose from the production tax. The larger the adjustment speed relative to the effective discount rate $(r-n)$, the smaller the loss. The reason for this is that rapid capital decumulation causes capital earnings to rise at a fast pace after their initial fall.

How the capital loss is distributed over the foreign and domestic owners of the capital stock depends on the share of the domestic capital stock owned by domestic households on the initial balanced growth path, which is denoted by s_k:

$$\tilde{A}(0) = s_k z^*\tilde{q}(0) \tag{13-41}$$

$$\tilde{F}(0) = -(1-s_k)\,z^*\tilde{q}(0) \tag{13-42}$$

Combining the public-budget constraint with the investment system, one derives the following solution for the return to human capital:

$$\tilde{\omega}(t) = \tilde{\omega}(\infty) + [\tilde{\omega}(0) - \tilde{\omega}(\infty)]e^{-ht} \tag{13-43}$$

$$a_\omega[\tilde{\omega}(0) - \tilde{\omega}(\infty)] = (1-t_f)(1-t_p)\alpha_k(-\tilde{t}_p) \tag{13-44}$$

$$a_\omega\tilde{\omega}(\infty) = t_c\tilde{F}(0) - (1+t_c)\left(\frac{h}{h+r-n}\right)t_p\alpha_k\left(\frac{\sigma_k}{1-\alpha_k}\right)(-t_p) \tag{13-45}$$

Short-run labor earnings exceed the long-run return to human capital because a declining capital-labor ratio reduces the marginal productivity of labor and, therefore, before-tax wages, over time. In the new steady state, the after-tax return to human capital falls below its initial steady-state level if the initial origin-based tax rate on production is positive (i.e., $t_p > 0$) and if a zero initial foreign-ownership share ($s_k = 1$) implies that international distributional effects are absent (i.e., $\tilde{F}(0) = 0$). This long-run decline in after-tax labor earnings is due to a loss in intertemporal efficiency on account of a lower capital-labor ratio.

The time path for economy-wide consumption (see Appendix C) is given by

$$\begin{aligned}\tilde{C}(t) &= \tilde{C}(0)e^{-h^*t} + \tilde{C}(\infty)(1-e^{-h^*t}) \\ &\quad + h\left(\frac{r+\theta}{r+\theta+h}\right)[\tilde{\omega})(0) - \tilde{\omega}(\infty)]\left(\frac{e^{-ht} - e^{-h^*t}}{h^*-h}\right)\end{aligned} \tag{13-46}$$

The initial and steady-state solutions for consumption are

$$\tilde{C}(\infty) = \tilde{\omega}(\infty) \tag{13-47}$$

$$\frac{r+\theta}{\Delta} a_c(1+t_c)\tilde{C}(0) = -\left(\frac{h}{h+r-n}\right)(1+t_c)t_p\alpha_k \frac{\sigma_k}{1-\alpha_k}(-\tilde{t}_p)$$

$$-s_k(n+\theta)\left(\frac{r+\theta}{h+r+\theta}\right)\frac{(1-t_p)(1-t_f)\alpha_k}{h+r-n}(-\tilde{t}_p) \tag{13-48}$$

$$+(1-s_k)\left(\frac{r+\theta}{h+r+\theta}+t_c\frac{(r-n}{h+r-n)}\right)(1-t_f)(1-t_p)\alpha_k(-\tilde{t}_p)$$

The long-run effect on net foreign assets is the result of changes in both national financial assets and the domestic capital stock:

$$\tilde{F}(\infty) = \frac{\sigma_k}{1-\alpha_k}\left[z-\left(\frac{\frac{r-\delta}{\sigma}]}{r+\theta}\right)\left(\frac{r-n}{h^*}\right)t_p\alpha_k\right](-\tilde{t}_p) \tag{13-49}$$

In the proceeding subsection, these expressions are interpreted by distinguishing among three cases. First, the case without adjustment costs is explored. In that case, the tax yields only efficiency implications, which are represented by the first term at the right-hand side of Eq. (13-48). There is no impact on the intergenerational and international distribution of resources because the value of the domestic capital stock, q, is unaffected. Second, the case with adjustment costs but without initial foreign ownership is examined. Adjustment costs reduce the consequences for overall efficiency. At the same time, they generate important effects on the distribution of wealth across generations at home. The second term at the right-hand side of Eq. (13-48) stands for these intergenerational effects. Finally, adjustment costs are combined with initial foreign ownership. In that case, the production tax yields a third effect (represented by the third term in Eq. [13-48]) in addition to that on overall efficiency and the intergenerational distribution, namely, on the international distribution of wealth.

4.1 No adjustment costs: efficiency effects

If adjustment costs are absent, the adjustment speed h becomes infinite. Hence, the origin-based tax leaves the per-unit value of the domestic capital stock and, therefore, initial financial wealth unaffected (see Eq. [13-41] with $h \to \infty$).[14] The reason for this is that physical capital can instantaneously leave the country and is, therefore, able to fully escape the tax burden on capital income. If the

[14] Without adjustment costs, the size of foreign ownership does not affect the results because the value of the equity claims on domestic capital is not changed.

initial tax rate is zero, a marginal increase in the origin-based production tax leaves the return to human capital (see Eqs. [13-43] and [13-45]) unaffected as well. At the margin, this tax reduces the after-tax earnings to labor only if it imposes a first-order distortion resulting from a positive initial tax on production. Thus, unlike the destination-based consumption tax with overlapping generations, the origin-based production tax does not influence saving if both first-order distortions and adjustment costs are absent. The reason behind this is that under these circumstances, a source-based capital income tax rebated to labor affects neither overall welfare nor the intergenerational and international distribution because of its neutral effect on both intertemporal efficiency (because $t_p = 0$) and the distribution between capital and labor (due to the absence of adjustment costs).

If the initial production tax is positive, the lower domestic capital-labor ratio implies a first-order loss in domestic welfare because the initial production tax drives a (positive) wedge between the marginal benefits and marginal costs associated with domestic investment. These efficiency losses result in lower tax revenues and are therefore absorbed by labor. Reflecting the lower value of human capital, aggregate consumption falls as indicated by the negative first term at the right-hand side of Eq. (13-48). National saving also decreases as households adjust the level of financial wealth to the decline in human wealth.

4.2 *Adjustment costs and no foreign ownership: effects on the intergenerational distribution*

The presence of adjustment costs reduces the discounted efficiency losses because it induces the capital-labor ratio to fall only gradually. Furthermore, adjustment costs change the distributional implications of the tax. In contrast to the case with perfect mobility of physical capital, the owners of the domestic capital stock bear part of the tax burden because adjustment costs force capital owners to temporarily settle for lower earnings on their capital.

Figure 13-1 shows a typical consumption path if adjustment costs are present and the initial tax on production is zero, so that overall efficiency is not affected. Immediately following the policy shock, aggregate consumption declines, reflecting the capital loss suffered by currently living generations owning the domestic capital stock; in contrast to the higher value of human wealth, the lower value of tangible wealth is fully capitalized by the generations currently alive. Consumption gradually rises. This development corresponds to a rising population share of generations who benefit from a higher return on human capital but who were not yet born when the then-living individuals suffered a capital loss on their tangible wealth. In fact, consumption rises above its original steady-state level when a large share of the then-alive individuals gain from the policy experiment.

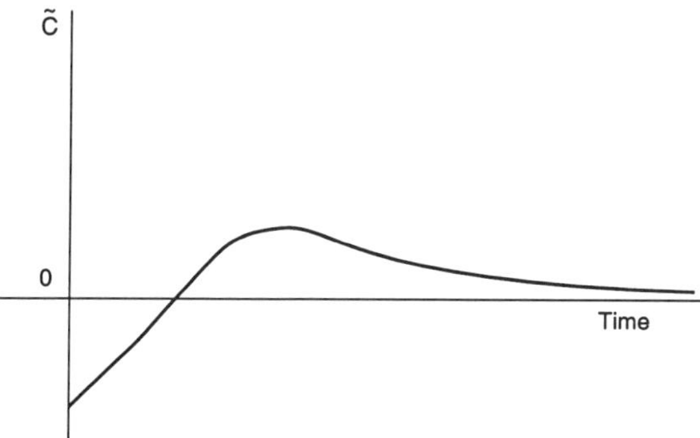

Figure 13-1. Source-based taxation and consumption

Aggregate consumption eventually starts to decline and returns to its initial steady-state level. After reaching a peak, aggregate consumption starts falling because the return to human capital gradually declines as the fall in the capital-labor ratio erodes the marginal product of labor. The fluctuations in consumption become larger if high adjustment costs (implying a low adjustment speed h) and a large birth rate, $n + \theta$, strengthen the intergenerational distribution effects. Intuitively, the adjustment costs produce the distributional effects between capital and labor, while a non-zero birth rate transforms these effects on the functional distribution of resources into consequences for the intergenerational distribution. If both the initial production tax and the birth rate are zero, consumption is unaffected.

If the initial production tax is positive, aggregate consumption is lower compared to the case with a zero initial tax. In fact, consumption may never rise above its original level if a high initial tax rate, t_p, and a large substitution elasticity in production, σ_k, yield large efficiency losses, and if a homogeneous population (i.e., the birth rate, $n + \theta$, is small) and rapid capital decumulation generate only small effects on the intergenerational distribution of resources.[15]

The origin-based production tax improves the initial trade balance due to one negative effect on investment and two positive effects on saving. First, capital decumulation yields an initial trade improvement, as investment demand falls while short-run supply is fixed. Second, consumption smoothing causes consumption to fall in anticipation of the loss in intertemporal efficiency. Third, the intergenerational distribution effect hurts those currently alive and, therefore, reduces aggregate consumption.

[15] In that case, the negative first term at the right-hand side of Eq. (13-48) dominates the positive second term.

4.3 *Adjustment costs and foreign ownership: effects on the international distribution*

The degree of foreign ownership of the domestic capital stock does not affect the macroeconomic implications of the efficiency losses because these losses continue to be absorbed by human capital at home. However, foreign ownership alters the distributional consequences of the origin-based production tax if adjustment costs imply that physical capital is not perfectly mobile internationally. In order to examine the implications of foreign ownership, this subsection assumes that foreigners initially own the entire domestic capital stock (i.e., $s_k = 0$) and that the efficiency effects are zero (i.e., $t_p = 0$).

With initial foreign ownership, the redistribution away from capital to labor hurts foreigners rather than current generations at home. In fact, current domestic generations benefit from higher labor earnings. Accordingly, domestic consumption rises on impact as indicated by the positive third term at the right-hand side of Eq. (13-48). Compared to the case without initial foreign ownership, the trade balance is weaker. Intuitively, the tax on foreigners enhances domestic welfare and, therefore, yields a higher level of domestic consumption. The effect on the international distribution is reflected in an initial jump in net foreign assets, as foreigners suffer a windfall loss due to the instantaneous fall in the value of their claims on the domestic capital stock (see Eqs. [13-40] and [13-42] with $s_k = 0$). As a direct consequence, the domestic economy can afford to run a larger discounted deficit on its trade balance. These macroeconomic effects originate in international rather than intergenerational redistribution. Hence, these effects occur even if the birth rate is zero, so that overlapping generations are absent.

5. An origin-based consumption tax

The origin-based tax examined in the previous section can be made neutral with respect to investment decisions by allowing investors to immediately expense their capital expenditures. The resulting tax can be interpreted as a value-added tax of the consumption type levied according to the origin principle.

Similar to the destination-based tax on consumption, the (time-invariant) origin-based consumption tax does not affect the investment side of the model and does not generate any first-order distortions. Nevertheless, the tax does impact upon domestic saving because it redistributes wealth away from capital to labor. Therefore, it has implications for the intergenerational distribution and, if foreigners own part of the domestic capital stock, for the international distribution of wealth as well. In particular, the origin-based tax hurts the owners of the domestic capital stock because it causes the per-unit value of the existing capital stock to fall (see Appendix A):

$$\tilde{q}(t) = -(-\tilde{t}_f) \quad t \geq 0 \tag{13-50}$$

The domestic ownership share of the capital stock determines the distribution of the capital loss over domestic and foreign residents (see Eqs. [13-39] and [13-50]) and is

$$\tilde{F}(0) = (1 - s_k)z^*(-\tilde{t}_f) \tag{13-51}$$

The declining value of the domestic capital stock reflects both the lower after-tax price of investment goods, which are substitutes for the existing capital stock, and the source-based tax on capital income. At the same time, the after-tax return to human capital rises:

$$a_\omega \tilde{\omega}(t) = [1 + t_c(1 - s_k)]z^*(-\tilde{t}_f) \tag{13-52}$$

The solution for aggregate consumption is given by (see Appendix C)

$$\tilde{C}(t) = \tilde{C}(0)e^{h^* t} + \tilde{C}(\infty)(1 - e^{-h^* t}) \tag{13-53}$$

Accordingly, just as in the case of a destination-based consumption tax, the time path of consumption is fully characterized by the adjustment speed h^* and the initial and long-run effects:

$$\tilde{C}(0) = \frac{\Delta}{a_c(1 + t_c)} \left\{ \frac{1\,(n + \theta)}{(r + \theta)(r - n)} + (1 - s_k)\left[\frac{1}{(r - n)} + \frac{t_c}{(r + \theta)} \right] \right\} z^*(-\tilde{t}_f) \tag{13-54}$$

$$\tilde{C}(\infty) = \tilde{\omega}(\infty) \tag{13-55}$$

Net foreign assets develop as follows:

$$\tilde{F}(t) = \tilde{F}(0)e^{-h^* t} + \tilde{F}(\infty)(1 - e^{-h^* t}) \tag{13-56}$$

$$\tilde{F}(\infty) = a_c \tilde{C}(\infty) \tag{13-57}$$

The short-run response of domestic saving and the growth-adjusted external account is found by differentiating Eq. (13-56).

5.1 Without foreign ownership

If domestic residents initially hold all claims on the domestic capital stock (i.e., $s_k = 1$) and the birth rate is positive (i.e., $n + \theta > 0$), the origin-based consumption tax unambiguously improves the external accounts by stimulating saving. Aggregate consumption falls on impact because currently living individuals suffer a welfare loss as they fully capitalize the lower value of the domestic capital stock but only partially internalize the higher returns to human wealth. Younger generations born after the time of the policy shock gain: They benefit from a higher return to human capital but escape the capital loss. Consequently, consumption, after falling on impact, starts to rise, and eventually exceeds its original steady-state level as a larger stock of net foreign assets allows a weaker trade balance. The higher the birth rate and the shorter the planning horizon of households, the larger the initial drop in aggregate consumption.

5.2 *With foreign ownership*

In contrast to the destination-based consumption tax, the origin-based tax affects the international distribution of wealth if foreigners own part of the domestic capital stock in the initial steady state. In particular, foreign owners of the domestic capital stock bear part of the burden of the origin-based tax. The welfare of living individuals at home may actually increase if their initial ownership of the domestic capital stock is small enough and if their planning horizon is sufficiently large due to a small birth rate. In that case, the rise in their human wealth may offset the fall in their tangible wealth with a resultant initial rise in domestic consumption (see Eq. [13-53]). Just as the origin-based production tax but unlike the destination-based consumption tax, the origin-based consumption tax has macroeconomic implications even if overlapping generations are absent (i.e., $n + \theta = 0$).

If consumption rises in the short run, the external trade balance worsens not only in the long run but also in the short run. Intuitively, an unanticipated origin-based tax expropriates foreign wealth, thereby instantaneously raising net foreign assets (see Eq. [13-52]). The short-run improvement in net foreign assets implies that the country can afford a larger trade deficit on a discounted basis, as foreigners need to transfer real resources to the domestic economy to service the larger claim of domestic residents.

5.3 *Neutralizing the distributional effects*

As with the destination-based consumption tax, the government can neutralize the distributional effects of an origin-based tax by employing a public debt policy. In particular, at the time the unanticipated tax is implemented, the government should provide a debt-financed wealth subsidy to the owners of the domestic capital stock. The time path for additional transfers that service the stock of public debt and leave per capita labor earnings constant (see Appendix B) is given by

$$\tilde{l}^* = -z^*(-\tilde{t}_f) = \tilde{B}(0)$$

6. Replacing destination-based by origin-based consumption taxes

This section uses the results from Sections 3 and 5 to compare the macro-economic implications of the two consumption taxes by examining the consequences of replacing a destination-based by an origin-based tax on consumption. Destination-based and origin-based taxes generally generate different macro-economic impacts because they involve different tax bases. In particular, a destination-based consumption tax implies a capital levy on tangible wealth held by domestic residents. An origin-based consumption tax, in contrast, taxes the domestic and foreign owners of the domestic capital stock. In an open economy, these two tax bases may differ and the two consumption taxes, therefore, typically yield different implications for the intergenerational and international distribution.

The two tax principles imply different impacts on the international distribution if foreigners own domestic equity on the initial balanced growth path. In particular, the origin-based tax exports the tax burden by reducing the value of the foreign claims on domestic capital. The destination-based levy, in contrast, taxes only financial wealth held by domestic residents and thus leaves the value of foreign claims unaffected. Accordingly, compared to a destination-based tax, the origin-based tax allows the domestic economy to run larger trade deficits, thereby expanding the consumption possibilities of domestic residents.

Without initial foreign ownership of domestic equity, the two consumption taxes do not affect the international distribution. However, in the presence of overlapping generations (i.e., a positive birth rate), the taxes still typically generate different macroeconomic consequences due to their differential impact on the intergenerational distribution. In particular, substituting an origin-based tax for a destination-based tax is neutral in the presence of overlapping generations (see Appendix D) only if:

$$\frac{A}{kq} = \frac{(w + l)}{w} \tag{13-57}$$

The left-hand side of Eq. (13-57) stands for the ratio of the base of the capital levy implied by the destination-based tax, which is tangible wealth held by domestic residents, and the base of the capital levy implied by the origin-based tax, which is the capital stock located within the home country. The right side represents the corresponding ratio for the tax on human capital implied by the two taxes. The destination-based tax amounts to a tax not only on after-tax wages, w, but also on public transfers, l. An origin-based tax, in contrast, includes in its base only the return to human capital earned in domestic production, which is after-tax wages w.

Equation (13-57) reveals that the macroeconomic implications due to intergeneration distributional effects originate in the distribution between human capital and financial capital. In particular, if Eq. (13-57) is realized, the burden on financial wealth relative to that on human wealth imposed by the destination-based tax, $[A/(w + l)]$, equals the same relative burden on these wealth components due to the source-based tax, (kq/w). Hence, the two taxes imply the same impact on the distribution between human capital and financial capital and thus on the intergenerational distribution. If the left side of Eq. (13-57) exceeds the right side, however, the destination-based tax implies the largest relative burden on financial capital while the origin-based tax bears heaviest on human capital. Hence, a shift from a destination-based to an origin-based tax benefits financial capital at the expense of human capital. Accordingly, older generations enjoy an increase in welfare, causing them to raise their consumption. The initial the expansionary effect associated with the redistribution in favor of older, currently living generations implies an initial worsening of the trade balance.

If public transfers are zero in the initial equilibrium, Eq. (13-57) can be written as

$$F = 0 \tag{13-58}$$

as $A = F + V$ (public debt is assumed to be zero on the initial balanced-growth path). If the condition in Eq. (13-58) is met, the base of the capital levy implied by the destination tax, which is tangible domestic wealth, coincides with the corresponding base of the capital levy implied by the origin-based tax, which is the domestic capital stock. This implies that both net trade and cross-border claims should be zero on the initial balanced growth path. Hence, the economy should effectively be closed in both commodity and capital markets in the initial equilibrium for the two consumption taxes to be equivalent.

7. Conclusions

Uniform destination- and origin-based consumption taxes are equivalent in traditional static models of international trade that do not allow for international factor mobility and optimizing overlapping generations. However, this chapter demonstrated that, once international capital mobility is allowed for in a dynamic framework, these two alternative principles of taxation typically generate different macroeconomic effects. It also identified the channels accounting for these differential consequences. In particular, the two consumption taxes typically yield different implications for the intergenerational and international distribution.

The two principles for taxing consumption are equivalent in an open economy if two conditions are met. First, foreign ownership of domestic equity should be absent, so that not only the destination-based but also the origin-based tax does not affect the international redistribution. Second, the relative burdens on human and financial capital implied by the two taxes should be the same. This ensures that the two taxes impact the intergenerational distribution in the same way. If the second condition is not met, the two principles are equivalent only if the birth rate is zero, so that overlapping generations are absent. In that case, a representative infinitely lived domestic household internalizes all distributional effects.

In general, however, the two consumption taxes yield different macroeconomic implications. The differences in macroeconomic impact of the two consumption taxes depend both on the initial foreign ownership of the domestic capital stock, which affects the international distributional effect, and the birth rate, which impacts upon the consequences for the intergenerational distribution. A higher birth rate implies that the population is more heterogeneous. Therefore, it tends to increase the differences between the two consumption taxes as it implies larger distributional effects across generations. If initial public transfers are zero, a destination-based tax reduces the external trade deficit the most if the economy has initially run a deficit on its foreign trade account corresponding to a positive net foreign asset position. In these circumstances, a destination-based tax puts a heavier burden on currently living generations than does an origin-based tax. Intuitively, positive net foreign assets imply that the base of the capital levy implied by a destination-based tax (financial wealth at home) is broader than the base of the capital levy corresponding to an origin-based tax (the domestic capital stock). If the economy is a net debtor initially, however, the origin principle is more beneficial for short-run trade performance, unless foreigners own a substantial share of the domestic capital stock on the initial balanced growth path. The reason for this is that origin-based taxes, by including the domestic capital stock in the tax base, imply the heaviest burden on current generations if domestically owned physical capital exceeds the tangible wealth held by these generations.

Consumption taxes typically improve the initial external trade balance by weakening consumption demand. Intuitively, these taxes typically imply a wealth tax on assets owned by current generations at home. However, there are conditions under which consumption taxes may worsen the trade balance in the short run. In particular, origin-based taxes may worsen the initial trade performance if foreigners own a large share of the domestic capital stock when the policy shock hits. In that case, current generations escape the wealth tax at the expense of foreign capitalists.

Origin-based production taxes impact upon the trade balance and net foreign assets by affecting not only saving but also investment. The investment effects importantly depend on adjustment costs in the installation of physical capital. These costs dampen the initial negative investment response and spread these investment effects over a longer time period. Furthermore, adjustment costs typically boost saving because they harm the wealth position of the currently living individuals who own domestic capital stock.

References

Berglas, E. (1981) "Harmonisation of Commodity Taxes." *Journal of Public Economics,* 16, 377-87.

Blanchard, O. J. (1985) "Debt, Deficits and Finite Horizons." *Journal of Political Economy,* 93, 223-47.

Bovenberg, A. L. (1986) "Capital Income Taxation in Growing Open Economies." *Journal of Public Economics,* 31, 347-76.

Buiter, W. H. (1988) "Death, Birth, Productivity Growth and Debt Neutrality." *Economic Journal,* 98, 279-93.

Chamley, C. and B. Wright (1987) "Fiscal Incidence in an Overlapping Generations Model with a Fixed Asset." *Journal of Public Economics,* 32, 3-24.

Frenkel, J. and A. Razin (1987) *Fiscal Policies in the World Economy.* Cambridge, MA: MIT Press.

Genser, B., A. Haufner, and P. B. Sørensen (1993) "Indirect Taxation in an Integrated Europe: Is There a Way of Avoiding Trade Distortions Without Sacrificing National Tax Autonomy?" Copenhagen: University of Copenhagen Business School, Economic Policy Research Unit, Working Paper. (English)

Hayashi, F. (1982) "Tobin's Marginal q and Average q: A Neoclassical Interpretation." *Econometrica,* 50, 213-24.

Judd, K. L. (1985) "Short-run Analysis of Fiscal Policy in a Simple Perfect Foresight Model." *Journal of Political Economy,* 93, 298-319.

Keuschnigg, C. (1991) "The Transition to a Cash Flow Income Tax." *Swiss Journal of Economics and Statistics,* 127, 113-40.

Lockwood, B., D. de Meza, and G. D. Myles (1994) "When are Origin and Destination Regimes Equivalent?" *International Tax and Public Finance,* 1, 5-24.

Nielsen, S. B. and P. B. Sørensen (1991) "Capital Income Taxation in a Growing Open Economy." *European Economic Review,* 34, 179-97.

Tait, A. A. (1988) *Value Added Tax: International Practice and Problems*. Washington D.C.: International Monetary Fund.

Weil, P. (1989) "Overlapping Families of Infinitely Lived Agents." *Journal of Public Economics,* 38, 183-98.

Whalley, J. (1979) "Uniform Domestic Tax Rates, Trade Distortions and Economic Integration." *Journal of Public Economics,* 11, 213-21.

Yaari, M. (1965) "Uncertain Lifetime, Life Insurance, and the Theory of the Consumer." *Review of Economic Studies,* 32, 137-50.

Appendix A: The investment system

The elasticities in the log-linearized model are assumed to be fixed at their values in the initial steady-state equilibrium. In order to express these elasticities in terms of observable shares, the paper uses two steady-state relationships ([A.1] and [A.2] below) that follow from Eqs. (13-2) and (13-6), respectively.

On a balanced growth path, the capital-labor ratio is constant. Accordingly, Eq. (13-2) yields the following steady-state relationship:

$$g(x) = n \tag{13A-1}$$

Setting the left-hand side of Eq. (13-6) equal to zero and using Eq. (13A.1), one derives the following steady-state relationship between the capital-output ratio and the share of the after-tax cashflow in net output, z^*:

$$(r-n)\frac{qk}{f(k)} = z^* = (1-t_f)\,[(1-t_p)\,\alpha_k - a_I] \tag{13A-2}$$

The log-linearized model

The dynamic equations are found by log-linearizing Eqs. (13-2) and (13-7), respectively:

$$\tilde{k} = g'(x)\,x\,\tilde{x} \tag{13A-3}$$

Here I have used

$$\tilde{q} = -\left(\frac{(1-t_f)\,(1-t_p)f''(k)k}{q}\right)\tilde{k} + \left(\frac{(1-t_f)\,(1-t_p)f'(k) - (1-t_f)x}{q}\right)\tilde{q}$$

$$-\left(\frac{(1-t_f)(1-t_p)f''(k)}{q}\right)(\tilde{t}_p+\tilde{t}_f)+(1-t_f)\frac{x}{q}(\tilde{x}+\tilde{t}_f)-g'(x)x\tilde{x} \tag{13A-4}$$

$$d\left(\frac{\dot{q}}{q}\right)=\frac{\delta\frac{dq}{q}}{\delta t}-\frac{\frac{\delta q}{\delta t}}{q}\frac{dq}{q}=\dot{\tilde{q}} \tag{13A-5}$$

where the second equality follows from $q = 0$ in the initial steady state.

Next, one uses the log-linearized version of Eq. (13-7) to eliminate $\tilde{x}$ from Eqs. (13A-3) and (13A-4). The steady-state elasticities in Eqs. (13A-3) and (13A-4) are rewritten by eliminating $g'(x)$ from Eq. (13-7) and eliminating q from Eq. (13A-2). This procedure gives rise to the following two-dimensional investment system:

$$\begin{bmatrix}\dot{\tilde{k}}\\ \dot{\tilde{q}}\end{bmatrix}=(r-n)\begin{bmatrix}0 & \frac{a_I}{\sigma_x z}\\ \left(\frac{1-t_p)\alpha_k}{z}\right)\left(\frac{1-\alpha_k}{\sigma_k}\right) & 1\end{bmatrix}\begin{bmatrix}\tilde{k}\\ \tilde{q}\end{bmatrix}+(r-n)\begin{bmatrix}0 & \frac{a_I}{z\sigma_x}\\ \frac{(1-t_p)\alpha_k}{z} & 1\end{bmatrix}\begin{bmatrix}-\tilde{t}_p\\ -\tilde{t}_f\end{bmatrix} \tag{13A-6}$$

where $z=z^*/(1-t_f)=(1-t_p)\,\alpha_k-a_I$. The adjustment speed (Eq. [13-38]) to the new long-run equilibrium, h, is computed as the absolute value of the stable (i.e., negative) root of the first elasticity matrix at the right side of Eq. (13A-6).

The investment system Eq. (13A-6) is solved by using Laplace transforms. The Laplace transform, $L_p(s)$, of a function $p(t)$ is defined by:

$$L_p(s)=\int_0^\infty e^{-st}p(t)dt \tag{13A-7}$$

The Appendix uses the following expression for the Laplace transform of the time derivative of a function $p(t)$

$$l_{\dot{p}}(s)=\int_0^\infty e^{-st}\dot{p}(t)dt=sL(s)-p(0) \tag{13A-8}$$

Taking Laplace transforms of Eq. (13A-6), one can solve for the Laplace transforms of $\tilde{k}$ and $\tilde{q}$ according to

$$D^*(s)\begin{bmatrix}L_{\tilde{k}}(s)\\ L_{\tilde{q}}(s)\end{bmatrix}=\begin{bmatrix}s-(r-n) & \frac{a_I}{\sigma_x z}(r-n)\\ \frac{(1-t_p)\alpha_k}{z}\left(\frac{1-\alpha_k}{\sigma_k}\right)(r-n) & s\end{bmatrix} \tag{13A-9}$$

$$\begin{bmatrix} \dfrac{a_I}{\sigma_x z}\left(\dfrac{r-n}{s}\right)(-\tilde{t}_f) \\ \dfrac{(1-t_p)\,\alpha_k}{z}\left(\dfrac{r-n}{s}\right)(-\tilde{t}_p)+\dfrac{r-n}{s}(-\tilde{t}_f)+\tilde{q}(0) \end{bmatrix}$$

where the determinant $D^*(s)$ of the elasticity matrix is defined by

$$D^*(s)=(s+h)\{s-(h+r-n)\} \tag{13A-10}$$

In order to find $\tilde{q}(0)$, I use the condition that $L_{\tilde{k}}(h+r-n)$ is bounded. This implies that the first row of the right-hand side of Eq. (13A-9) should be zero if $s = h + r - n$. This condition yields Eqs. (13-40) and (13-50). The Laplace transform for capital accumulation is derived by substituting the solution for $\tilde{q}(0)$ into the second row of Eq. (13A-9). Inverting the Laplace transform, one arrives at Eqs. (13-36) and (13-37).

The initial jump in domestic financial wealth is found by using $dA(0) = s_k k dq(0)$ and the definition of $\tilde{A} = (r - n)(dA/y)$. This yields:

$$\tilde{A}(0)=s_k\frac{(r-n)qk}{f(k)}\tilde{q}(0) \tag{13A-11}$$

Substituting Eqs. (13A-2) into (13A-11), one finds Eq. (13-39). The initial jump in net foreign assets Eq. (13-42) is found analogously by using $dF(0) = -(1 - s_k)kdq(0)$. Furthermore, one derives the required initial jumps in public debt to offset the capital losses suffered by capitalists in this way (see Eqs. [13-34] and [13-58]).

The short-run effect on investment Eq. (13-39) is derived from Eq. (13A-3) by eliminating $g'(x)$ from Eq. (13-7) and using Eq. (13A-2) to eliminate q.

Appendix B: The public budget constraint

To find the increases in the tax rates that are required to finance a given constant increase in lump-sum transfers, one linearizes the public and national budget constraints (Eqs. [13-20] and [13-22], respectively). The relationship between the changes in tax rates and the increase in transfers is found by eliminating the Laplace transform of consumption and using $(r-n)\,L_{\tilde{l}}(r-n)=\tilde{l}$ (because $\tilde{l}$ is constant over time) and $\tilde{B}(0) = 0$:

$$\begin{aligned}&\tilde{l}-t_c\tilde{F}(0)-(1+t_c)t_p\alpha_k(r-n)L_{\tilde{k}}(r-n) \\ &=(1+t_c)a_c\tilde{t}_c+(1-t_p)(1-t_f)(-\tilde{t}_p)+(1-t_f)\,[(1-t_p)-a_I](-\tilde{t}_f)\end{aligned} \tag{13B-1}$$

The effect on the return to human capital is found by log-linearizing:

$$\omega=l+(1-t_f)\,(1-t_p)\,[f(k)-kf'(k)] \tag{13B-2}$$

This yields

$$a_\omega\tilde{\omega}=\tilde{l}+(1-t_f)\,(1-t_p)\,(1-\alpha_k)\,(\tilde{t}_i+\tilde{t}_f) \tag{13B-3}$$

$$+ (1-t_f)(1-t_p)\frac{\alpha_k(1-\alpha_k)}{\sigma_k}\tilde{k}$$

Substituting Eqs. (13B-1) into (13B-3) to eliminate $\tilde{T}$ and substituting the solution for the capital-labor ratio (from Eqs. [13-36] and [13-37]), one arrives at

$$a_\omega\tilde{\omega}(t) = (1+t_c)\,a_c\tilde{t}_c + z^*(-\tilde{t}_f) + (1-t_f)(1-t_p)\,\alpha_k(-\tilde{t}_p)e^{-ht} + t_c\tilde{F}(0) - (1+t_c)\,t_p\alpha_k\frac{h}{(h+r-n)}\left(\frac{\sigma_k}{1-\alpha_k}\right)(-\tilde{t}_p) \qquad \text{(13B-4)}$$

which yields Eqs. (13-43), (13-44), and (13-45) if $\tilde{t}_c = \tilde{t}_f = 0$. Equation (13-52) is derived from Eq. (13B-4) by substituting Eq. (13-51) and setting $\tilde{t}_p = \tilde{t}_c = 0$.

Appendix C: The saving system

In order to manipulate the elasticities, this appendix derives a number of steady-state relationships. Imposing the steady-state condition on Eq. (13-19), one finds the following expression linking A and C on a balanced-growth path:

$$A = \frac{(r-\sigma/\sigma)}{\Delta(n+\theta)}C(1+t_C) \qquad \text{(13C-1)}$$

The steady-state value of human wealth is given by (from Eq. [13-14])

$$H = \frac{\omega}{r+\theta} \qquad \text{(13C-2)}$$

Combining Eqs. (13C-1), (13C-2), and (13-16), one finds

$$\frac{\omega}{(1+t_c)C} = \frac{a_\omega}{a_c(1+t_c)} = \frac{h^*(r+\theta)}{\Delta(n+\theta)} \qquad \text{(13C-3)}$$

$$\frac{A}{\omega} = \frac{(r-\sigma/\sigma)}{(r+\theta)\,h^*} \qquad \text{(13C-4)}$$

where h^* is defined in Eq. (13-30) and

$$a_\omega = (1-\alpha_k) + t_p\alpha_k + t_c a_c + t_f\{(1-t_p)\alpha_k - a_I\}.$$

Log-linearizing Eqs. (13-17) and (13-19), one arrives at the saving system:

$$\begin{bmatrix}\dot{\tilde{C}}(t)\\ \dot{\tilde{A}}(t)\end{bmatrix} = \begin{bmatrix}\dfrac{(r-\sigma)}{\sigma} & -\dfrac{(n+\theta)\Delta}{(1+t_c)\,a_c(r-n)}\\ -(r-n)a_c(1+t_c) & r-n\end{bmatrix}\begin{bmatrix}\tilde{C}(t)\\ \tilde{A}(t)\end{bmatrix} \qquad \text{(13C-5)}$$

$$+\begin{bmatrix} \frac{r-\delta}{\sigma}\tilde{t}_c \\ (r-n)a_\omega\tilde{\omega}-(r-n)a_c(1+t_c)\tilde{t}_c \end{bmatrix}$$

where the time path $\tilde{\omega}(t)$ is derived in Appendix B (see Eq. [13B-4]). In particular, one can write the last element in the last vector in Eq. (13C-5) as

$$(r-n)a_\omega\tilde{\omega}(t)-(r-n)a_c(1+t_c)\tilde{t}_c=(r-n)a_\omega\tilde{\omega}_c(t) \tag{13C-6}$$

where

$$\tilde{\omega}_c(t)=\tilde{\omega}_c(\infty)+[\tilde{\omega}_c(0)-\tilde{\omega}_c(\infty)]e^{-ht} \tag{13C-7}$$

$$\begin{aligned} a_\omega\tilde{\omega}_c(\infty) &= t_c\tilde{F}(0)+z^*(-\tilde{t}_f) \\ &\quad +(1+t_c)t_p\alpha_k(r-n)L_{\tilde{k}}(r-n) \end{aligned} \tag{13C-8}$$

$$a_\omega[\tilde{\omega}_c(0)-\tilde{\omega}_c(\infty)]=(1-t_f)\,(1-t_p)\alpha_k(-\tilde{t}_p) \tag{13C-9}$$

Equation (13C-5) is solved by taking Laplace transforms. h^* is found as the absolute value of the negative root of the first elasticity matrix at the right-hand side of Eq. (13C-5). $(r+\theta)$ is the unstable root.

The short-run change in financial wealth, $\tilde{A}(0)$, is given from the investment system (combine Eqs. [13-32] and [13-33]). To pin down the initial change in consumption, $\tilde{C}(0)$, one uses the condition that $L_{\tilde{C}}(r+\theta)$ is bounded:

$$\frac{(1+t_c)a_c}{\Delta}\begin{bmatrix}\tilde{C}(0)+\dfrac{\frac{r-\delta}{\sigma}}{(r+\theta)}\tilde{t}_c\end{bmatrix}=\frac{\tilde{A}(0)}{(r-n)}+a_\omega L_{\tilde{\omega}_c}(r+\theta) \tag{13C-10}$$

Substituting Eqs. (13C-7), (13C-8), (13C-9) into (13C-10), one derives Eqs. (13-28), (13-48), and (13-53) for $\tilde{C}(0)$. The time path for aggregate consumption is derived by substituting Eq. (13C-10) into the first row of the Laplace transform of Eq. (13C-5) to eliminate the initial change in financial wealth.

Appendix D: Comparing consumption-based taxation

In order to find the changes in the tax rates $(-\tilde{t}_f)$ and $\tilde{t}_c$ that yield the same increase in the lump-sum transfer $\tilde{l}$, one uses Eq. (13B-1). Without initial foreign ownership, $\tilde{F}(0)=0$ (because $s_k=1$). Furthermore, $\tilde{k}=0$ because the consumption-based taxes do not affect domestic capital accumulation. Accordingly, one finds

$$\tilde{l}=(1+t_c)a_c\tilde{t}_c=(1-t_f)\,[(1-t_p)-a_l]\,(-\tilde{t}_f) \tag{13D-1}$$

The two tax changes yield the same macroeconomic effects if and only if they produce the same initial effect on consumption. These short-run impacts are given by, respectively, Eqs. (13-28) and (13-53). Substituting Eq. (13C-1) into (13-38) to eliminate $\{(r-\delta)/\sigma\}$, one finds that the following relationship has to hold for the two taxes to yield the same effects on initial consumption:

$$A(r-n)=\frac{z^{*}f(k)}{\{(1-t_f)\,[(1-t_p)\,f(k)-xk]\}}\,(1+t_c)C \tag{13D-2}$$

Setting the left-hand side of Eq. (13-17) equal to zero, one derives for consumption in the initial steady state

$$(1+t_c)C=(r-n)\,A+\omega \tag{13D-3}$$

Substituting Eq. (13D-3) and

$$(1-t_f)\,[\,(1-t_p)\,f(k)-xk]=z^{*}f(k)+w \tag{13D-4}$$

into Eq. (13D-2), and using Eq. (13A-2) to eliminate z^*, *one arrives at Eq. (13-59).*

CHAPTER 14

Factor mobility, risk, inequality, and redistribution

David E. Wildasin

1. Introduction

Economic integration is not easy to define in a precise way, but in general it is clear that technological and political change over the past half-century or more has lowered the cost of many types of transactions among spatially separated agents. Better communication and transportation, the spread of knowledge about market opportunities and commercial practice, the liberalization of many types of economic policy through such institutions as the European Union and the North American Free Trade Agreement, and the collapse of the planning mechanisms of the state-dominated economies of Eastern Europe and the former Soviet Union all exemplify and contribute to this trend. Goods and services now flow more freely within and among regions, businesses can attract capital from more fully developed and interlinked capital markets, and workers can move more freely among different jurisdictions. Increased interjurisdictional linkages among markets for goods and factors are significantly changing the economic environment within which government fiscal and other policies are implemented. In particular, income redistribution and social insurance policies, which more than any others define the modern welfare state, directly impinge upon and attempt to alter the equilibrium outcomes of factor markets.[1] Their effects

* Earlier versions were presented at meetings of the Regional Science Association (Niagara Falls), the Allied Social Science Associations (Washington, DC), and the International Institute of Public Finance (Lisbon) and at conferences on "The Future of the Welfare State" (Ebeltoft, Denmark), "Topics in Public Economics" (Tel Aviv University), and "Distributional Aspects of Fiscal Policy: The Implications of Economic Integration," (University of Essex). I am grateful to J. Burbidge, G. Eskeland, P. Mieszkowski, R. Musgrave, J. Rust, R. Schoeb, Y. Weiss and conference participants for many useful comments. This chapter is an expanded version of an article entitled "Factor Mobility, Risk, and Redistribution in the Welfare State," which appeared in the *Scandinavian Journal of Economics*. The reader familiar with that paper may wish to omit Sections 2, 3.1, 3.2, and 4.1. The new title reflects the broader scope of the current chapter, reflected especially in Sections 3 and 4. This research was initiated during a visit to the Norwegian School of Economics and Business Administration and continued at the Public Economics Division of the World Bank. I am grateful to these institutions for their hospitality and support.

[1] In a "short-run" and ex post sense, many welfare-state policies are redistributive in nature. From a "long-run" and ex ante perspective, however, they can also be viewed as insurance programs. Many authors have commented upon the "social insurance" view of government income redistribution policy, and this view may indeed be one of the foundations of the modern welfare state. See, for example, Atkinson (1987: Section 2.3) and references there to work by Harsanyi, (*cont.*)

are likely to be sensitive to the nature of these markets. How does factor market integration affect income inequality and risk and what are its implications for social policies that deal with inequality and risk?

It may be noted, first, that increased integration of factor markets can impose new constraints on the ability of governments to engage in income redistribution. The potential mobility of factors of production in response to fiscal differentials underlies traditional arguments for centralization of the redistributive functions of government (see for example Oates [1972]). Increased internationalization of factor markets implies that such a "central" government, i.e., one whose geographical extent coincides with that of the relevant factor market, cannot ordinarily be understood as a "national" government. The redistributive function of government has become increasingly decentralized over time due to the expanded geographical scope of the ambient factor markets within which redistributive policies are executed. However, while greater factor mobility may add constraints to the ability of governments to redistribute income, it can also in itself provide a form of market insurance against income risk. Access to "external" factor markets limits the extent of factor price variation through spatial arbitrage and may, to some degree, obviate the need for public sector insurance of such risks. The present paper investigates this aspect of increasing factor market integration for the insurance and redistributive role of the public sector. Recent macroeconomic literature (such as analyses of optimal currency areas; see De Grauwe [1992] and Eichengreen [1993] and the references therein) have emphasized the possibility of risk *pooling* through centralized fiscal systems with immobile factors of production. As discussed further below, the analysis here emphasizes risk *shifting*, and changes in the welfare costs of redistribution, due to the increased mobility of some but not all factors of production.

Section 2 develops a model in which one immobile and one potentially mobile factor of production are employed together in a risky production process. The degree of integration of the market for the potentially mobile factor is parameterized by a mobility cost parameter. Section 3 investigates the impact of variations in this parameter to show how changes in factor mobility affect factor pricing and income risk, with or without government redistributive policies. While many of the most important results are quite general, the analysis is worked out in particular detail for a special case in which the possible consequences of factor market integration are especially striking. Section 4 discusses issues of factor market integration in the context of developing and

(*cont.*)
Buchanan, Rawls, Varian, and others. The notion that income taxation contributes to risk pooling, and perhaps to risk taking, appears in Domar and Musgrave (1944) and Blum and Kalven (1963); for a survey and additional references, see Sandmo (1987). Grossman and Eaton (1985) and Lawrence and Litan (1986) emphasize the role of protectionist trade policies as forms of insurance against trade shocks.

developed countries and the implications of the analysis in those contexts. Section 5 identifies some questions for further research.

2. The model

It is helpful to begin by illustrating some of the basic ideas of the model with a simple parable.

Imagine a group of specialized regions, in each of which workers produce a region-specific commodity for export, and suppose that regional weather conditions and the prices of export goods on external markets vary randomly and, to at least some degree, independently. If workers are unable to leave their native regions for alternative types of employment, the regional market-clearing wages will depend on region-specific weather and price realizations so that, in a given year, some workers will experience high, while others will have low incomes. If all of these regions were within the jurisdiction of a single government, it would be possible, in principle, to devise a system of taxes and transfers that would pool some or all of this income risk. If there is no such government and no market mechanisms through which to insure against these risks, however, the workers must simply absorb their regional income shocks.

Now suppose that it becomes possible for workers to move from one region to another after they observe the weather and the market price for the goods produced in each region. As long as the random shocks to each region are not perfectly correlated, the returns to workers will be higher in some regions than in others, and workers will tend to move from low-wage to high-wage regions. In doing so, they carry out a form of spatial arbitrage that brings wages in different regions closer together. They also improve the efficiency of resource allocation, increasing the total value of production. At the limit, if migration is costless, wages must be equalized among regions, so that all region-specific risk is perfectly pooled and the ex post distribution of income among workers is perfectly equal. In short, *the integration of labor markets can itself insure workers against income risk, obviating the need for any explicit private or public insurance*. Indeed, whereas such insurance might be valuable when the regional labor markets are completely isolated from each other, it might be harmful in the case where the markets are integrated. At a minimum, it would reduce the incentives for workers to relocate from low- to high-wage regions.

This parable suggests how the integration of factor markets can bring about both greater efficiency of resource allocation and greater equality in the distribution of income. It suggests that government policies that attempt to mitigate income risk may be more harmful to the efficiency of resource allocation as markets become more integrated, and it also suggests that the benefits of those policies may diminish as well. Perhaps, then, increased factor mobility associated with economic integration weakens the rationale for some of the traditional redistributive functions of the welfare state, by making those functions more costly as well as by reducing whatever insurance benefits they might have provided.

Although the parable is suggestive, it is both imprecise and incomplete. Equilibrium models of factor mobility are, most naturally, based on the existence of some *immobile* factor. The presence of immobile factors implies that production in each region exhibits diminishing returns to mobile factors, giving rise to equilibrating adjustments of factor prices in response to factor migration.[2] The presence of immobile factors is also important in the analysis of income redistribution policy, since some degree of immobility is necessary for such policies to have any real effects on income distribution. If the existence of immobile factors is acknowledged, one must ask how the increasing mobility of some factors interacts with the pricing of other, less mobile factors and the income risk to which they are exposed. How do the incidence and allocative eefects of redistributive policies depend on the presence of multiple factors with simultaneously determined prices? The interplay between mobile and immobile factors features prominently in the following analysis and differs from many macro models which assume complete factor immobility (such as models of optimal currency areas with centralized fiscal systems that pool risk among regions).[3]

To address these questions, a more formal analysis is necessary. Thus, consider an economy in which a single homogeneous output x is produced using one potentially variable factor of production, m, and one or more fixed factors. The production technology is subject to uncertainty, represented by a random variable θ, and is characterized by diminishing returns to m:

$$x = f(m,\theta), \quad f_m > 0 > f_{mm}. \tag{14-1}$$

Note that the model is fundamentally static, with production occurring once after the realization of a single random shock. Factor markets are perfectly

[2] In the absence of fixed factors, there is no mechanism to stop the flow of factors from low- to high-return locations, other than *a priori* given migration costs. While such migration costs are certainly important, they do not in themselves offer a very complete or insightful theory of interregional factor allocations.

[3] See, for example, De Grauwe (1992), Bureau and Champsaur (1992), Drèze (1993), and Persson and Tabellini (1993); for a survey and additional references to the literature, see Eichengreen (1993). Factor mobility and its implications for general equilibrium factor pricing and the sharing of risk through factor markets are not generally considered in these discussions. By assuming a given degree of factor market integration, previous analyses take underlying income risks as given, whereas the impact of integration on the magnitude and distribution of these risks is a central issue here. Bureau and Richard (1994) provide a recent analysis of some of the implications of factor mobility for public insurance mechanisms. Analyses of convergence among regions (for example, Barro and Sala-i-Martin [1991]) have drawn attention to the potential importance of factor mobility but tend to focus on total per capita income variation among regions rather than the implications of partial factor mobility for the distribution of income and income risk within regions by type of factor. The analytical framework of Boadway and Wildasin (1990) is similar to that presented here but the focus there is on centralized rather than decentralized redistributive policy.

competitive and the price of the variable factor is determined after the state of the world is known. Expressing all prices relative to the homogeneous output, the return per unit of the variable factor is thus

$$w = f_m(m,\theta) \tag{14-2}$$

which, in general, is random. The returns to the fixed factors are given by

$$r = f(m,\theta) - wm \tag{14-3}$$

and are random, in general. It is assumed here that *factor owners are unable to buy private insurance against factor price fluctuations, so that they do bear income risk when factor prices vary*. Some of the issues that arise in the presence of such insurance are briefly discussed in the conclusion.

Factor supplies are perfectly inelastic at the level of individual households, so that labor/leisure, consumption/saving, and human capital investment decisions are ignored. The initial domestic endowment of the variable factor is denoted by $\overline{m}$. When this factor is mobile, the amount of the input used in local production, m, may differ from $\overline{m}$ either because of imports from external sources ($\overline{m} < m$) or because of exports to the external market ($\overline{m} > m$); mobility is the only source of factor variability. As a central case, one may think of the variable factor as labor, with $\overline{m}$ the initial native population of mobile workers, and think of the fixed factor as land and capital owned by other (nonmobile worker) native residents. In this case, movement of the variable factor corresponds to immigration or emigration. The analysis does not however require factors of production to be owned by (initial) domestic residents.

The domestic government may drive a wedge between gross and net factor returns through the use of (source-based) taxes and transfers. Let t denote a tax (or transfer, if negative) paid by (or to) the owners of the variable factor, so that its net domestic return is $w - t$. In general, t is allowed to depend on the state of nature or, equivalently, to depend on the realized income of the variable factor. The government budget constraint requires that taxes paid by the owners of one factor be transferred to the owners of the other factor, so that the net return to the owners of the immobile factors is given by $r + tm$.[4]

[4] It is trivial to allow for other exogenously fixed government expenditures or revenues, but since none of the results are affected by ignoring such policies, they are omitted for ease of exposition. If provision levels are held fixed, expenditures on pure or nonrival public goods would not vary with factor movements. Differences in levels of provision among regions, like differences in climate and other amenities, would give rise to compensating differentials in equilibrium wages in the presence of full factor market integration, a fact that many authors have exploited to estimate revealed valuations of amenities and public goods. Allowing explicitly for such differences among regions would complicate the details of the following analysis but not its essential features. The benefits from provision of rival or congestible public goods, including cash subsidies as well as various in-kind transfers and public services, are captured in the model through the fiscal variable t. This variable should be interpreted to represent the fiscal contribution per unit of the variable factor, net of any costs incurred for the provision of rival public (*cont.*)

The level of employment of the variable factor is determined by factor mobility, which may be costly. Let $\overline{w}$ denote the certain net return to the variable input on external markets, taken as exogenously fixed. Let c be the per-unit cost of moving the variable factor into or out of the domestic economy. Migration equilibrium requires that the net return to the variable factor be equalized across locations, net of migration costs, i.e.,

$$\overline{w} - c \leq w - t \leq \overline{w} + c \tag{14-4a}$$

$$m > \overline{m} \rightarrow w - t = \overline{w} + c \tag{14-4b}$$

$$m < \overline{m} \rightarrow w - t = \overline{w} - c \tag{14-4c}$$

$$\overline{w} - c < w - t < \overline{w} + c \rightarrow m = \overline{m} \tag{14-4d}$$

Substituting from Eq. (14-2), Eqs. (14-4a) to (14-4d) determine the equilibrium value of m conditional on the state of the world θ and on the tax/transfer policy t.

A special case. Given the state of the world and the redistributive policy of the domestic government, the system of equations and inequalities in Eq. (14-2) and Eqs. (14-4a) to (14-4d) constitutes a simple general equilibrium model that can be used to determine equilibrium levels of the variable factor and output, equilibrium gross and net factor prices, and the distribution of income. It is possible to study this model in its most general form, and the analysis below does indeed contain several results that apply in the general case. However, the nature and mechanics of equilibrium in the model are most easily understood by considering an illustrative special case.

The special case involves restrictions on the production function and on the distribution of the random variable θ. First, the production function is assumed to be quadratic in m with a marginal product for the variable factor that is subject to additive uncertainty, that is, $f(m,\theta) = (a + \theta)\, m - bm^2/2$, so that $f_m = a + \theta - bm$. For the sake of brevity, let us call this the *additive-quadratic* production technology. Second, suppose that θ is a discrete random variable, taking on only the values θ_1, θ_2 with equal probability. Without loss of generality, assume that $\theta_1 > \theta_2$ (so that θ_1 is a "good" state of the world) and that $\theta_1 + \theta_2 = 0$ (that is, the parameter a is adjusted so that the θ_i's have a zero mean). Figure 14-1 shows the linear downward-sloping marginal productivity curves for the variable factor for each of the two states of the world. Assume, finally, that $a - b\overline{m} = \overline{w}$, so that the mean domestic marginal product of the variable factor, when only the domestic endowment of the factor is employed, is equal to its external net rate of return. This assumption provides a reference point or normalization for the analysis by anchoring the expected return to the variable

(*cont.*)

goods and services. There is some loss of important detail in this interpretation insofar as the value of the benefits provided by public expenditures differ from the cost of provision but the analysis would not be affected in its essential features by explicit inclusion of congestible public goods in the model.

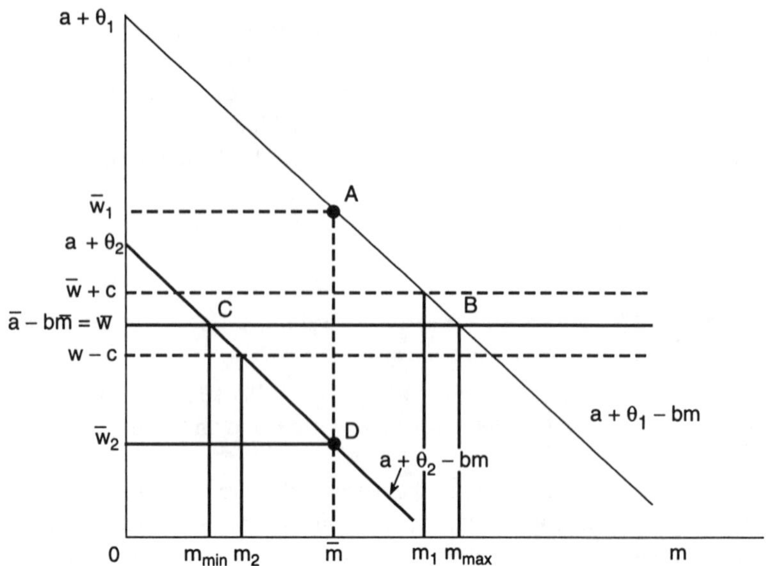

Figure 14-1. Factor mobility and income risk

input to that obtainable externally.[5] To depict the equilibrium, suppose first that there is no government redistributive policy so that $t = 0$. If c is sufficiently large – specifically, if $c > \theta_1 = |\theta_2|$ – there will be no movement of the variable factor in either state of the world. Hence $m = \overline{m}$ in equilibrium, and the equilibrium price of the variable factor is $\overline{w}_i \equiv f_m(\overline{m},\theta_i)$ in state θ_i, as shown in Fig. 14-1. This corresponds to the equilibrium condition Eq. (14-4d). Total output and the return to the fixed factor are given by $0\,(a + \theta_1)A\overline{m}$ and $(a + \theta_1)A\overline{w}_1$, respectively, for the good state, and by $0\,(a + \theta_2)\,D\overline{m}$ and $(a + \theta_2)\,D\overline{w}_2$ for the bad state.

If $c < \theta_1$, factor migration will occur in each state of the world. In the extreme case where $c = 0$, migration will occur in either state of the world, with $m = m_{max}$ if $\theta = \theta_1$ and $m = m_{min}$ if $\theta = \theta_2$, as shown in Fig. 14-1. The net domestic return to the variable factor will be equal to that on the external market, $\overline{w}$, independently of the realization of θ. Total output and the return to the fixed factor will be $0\,(a + \theta_1)Bm_{max}$ and $(a + \theta_1)B\overline{w}$ in the good state, and $0\,(a + \theta_2)\,Cm_{min}$ and $(a + \theta_2)\,C\overline{w}$ in the bad state. More generally, if $0 < c < \theta_1$, the equilibrium domestic price for the variable factor is $\overline{w} + c$ in the good state (corresponding to equilibrium condition Eq. [14-4b]) and $\overline{w} - c$ in the bad state (corresponding to equilibrium condition Eq. [14-4c]). The equilibrium level of employment of the variable factor is m_i in state i, with $m_{min} < m_1 < \overline{m} < m_2 < m_{max}$, as shown in

[5] If the mean domestic return is higher or lower than that in the external market, the owners of the variable factor would obtain a higher or lower expected return, respectively, when factor markets are integrated.

the figure. Total output and the return to the fixed input can be read from the diagram as before.

It is straightforward to show how taxes or transfers are incorporated into this model. If, for instance, the variable factor is subject to a positive per-unit tax of t in the good state, the curve $a + \theta_1 - bm$ in Fig. 14-1, shifted down by the amount t, would show the *net* return to the variable input as a function of the level of employment. The level of m at which this net return is equal to $\overline{w} + c$ would determine the equilibrium level of m in the good state, assuming that it exceeds $\overline{m}$. If the variable input receives a subsidy (i.e., $t < 0$) then the curve would be shifted upward by the appropriate amount to determine the equilibrium. The level of employment of the variable input generally depends on the tax-transfer policy t.

Although this special case of the model entails quite restrictive assumptions, it clearly illustrates the essential elements of the determination of equilibrium. Most importantly, it shows how the equilibrium level of employment as well as gross and net factor prices depend on the state of nature, government redistributive policies, and the level of migration costs. If migration costs are sufficiently high, the variable factor is effectively immobile and external factor prices do not affect domestic factor prices. If migration costs are sufficiently low, domestic factor prices are linked by spatial arbitrage, through factor mobility, to external prices. These are important and *general* properties of the model, not dependent on specific assumptions about the form of the production function or the nature of uncertainty.

In closing the description of the basic model, it is worth noting some possible interpretations and extensions. First, the underlying source of risk in the economy, the random variable θ, has several possible interpretations. It could refer to technological uncertainty in an economy where the homogeneous output is "corn," an all-purpose commodity used directly for consumption. Alternatively, one might suppose that the domestic economy is small and open with respect to commodity trade and that it is specialized in the production of particular goods which trade on world markets at uncertain prices. This corresponds to the special case of Eq. (14-1) where θ enters f multiplicatively and is interpreted as the world price of the domestically-produced good relative to the price of "corn"; "corn" itself could be a Hicksian composite commodity that encompasses all other tradeable goods that have fixed relative prices in world markets.

It is straightforward to extend the model to allow explicitly for other traded factors of production or for many traded goods, provided that these commodities trade at fixed external prices and that they are not the subject of any fiscal policies or other distortions. Adding extra inputs to the production process at fixed prices does not change the nature of factor price determination for the two inputs described already. (See Sandmo and Wildasin [1994] for further discussion.) Trade in goods can lead to factor price equalization, in which case "commodity movements and factor movements are substitutes" (Mundell 1957). Although factor price equalization could obviate much of the present analysis by eliminating migration incentives, it is worth recalling that the underlying assumptions of identical production technologies among jurisdictions and free intersectoral factor mobility are quite strong.[6] In the present model, the random variable θ can be interpreted as random departures from the production technology prevailing in the rest of the world. Under this interpretation, factor price equalization is precluded by jurisdiction-specific production technologies built directly into the model. Alternatively, one could think of θ as a terms-of-trade shock which affects factor prices because some factors of production are not only interjurisdictionally but intersectorally immobile (at least over the relevant time horizon). At the empirical level, observed factor mobility as well as (binding) constraints on factor mobility (such as immigration quotas or capital controls) testify to the existence of spatial variations in net factor returns, suggesting the value of models in which factor price equalization does not hold.

3. Economic integration and income risk

3.1 *Income risk in the absence of income redistribution policy*

Consider now the nature of income risk in the foregoing model. We begin with the case where the government does not intervene to change the distribution of income.

Suppose first that migration costs are prohibitively high, so that no factor reallocations occur in any state of the world. Domestic factor prices and incomes will generally be stochastic, with distributions that depend both on the distribution of the underlying random variable θ and on the way that uncertainty enters the production technology. When the production function is additive-quadratic, the gross price of the variable factor has a variance equal to the variance of θ itself, while the gross return to the fixed input is nonstochastic.[7] This is illustrated for the particular case of a two-point distribution of θ in Fig. 14-1, where the return to the fixed factor is the area under the marginal product curve for m and above its equilibrium price, i.e., the triangular area $(a + \theta_1)A\overline{w}_1$ in the

[6] Indeed, any plausible theory of technological uniformity requires an explanation of technological diffusion; since technology is frequently embodied in either human or non-human capital, factor mobility may actually contribute importantly to the establishment of identical production technologies in different regions or countries.

[7] Given $f(m,\theta) = (a + \theta)\, m - bm^2/2$, the equilibrium price of the variable factor with no migration is $a - b\overline{m} + \theta$. Since $E(\theta) = 0$, the expected return to the variable factor is just $a - b\overline{m}$ and the variance is $E\,(a - b\overline{m} + \theta - [a - b\overline{m}]\,)^2 = E\,(\theta)^2 = \mathrm{Var}\,(\theta)$. From Eq. (14-3), $r = (a + \theta)\overline{m} - b\overline{m}^2/2 - ([a + \theta]\overline{m} - b\overline{m}^2) = -\, b\overline{m}^2/2$, which is independent of the value of θ.

good state and $(a + \theta_2)D\overline{w}_2$ in the bad state. These triangles are clearly equal in size, showing that the return to the fixed factor is state-independent.

In the opposite extreme case, where migration costs are negligible, the equilibrium domestic factor price for the variable input is equal to the price fixed on external markets and is thus completely certain. Although income risk for the owners of the variable factor disappears in this case, it does not disappear for the economy as a whole. Rather, all risk is shifted to the owners of the immobile factor. A complete opening of the economy to the external market for the variable input does not merely imply that the fixed factor absorbs all risk, however. It also changes the mean return to the fixed factor. In the special case illustrated in Fig. 14-1, for example, the mean return to the variable input is unchanged when it becomes perfectly mobile, but the mean return to the fixed input becomes $.5\,(a + \theta_1)B\overline{w} + .5\,(a + \theta_2)C\overline{w}$, in contrast to a mean return of $.5\,(a + \theta_1)\,A\overline{w}_1 + .5\,(a + \theta_2)\,D\overline{w}_2$ when the variable input is completely immobile. Moving from complete immobility to perfect mobility of the variable input thus increases the mean return to the fixed input by the amount $\overline{w}_1 AB\overline{w} - \overline{w}CD\overline{w}_2 = (\overline{m} - m_{\min})\theta_1$. There is an "efficiency gain" that results from an increase in the mobility of the variable input which takes the form of an increase in the mean income accruing to the factor owners in the domestic economy.

Although the comparison of the polar extreme cases of complete immobility and complete mobility of the variable input is informative, the process of economic integration does not occur all at once, as represented in the model by a reduction in c from some very high level to zero. A more realistic view of the process is that the variable input is partially mobile initially, but that it becomes increasingly mobile over time. What happens to income and income risk for each type of factor as the domestic market for the variable input becomes *increasingly* integrated with the external market? This amounts to asking for a comparative-statics analysis of the effect of a reduction in c on the distribution of returns to both factors.

When the variable input is immobile (for instance, if c is infinite), the cumulative distribution of w is given by

$$\text{prob}\left\{ w \le w_0 \right\} = \text{prob}\left\{ f_m(\overline{m},\theta) \le w_0 \right\} \tag{14-5}$$

for any $w_0 \ge 0$, a distribution that can be determined for any given production technology and distribution of θ. For instance, in the additive-quadratic case, the distribution of $w - a + b\overline{m}$ is identical to that of θ. Reductions in c truncate the distribution of w at both tails, such that

$$\text{prob}\left\{ w = \overline{w} + c \right\} = \text{prob}\left\{ f_m(\overline{m},\theta) \ge \overline{w} + c \right\} \equiv P_1 \tag{14-6a}$$

$$\text{prob}\left\{ w = \overline{w} - c \right\} = \text{prob}\left\{ f_m(\overline{m},\theta) \le \overline{w} - c \right\} \equiv P_2 \tag{14-6b}$$

$$\begin{aligned} \text{prob}\left\{ w \le w_0 \right\} = P_2 + \text{prob}\left\{ \overline{w} - c \le f_m(\overline{m},\theta) \le w_0 \right\} \supset \\ \in [\overline{w} - c, \overline{w} + c] \end{aligned} \tag{14-6c}$$

In particular, if θ is symmetrically distributed and if $\overline{w} = a - b\overline{m}$, reductions in c trim the tails of the distribution of w without changing its mean, so that *the only effect of increased integration on the return to the variable factor is to reduce its risk.* If the external rate of return to the variable factor were higher or lower than $a + b\overline{m}$ *or if* θ *were not symmetrically distributed, greater integration would raise or lower its mean return while still limiting the range of its variation.*

The effect of reductions in c on the distribution of returns to the immobile factor is more difficult to ascertain in general. However, analysis of a useful special case – that of an additive-quadratic production technology and uniformly-distributed technology shocks – confirms what the polar cases of complete immobility and complete immobility suggest should be true. First, as shown in Fig. 14-2, *reductions in the cost of factor mobility raise the expected return to the fixed input.* That is, there is an "efficiency gain" from improved mobility of the variable input since it can be allocated more easily where its productivity is higher. (The subscript "LF" in these figures denotes "laissez faire," in reference to the absence of a government redistributive policy.) Second, *the variance of the return to the variable input diminishes as its mobility improves,* as shown in Fig. 14-3. Third, *the variance of the return to the fixed factor rises as the mobility of the variable input increases.*

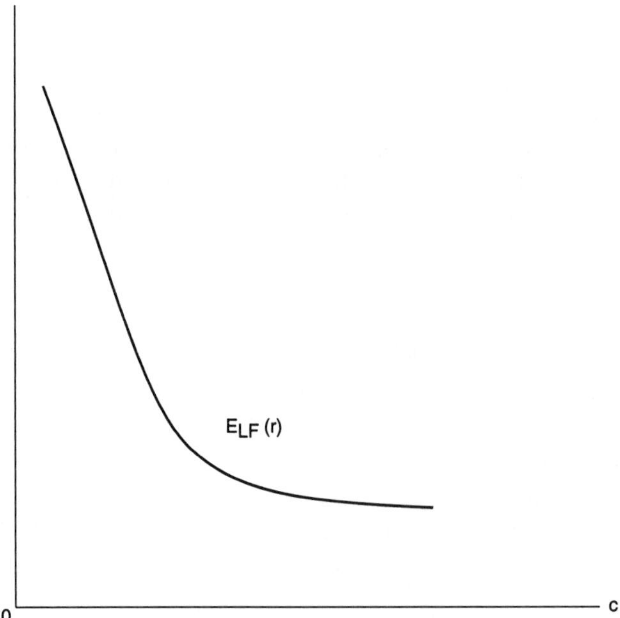

Figure 14-2. Expected return to fixed factor

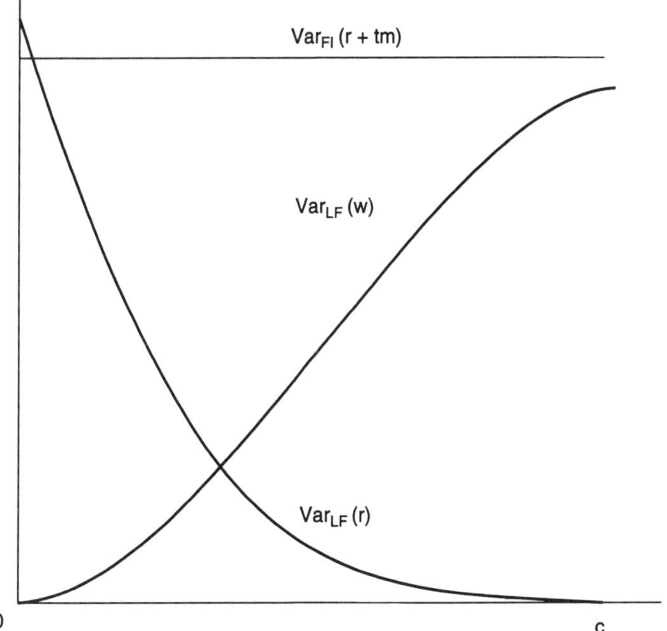

Figure 14-3. Variations of factor returns

3.2 Economic integration, risk, and income redistribution

Let us now consider the impact of government redistribution policy as the mobility of the variable factor changes.

Full insurance for the variable factor. Begin with the case where the variable factor is completely immobile. As noted above, the gross income of this factor varies with the state of nature in this case; the income of the immobile factor may not. Government policy cannot eliminate income risk under the assumptions that we have made, but it can change how that risk is distributed. For instance, it would be possible to impose a tax/transfer policy such that the net income of the variable input would be the same in all states of the world, the case of *full insurance* for the variable factor. This outcome can be achieved by setting $t = f_m(\overline{m},\theta) - \overline{w}$, in which case the net income of the variable input would be equal to $\overline{w}$ in every state while the income of the fixed input would be equal to $f(\overline{m},\theta) - \overline{wm}$, thus absorbing all income risk. Income redistribution policy has no effect on the physical allocation of resources in this case.

Now suppose that the variable input is potentially mobile, at a cost of c per unit, and that the government continues to use redistributive policies that keep the net income of the variable input fixed at $\overline{w}$. As long as this policy is in place, there is no incentive for domestic or foreign owners of the variable input to incur the cost of removing it from or bringing it to the domestic economy; in other words, this policy forestalls any factor mobility for any positive value of c. Under this policy, then, changes in the level of c have no effect on input or output levels or on gross or net incomes in any state of the world. By comparison with the *laissez-faire* case, for each value of c, the mean return to the variable input is the same, but its variance is lower (specifically, zero) in the presence of this government policy. On the other hand, the mean return to the immobile factor is lower because the efficiency gains from factor mobility are not exploited. This is an "efficiency loss" from the imposition of the government's redistributive policy.

How does this policy of full insurance for the variable factor affect the variability of the net return to the fixed factor? The answer is clear in general terms: The fixed input absorbs all income risk in the economy and this risk is independent of the level of c (because the allocation of resources is independent of c in the presence of full public insurance for the variable input). The horizontal line in Fig. 14-3 labeled "$\text{Var}_{FI}(r + tm)$" (for "full insurance") illustrates. Interestingly, it is possible that the variability of the return to the fixed factor can be *lower* in the full insurance case than under *laissez faire* for sufficiently small values of c. In the case illustrated in Fig. 14-3, however, this occurs only at very low values of c.

Partial insurance of the variable input. An extreme policy of using taxes and transfers to shift all income risk from the variable to the fixed factor destroys all incentives for the variable factor to relocate after the state of nature is known. This policy thus completely negates any allocative gains from reductions in the cost of factor mobility. While this extreme case is illustrative, it is clearly quite special; *a priori*, findings for this case may not extend to more interesting intermediate cases. For instance, suppose that the government imposes a proportional tax or subsidy on deviations from the mean return of the variable input, such that

$$t = \alpha (w - \overline{w}) \quad \alpha \in [0,1] \tag{14-7}$$

This policy encompasses the *laissez faire* and perfect insurance policies as polar extremes, corresponding to $\alpha = 0$ and $\alpha = 1$, respectively. More generally, a policy with $\alpha \in (0,1)$ proportionally shrinks the variation in w, and can be viewed as a proportional income tax/negative income tax scheme with a constant marginal tax rate of α and a break-even level of income of $\overline{w}$. The net return to the variable input under this policy is a simple weighted average of the gross return w and the mean return $\overline{w}$:

$$w - t = \alpha\overline{w} + (1 - \alpha)w \tag{14-8}$$

Although it is quite difficult to derive general conclusions about the effects of increased factor mobility on factor allocations and income distribution under this policy, results can be computed for the simple special case where the production technology is additive-quadratic and θ is uniformly distributed. A policy of partial insurance for the variable input implies that the gross and net returns to each factor diverge due to the presence of the taxes and transfers through which the insurance is implemented. For any *given* value of the cost of migration c, one can show that (i) the expected gross and net return to the variable input is equal to $\overline{w}$ in the presence of partial insurance (by construction); (ii) the variance of the net return to the variable input is less than the variance of the gross return; (iii) the expected net return to the fixed input is less than its expected gross return; and (iv) the variance of the net return to the fixed input exceeds that of the gross return.[8] What is of most interest for present purposes, however, is how these moments of the factor price distributions change with the cost of mobility. Essentially, the results parallel those for the *laissez-faire* case. As economic integration proceeds, the variance of both the gross and net return to the variable input falls. In the extreme case of perfect mobility, both variances drop to zero as a result of perfect arbitrage between the internal and external factor markets. Reductions in c raise the expected gross and net return to the fixed factor and also raise the variance of both the gross and the net return. These impacts are qualitatively in the same direction as for the *laissez-faire* case, though of course their quantitative magnitudes are different.

3.3 Alternative assumptions about factor mobility

In applying the preceding analysis, the question naturally arises as to which factors of production, in practice, are relatively mobile or immobile. A case could be made, in some circumstances, for the stylized assumption that "capital is mobile but labor is immobile," whereas the reverse assumption might be equally defensible in other circumstances. Actually, an attempt at rigid *a priori* determinations of "fixed" and "variable" inputs will probably not be fruitful since, in practice, almost all inputs are variable, but only at a cost. Factor migration is intrinsically a dynamic process, and the responsiveness of capital and labor allocations to rate of return differentials in different locations will depend on the persistence of the differentials and on the length of the decision horizons of workers and firms. For example, U.S. census data show that the proportion of young adults (for instance, those aged 20–24) who relocate in a given year is much higher than the proportion of older adults (for instance, those in the age groups 55–64 or 65–74) who move. Formal empirical analysis (such as Topel [1986]) confirms that younger workers are more likely than older

[8] Details and illustrations of the calculations are omitted to save space. These properties are as expected: (ii) implies that the partial insurance policy actually does lower the variance of net relative to gross income for the "insured" factor; (iii) implies that there is an "efficiency loss" from the policy; and (iv) implies that the policy shifts risk from the variable to the fixed input.

workers to relocate in response to a given wage differential. An obvious explanation for this pattern of behavior is that young workers have lower moving costs and have a longer period during which they can reap the benefits of higher incomes in a new location. A corollary of this finding is that spatial net income differentials that are persistent or that are expected to persist will give rise to more factor reallocation than short-lived fluctuations in factor returns.

The dynamic nature of the migration process raises a number of difficult questions for empirical analysis. First, the demographic, health, and occupational status of migrants is likely to change over the horizon of relatively costly moves. Potential migrants may well marry, have children, become employed or unemployed, acquire new skills, or become ill or elderly during the time that they expect to reside in a new location. The "net income" measure that is relevant for modeling the migration decision should thus include benefits and costs accruing to other family members, perhaps extending over more than one generation and varying among households.[9]

Second, changes in migrant status over time are also likely to be crucial for understanding how potential migrants interact with fiscal systems and other policies. Many welfare-state policies affect people at the extremes of the life cycle (family allowances, education, child care, retirement benefits, and health care for the elderly), so their effect on migration choices may be especially dependent on the length of the potential migrant's planning horizon and on current and anticipated family demographic structure. Public pension systems affect the entire lifetime income stream of participants. Rough estimates (Wildasin 1994a) indicate that 20-year-old workers moving from one EU country to another may experience changes in net public pension wealth amounting to several years' worth of earnings. Quantitatively large effects of policy on net factor returns are of course to be expected, since public expenditures in modern welfare states often amount to half of GDP.

Third, the degree of factor mobility may be obscured, empirically, by endogenous policy adjustment. As an illustration, suppose that unrest and economic breakdown in one country induce neighboring countries to reinforce their immigration constraints. Wide fluctuations in factor returns may only give rise to small changes in factor allocations under such circumstances because policy responses are designed to ensure this is the case. Another way to say this is that the data are generated by a simultaneously-determined equilibrium in

[9] Empirical research on savings behavior suggests that while some households are relatively myopic, others plan for retirement consumption in accordance with the life-cycle hypothesis and still others appear to accumulate wealth for the purpose of making intergenerational transfers. Planning horizons for migration decisions are presumably likewise heterogeneous. See, for example, King and Dicks-Mireaux (1982) and, for a survey and additional references, Boadway and Wildasin (1994).

policies and market variables, and models that focus only on the latter will be misspecified.[10]

A final important issue for empirical analysis of factor mobility concerns factor aggregation. The migration costs of old and young workers or of low-skilled, higher-skilled, professional, and managerial workers are likely to differ substantially. Indeed, one important benefit of certain types of skill acquisition (including language skills and general education) is precisely the increased greater interoccupational and interregional mobility that it affords. The possibility of substitute/complement relationships among different types of labor, the role of skill and human capital heterogeneity as a contributing factor to earnings inequality, and the importance of intergenerational distributional issues and their interaction with intergenerational tax/transfer policies such as public pensions and debt policy, are all important issues the study of which hinges on explicit recognition of labor heterogeneity. The private nonhuman capital stock is also heterogeneous and of variable durability. The same is true for public capital. Major public infrastructure may be quite long-lived, while other types of public capital can be adjusted relatively quickly.

A more general analysis would allow for many heterogeneous factors of production, each of which is potentially mobile with costs of adjustment, varying by factor, that depend on the speed of adjustment. Pending the formulation and analysis of such models, there is still much to be learned from the study of simple static general equilibrium models based on stylized assumptions about factor mobility and factor aggregation. These models can be viewed as special cases of more general formulations, yielding results which therefore serve as benchmarks for further analysis. In this exploratory spirit, it is useful to entertain a variety of assumptions about factor mobility. With specific reference to the model developed above, it may be useful, for the purposes of some questions relating to some regions over some periods of time, to aggregate all inputs into capital and labor and to assume that labor is mobile and that capital is immobile. For other purposes, one might reverse the assumptions about labor and capital mobility. For still other purposes, other factor aggregations might be more useful. The most fruitful approach to the analysis of public policy questions facing the welfare states of modern Europe and elsewhere is not to insist that either "capital" or "labor" is mobile or immobile, but rather to recognize the appropriateness of different stylized assumptions for different purposes.

[10] Summers (1988) has made this point in the context of trade policy and capital mobility. When these lines were first written, the U.S. government was attempting to discourage Haitians and Cubans from entering the U.S., fearing a repetition of the Mariel boatlift. Such situations arise with increasing frequency, illustrated, for instance, by the recent attempts by Albanians to move to Italy which met with considerable Italian resistance.

4. The experience of factor market integration

As already discussed, assessing the extent of factor mobility and factor market integration presents a number of difficult empirical questions, so the application of the foregoing analysis to practical cases must be undertaken carefully. Nevertheless, despite (or perhaps because of) the simplicity of the analysis developed in the preceding sections, it can shed some light on the experience of factor market integration and on the formulation of economic policy in a variety of contexts. This section discusses some aspects of factor market integration and its fiscal implications in developed and developing countries.

4.1 Factor market integration in developed countries

The welfare states of the advanced democracies face an increasingly liberalized economic environment. In part this is a result of more or less deliberate policy choices, and in part it is a result of long-run technological and other trends. One aspect of this liberalization is an increase in factor mobility. Freer markets generally create incentives for greater responsiveness to shocks, with resulting gains in efficiency. The analysis of Sections 2 and 3 bears this out: As factor mobility increases, expected income rises. Shocks give rise to larger fluctuations in input and output levels, with higher levels of employment in high-productivity states of the world and lower levels in states where productivity is low. Efficiency is improved and expected returns rise. In the specific model used, the increase in efficiency of resource allocation accrues only to the immobile input, while the expected return to the variable input remains unchanged. These efficiency gains may be lost, however, if government redistributive policies dull the incentives for state-contingent reallocations of the variable input. In the extreme case of full insurance, none of the potential efficiency gains from greater factor mobility may be realized.

What are the distributional implications of greater factor mobility? Do the efficiency gains of greater factor mobility come at the cost of equity? These questions are, by their very nature, not easily resolved due to the difficulty in defining what is equitable. Still, some useful lessons can be drawn from the foregoing analysis by considering different possible scenarios.

Suppose, for example, that there are only two factors, labor and capital, and that labor is the variable input. In the *laissez-faire* economy, greater labor mobility raises the expected return to capital. Workers do not, on average, obtain higher incomes. They do, however, experience reduced income risk, as greater mobility provides them with better access to external market opportunities. Capital income becomes increasingly risky as labor mobility improves. Government policies that pool income risk bring about efficiency losses but also shift income risk from labor to capital. If protection of labor income through market mechanisms is infeasible, then there may be substantial benefits from government redistributive policies in a relatively closed economic environment where workers in unproductive regions have very few opportunities to escape to more rewarding pursuits. However, the benefit from these policies is diminished, and their cost is increased, when labor mobility increases. These policies now inhibit state-contingent factor reallocations that both increase efficiency and reduce income risk for workers. Although a more open economic environment may limit the ability of policymakers to redistribute income and cause some retrenchment of programs aimed at insuring wage incomes, it does not necessarily follow that the *objectives* of those programs are compromised. Rather, the mechanism of wage income insurance may simply shift from public sector redistribution to private sector wage equalization through migration.

Suppose now that capital rather than labor is "the" mobile factor of production. The foregoing analysis implies that greater integration of factor markets may increase earnings risk for labor. Greater capital mobility may reduce the riskiness of investment returns at their source. To the extent that capital income streams are tradeable through financial markets, however, the risks to capital income recipients may already be widely shared. Reductions in capital income risk at source may therefore not reduce the income risk of capital owners very substantially. The riskiness of wage income, however, may increase significantly. The analysis presented in Section 3 suggests that such wage risk can be diminished by reductions in the degree of insurance provided to capital income. One way to do this is by restructuring fiscal and other policies. Reductions in effective corporate income tax rates, for example, could reduce the burden of risk shifted from capital income to labor income while simultaneously raising the net return to labor by improving the efficiency of resource allocation.

As a further variation on the model, suppose that there are three factors of production. Suppose that highly skilled and (generally) high-income workers are treated as a variable input while low-skilled and (generally) low-wage workers are relatively immobile. Capital is freely mobile and untaxed and, as indicated in Section 2, can be subsumed within the model with no change in the analysis. In this world, greater mobility of high-skilled workers does not raise their average incomes, but it does result in an increase in the average income of *low-skilled* workers, as illustrated in Fig. 14-2. In this respect, greater mobility of high-skilled labor would be inequality-reducing. Nevertheless, low-skilled workers may experience greater income risk as a result of greater mobility of high-skilled workers, while the income risk of the latter may diminish. The allocative losses due to government policies such as personal income taxes, payroll taxes, and consumption taxes increase if the market for the highly skilled workers becomes freer. Since these policies also shift income risk to less skilled workers, scaling back the extent of income-conditioning of tax-transfer policies that apply to high-skilled workers may reduce some of the income shocks to which less skilled workers might otherwise be exposed.

German unification provides a modern European example of a situation where factor market integration is playing an important role in income distribution and where it presents new challenges for policymakers (see Sinn and Sinn [1992] for an insightful discussion). East-west migration within Germany has to some extent provided an opportunity for workers in the east to raise their incomes. The magnitude of this flow would undoubtedly be much larger if the government were to refrain from providing generous unemployment benefits and other "social benefits" to workers in the east, along with operating subsidies to outmoded and uneconomic firms there in order to maintain the demand for labor. As in the model of Section 3, government insurance of wage income has reduced the labor flow that would otherwise have taken place, but at the cost of lost efficiency. This picture of factor market relationships between eastern and western Germany can be extended to a characterization of western Europe, or to Europe as a whole. (See Straubhaar and Zimmermann [1992] and Flanagan [1993] for recent assessments of labor mobility in Europe.) The admission of Greece, Spain, and Portugal to the EU facilitates labor mobility and equalization of earnings among workers within western Europe. The prospect of such migration presumably underlies, at least in part, the rejection of Turkey's application for EU membership. Similarly, the relatively rapid admission of the Nordic countries and Austria to the EU can be attributed, in part, to the absence of concerns about strong negative labor-market impacts on existing member states. East-west migration from the states of the former Eastern-bloc countries also affords an opportunity for equalization of earnings through labor movements, as does migration from Latin America to North America.

In Canada, there has been considerable debate over the extent to which intergovernmental transfers have inhibited labor migration from poor provinces, perhaps thereby forestalling interprovincial wage equalization. An analysis by Boadway and Green (1981) indicates that better-educated workers in Newfoundland tend to be more mobile, indicating both the importance of mobility costs for some workers and ways that mobility costs can be reduced through policy interventions. They find that better education contributes not just to increases in *net* migration (a "brain drain") but also to increases in *gross* migration, in which one region exchanges well-educated workers with other regions. This suggests that reductions in mobility costs through education may increase the integration of a region (industry, occupation) with the rest of the economy and lead to more productivity-enhancing "matching migration" as opposed to "expansion or contraction" migration. Presumably, such migration also reduces inequality among mobile workers.

4.2 *Factor market integration in LDCs and in a historical context*

One can find numerous examples where labor mobility has contributed or clearly could contribute to reduced inequality in earnings. Some of the most interesting examples appear in economies where public sector insurance/redistribution programs are poorly developed and where mobility of labor may thus assume a particularly prominent role. Modern less-developed countries often have very rudimentary and limited tax and transfer systems; the same was true of the now-developed countries in earlier periods, before the modern welfare state assumed its present standing.[11]

As a first illustration, one might consider the "great migration" of blacks (and non-black low-wage workers) from the rural South to the urban North of the United States during the first decades of this century (see Margo [1990] for a discussion and references). The consequences of this migration are still being felt, and they have not by any means been entirely benign. Nevertheless, access to labor market opportunities for blacks outside the South and the accompanying migration undoubtedly raised black incomes relative to what they would otherwise have been and thus contributed to a reduction in economic inequality. The system of *apartheid* in South Africa provides an interesting comparison. *Apartheid* limited the freedom of contract of black South Africans in many respects; the restrictions on freedom of movement were among the most important and contributed substantially to the creation and entrenchment of extreme economic inequality. Many job opportunities for blacks were thus destroyed by artificial separation of the races among regions (including so-called "homelands") and within metropolitan areas. The establishment of black townships limited the geographical scope of the labor market for blacks, artificially depressing their earnings, perhaps raising the earnings of some segments of the white labor force and, in the process, creating substantial economic inefficiency. (In accordance with standard principles of fiscal federalism, the South African case provides a striking illustration of the role of political and fiscal centralization in facilitating the income-redistributive functions of the public sector. A highly centralized system was used, under *apartheid*, to carry out redistribution from poor to rich, probably at great economic cost. It would have been difficult for any single province or metropolitan area within South Africa to implement a policy like *apartheid* in isolation because of the efficiency losses associated with it.) The dismantling of *apartheid* and the still-immature decentralization of political authority in South Africa should lead to a substantially more liberal economic environment that both improves economic efficiency and reduces earnings inequality.

[11] Needless to say, it is impossible here to give more than a few illustrative examples of the extremely diverse experience of developing countries. See Stark (1991) and Razin and Sadka (1995) for a discussion of migration issues in LDCs and further references to relevant literature.

Of course, reductions in earnings inequality associated with more intense labor market competition are unlikely to be welcomed by workers facing the erosion of a previously protected situation. This is one of the pressing dilemmas facing China today. As in South Africa under *apartheid*, households in China faced severe restrictions on mobility during the Mao period. The household registration *(hukou)* system (see, for example, Cheng and Selden [1994] for a description) specified where people could work and, in particular, classified workers as rural or urban workers. A worker seeking to move from rural agricultural employment to urban nonagricultural work would have to apply through the relevant bureaucracies, and the number of workers allowed to make such moves was tightly controlled. The enforcement of these controls was closely intertwined with state controls on essential goods and services. For instance, unauthorized workers would not qualify for grain rations, employer-provided housing, or health care. The absence of freely functioning markets for such basic goods meant that households would likely bear substantial costs if they relocated without proper bureaucratic approval. Substantial interregional income inequality has arisen from this system, with incomes in coastal regions and urban areas of China substantially greater than in interior and rural areas. Liberalization of food markets has already taken place to a substantial extent and liberalization of housing and labor markets, including the unbundling of health and social service provision from the employment relationship, rank very high on the agenda for economic reform (see Harrold and Lall [1993]). As liberalization occurs, migration is increasing substantially, no doubt helping to close some of the gaps in income between regions and among differently-classified workers. This process has given rise to some concern that the comparative and perhaps absolute reduction in economic status of the established urban population may give rise to unrest. However that may be, it is quite apparent that there are large potential efficiency gains from enhanced labor mobility in China and that this is also likely to reduce earnings disparities.

Analyses of migration of labor and capital from the old world to the new in the nineteenth century also illustrate the role of spatial arbitrage in the equalization of factor prices. Research by economic historians, especially a series of recent studies by O'Rourke et al. (1993), O'Rourke et al. (1994), and others (see Hatton and Williamson [1994] for a review) reveals that migration from the Old World to the New in the late nineteenth century contributed substantially to equalization of wage rates among countries. These authors emphasize that both capital and labor tended to flow in the same direction, leading to greater equality of returns for capital as well. The remaining immobile factors (land and natural resources) experienced offsetting adjustments in returns. Although this historically very important migration antedates the rise of the welfare state, its effects were presumably inequality-reducing. It would be quite interesting to compare quantitatively the distributional impact of these factor movements with direct policy interventions aimed at achieving changes in the distribution of income.

5. Conclusion

There are many issues relating to factor market integration and risk that have been ignored here. For this reason, the analysis should be regarded only as suggestive. Several important and difficult empirical questions have already been mentioned. It is useful, in closing, to highlight some additional topics that warrant further investigation.

Markets for risk. The foregoing analysis applies, in principle, to any situation where there is one potentially mobile variable input that is employed, along with a fixed input, subject to uncertainty. The focus of the analysis has been on the mean and variance of the income stream at its source. Some income streams, however, notably those accruing to capital investments, can be traded and thus diversified. Increases in capital market integration may not, therefore, reduce the *cost* of risks that can be pooled by other means but may, instead, substitute for some of the functions of financial markets; conversely, development of financial markets may reduce some of the benefits of interjurisdictional capital flows.

Risk-pooling among jurisdictions generally requires cross-ownership of claims on income streams; complete diversification across many jurisdictions implies that the tradeable assets employed in a given jurisdiction will be owned, in equilibrium, by nonresidents. This, however, creates an incentive for each local jurisdiction to tax away the income of diversifiable assets, or to seize the assets themselves (see Wildasin and Wilson [1994], Nielsen [1994] and the literature on sovereign debt, such as Eaton and Gersovitz [1989]). Therefore, a real question exists regarding the sustainability of a regime with diversified cross-ownership of assets unless governments can agree, in a *credible* fashion, to restrain themselves from source-based taxation of income or assets owned by nonresidents. Liberalization of regulatory constraints on factor movements may provide one means by which such commitments could be made or signalled, and perhaps thereby facilitating trading of risky assets.

A related issue concerns the possibility of rent extraction by owners of immobile factors from owners of partially mobile factors. In a model of land-rent maximizing localities with imperfectly mobile households, Wildasin and Wilson (1996) show how local fiscal policy can be used to exploit monopsony power on behalf of landowners, giving rise to *ex post* inequality among *ex ante* identical individuals and thus creating, rather than reducing, income risk. In that model, increases in uncertainty are accompanied by efficiency losses. Resolution of these issues requires a predictive model of the formulation of local tax policy, an undertaking that lies beyond the scope of the present chapter.

Localization economies and factor market integration. Urban agglomerations may provide another market mechanism for pooling risk. Krugman (1991, esp. Appendix C) presents a model in which firms with uncorrelated production risks locate together, providing risk-averse workers with protection from wage risk. If firms can bear risk more easily than workers, agglomerations can arise. In its emphasis on pooling of risk through access to dense markets, the present analysis parallels that of Krugman. However, in Krugman's case, dense markets arise through urban agglomerations, whereas in the present analysis it is lower costs of movement to other regions that allow owners of mobile factors to access markets with more stable factor prices. This raises several interesting issues for further analysis, formulated here as conjectures. First, to the extent that agglomerations arise from pooling of labor market risk, greater mobility of labor among regions or countries reduces the benefits of agglomeration and may lead to smaller equilibrium city sizes. By the same token, increases in labor mobility among uncorrelated employers within a metropolitan area, due to urban growth or diversification of urban industry, reduces the attractiveness of interregional migration. Second, although the analysis here has suggested that redistributive policies may reduce interregional factor mobility and the sharing of risks through factor markets, there would seem to be a corollary in the localization-economies context: Social insurance reduces the benefits of urban agglomeration and, presumably, leads to smaller equilibrium city size.

Unequal regions and the gains and losses from federation. As noted at the outset, a public policy that provides "insurance" in a long-run sense may be viewed as "redistributive" in the "short run." Incomes *per capita* in different regions of the U.S. have converged substantially over the course of the past century (see, for example, Mills and Hamilton [1984: Figure 2.1]), and comparatively free migration of labor and capital within the U.S. has surely assisted that process. For most of the century, however, some regions (notably the South) have been poor relative to other regions. To the extent that labor and capital mobility have contributed to equalization of factor returns, there have been losers in this process as well as gainers. Within the long-run perspective of the U.S. Constitution, such gains and losses may not in themselves be of much concern. For a period of decades, workers or capital owners in one region may suffer reductions in income because of competition from immigrant capital or labor from other regions, but workers and capital owners in each region (locality, etc.) value the option of being able to move elsewhere should economic prospects in their current location take a turn for the worse. Indeed, relative freedom of factor movements within countries is commonplace, and it is clear that restrictions on such freedom (e.g., a prohibition on seeking employment outside of one's city of birth) would result in significant increases in income risk.

Consider, by contrast, the issue of freedom of migration between eastern and western Europe. Rather like the American South, the countries of eastern Europe have incomes much below that of their neighbors to the west. Unrestricted movement of labor and capital among these countries would certainly contribute to "pooling of income risks" or equalization of factor returns. However, it is not clear that this is in the interest of affluent western countries. The analysis in Wildasin (1994b) shows that immigration is necessarily harmful to at least some of the initial residents (or, more precisely, the initial owners of the factors of production) of a region if immigrants are net beneficiaries of the fiscal system. (It is even possible that the initial residents may benefit from making transfers to a source jurisdiction if this inhibits immigration.) In the "short run," then, the welfare states of western Europe may be net losers from increased factor mobility. In the "long run," residents in these countries value the option of being able to employ their productive resources outside of their home countries, and might therefore wish to commit themselves to institutional arrangements, such as EU membership, that expand such options. Whether a country gains or loses from membership in a common market, or from allowing another country to join a common market, is therefore a complex question that depends, in part, on the durability of the institutional arrangements.

References

Atkinson, A. B. (1987) "Income Maintenance and Social Insurance." In A. J. Auerbach and M. S. Feldstein, eds. *Handbook of Public Economics.* Amsterdam: North-Holland.

Barro, R. J. and X. Sala-i-Martin (1991) "Convergence Across States and Regions." *Brookings Papers on Economic Activity,* 107-82.

Blum, W. and H. Kalven (1963) *The Uneasy Case for Progressive Taxation.* Chicago: University of Chicago Press.

Boadway, R. W. and A. G. Green (1981) "The Economic Implications of Migration to Newfoundland." Economic Council of Canada, Discussion Paper No. 189.

Boadway, R. W. and D. E. Wildasin (1990) "Optimal Tax-Subsidy Policies for Industrial Adjustment to Uncertain Shocks." *Oxford Economic Papers,* 42, 105-34. Reprinted in P. J. N. Sinclar and M. D. E. Slater, eds. *Taxation, Private Information, and Capital.* Oxford: Clarendon Press.

Boadway, R. W. and D. E. Wildasin (1994) "Taxation and Savings: A Survey." *Fiscal Studies,* 15, 19-63.

Bureau, D. and P. Champsaur (1992) "Fiscal Federalism and European Economic Unification." *American Economic Review Papers and Proceedings,* 82, 88-92.

Bureau, D. and C. Richard (1994) "Public Insurance and Mobility: An Exploratory Analysis in the Context of European Economic Unification." Ministère de l'économie, Direction de la prévision. Paper presented at the conference on "Decentralization and the Economic Organization of Space," GREQAM, Marseille.

Cheng, T. and M. Selden (1994) "The Origins and Social Consequences of China's *Hukou* System." *China Quarterly,* 139, 644-68.

Domar, E. D. and R. A. Musgrave (1944) "Proportional Income Taxation and Risk Taking." *Quarterly Journal of Economics,* 58, 387-422.

De Grauwe, P. (1992) *The Economics of Monetary Integration.* Oxford: Oxford University Press.

Drèze, J. (1993) "Regions of Europe: A Feasible Status, To Be Discussed." *Economic Policy,* 17, 265-307.

Eaton, J. and M. Gersovitz (1989) "Country Risk and the Organization of International Capital Transfer." In G. Calvo et al., eds. *Debt, Stabilization, and Development.* Oxford: Basil Blackwell.

Eichengreen, B. (1993) "European Monetary Integration." *Journal of Economic Literature,* 31, 1321-57.

Flanagan, R. J. (1993) "European Wage Equalization Since the Treaty of Rome." In L. Ulman et al., eds. *Labor and an Integrated Europe.* Washington DC: Brookings Institution.

Grossman, G. M. and J. Eaton (1985) "Tariffs As Insurance: Optimal Commercial Policy When Domestic Markets Are Incomplete." *Canadian Journal of Economics,* 18, 258-72.

Harrold, P. and R. Lall (1993) "Reform and Development in 1992—93." World Bank Discussion Papers, China and Mongolia Department, No. 215.

Hatton, T. J. and J. G. Williamson (1994) "International Migration 1850—1939: An Economic Survey." In T. J. Hatton and J. G. Williamson, eds. *Migration and the International Labor Market 1850—1939.* London: Routledge.

King, M. A. and L.-D. L. Dicks-Mireaux (1982) "Asset Holdings and the Life-Cycle." *Economic Journal,* 92, 247-67.

Krugman, P. (1991) *Geography and Trade.* Cambridge: MIT Press.

Lawrence, R. Z. and R. E. Litan (1986) *Saving Free Trade.* Washington DC: Brookings Institution.

Margo, R. A. (1990) *Race and Schooling in the South, 1880—1950: An Economic History.* Chicago: University of Chicago Press.

Mills, E. S. and B. W. Hamilton (1984) *Urban Economics.* Third edition. Glenview: Scott Foresman.

Mundell, R. A. (1957) "International Trade and Factor Mobility." *American Economic Review,* 47, 321-35.

Nielsen, S. B. (1994) "Withholding Taxes and Country-Specific Shocks." Unpublished.

Oates, W. E. (1972) *Fiscal Federalism.* New York: Harcourt, Brace, Jovanovich.

O'Rourke, K. A., A. M. Taylor, and J. G. Williamson (1993) "Land, Labor, and the Wage-Rental Ratio: Factor Price Convergence in the Late Nineteenth Century." NBER Historical Paper No. 46.

O'Rourke, K., J. G. Williamson, and T. J. Hatton (1994) "Mass Migration, Commodity Market Integration and Real Wage Convergence." In T. J. Hatton and J. G. Williamson, eds. *Migration and the International Labor Market 1850—1939,* London: Routledge.

Persson, T. and Tabellini, G. (1993) "Federal Fiscal Constitutions: Part I: Risk Sharing and Moral Hazard." Copenhagen Business School, EPRU, Working Paper 1993-4.

Razin, A. and Sadka, E. (1995) *Population Economics.* Cambridge: MIT Press.

Sandmo, A. (1987) "The Effects of Taxation on Savings and Risk Taking." In A. J. Auerbach and M. S. Feldstein, eds. *Handbook of Public Economics.* Amsterdam: North-Holland.

Sandmo, A. and D. E. Wildasin (1994) "Taxation, Migration, and Pollution." Norwegian School of Economics and Business Administration, Institute of Economics, Discussion Paper No. 3/94; Vanderbilt University, Working Paper No. 94-W02.

Sinn, G. and H. W. Sinn (1992) *Jumpstart: The Economic Unification of Germany.* Cambridge: MIT Press.

Stark, O. (1991) *The Migration of Labor.* Cambridge: Basil Blackwell.

Straubhaar, T. and K. F. Zimmermann (1992) "Towards a European Migration Policy." CEPR, Discussion Paper No. 641.

Summers, L. (1988) "Tax Policy and International Competitiveness." In A. M. Spence and H. A. Hazard, eds. *International Competitiveness.* Cambridge: Ballinger.

Topel, R. H. (1986) "Local Labor Markets." *Journal of Political Economy,* 94, Part 2, 111-43.

Wildasin, D. E. (1994a) "Public Pensions in the EC: Migration Incentives and Impacts." Unpublished.

Wildasin, D. E. (1994b) "Income Redistribution and Migration." *Canadian Journal of Economics,* 27, 637-56.

Wildasin, D. E. and J. D. Wilson (1994) "Risky Local Tax Bases: Risk Pooling vs. Rent Capture." Vanderbilt University, Working Paper.

Wildasin, D. E. and J. D. Wilson (1996) "Imperfect Mobility and Local Government Behavior In an Overlapping Generations Model." *Journal of Public Economics,* 60(2), 177-98.

Index

Admission price equilibrium, 76-78, 102-3
Admission prices, 100-101, 123
Admission price system, 101-2
  defined, 76, 101
Agents, 60-61, 101, 136
Anonymous Lindahl price equilibrium, 103
Anonymous Lindahl price system, 102-3
Anonymous pricing in Tiebout economies, 89-120
  admission price equilibrium, 102-3
  admission prices, 101, 123
  admission price system, 101-2
    defined, 76, 101
  asymptotic constant returns to scale, 108-9
  core, 95-99
    emptiness of, 96-99
  crowding types, market games with, 113-16
  crowding types model, 94-95, 112-13
  differentiated crowding model, 92-94, 111-12
  equilibrium and prices, 99-105
  feasible state of the economy, 95
  jurisdictions, optimal size of, 105
  Lindahl price system, 100-103
  local public goods economies:
    crowding types model, 94-95
    models of, 91-95
    nondifferentiated/differentited crowding models, 92-94
  nondifferentiated crowding model, 109-11
  per capita boundedness, 108
  strict small group effectivenss, 106-8
  Taste Anonymity in Consumption (TAC), 95
  Taste Anonymity in Production (TAP), 95
  Tiebout assumption six, 105-9
  uniform Tiebout equilibrium, 104
  uniform Tiebout price system, 104
Anonymous Revelation Game (ARG), 149
Apartheid system, and factor integration, 333-34
Asymptotic constant returns to scale, 108-9

Benchmark case of global destination regime, 267-68
Blocking opportunities, exhaustion of, 130, 132
Boundedness, per capita, 108

Capacity:
  added at fixed time intervals, 172-74
  continuous additions to, 165-67
  fixed increments in, 178-80
  intermittent capacity additions, 162, 171-80
  replacement, 174-75
City formation, "slime mold" model of, 15-32
Club, defined, 130
Club economies:
  anonymous pricing in Tiebout economies, 89-120
  complementarities between private and club goods, 122
  decentralization in, 121-38
  defined, 130
  and existence problems, 135-36
  main feature of, 130
Club structure, 130
Club theory, basis of, 121
Club type system, 131
Coalition structure, 130
Competitive equilibrium, 128-30
  and decentralization in club economies, 129-30
  defined, 128
  and First Welfare Theorem, 68-78
    equivalence of core/equilibrium outcomes, 72
    two-part equilibrium outcomes in core, 71-72
    wage/price-taking equilibrium for economies with collective goods, 69-72
Conjectural prices, 126
Consumption-based taxation, comparing, 312-13
Continuous additions to capacity, 165-71
  depreciation/maintenance, 168-69
  irreversibility/adjustment costs, 169-71
  simplest case, 165-67
Cost share equilibrium, 103
Cross-border income shifting:
  behavior of multinationals with, 246-49
  optimal tax policy in home country, 250-52
  optimal tax policy in host country, 249-50
  tax policy with, 244-54

Crowding types, market games with, 113-16
Crowding types model, 94-95, 112-13

Decentralization in club economies, 121-38
  club, defined, 130
  club economy:
    defined, 130
    main feature of, 130
  club structure, 130
  club type system, 131
  coalition structure, 130
  and competitive equilibrium, 129-30
  complementarities between private and public goods, 122-27
  decentralization, defined, 122
  efficient scale, 134-35
  equal-treatment core, 131
  "exhaustion of blocking opportunities," 130, 132
  existence, 135-36
  nonanonymous crowding, 121, 123
  and price systems, 129-35
  replication and optimal size, 127-29
  unreplicated club economy, 122
Decentralized tax autonomy, 262-85
Depreciation, as continuous addition to capacity, 168-69
Destination- and origin-based taxation, 286-313
  consumption-based taxation, comparing, 312-13
  destination-based consumption tax, 294-96
    replacing by origin-based consumption taxes, 304-6
  investment system, 308-10
    log-linerarized model, 308-10
  model, 289-94
    consumption and saving behavior, 290-92
    government, 293
    production and investment, 289-90
    solution, 294
  origin-based consumption tax, 302-4
    with foreign ownership, 304
    neutralizing distributional effects, 304
    without foreign ownership, 303
  origin-based production tax, 297-302
    effects on intergenerational distribution, 300-301
    effects on international distribution, 302
    efficiency effects, 299-300
  public budget constraint, 310-11
  saving system, 311-12

Differentiated crowding model, 92-94, 111-12
Domestic income shifting, 239-43
  optimal tax policy in home countries, 241-42
  optimal tax policy in host countries, 242-43

Economic integration, 314-39
  and income redistribution, 325-27
    full insurance for the variable factor, 325-26
    partial insurance of variable input, 326-27
  and income risk, 322-29
    in absence of income redistribution policy, 322-24
Efficient scale, 134-35
Equal-treatment property, 60
Equal-treatment redistribution, 79
"Exhaustion of blocking opportunities," 130, 132
Existence problems, and club economies, 135-36
External economies of scale, 47-49

Factor mobility:
  alternative assumptions about, 327-29
  economic integration, 314-39
    and income risk, 322-29
  factor market integration:
    in developed countries, 330-32
    experience of, 330-35
    in LDCs and in historical context, 333-35
    and localization economies, 336
  factor supplies, 318
  model, 316-22
  special case, 319-22
First-best theory of public goods, 147
First Welfare Theorem, 57-78, 89-90, 112
  admission equilibrium, 76-78
    and equivalence of core and outcomes, 77-78
    and two-part equilibrium outcomes, 77
  agents, 60-61
  competitive equilibrium, 68-78
    equivalence of core/equilibrium outcomes, 72
    two-part equilibrium outcomes in core, 71-72
    wage/price-taking equilibrium for economies with collective goods, 69-72
  core, 64-68
    equal-treatment property of, 65
    and equivalence of set of type-optimal allocations, 67-68
    nonemptiness of, 68

endowments, 60-61
goods, 60-61
jurisdictions, 60-61
type-optimal, 63-64
jurisdiction structure, 61
Lindahl equilibrium, 72-75
equivalence of core and Lindahl outcomes, 75
equivalence of equilibrium concepts, 75
nonanonymous Lindahl price system, 73
outcomes in the core, 74-75
production, 61-62
states of the economy, 62-63
Tiebout equilibria and contestibility, 76
See also Second Welfare Theorem
Fully Anonymous Prices (FAP), 101-2

"Generic" information, defined, 154
Global destination-based VAT regime, 265-67
benchmark case of global destination regime, 267-68
implementation of, 268-73
model, 265-67

Heterogenous consumers, 192-94
and utility function, 194

Identical consumers, 186-92
willingness to pay, comparison of demand compensation and, 189-92
Incentives and disagglomerative forces, 139-60
agglomeration forces in simple taxation model, 140-48
one-dimensional second-best taxation model, 140-42
second-best taxation as a game, 142-44
summary of results/discussion, 144-48
significance of core, 151-53
taxes as incentive devices, 148-51
Income redistribution, and economic integration, 325-27
Income shifting:
cross-border, tax policy with, 244-54
domestic, tax policy with, 239-43
tax implications of, 254-58
Intermittent capacity additions, 162, 171-80
capacity added at fixed time intervals, 172-74
capacity replacement, 174-75
simplest case, 171-72
Irreversibility/adjustment costs, 169-71

Jurisdictions, 60-61
interjurisdictional transfers, property taxation, 215-17
optimal size of, 105
risk-pooling among, 335
structure, 61
type-optimal, 63-64

Large external economies of scale, 48
Lindahl equilibrium, 72-75, 124-25
equivalence of core and Lindahl outcomes, 75
equivalence of equilibrium concepts, 75
nonanonymous Lindahl price system, 73
outcomes in the core, 74-75
Lindahl price system, 100-103
Localization economies, and factor market integration, 336
Local public goods economies:
crowding types model, 94-95
models of, 91-95
nondifferentiated/differentiated crowding models, 92-94

Maintenance, as continuous addition to capacity, 168-69
Markets for risk, 335-36
Mixed origin/destination principle, implementation of, 278-81
Monopolistic provision of public goods, 185-96
heterogenous consumers, 192-94
and utility function, 194
identical consumers, 186-92
comparison of willingness to pay/demand compensation, 189-92
consumuer maximization, 189-90
efficient solution, 188-89
monopoly solution, 187
Musical-suburbs problem, 197-219
definition of, 198-99
entry barriers, 209-12
interjurisdictional transfers, 207-9
many types of workers, extension to model with, 212
model, 200-202
properties of the equilibrium, 202-7
property taxation, 212-17
equilibrium, 214-15
interjurisdictional transfers, 215-17
model, 212-14

Nationalism:
economically viable fiscal federation, 221-23
secession from, 223-27
and secession, 220-34
tolerating, 227-29
Nonanonymous crowding, 121, 123

Nonanonymous Lindahl equilibrium, 58-59, 73
Nonanonymous Lindahl price system, 73
Nondifferentiated crowding model, 92-94, 109-11
Nonreciprocal restricted origin principle, implementation of, 275-78

Origin-based consumption tax, 302-4
with foreign ownership, 304
neutralizing distributional effects, 304
without foreign ownership, 303
Origin-based production tax, 297-302
effects on intergenerational distribution, 300-301
effects on international distribution, 302
efficiency effects, 299-300

Pareto optimum, 78-84
Peer-group effects, 197
Per capita boundedness, 108
Price systems:
admission, 101-2
defined, 76, 101
anonymous Lindahl, 102-3
and decentralization in club economies, 129-35
in economies with public goods, 58
Fully Anonymous Prices (FAP), 101-2
Lindahl, 100-103
nonanonymous Lindahl price system, 73
uniform Tiebout, 104
Property taxation, 212-17
equilibrium, 214-15
interjurisdictional transfers, 215-17
model, 212-14
Purchasing power, regional distribution of, 50-51

"Racetrack" economy, 16-17
Ratio equilibrium (Kaneko), 103
Regions, size of, 33-54
Relative prices, 36-38
Relative utilities, 38-39
and low transport costs, 53
Replacement, capacity, 174-75
Restricted origin principle, implementation of, 273-75
Risk-pooling, among jurisdictions, 335

Samuelson rule, 203, 205
Secession, and nationalism, 220-34
Second Welfare Theorem, 60, 78-88, 90, 112
Pareto optimum, 78-84
Self-financing of congestible facilities, 161-84
continuous additions to capacity, 165-71
depreciation/maintenance, 168-69
irreversibility/adjustment costs, 169-71
simplest case, 165-67
intermittent capacity additions, 162, 171-80
capacity added at fixed time intervals, 172-74
capacity replacement, 174-75
simplest case, 171-72
literature review, 180-81
more general capacity expansion technology, 175-78
fixed increments to capacity, 178-80
static self-financing results, review of, 162-65
Size of regions, 33-54
agglomeration, 33-34
basic model, 35-39
questions addressed by, 35-36
relative prices, 36-38
relative utilities, 38-39
comparison with Krugman, 49-53
dispersion, 33-34
equality of utility levels, 40fn
equilibrium size of regions, 39-43
external economies of scale, 47-49
purchasing power, regional distribution of, 50-51
purpose of study, 33
unbounded transport costs, 40-41
welfare, 43-47
"Slime mold" model of city formation, 15-32
definition of, 15-16
diffusion, 25-26
dynamic spatial model, 16-20
market potential funciton, 19-20
"racetrack" economy, 16-17
flat distribution of manufacturing, 22-25
fluctuations, growth of, 27-31
heuristic analysis, 20-27
"racetrack" economy, 16-17
immoble "farmers," 16-17
mobile "firms," 16-17
transport costs, 17
self-organization, 20-27
condition for, 24
simulations, 20-27
Small external economies of scale, 48
Strict small group effectivenss, 106-8

Taste Anonymity in Consumption (TAC), 95
Taste Anonymity in Production (TAP), 95
Tax arbitrage and decentralized tax autonomy, 262-85
decentralized VAT regime, scope for, 281-84

global destination-based VAT regime, 265-68
benchmark case of global destination regime, 267-68
implementation of, 268-73
model, 265-67
mixed origin/destination principle, implementation of, 278-81
nonreciprocal restricted origin principle, implementation of, 275-78
restricted origin principle, implementation of, 273-75
Theory of Clubs (Berglas), 185-86
Tiebout admission equilibrium, 76-77
Tiebout economies, anonymous pricing in, 89-120
Tiebout equilibrium, 104
Tiebout Program, 60
Transfer pricing and income shifting, 237-61
cross-border income shifting, tax policy with, 244-54
domestic income shifting, tax policy with, 239-43
Type-optimal demands, 59-60
Type-optimal jurisdictions, 63-64

Uniform Tiebout equilibrium, 104
Uniform Tiebout price system, 104

Variety, and economies of scale, 48

Welfare, 43-47